Helping Children Left Behind

State Aid and the Pursuit of Educational Equity

Edited by John Yinger

The MIT Press
Cambridge, Massachusetts
London, England

This book was set in Palatino on 3B2 by Asco Typesetters, Hong Kong, and was printed and bound in the United States of America.

Library of Congress Cataloging-in-Publication Data

Helping children left behind : state aid and the pursuit of educational equity / edited by John Yinger.
    p.   cm.
Includes bibliographical references and index.
ISBN 0-262-24046-7 (hc. : alk. paper)
1. Government aid to education—United States—States—Case studies. 2. Educational equalization—United States—States—Case studies. I. Yinger, John, 1947–
LB2825.H38   2004
379.2′6—dc22   2003066825

10 9 8 7 6 5 4 3 2 1

Contents

Appendixes

Preface and Acknowledgments

In recent years, many state supreme courts have declared that the education finance system in their state does not satisfy state constitutional requirements, and policymakers throughout the nation have been searching for an education finance system that provides all school districts with the support they need to meet high performance standards. As a result, the recent history of education finance is full of litigation, debate, and reform. On April 5–6, 2002, about three dozen scholars gathered at the Maxwell School of Citizenship and Public Affairs at Syracuse University for a conference on this important topic. This book is the direct descendant of the papers presented at this conference.

The success of any conference or conference volume obviously depends primarily on the participants, and this volume is fortunate to build on the contributions of an exceptionally qualified cast of scholars. The authors of chapters 2 through 9 of this book are the scholars who presented papers at the April 2002 Conference on State Aid to Education. Brief biographies of these scholars can be found at the end of the book. The discussants for these papers at the conference were Katharine Bradbury, Federal Reserve Bank of Boston; Timothy Gronberg, Texas A&M University; Robert Inman, University of Pennsylvania; Therese McCarty, Union College; Robert Schwab, University of Maryland; David Sjoquist, Georgia State University; Leanna Stiefel, New York University; and Robert Strauss, Carnegie Mellon University. Several of my colleagues at the Maxwell School graciously served as chairs of the conference sessions, namely, Stacy Dickert-Conlin, Mary Lovely, Larry Schroeder, Michael Wasylenko, Stuart Rosenthal, and William Duncombe.

Other scholars and policymakers who attended the conference were Robert Bifulco, Duke University; Sherrilyn Billger, Union College; Ronald Ehrenberg, Cornell University; Kathleen Fazio, Office of the

New York State Comptroller; Brandon Gordon, Midstate School Finance Consortium; Molly Hunter, Campaign for Fiscal Equity; Karen Kaplan, New York City Partnership; Alex Stricker, Fannie Mae; and Charles Szuberla, New York State Department of Education. All the conference sessions were open to the university community, and other Maxwell faculty, along with graduate students from Maxwell and from Cornell University, also attended some of the sessions.

The conference was sponsored by the Education Finance and Accountability Program (EFAP), of which I am the director and Bill Duncombe, the coauthor of chapter 5, is the associate director. EFAP is a subunit of the Center for Policy Research (CPR) in the Maxwell School of Syracuse University. CPR is a research center that supports a wide range of policy-related research. EFAP helps give focus to CPR's research in education. My job was to provide the conceptual framework for the conference and to invite people to participate. My main objective was to combine discussions of general conceptual issues that arise in designing a state aid system with detailed evaluation and comparison of recent reform efforts in several key states. I hope the readers of this book agree with me that, thanks particularly to the contributions of the authors and discussants, this objective has been fully achieved.

The conference, and hence this volume, would not have been possible without the efforts of many people in addition to the participants. The conference was financed largely through funds given to EFAP by Syracuse University. I would particularly like to thank John Palmer, then dean of the Maxwell School, for his support of this program. The conference also benefited from the backing of Tim Smeeding, CPR's director, who contributed some funds from CPR. Tim was out of the country and could not attend the conference himself, but he wrote a welcoming letter to the participants and was supportive throughout.

The conference also would not have been possible without the administrative efforts of Kitty Nasto, who arranged everything from the conference materials to new entries on the EFAP Web site to travel schedules to room reservations to meals and coffee breaks. Kitty made all of these arrangements with unfailing skill and good humor. The CPR staff also provided administrative support, including assembling the notebooks given to every conference participant. (Kitty and the CPR staff, especially Kim Desmond, Emily NaPier, Mary Santy, and Mindy Tanner, also helped check all the references and format the revised papers for inclusion in the book.) Four graduate students at the Maxwell School, Tariq Al-Alawi, Yao Huang, Kristina Lambright, and

Tabo Maboguane, also helped with a variety of tasks. I am very grateful for all of these contributions.

A special word of thanks goes to William Upwood, who runs the Global Collaboratory at the Maxwell School, where the conference was held. Because of his efforts, we were able to have two people participate in the conference all day on April 6 via live video feed from the University of Michigan, to play from the Internet a taped presentation by one of the paper authors who was unable to attend the conference at the last minute, and to deliver tapes of the conference proceedings to several participants who could not attend every session. Kim Leven at Syracuse and Pam Dietz at the University of Michigan also helped with these arrangements.

State education finance systems are complex and difficult to reform. Nevertheless, these systems are an essential part of any effort to meet educational objectives expressed by a state supreme court or selected by state policymakers. It is my hope that people around the country, both public officials and private citizens, will find this volume helpful as they learn about education finance and search for the best school finance reforms for their own states.

John Yinger
June 2003

I   General Analysis of State Aid Reform

1

State Aid and the Pursuit of Educational Equity: An Overview

John Yinger

1.1 Introduction

In 1971 the California Supreme Court ushered in a new era in education finance by ruling, in *Serrano v. Priest*, that California's system for financing elementary and secondary education violated the state's constitution.[1] Relying heavily on a property tax to finance education was unconstitutional, the court declared, because it made a child's education dependent on the wealth of his or her school district.

Since then, forty-three additional state courts have heard challenges to the constitutionality of the education finance system in their state. Although the legal standards vary from state to state and have shifted over time, seventeen more education finance systems have been declared unconstitutional by state supreme courts since *Serrano v. Priest*.[2] The most recent such decision was in New York in June 2003. In most cases, these court decisions have been followed by significant education finance reforms.

The impact of state courts goes far beyond these eighteen state supreme court decisions. Reforms passed in response to one of these decisions have been upheld by the supreme court in Texas, and further education reform litigation is ongoing in Arizona, California, Connecticut, Kentucky, Massachusetts, Montana, New Hampshire, New Jersey, and West Virginia. State supreme courts also have reversed lower-court decisions rejecting education reform in Idaho, Kansas, North Carolina, and South Carolina, and litigation continues in all of these states.[3] Moreover, the Missouri Supreme Court upheld a reform that was passed in response to a trial court decision,[4] and trial courts in Alaska and New Mexico have rejected their states' systems for funding school facilities.

State supreme courts have upheld the existing education finance systems in eighteen states, but these decisions have not prevented education finance reform or further litigation in many cases. Among the states in this category, for example, additional lower-court litigation spurred major education finance reforms in Colorado (National Center for Education Statistics 2001c) and Maryland (Montgomery 2002), and Michigan (Cullen and Loeb, chapter 7) passed a major education finance reform without any further court involvement. Moreover, voters in two states, Florida and Oregon, responded to state supreme court decisions upholding the education finance systems in those states by passing an amendment to the education clauses of their state constitutions. The Florida amendment calls for "a uniform, efficient, safe, secure, and high quality system of free public schools," which is one of the strongest equity standards in the nation (Advocacy Center for Children's Education Success with Standards 2003). Finally, new education finance litigation is pending in Colorado and Florida.

All this litigation and reform reflects, of course, the dramatic disparities in school spending and student performance that divide school districts in most states. In the average state in 2000, for example, low-poverty school districts spent almost $1,000 more per pupil than did high-poverty districts (The Education Trust 2002). Some evidence on performance gaps is provided in Casserly 2002, which compares 2001 reading and math test scores in large cities, where poverty is concentrated, and the states in which they are located. The gaps in eighth-grade reading and math scores are presented in tables 1.1 and 1.2, respectively.[5] These tables indicate the extent to which large cities lag behind the remainder of their states in bringing eighth-grade students up to a target score on the state's standardized tests. Student performance falls short of the state average in virtually every big city in the United States, and the test score gaps are often very large. In the case of reading, the share of students reaching the target score is almost 70 percent below the state average in St. Louis and more than 40 percent below the state average in eleven other cities. The disparities in math scores are even larger. Milwaukee falls almost 80 percent below its state average in the number of its students reaching the state's target score in math, and twenty-one other cities are more than 40 percent below the averages in their states.

The new state aid programs that were passed in response to the 1971 *Serrano v. Priest* decision (*Serrano I*) and the related 1977 *Serrano v. Priest* decision (*Serrano II*) dramatically reduced the disparities in

Table 1.1
Eighth-grade reading test score gaps between big cities and states, 2001

>60%	St. Louis, Baltimore, Philadelphia
50–59%	New Orleans
40–49%	Milwaukee, Buffalo, Detroit, Providence, Rochester, Denver, Oakland, Newark
30–39%	Boston, Los Angeles, Indianapolis, Minneapolis, Richmond, Fresno, St. Paul, Miami
20–29%	Pittsburgh, Chicago, New York City, Oklahoma City, Dayton, Norfolk
10–19%	Cleveland, Long Beach, Columbus, Atlanta, Dallas, Toledo, Sacramento
0–9%	Austin, Fort Worth, Nashville, Charlotte, San Francisco, Houston, Portland, Greensboro, Seattle
−4–0%	San Diego

Source: Casserly 2002.
Note: Results for cities in Ohio and Tennessee are for ninth-grade scores, and results for Denver, Detroit, St. Louis, and Seattle are for seventh-grade scores.

Table 1.2
Eighth-grade math test score gaps between big cities and states, 2001

>70%	Milwaukee, Rochester, Baltimore
60–69%	Philadelphia, Providence, Denver, New Orleans, Newark, St. Louis
50–59%	Buffalo, Dayton, Cleveland, Chicago
40–49%	Indianapolis, Pittsburgh, Oakland, Detroit, Richmond, Los Angeles, Minneapolis, Boston, New York City
30–39%	St. Paul, Toledo, Columbus, Oklahoma City, Fresno, Atlanta
20–29%	Memphis, Miami, Norfolk
10–19%	Dallas, San Diego, Long Beach, Nashville
0–9%	Austin, Fort Worth, Charlotte, Sacramento, Greensboro, Houston
−17–0%	Portland, Seattle, San Francisco

Source: Casserly 2002.
Note: Results for cities in Ohio and Tennessee are for ninth-grade scores, and results for Denver, Detroit, and Seattle are for seventh-grade scores. The results for Detroit refer to scores on 2000 tests.

spending per pupil across school districts in California. In contrast, these programs do not appear to have significantly reduced across-district disparities in student achievement or raised the performance of students in high-poverty urban districts (see Downes 1992 and Sonstelie, Brunner, and Ardon 2000).

The same patterns emerge in other states that have implemented reforms. Evans, Murray, and Schwab (1997, 1999) and Murray, Evans, and Schwab (1998) demonstrate that court-induced reforms in state aid reduce per-pupil spending disparities across school districts in the state. These reforms have not had nearly as large an effect on disparities in student performance, however, as they have had on disparities in spending. Indeed, some scholars argue that they have not affected performance disparities at all, and the available evidence indicates that students in many districts, especially high-poverty urban districts, still perform far below the state average even after major school aid reform. Tables 1.1 and 1.2 reveal significant test score gaps facing Los Angeles, Oakland, Dallas, and Fort Worth, for example, despite significant education finance reform efforts in California and Texas. There is no agreement, however, about the meaning of this evidence. Some scholars interpret it as a sign that equalization of education financing across districts is ineffective and should not be tried;[6] others, including myself, interpret it as a sign that many existing equalization efforts are flawed and that new approaches are needed.

The persistence of large across-district disparities in educational performance in many states is one of the factors that have pushed state legislatures and education departments toward a new focus on student performance and toward new programs to promote school district accountability. Forty-eight states now require local schools to administer state-selected tests in reading and mathematics (Goertz and Duffy 2001).[7] A majority of states also require tests in writing, social studies, and science.

These tests are accompanied by various types of accountability systems. Goertz and Duffy (2001) classify accountability systems into three categories: public reporting, locally defined, and state defined.[8] Thirteen states fall into the first category, in which requirements are imposed on school districts to report on various performance measures determined by the state. The second category, which involves only two states, is similar, except that in states in this category, each district selects its own performance measures. State-defined accountability systems, which are found in thirty-three states, set targets for student performance on achievement tests and then reward districts that meet their targets and/or sanction districts that fall short.[9] These rewards and sanctions obviously constitute a new element of the education finance system.

This book provides an overview of the research on state aid to education and a detailed look at state aid reform in five key states: Kansas, Kentucky, Michigan, Texas, and Vermont. The state aid reform efforts in these states are particularly ambitious, and they illustrate the range of recent reform strategies.

To be more specific, part I of the book addresses the general issues involved in state aid reform. Chapter 2, by Anna Lukemeyer, provides an introduction to the court cases and legal theories at the center of state aid reform efforts over the last thirty years. Chapter 3, by David Figlio, examines several central conceptual issues in state aid reform, and chapter 4, by Thomas Nechyba, explores the effects of state aid reform on residential patterns and other noneducational outcomes and the feedback from these effects to education. Part II includes chapters by William Duncombe and Jocelyn Johnston, Ann Flanagan and Sheila Murray, Julie Cullen and Susanna Loeb, Jennifer Imazeki and Andrew Reschovsky, and Thomas Downes on each of the five states mentioned (Kansas, Kentucky, Michigan, Texas, and Vermont, respectively). The book also includes some general reference material: Appendix A describes significant education finance decisions by state courts, Appendix B describes state operating aid programs, and Appendix C describes state building aid programs.

This chapter provides some background information regarding the debate about state aid, introduces the key themes that arise in discussions of state aid reform, and presents a guide to the examination of these themes in later chapters. The rest of the chapter is organized in four sections. Section 1.2 provides background information on some important analytical issues. Section 1.3 reviews the main choices that a state must make in designing a package for reforming its education aid system. Section 1.4 discusses a variety of issues that arise in evaluating the effects of aid reform efforts. Section 1.5 offers some conclusions from the chapter's discussion.

1.2 Background

Any discussion of state aid to education must build on several key concepts and on an understanding of state aid formulas. These topics

are introduced in this section and discussed throughout this book, particularly in chapter 2 (Lukemeyer) and chapter 3 (Figlio).

1.2.1   Selecting a Method for Measuring Education and an Equity Standard

Most scholars agree that any education finance system needs to be
based on a method for measuring the education provided by a school
district and the selection of an equity standard (see, for example, Berne
and Stiefel 1984, 1999; Monk 1990). The three most widely discussed
methods for measuring education are *spending* per pupil, *real resources*
per pupil, and *student performance* based on test scores and perhaps
other measures. Spending per pupil is obviously a simple method to
work with, but it is widely regarded as unsatisfactory, because it does
not recognize that educational costs vary across districts for reasons
outside the control of school officials. The other two methods, however, explicitly account for educational costs.

Measuring education using real resources per pupil is a way to account for the fact that teacher wages (and perhaps other input
prices) are not the same in every district. Teacher wages vary across
districts for two fundamental reasons that are outside the control of
school officials.[10] First, it costs more to attract teachers into education
from the private sector in high-wage than in low-wage regions.
Second, some districts have to pay more than others to attract teachers
of a given quality because they have more disadvantaged students
or special-needs students, who pose extra challenges in the classroom (see Chambers 1998; Duncombe, Ruggiero, and Yinger 1996;
Duncombe and Yinger 1999; Guthrie and Rothstein 1999; and Odden
1999).

Educational-performance measures, such as test scores, can, of
course, stand on their own without any reference to educational costs.
However, incorporating a performance-based method for measuring
education into a state aid formula requires a translation of spending
into performance; in other words, such an incorporation must recognize that it costs more to obtain a given level of performance in some
districts than in others. This cost variation arises not only because of
teacher wage differences but also because districts with more at-risk
students must spend more than other districts to obtain the same student performance (Downes and Pogue 1994b). School districts with a
high concentration of poor students, for example, may need lower

student-teacher ratios or additional prekindergarten, health, or counseling programs to overcome the disadvantages their students bring to school.[11]

Spending can be translated into performance in a way that accounts for both of these factors using a comprehensive educational-cost index (see Duncombe, Ruggiero, and Yinger 1996; Duncombe and Yinger 1997, 1998; Reschovsky and Imazeki 1998, 2001). As discussed in the next section, it may also be possible to accomplish this step with an aid formula that gives more weight to at-risk students.

Several standards for establishing the equity of an education finance system have been discussed in court opinions and in the academic literature. The most basic standard is educational *adequacy*, which is said to exist when students in every school district receive an education that meets some minimum standard. The impact of this standard depends, of course, on how high it is set, and as is shown throughout this book, some states have set a much higher standard than others.

Another key equity standard is *access equality*, defined as a situation in which an increase in taxpayer effort, as measured by the effective property tax rate, has the same impact on per-pupil revenue in every district. This standard was proposed in Coons, Clune, and Sugarman 1970, and it played an important role in the original *Serrano* decision (see Sonstelie, Brunner, and Ardon 2000). Access equality is similar to, but distinct from, another standard, known as *wealth neutrality*, which is achieved when district wealth and district education are not correlated. These two standards were initially thought to be the same, but Feldstein (1975) demonstrated that they are not. They differ in that one of them, access equality, refers to school districts' budget constraints, and the other, wealth neutrality, refers to the outcome of decisions made by the school district. Any policy that alters school districts' budget constraints will have an impact on what districts decide to do; the magnitude of this impact is difficult to predict, however, and no particular distribution of education across districts can be guaranteed, no matter how education is measured.

A final standard is *equality*, defined as the same education in every school district. Several state supreme courts have used language that appears to set equality as the required constitutional standard. No court, however, has combined an equality standard with a clear statement about how education should be measured or a clear statement about the steps a state must take to achieve this standard.[12]

1.2.2   Aid Formulas and Equity Objectives

The equity objective of an education finance system is defined by one of these equity standards combined with any of these methods for measuring education. Policymakers in a particular state might decide, for example, that they want an education system that achieves an adequate education as measured by real resources per pupil. After describing the two main types of formulas for awarding state educational aid, I show how these types of formulas can be modified to achieve any combination of these equity standards and education measurements.

1.2.2.1   Foundation Aid   The most basic type of education-aid formula is called *foundation aid*. This type of formula sets aid per pupil to district i, A_i, equal to a foundation amount of spending per pupil, E^*, which is the same for all districts, minus the amount of money the district can raise at a state-determined minimum tax rate, say t^*. If V_i is property value per pupil in district i, then this amount is t^*V_i, and the aid formula is

$$A_i = E^* - t^*V_i. \tag{1.1}$$

This standard foundation formula is suited for education as measured by spending per pupil and for an adequacy objective. Specifically, E^* equals the minimally adequate spending per pupil selected by state policymakers.

As shown by Ladd and Yinger (1994), however, this formula can easily be altered to accommodate the other two methods for measuring education. Let W_i be an index of teacher wage costs and C_i be a comprehensive index of educational costs in district i that reflects both wage costs and the extra costs associated with educating disadvantaged students. Then multiplying E^* by W_i is equivalent to measuring education using real resources per pupil, and multiplying E^* by C_i is equivalent to measuring education using student performance.[13] In principle, an equivalent adjustment for the cost impact of student characteristics can be made by giving aid on the basis of "weighted" pupils, such that more disadvantaged students receive higher weight in the funding formula.[14]

This analysis reveals that educational-cost indexes play a critical role in helping education finance systems catch up with the new focus on student performance in the broader debate about education policy. Unless it adjusts for differences in educational costs from district to district, a state education aid program simply is not compatible with performance objectives. Although scholars do not agree on the best method to account for these cost differences, there is widespread agreement that state aid formulas should include cost adjustments.[15] The need for cost indexes was emphasized, for example, in a recent report by the National Research Council's Committee on Education Finance (Ladd and Hansen 1999). See also Duncombe and Yinger 1999; Guthrie and Rothstein 1999; and Odden 1999.

To design a foundation aid program, a state not only must decide how to measure education, but it also must (1) select a foundation level, (2) select a minimum tax rate for districts, (3) decide whether districts are required to comply with this minimum tax rate, and (4) decide whether to restrict district supplementation of the foundation amount. Selecting the appropriate foundation level corresponds to deciding what level of education the state will regard as adequate. Because a higher foundation level implies a higher budgetary cost, each state must balance the educational benefits of a higher standard against the costs of achieving it.

The higher the minimum tax rate imposed on districts, the higher the local contribution to the education finance system. Thus, one way for a state to lower the burden of local property taxes is to lower t^* and to fund the resulting increases in aid payments required to reach the foundation spending level through state-level taxes. A decision about t^* is therefore one aspect of the broader issue of financing education aid reform, which is discussed in section 1.3.4. So long as the districts are required to impose at least the minimum tax rate, all districts will reach the foundation spending level.[16] If districts are not required to tax at the minimum rate, however, many districts receiving a relatively high amount of aid will cut their tax rates below t^* to free up taxpayers' resources for nonschool purposes.

The final decision, involving supplementation, is perhaps the most controversial. If *adequacy* is the equity standard, there is no reason to prevent spending beyond the foundation amount by the least-needy districts. To achieve educational *equality* across its districts, however, a state would have to prevent any district from spending more than the foundation amount.[17] Other standards may call for some restrictions on supplementation.

One way to reduce supplementation can be built right into a foundation plan. (Other ways are discussed in section 1.3.3.) To be specific, a state can recapture aid from the wealthiest or lowest-cost districts, that is, from the districts that have negative aid according to the above formula. Making aid payments negative, that is, requiring direct payments from low-need school districts to the state, is not politically feasible and has never been attempted, but a state can accomplish the same thing by eliminating the property tax at the district level and turning it into a state tax. As I show in subsequent sections, a few states have used modified versions of this approach. When a state property tax is used to finance a foundation program, more property tax revenue is collected in low-need school districts than is required to fund their foundation payments. Consequently, shifting to a state property tax lowers the disposable income of voters in low-need districts below the point where it was with a local property tax and therefore lowers their desired level of school spending.[18]

1.2.2.2 Guaranteed Tax Base Aid The second main type of aid formula is called a district power–equalizing or guaranteed tax base (GTB) program. This type of formula is derived from the principle that per-pupil spending in a district, E_i, should depend only on the effective property tax rate the district is willing to impose, t_i; that is, $E_i = t_i V^*$, where V^* is a policy parameter selected by the state. Because aid per pupil, A_i, equals total spending per pupil minus local property taxes per pupil, $t_i V_i$, this principle leads to the following formula for a GTP program:

$$A_i = E_i(1 - V_i/V^*). \tag{1.2}$$

This formula describes a matching grant in which the state's share of spending per pupil (A_i/E_i) is much higher for low-wealth districts than for high-wealth districts. The high rate at which the state matches education spending in low-wealth districts greatly lowers the price of education in those districts, thereby inducing them to increase their spending on education substantially.[19] The price of education falls by a smaller amount in middle-wealth districts, so they have a more modest incentive to raise their education spending.

From a state's point of view, the key issue in a GTB formula is the selection of V^*. If V^* is set equal to property value per pupil in the wealthiest district, then every district in the state except the wealthiest receives some aid through the program, the price subsidy for the poorest districts is very large, and the cost to the state is very high. Lowering V^* lowers the magnitude of the subsidies and the cost to the state.

A state also can use a GTB formula to limit spending by high-wealth districts if it lowers V^* and reclaims funds from districts with negative aid according to the above formula, that is, from the richest districts. As discussed more fully in section 1.3.3, an approach of this type, often referred to as "recapture," is included in the reforms enacted in Texas (Imazeki and Reschovsky, chapter 8) and Vermont (Downes, chapter 9). A recapture provision in a GTB formula limits spending by high-wealth districts because it confronts these districts with a negative matching rate and hence a higher price of education. If a district's property value per pupil is 50 percent higher than V^*, for example, then its matching rate is $(1 - 1.5) = -0.5$, and it must pay the state an amount equal to half of its total spending. This is equivalent to a 50 percent increase in the price of education, which may easily result in a 20 or 30 percent decrease in school spending in the district (see Fisher and Papke 2000).

The standard GTB formula is designed for education measured by spending per pupil. As shown by Ladd and Yinger (1994), however, it can easily be adjusted to accommodate either of the other ways of measuring education simply by replacing the 1 in equation (1.2) with either W_i (for measurement by real resources) or C_i (for measurement by performance). A similar approach, which is used by Texas (Imazeki and Reschovsky, chapter 8) is to express the GTB formula in terms of weighted pupils, with weights for pupils that reflect the higher costs of educating disadvantaged students. Despite the contradiction between a GTB formula based on spending per pupil and the current focus in other realms of education policy on education performance, however, adjustments of this type are rare.

In principle, a GTB formula also could be adjusted to achieve wealth neutrality. As shown by Feldstein (1975), this would require that the (V_i/V^*) term in equation (1.2) be raised to a power that reflects the estimated behavioral response to the matching grant provided by the state under the formula.[20] Because a matching grant is a type of price subsidy, this estimated behavioral response is a type of price elasticity. Alternatively, Duncombe and Yinger (1998) argue that wealth neutrality could be approximated by defining a formula in which the (V_i/V^*) term is raised to a power, say α, and then adjusting α every year until the correlation between district wealth and district education falls below some acceptable threshold.

The recognition that some districts face higher educational costs than others leads not only to a change in the method for measuring education, but also to a reconsideration of the wealth neutrality standard. A student is just as disadvantaged, after all, by living in a district with relatively high costs as he or she is by living in a district with relatively low wealth. So an alternative, more general equity standard is "fiscal" neutrality, which is said to exist when a district's education is not correlated with the balance between its taxing capacity (i.e., wealth) and spending requirements outside its control (i.e., costs). Duncombe and Yinger (1998) show how the GTB approach can be modified to yield this type of neutrality. To be specific, they measure the balance between wealth and costs in a district using the ratio of its property value index (V_i/V^*) to its cost index (W_i or C_i). Fiscal neutrality can then be approximated by replacing the property value index in equation (1.2) with this ratio and by introducing an adjustable policy parameter, as in the previous paragraph.

Although wealth neutrality is the equity standard that has been set by several state supreme courts and touted by several policymakers, no state has implemented an aid program designed to achieve it, that is, a program that incorporates the adjustments required to account for districts' behavioral responses to the aid formula. Aid programs of this type are simply too complicated to implement. The inconsistency between access equality and a performance-based method for measuring discrimination has been recognized, at least implicitly, by several state supreme courts. In its 1997 decision, *Brigham v. State*, for example, the Vermont Supreme Court calls for access equality but also says that "differences among school districts in terms of size, special educational needs, transportation costs, and other factors will invariably create unavoidable differences in per-pupil expenditures" (p. 22). Nevertheless, Vermont, unlike Texas, does not use a performance-based method for measuring education in its GTB formula, and no state has even considered a performance-based expression of its GTB program's equity objective.

Duncombe and Yinger (1998) also show that GTB formulas are not very good for achieving educational adequacy; even if wealth neutrality or fiscal neutrality is achieved through the implementation of the formula, some districts will decide to levy tax rates that are well below the rate needed to fund any reasonable adequacy target. Moreover, foundation formulas cannot eliminate the correlation between educational outcomes and wealth (or fiscal health) without an extremely high value for the foundation level and a required minimum tax rate. Different aid formulas clearly satisfy different equity objectives.

Table 1.3
Aid formulas and equity objectives

Equity standard	Definition of education		
	Spending per pupil	Real resources per pupil	Student performance
Adequacy	Standard foundation formula (with required minimum tax rate)	Foundation formula with foundation level adjusted for resource costs	Foundation formula with foundation level adjusted for educational costs
Access equality	Standard GTB formula	GTB formula with adjustment for resource costs	GTB formula with adjustment for educational costs
Fiscal neutrality	Standard GTB formula with adjustment for behavioral response	GTB formula with adjustments for resource costs and behavioral response	GTB formula with adjustments for educational costs and behavioral response
Equality	Standard foundation formula with prohibition of supplementation	Foundation formula with adjustment for resource costs and no supplementation	Foundation formula with adjustment for educational costs and no supplementation

1.2.2.3 Summary The foregoing discussion is summarized in table 1.3, which indicates the type of aid formula that is required to achieve each possible combination of the three methods for measuring education and the four equity standards presented in section 1.2.1. Many of the aid formulas specified in this table have never been tried. As I show in section 1.3, however, examples can be found among the states of all the formulas in the first row, and some of these have been combined with restrictions on supplementation that move them toward an equality standard, as in the table's last row. It is not surprising that most of the other formulas in the table have not been tried because, as explained earlier, they involve complex adjustments either for educational costs or for behavioral responses by school districts or both.

1.3 Policy Choices in State Aid Reform

With the background presented in the previous section, we can now turn to a discussion of the themes raised by the chapters in this book. The first set of themes, which is considered in this section, involves the policy choices that states must make in reforming their education finance system. The second set of themes, which is considered in the following section, involves an evaluation of existing efforts to reform education finance in the states.

1.3.1   What Is the Appropriate Aid Formula?

Perhaps the most fundamental step in any effort to reform education funding is the selection of a formula for awarding a state's educational aid to localities. This selection is usually guided by the legal requirements in court decisions, but of course it also reflects the interests of state policymakers. As discussed in Lukemeyer (chapter 2), many of the early state court decisions in the area of education finance equity focused on access equality. On the basis of these decisions, several states, including California, adopted GTB formulas (Sonstelie, Brunner, and Ardon 2000). Lukemeyer also points out that several state courts have not distinguished among access equality, wealth neutrality, and equality, so that the signals they are sending about the right aid formula to select are, to say the least, confusing.

Recent state court decisions have emphasized adequacy as the objective of the education finance system. According to the widely cited 1989 Kentucky Supreme Court decision in *Rose v. Council for Better Education*, for example, all students have the constitutional right to "an equal opportunity to an adequate education." The recent decision by New York's highest court in *Campaign for Fiscal Equity v. New York* (2003) also emphasized adequacy. According to this decision, the state must provide "schoolchildren the opportunity for a meaningful high school education, one which prepares them to function productively as civic participants" (slip op. at 15). It is perhaps not surprising, therefore, that all five of the states discussed in part II of this book have based their education finance reforms on a foundation plan.

With or without a court case to guide a state in its choice of a method for financing education, foundation aid formulas are very popular. In fact, forty-one states employ a foundation formula (appendix table B.3).[21] In many cases, therefore, "reform" of a state's education finance system involves passing a significant increase in the foundation level (E^*), instead of coming up with a new funding formula altogether.

Regardless of whether the foundation formula in a state is old or new, the generosity of a reform program based on it is determined largely by the foundation level. The *Rose* decision in Kentucky implicitly called for a high foundation level by ruling that the state constitution required an education system providing each student with a set of seven capacities, such as "sufficient oral and written communication skills to enable students to function in a complex and rapidly changing civilization." Other states have set less ambitious, and hence less costly, standards (see appendix B).

A second key issue in regard to the use of a foundation formula is whether localities are required to impose the minimum property tax rate specified in the formula. As explained earlier, the foundation level of spending in the formula is unlikely to be reached without such a requirement. Although twenty-eight of the states with foundation formulas require a minimum tax rate to be imposed in the state's localities or, equivalently, that localities provide a minimum local share of education costs, the others do not (appendix table B.4).

Only three states, Indiana, Missouri and Wisconsin, rely exclusively on a GTB formula to finance education in the state. However, four of the states considered in this book (Kansas, Kentucky, Texas, and Vermont) combine their foundation programs with a second tier of aid based on a GTB formula. Such an approach is also used in six other states, and Delaware combines flat grants with a GTB-like formula (appendix table B.3). In states that use this type of approach, the foundation aid is given first, and the GTB applies to taxes above the minimum rate in the foundation formula, generally up to some maximum.[22] Such an approach is designed to ensure that a minimum education level is achieved throughout the state via the foundation formula and then to place districts on an equal footing if they want to supplement the foundation level by raising additional taxes. In other words, it combines the adequacy standard with the access equality standard for supplementation.

This type of approach has been recommended by several scholars (Gess et al. 1996; Odden and Picus 1992), but on the basis of the results of some simulations, one of those scholars (Odden 1999) recently changed his mind. These simulations showed that adding a second-tier GTB formula on top of a foundation formula may actually lower the equity of educational outcomes in a state on a variety of measures, despite the large price subsidy it provides to low-wealth districts.[23] This result reflects a point made earlier in this chapter about the tax rate employed in a foundation formula: If districts are not required to tax at this rate at a minimum, many low-wealth districts will decide to set their tax rates below the rate in the formula so that they can free up money for nonschool spending.[24] This type of response is clearly evident in states that impose no minimum tax rate on localities.[25] It follows that when a minimum tax rate is imposed, most low-wealth districts are forced to tax at a rate that is above the one that they would select if they were unconstrained. When a GTB plan is added, most low-wealth districts find that the required minimum rate is so far above the one they would otherwise prefer that they do not want to increase their tax rate any further, despite the large price subsidy they stand to receive through the GTB plan. As a result, only districts with property values that are relatively high but still below V^* are affected by the GTB plan; these districts do not feel constrained by the requirement of a minimum tax rate and respond to the modest price subsidy they receive from the GTB formula.

This analysis provides a reminder of how important it is to distinguish between access equality and wealth neutrality or any other equity standard based on the distribution of education (however defined) across districts. A second-tier GTB does equalize the ability of all districts in a state to supplement the foundation level of spending, but it does not equalize spending or cost-adjusted spending across districts, because it fails to recognize that the tax rate in low-wealth districts is already far above the level that they would choose if they were unconstrained. In this context, granting access equality is essentially meaningless, because low-wealth districts are not in a position to take advantage of the access they have been given.

When it is used as a second tier on top of a foundation program, therefore, a GTB program is a poor tool for boosting educational spending in an equitable manner. For any equity objective except strict access equality, a better approach is to repeal the GTB program and use the resulting savings to fund a higher foundation level.

1.3.2 Should the Formula Account for Student Characteristics and Wage Costs?

A second key policy choice is whether to bring educational costs into state aid reform. In the terms of table 1.3, the issue is whether to shift the measurement of education from spending per pupil to real resources per pupil or to performance. The highest courts in some states, such as New York and Tennessee, have explicitly rejected spending as a way to measure education because it does not account for educational costs, and many other courts implicitly reject spending by talking about "educational quality" (Lukemeyer, chapter 2).[26]

Perhaps the clearest signals on educational costs have come from New Jersey. In 1998, for example, the New Jersey Supreme Court ruled, in *Abbott v. Burke* (*Abbott v. Burke V*), that the state was responsible for providing supplementary programs in twenty-eight urban school districts to bring student performance in these districts up to an adequate level (Goertz and Edwards 1999).[27] To be specific, the court required the state to provide these urban schools with whole-school reform, kindergarten, a half day of preschool for three- and four-year-olds, coordination with health programs, and programs to deal with security and technology.[28] Additional requirements for the preschool programs, such as student-teacher ratios, were spelled out in *Abbott v. Burke* in 2000 (*Abbott v. Burke VI*).

All these requirements explicitly recognize that educational costs are higher in urban districts, with their concentration of disadvantaged students, than in others.[29] As the court put it in an earlier decision,

We have decided this case on the premise that the children of poorer urban districts are as capable as all others; that their deficiencies stem from their socioeconomic status; and that through an effective education and changes in that socioeconomic status, they can perform as well as others. Our constitutional mandate does not allow us to consign poorer children permanently to an inferior education on the theory that they cannot afford a better one or that they would not benefit from it. (*Abbott v. Burke* [1990] [*Abbott v. Burke II*], 385–386)

The New Jersey court has not recognized, however, that educational costs also may vary across nonurban districts (see Lauver, Ritter, and Goertz 2001).

These court decisions, along with the growing emphasis on performance in state education policy, appear to have encouraged states to include cost adjustments in their state educational aid formulas. A recent survey finds that "38 states currently distribute some education funds on the basis of poverty" (Carey 2002, 1), which is a key determinant of educational costs. Of these states, thirteen incorporate district poverty into their main aid formula, eighteen have supplementary aid programs weighted toward districts with poor children, and seven use both of these approaches.[30] Using a slightly broader definition than poverty, the U.S. Census finds that twenty states have categorical "compensatory" programs for "economically disadvantaged" students (appendix table B.2). Aid formulas in several states also reflect other factors known to affect educational costs, such as the cost of living or the share of students with limited English proficiency or with a handicap.[31] For example, thirty-three states have categorical aid programs for handicapped students (appendix table B.2), and only three states

(Delaware, Nevada, and South Dakota) have aid programs that ignore educational costs altogether (appendix table B.3).

Adjusting aid formulas for educational costs is difficult, however, and existing methods for doing so range from ad hoc cost adjustments in many states to a regression-based comprehensive cost index in Massachusetts during the 1980s (Bradbury et al. 1984). To account for the higher cost of educating poor students, sixteen states use pupil weights, five states make cost-based adjustments to their main aid formula, and twenty-four states use categorical grants; these figures include seven states that combine two of these approaches and leave out the twelve states with no cost-based aid (appendix table B.5). Clearly, no consensus has emerged on the best way to proceed, and existing methods almost certainly understate the variation in educational costs across districts.[32] Carey (2002) finds, for example, that the average state provides 17.2 percent more funding for a poor student than for a nonpoor student, whereas existing research suggests that the cost of educating a poor student is at least 100 percent higher than that of educating a nonpoor student.[33] Only one state, Maryland, gives every poor student an additional weight this high (appendix B).

All of the reforms reviewed in this book also involve some form of cost adjustment in the state educational aid formula. Kansas, Kentucky, Texas, and Vermont adjust their basic foundation amount for the share of a district's students in poverty, with special needs, or with limited English proficiency, but the adjustments are fairly ad hoc. Texas also adjusts for the geographic cost of living. Michigan does not include cost adjustments in its foundation amount but does provide categorical programs with ad hoc adjustments for concentrations of poor students or other students with special needs; unfortunately, these programs have never been fully funded and may therefore have relatively little impact on the state educational aid received by high-cost districts (see Cullen and Loeb, chapter 7).[34]

Perhaps the main issue in these cost adjustments, along with the ones in other states, is their ad hoc nature. As a result, existing cost adjustments move states away from the first column in table 1.3 toward the third column (usually in the first row), but none of them can be considered fully consistent with a performance-based method for measuring education. Several of the chapters in part II explore alternative, more accurate ways to account for educational costs.[35] Given the emphasis of state education policy on student performance, this is a key issue for scholars and policymakers to pursue.

Cost adjustments in state aid reforms in the five states examined in part II raise two additional issues. First, the reforms in Kansas, Texas, and Vermont include a cost adjustment that raises the foundation level for the smallest districts. Size adjustments also appear in the aid programs of fourteen other states (appendix table B.5). This type of adjustment is not about transportation costs, which are considered separately. Instead, the rationale for this type of adjustment is the well-known result (surveyed in Andrews, Duncombe, and Yinger 2002) that the per-pupil cost of education is higher in very small districts than in medium-sized ones. It is not clear, however, that a cost adjustment is the appropriate response to this finding, because the cost disadvantage of small districts can be eliminated in many cases through district consolidation (Duncombe and Yinger 2001b). If per-pupil costs can be lowered through consolidation, a state is wasting money by rewarding districts that refuse to consolidate.[36] More research is needed to determine the circumstances under which consolidation of school districts is a cost-effective option.

Second, four of the states examined in this book, Kansas, Kentucky, Michigan, and Texas, provide more aid to districts with a relatively high concentration of "exceptional" or gifted students. The aid programs in thirty other states follow suit (appendix table B.6). These provisions have nothing to do with ensuring adequacy in student performance. An educational cost adjustment is designed to recognize that some districts must spend more than others to achieve a given level of student performance. Districts with many exceptional students may decide to spend money on special programs for these students, but these districts have to spend *less* than other districts to reach any given performance target. Policymakers and courts may want to encourage the creation of programs for gifted students with provisions such as these, but if they do, they should recognize that these provisions are not cost adjustments and have nothing whatsoever to do with achieving performance objectives.[37]

1.3.3 Should Supplementation by Wealthy Districts Be Reduced?

Another key issue facing policymakers is whether education finance reform should reduce the extent to which wealthy (or otherwise low-need) districts supplement the foundation amount specified in the aid formula. The recent emphasis on adequacy in state court decisions indicates that restrictions on supplementation may not be required, but the continuing role of other equity standards in some states, including some that emphasize adequacy, suggests that reductions in supplementation may be called for in many, if not most, cases.[38] In fact, all five of the reform efforts reviewed in this book explicitly restrict supplementation by high-wealth districts to some degree.[39] These limits tend to be complicated and are often politically unpopular, so the debate on supplementation in these states is likely to continue for many years.[40] Moreover, virtually any aid reform plan includes some provisions that reduce this type of supplementation, even if those provisions are not explicitly designed to do so.

States limit supplementation in five ways. The most direct approach is simply to prohibit supplementation or to prohibit it beyond some limit. The Kansas reform, for example, prohibits supplementation beyond the spending level supported by its second-tier GTB program (Duncombe and Johnston, chapter 5), the Kentucky reform prohibits supplementation beyond 30 percent above the spending level supported by the state's second-tier GTB program (Flanagan and Murray, chapter 6), and the Michigan reform calls for phased-in provisions that will eventually allow only a limited amount of supplementation even in the wealthiest districts (Cullen and Loeb, chapter 7).

These limitations on supplementation build on a long tradition of local tax and expenditure limitations, which exist in one form or another in forty-four states, usually with some form of override provision (O'Sullivan 2001).[41] In fact, all of the states examined in this book except Vermont had school property tax limitations before they implemented their school finance reform plans, and they either replaced their tax limitations with features of the reform plan or, as in Texas, incorporated the tax limitations into their reforms. Five other states with court-mandated school reform also already had school property tax limitations in place before the reforms, and four more states added such limitations after the implementation of a reform ordered by the state supreme court (see Evans, Murray, and Schwab 2001).[42] The last category includes the well-known case of California, which passed a property tax limitation, Proposition 13, in 1978, after the *Serrano I* and *Serrano II* decisions. This proposition dramatically limited school spending (Sonstelie, Brunner, and Ardon 2000).

A second approach to limiting supplementation, used by a few states, involves a second-tier GTB program with a recapture provision that raises the price of supplementation in high-wealth districts.[43] This approach does not forbid spending above the foundation level but instead discourages it by making its price very high. As noted earlier in the chapter, a large literature demonstrates that school districts are sensitive to price changes, so this approach can significantly lower spending by low-need districts. Versions of this approach are used by Texas and Vermont.

This approach has two weaknesses, however. First, it is likely to be unpopular in wealthy districts, where voters may resent the extra "tax" that it imposes. Second, the amount of revenue that it recaptures depends on the spending decisions of the high-wealth districts and therefore cannot be known when the state aid budget is determined. These problems are illustrated by the original second-tier GTB formula in Vermont, which applied to all revenue above the foundation amount (Downes, chapter 9). Vermont collected recaptured funds in an account and then returned them to districts based on the tax rate they imposed and (inversely) on their wealth. No state funds were involved. The key problem with this design was that it left all districts uncertain about the revenue consequences of their tax rate decisions.[44] This uncertainty was eliminated in 2003, when Vermont switched to a more traditional GTB formula (ACCESS 2003). The recapture provisions in the Texas reforms are less dramatic, primarily because they apply to only 88 (out of 965) school districts in the state (Imazeki and Reschovsky, chapter 8).[45] Moreover, the Texas provisions give wealthy districts five options for meeting their recapture obligations, thereby eliminating the uncertainty that was present in the original Vermont approach.

Both Texas and Vermont use their second-tier GTB formulas both to promote access equality and to limit supplementation. As explained earlier in the chapter, the promise of access equality is an empty one, and a better approach would be to use a GTB solely to promote the second objective. This requires a relatively low value for V^*, as in Vermont.[46] However, lowering V^*, magnifies the negative matching rates in the wealthiest districts and is therefore likely to increase their opposition to a reform plan. One way to mitigate this opposition would be to multiply the matching rate in equation (1.2) by a fraction, thereby lowering both the price increase that wealthy districts face and the reduction in supplementation.

The third way for a state to limit supplementation in low-need districts is to transform the property tax into a state tax and use the revenue to finance the foundation plan. As explained in section 1.2.2.1, this approach lowers the disposable income of high-wealth districts (or low-cost districts, if a cost adjustment is included in the foundation plan) relative to a foundation plan based on a local property tax. The resulting income effect results in a decline in the desired education spending level, and hence in the level of supplementation, in those districts. Although not definitive, the available evidence suggests that this approach, which operates through an income effect, is likely to have a smaller impact on supplementation than the GTB approach, which operates through a price effect.

The local property tax was transformed into a state tax as part of education finance reform efforts in Kansas (Duncombe and Johnston, chapter 5), Michigan (Cullen and Loeb, chapter 7), and Vermont (Downes, chapter 9), but the impact of these changes on supplementation was mitigated, if not eliminated, by the details of the transformation. In Kansas, the transformation was accompanied by large increases in state aid funded by other state taxes, primarily the sales tax, so that the current state-set property tax rate is below the prereform local property tax rate except in a few wealthy districts. State aid from other sources also increased in Vermont after the transformation, although to a lesser degree than in Kansas. In Michigan, the transformation was accompanied by a dramatic reduction in the property tax rate, so that the condition required to reduce supplementation, namely, a state tax rate above the prereform local tax rate, does not exist in any district.

The fourth way a state can limit supplementation in low-need districts is by redistributing state aid away from these districts toward high-need districts. This approach faces political obstacles, because it involves cutting the aid of low-need districts, but it is a relatively low-cost way to shift a state's focus away from general school support toward an adequacy standard. It builds on the relationship between state aid and local spending, which is another form of an income effect. According to a large literature, cutting aid to low-need districts lowers their effective income and induces them to choose a lower spending level for education (see Fisher and Papke 2000). Moreover, extensive empirical evidence indicates that the impact on school spending of a change in state aid is significantly larger than the impact of an equivalent change in voters' disposable income.[47] As a result, the type of redistribution involved in this approach is likely to have a larger impact on supplementation by low-need districts than is state takeover of the property tax, and it might have a larger impact than a GTB plan with recapture.

Finally, any state aid reform plan that raises state taxes in high-wealth (or otherwise low-need) districts will reduce supplementation in those districts to some degree. The more progressive the increase in state taxes, the larger this effect is likely to be. The education finance reform undertaken in Kentucky falls into this category; the state financed an increase in its foundation level through a significant increase in state taxes, along with an increase in the required minimum local tax rate (Flanagan and Murray, chapter 6).[48] This approach, like the previous two, works through income effects; that is, supplementation is reduced because of a decline in the resources available in high-wealth districts. In this case, however, the changes in financing affect voters in high-wealth districts only to the extent that variables predicting which voters experience an increase in taxes, such as their income, are correlated with district wealth. An income tax increase, for example, will lower supplementation in districts that have high wealth because their residents have high incomes and are able to buy expensive houses, but it will not lower supplementation in districts that have poor residents along with a power plant that results in high property wealth per pupil.

This discussion of ways to limit supplementation leads to four main conclusions. First, it is virtually impossible to reform state aid through an expanded foundation aid program without limiting supplementation by low-need districts. The limits on supplementation can be severe, as are those that have been imposed in Kansas, Michigan, and Vermont; moderate, as is that implemented in Texas; or weak, as is that applied in Kentucky. But the only way to increase the foundation spending level, E^*, in equation (1.1) without limiting supplementation is to pay for the increase entirely through an increase in the required local tax rate, t^*. This approach shifts resources toward the districts with the lowest wealth without influencing districts that are too wealthy to receive funding under the original foundation plan.[49] No existing state aid reform plan has relied exclusively on this approach, although, as noted earlier, it is part of the Kentucky plan.

The literature recognizes that state aid reform can promote educational equity by providing more resources to districts with low student performance (called "leveling up") or by restricting the ability of districts with high student performance to go beyond the provision of basic educational services ("leveling down"). As the cases considered in this book illustrate, all aid reform plans involve elements of both of

these strategies. Scholars disagree, however, on the net impact of the
typical reform; that is, they disagree about the impact of reform on
spending in the average district or on performance by the average student in the state. Murray, Evans, and Schwab (1998) and Dee (2000)
find that the typical reform involves more leveling up, whereas Hoxby
(2001) finds that many reform plans, especially the most dramatic, involve more leveling down.[50] According to Hoxby, this outcome reflects
the fact that some types of leveling down allow the state to keep its
own costs down. As she puts it: "It is expensive to bribe districts that
would prefer low spending into spending a lot. It is inexpensive to forbid high spending" (1222).

The analysis presented in this book does not reveal, of course,
whether the average reform levels up or levels down, but it does indicate that the choice for policymakers is not whether to reduce supplementation by low-need districts, but instead how much to reduce
supplementation using which approach. Some leveling down arises,
after all, even when a state uses state taxes to pay for an increase in the
foundation spending level. Thus, each state must select the approach to
supplementation that best fits the mandates of its courts and its policy
objectives.[51]

The second conclusion arising from the discussion of supplementation is that reductions in supplementation by high-wealth districts accompany state aid reforms designed to meet legitimate educational
objectives and do not necessarily arise simply from a state's desire to
minimize its own costs. It is true, of course, as Hoxby (2001) points out,
that a state may be able to minimize how much it must pay to meet
an equality standard by explicitly limiting supplementation in high-
wealth districts. It is also true, however, that supplementation by high-
wealth districts is reduced whenever a state decides, in the name of
fairness, to redistribute some of its aid money from wealthy to poor
districts or to pay for a higher foundation amount by turning a local
property tax into a state tax.

It is tempting to regard reductions in supplementation as part of education finance reform as somehow punitive or inappropriate because
they pull wealthy districts below their preferred level of school spending. In fact, however, the level of spending wealthy districts "prefer" is
heavily influenced by the education finance system in place prior to
any reform. This preferred level of spending is boosted by state aid, for
example, and it is boosted by a state's decision to set an extremely low
foundation spending level and thereby to forgo the high state taxes

needed to bring foundation spending up to a level courts or education experts regard as adequate. Indeed, this preferred level of spending is even influenced by the way the state draws school district boundaries, which are the principal determinant of a school district's wealth and of the extent to which its students are disadvantaged.[52] As a result, rejecting reductions in supplementation as part of a reform package is equivalent, in many cases, to endorsing the prereform education finance system created by the state.

A better approach to the issue of supplementation would be for a state considering reform to decide on its educational objectives, on constitutional or policy grounds, and then to determine which methods for reducing supplementation by wealthy districts are most consistent with those objectives. The analysis surrounding this determination should recognize that preventing wealthy districts from using their own funds to supplement the state's foundation amount may promote an equality objective but also imposes costs on society in the form of lost educational benefits in those districts.[53] It should also recognize, however, that a state may not be able to meet its constitutional or policy-based equity objectives without removing some of the existing subsidies that wealthy districts receive in the form of state aid or tax relief.

The third conclusion is that supplementation by wealthy districts can be reduced through a variety of policies, but little is known about the relative impact of different approaches. Explicit limits on supplementation may appear to be the most effective policy, but these limits can be set to permit such high levels of supplementation that they have little impact on behavior. Moreover, inferences about the income and price effects of many policies on school district spending can be made on the basis of related studies, but there is no direct evidence on the extent to which supplementation is reduced by GTB programs with recapture, state takeover of local property taxes, redistribution of existing aid funds, or tax increases to pay for a higher foundation spending level. As indicated earlier in the chapter, my own ranking based on existing indirect evidence is that GTB programs and redistribution of existing aid funds have the largest effects on supplementation, followed by state takeover of the property tax, and then by increases in other state taxes, but more research on this topic is clearly needed.

The fourth conclusion is that the reforms in Kansas, Kentucky, Michigan, and Texas all combine some adjustments of aid amounts for differences in educational costs with some limits on supplementation.

In effect, therefore, these reforms bear some resemblance to the entry in the bottom right of table 1.3, which involves full cost adjustment and no supplementation. The actual reforms do not go all the way to the system described in that entry, however, because both their cost adjustments and their equalization efforts are incomplete.

1.3.4   How Should State Aid Reform Be Financed?

Another fundamental issue in any school aid reform plan is how to pay for it. This issue has two parts. The first part is the extent to which the burden for funding a state's schools should be shifted from school districts to the state, and the second part is the choice of taxes to fund the state's share of the burden.

The average state provides half of the revenue for elementary and secondary education, but this share varies widely from state to state (see appendix table B.1). Concern about the state's contribution has been central to the education finance debate since *Serrano I* identified the local property tax as a source of educational inequity. Because other local taxes are generally not available to school districts, any funding plan for education that reduces reliance on the local property tax almost inevitably involves an increase in the state's share of educational funding. With one exception, every education funding reform plan discussed in this book both reduces local property taxes and increases the state's share of the funding burden. The exception is the reform in Kentucky, in which the state share of funding was already very high and, as noted previously, both state and local taxes were increased.

In many states that have undertaken reform of their systems for funding education, including Michigan and Vermont, voter dissatisfaction with high property taxes was also a key motivation for the reform. In Michigan, for example, a frustrated legislature decided to eliminate the state's property tax to force the state to design a better education finance system (Cullen and Loeb, chapter 7). Moreover, concern for high property tax burdens is such a powerful issue in some states that it gets in the way of school aid reform.

Consider the case of New York, which passed a $3 billion School Tax Relief Program (STAR) in 1997. This program takes the form of a state-funded homestead exemption, which exempts homeowners from school property taxes on the first $30,000 of the market value of their home. STAR provides little, however, help for districts with a high concentration of renters, particularly the poor urban districts, which are the neediest school districts in the state (Duncombe and Yinger 2001a).[54] Its cost represents over 20 percent of the state's budget for education aid. With this much money, New York could have implemented a new state aid program that would have gone a long way toward eliminating the educational inequities that are currently under debate after the *CFE v. New York* decision by the state's highest court.[55] This type of aid increase would also provide property tax relief, because aid increases are not fully translated into spending increases, and it could be designed to promote widely recognized educational-equity standards.

The extent of any shift from local to state funding that results from school finance reform is largely controlled through decisions about the parameters of the school aid formula. With a foundation formula, the key issues are the magnitudes of the foundation spending level and of the required minimum local property tax rate. Raising the foundation spending level with the required tax rate held constant raises the state's share of education funding. Moreover, the lower this tax rate for a given foundation level, the higher the state share of education funding must be.[56] If the property tax is turned into a state tax—that is, if the revenue from the property tax is sent directly to the state rather than to the localities—then the decision about the property tax rate determines the share of education revenue that comes from the property tax, instead of from other state taxes.

One implication of this analysis is that a state can minimize the increase in state taxes (or, if the property tax is a state tax, in other state taxes) needed to finance a higher adequacy standard by raising the minimum required property tax rate school districts must charge. With a local property tax, however, a state obviously cannot fully fund reform in this way, because it places the burden for financing reform on the neediest districts. Moreover, any preexisting voter dissatisfaction with the property tax may undermine this approach, regardless of whether the property tax is collected by school districts or the state.

Policymakers also must decide whether to pay for any increase in the state's contribution to education that may result from education finance reform by increasing the state income tax or the state sales tax. This choice raises complex issues of equity and efficiency that will not be addressed here. Suffice it to say that a debate about the best state tax to use to finance a state aid reform plan is an appropriate, and almost inevitable, part of designing such a plan. One interesting example comes from Michigan, where the voters explicitly selected a higher sales tax over a higher income tax as a way to pay for education aid reform in the state (Cullen and Loeb, chapter 7).

1.3.5   Should Aid Reform Be Linked to Accountability?

A fourth choice that policymakers designing a plan for state aid reform must make is whether state education aid should be linked to an accountability program. As noted earlier, virtually all states have some type of accountability program, and a majority of states have a program that imposes some type of financial rewards and punishments. The courts did not link accountability to state aid reform until fairly recently, but the Kentucky Supreme Court's *Rose* decision in 1989 threw out the state's existing system of school governance and brought new visibility to accountability programs. Moreover, the recent state aid reforms in Kentucky, Michigan, and Texas have all been accompanied by accountability programs that include district-level rewards and sanctions.

It is now widely recognized that state aid reform and accountability are inextricably linked (Figlio, chapter 3). State legislatures are often reluctant to give more money to school districts without assurances that the money will be well spent, and some scholars have found that increases in state aid are likely to undermine school district efficiency (Duncombe and Yinger 1997, 1998). (In this context, efficiency is a measure of a school district's success in translating inputs into student performance, after accounting for factors outside the district's control, such as concentrated poverty among its students.) Indeed, some scholars have argued that aid increases are unlikely to boost student performance at all, either because their negative impacts on school district efficiency are so large or because additional inputs are unable to influence performance.[57] Because of these concerns it seems reasonable to combine aid increases for needy school districts with accountability programs that preserve the efficiency with which these districts operate and even encourage them to operate with greater efficiency.

The problem is that our knowledge of accountability programs is distressingly limited. Many of the early accountability programs were seriously flawed because they set up rewards based solely on student test scores. Approaches of this sort fail to recognize that poor performance depends both on a school district's efficiency and on cost factors, such as wage rates and student characteristics, that are outside the district's control. An "accountability" system that punishes a district because it contains many disadvantaged students obviously makes no sense.

Unfortunately, however, it is difficult to separate these two causes of poor performance. Some existing accountability programs have made steps in this direction (Clotfelter and Ladd 1996; Hanushek and Raymond 2001; Ladd 2001; Murnane and Levy 2001), but to some degree all existing programs reward some districts and punish others for factors that are outside the districts' control.[58] These points are nicely summarized by Hansen (2001, 2):

Research is just beginning into the reliability and stability of different methods of ranking and rating schools for the purposes of determining rewards and sanctions. Differences in school size and in the size of relevant cohorts of students ... can result in accountability systems with perverse incentives.... Improperly designed incentives can have serious effects on the morale and motivation of school personnel.

Moreover, there is no compelling evidence on the impact of accountability programs on student performance. One study (Ladd 1999) finds some evidence consistent with a positive impact on student achievement resulting from Dallas's accountability program, but this study observes only a single year before the program was implemented and cannot rule out the possibility that the observed increases in student performance in later years reflect something unusual about this year, instead of the impact of the accountability program. Ultimately, accountability programs themselves must be held accountable. If they do not result in higher student performance, then they should be dropped. There is obviously room for more research on this important topic and for experiments with more accountability programs.

The objective of accountability programs is to give school districts incentives to be more efficient, that is, to improve student performance with no increase in resources. An alternative method for promoting this objective is to mandate certain teaching or management practices that, in the opinion of state officials, will result in higher school efficiency. This approach was taken by the New Jersey Supreme Court, which, as noted earlier, required the state to implement a specific whole-school reform program in twenty-eight (later thirty) low-performing urban school districts. Moreover, in its 1989 *Rose* decision, the Kentucky Supreme Court found constitutional violations in school curriculum and governance, as well as in school finance. The subsequent reforms included major changes in curriculum and management (see Flanagan and Murray, chapter 6).

1.3.6   Should Aid Reform Be Linked to School Choice?

Expanding school choice is another type of policy that is linked to education finance reform in several states. School choice plans, which come in many different forms, give parents alternatives to sending their children to the local public schools in their neighborhood. Choice plans allow parents to send their children to other schools in the same district or to schools in other districts, enable the creation of public charter schools subject to fewer restrictions than existing public schools, or provide vouchers that parents can use to help send their children to private schools. These plans are intended not only to provide parents with choices regarding their children's education but also to promote competition among schools. Some people argue that such competition will force existing public schools to improve, that is, to become more efficient (see chapter 4).

The potential role of school choice in school aid reform is illustrated by the case of Michigan (Cullen and Loeb, chapter 7). The school aid reforms implemented in Michigan in 1994 included strong encouragement of charter schools, and these reforms were complemented with a new school choice plan a few years later. Michigan now has about 180 charter schools, three-quarters of which are run by private, for-profit companies (*New York Times* 2002).

. Charter schools and school choice plans are difficult to evaluate, but the limited available evidence does not suggest that charter schools provide significantly better education than other public schools or that competition from charter schools or choice plans forces public schools to become more efficient (Gill et al. 2001). Nevertheless, these approaches continue to have many supporters, and they will undoubtedly continue to be the subject of further experiments and further research.

School vouchers have not been part of any major school finance reform plan implemented to date, but vouchers have been used in several places, including Milwaukee, Cleveland, and Florida. The Florida voucher plan blends the notions of choice and accountability by making vouchers available to students in schools rated "failing" by the state (see Figlio, chapter 3). So far, however, only a handful of students have made use of the voucher option. A 2002 U.S. Supreme Court decision, *Zelman v. Simmons-Harris*, upheld the constitutionality of the Cleveland vouchers, which are used primarily to send children to Catholic schools. As a result, voucher plans may become more widely used in the future.

The available evidence indicates that some existing voucher programs have a small positive impact on the performance of participating students, at least in mathematics, whereas other voucher programs have no impact on performance at all (Rouse 1998). This evidence, however, is difficult to interpret. Rouse (2000) presents some evidence, for example, suggesting that the Milwaukee voucher program has a small positive effect on math performance because of smaller class sizes in the private schools attended by Milwaukee voucher recipients than in the public schools these students would otherwise attend. The cause of this class size difference is not known, however. Voucher proponents might argue that it arises because private schools are more efficient than public schools and can hire more teachers with the money they save. Voucher opponents can counter that these extra teachers could be hired thanks to cost savings associated with a smaller concentration of disadvantaged students in participating private schools than in the public school population as a whole. Moreover, participants in the Cleveland program primarily send their children to Catholic schools because subsidies to these schools from the Catholic Church keep the tuition low enough that the voucher can cover it. Subsidies of this type obviously would not be available in a large voucher program.

1.3.7   Should Capital Spending Be Included?

A final choice for policymakers confronting education aid reform is whether the reform plan should attempt to promote equity in capital spending. With some notable exceptions, most of the court cases have focused on the equity of operating spending in the state, not of capital spending. One important exception can be found in New Jersey, where capital spending was included in the original *Robinson v. Cahill* ruling in 1973 and where the 1997 *Abbott v. Burke* ruling (*Abbott v. Burke IV*) explicitly called for more capital spending in poor urban school districts (Goertz and Edwards 1999).[59] Capital spending was not included in the initial court cases involving school aid reform in Texas, but in its 1995 decision in *Edgewood Independent School District v. Meno*, known as *Edgewood IV*, the Texas Supreme Court ordered the state to deal with inequity in capital spending among the state's school districts (see Imazeki and Reschovsky, chapter 8). Moreover, as noted earlier, a recent supreme court decision in Arizona and recent trial court decisions in Alaska and New Mexico declared that these states' systems for funding capital spending are unconstitutional (see appendix A).

At one level, it obviously makes no sense to eliminate inequities across districts within a state in operating spending but to allow them in capital spending; after all, both types of spending are crucial for providing education. It is also true, however, that capital spending has a less direct connection to student performance than does operating spending and that state formulas for building and operating aid tend to be fundamentally different from one another (Sielke 2001).

Compared to operating aid, for example, building aid relies much more heavily on matching grants (appendix C). In fact, only six states rely exclusively on lump-sum grants for capital spending, whereas twenty-three states use only matching grants, and nine states use a combination of the two. Regardless of the formula used, many of these grants also require that individual building projects be approved by the state. In contrast, eleven states do not provide any building aid to localities at all, and Hawaii, with its state school system, fully funds school capital spending. Finally, building aid programs are far less likely than operating aid programs to adjust for district property wealth. To be specific, only twenty-five states have at least one building aid program weighted toward low-wealth districts.

Unfortunately, the principles behind and the behavioral consequences of these building aid formulas are not well understood. More work by both policymakers and scholars is clearly needed to shed light on inequities involved in capital spending—and on the best ways to alleviate them.

1.4   Analyzing the Effects of State Aid Reform

A second set of themes in this book involves the effects of reforms to state education-aid programs. Are court mandates actually implemented? Do state aid reforms eliminate disparities in spending and in student performance? Do these reforms have unintended consequences, and are they undermined or reinforced by behavioral responses unanticipated by policymakers? We now turn to an examination of these questions.

1.4.1   To What Extent (and Over What Period) Are Court Mandates Implemented?

In most cases, state education-aid reform is stimulated by a state supreme court decision. One of the key factors influencing the effectiveness of the eventual reform, therefore, is the process that leads from a court decision to an actual aid reform program. This process appears to depend on the willingness of the state's legislative and executive branches to respond to a court decision that overturns the state's education finance system and on the willingness of the state supreme court to impose specific requirements on the other branches of government in the state. To some degree, of course, the legislative and executive branches must defer to the court on constitutional matters, and courts traditionally have deferred to the other branches of government on matters of educational policy. But despite this general standard of deference, the range of outcomes for this process is amazingly large.

In some states, a relatively weak signal from the courts results in dramatic reform by the legislative and executive branches. Kansas (Duncombe and Johnston, chapter 5) provides one example of this type of situation. Maryland provides another. In 1994 a trial court in Maryland approved a settlement that called for the state to increase its funding for Baltimore's schools. In 2000, this court ruled that this decree had not been followed and ordered the state to increase its funding to Baltimore. The legislature and governor did not immediately comply with the court's ruling but instead set up a commission to make recommendations for improving the adequacy and equity of education in Maryland. This commission issued its final report in January 2002 and recommended a dramatic increase in state education aid to localities, particularly for schools with high concentrations of poor students, students with special needs, or students with limited English proficiency. A grassroots campaign convinced the legislature to pass legislation based on the commission's recommendations, and these recommendations were signed into law in April of the same year (Montgomery 2002; Hunter 2003).

Another common route to state aid reform is a clear state supreme court decision that is taken seriously by the legislative and executive branches. This route is illustrated by Kentucky (Murray and Flanagan, chapter 6) and Vermont (Downes, chapter 9). The Vermont case is somewhat unusual in that voter dissatisfaction with high property taxes was reflected in the legislature that was elected right before the state supreme court handed down its decision in 1997 striking down the state's education funding system. As a result, this legislature acted promptly to put a new system in place.

Other states have witnessed a drawn-out tug-of-war between the legislative and executive branches on the one hand and the courts on the other. Texas (Imazeki and Reschovsky, chapter 8) provides one example of this pattern and Ohio (ACCESS 2003) provides another.[60] The most dramatic example, however, is undoubtedly New Jersey (Goertz and Edwards 1999; ACCESS 2003), which has experienced decades of legislative and executive resistance to reform of the state's school finance system combined with gradual strengthening of requirements imposed on the state by the state's highest court. The original lawsuit challenging the education finance system in New Jersey was filed in 1970, and in 1973 the New Jersey Supreme Court ruled, in *Robinson v. Cahill*, that the state's education finance system did not meet the constitutional requirement in the state for "thorough and efficient" schools. The New Jersey Supreme Court has issued twelve more decisions in the area of education finance since then, and the battle between policymakers and the courts continued into 2003. The legislature responded to the early decisions by increasing the state's share of education funding, but not until *Robinson v. Cahill* in 1976 (*Robinson v. Cahill V*) did the court give tentative approval to a state aid system. Despite this approval, the legislature refused to appropriate money for its own legislation, so the court briefly shut down the schools in the summer of 1976. This action led to a state income tax to fund school aid followed by the reopening of the schools in time for the 1976–77 school year.

A second round of litigation, known as *Abbott v. Burke*, began when the Education Law Center filed a lawsuit on behalf of the state's urban school districts. After a series of preliminary decisions, the court ruled in favor of the plaintiffs; that is, it required education finance reform. Twice the state passed legislation in an attempt to satisfy the court, and twice the court ruled that the new legislation was still unconstitutional. The court's frustration with state policymakers finally led it to impose specific spending requirements on the state. As noted above, the court ruled, in *Abbott v. Burke V* in 1998 and in *Abbott v. Burke VI* in 2000, that the state was responsible for funding a variety of specific programs in urban schools. The long-standing battle between policymakers and the court appeared to end early in 2002, when the new governor of New Jersey, James McGreevey, dropped the state's opposition to the court orders issued in the *Abbott* decisions and set up a panel to oversee the state's implementation of the requirements the court had imposed (Kocieniewski 2002).[61]

Overall, anyone trying to understand state aid reform in a given state would do well to begin by looking into the role of the state courts in the reform process and the interplay between courts and policymakers. These factors are, of course, different in every state, but they almost always have a significant impact on the nature of the reform package that is ultimately adopted.

1.4.2 Effects on the Equality of Spending

A key issue in evaluating state aid reform is whether it actually makes school spending more equitable, that is, whether it reduces disparities in spending across school districts, as required by several state supreme court decisions. All five chapters in part II of this book examine this issue, and all find that reform does reduce spending disparities, sometimes substantially, but does not lead to complete spending equality.[62] These chapters build on the work of several scholars who have studied the link between aid reform and spending equality using national data.

Murray, Evans, and Schwab (1998) examine data for over 10,000 school districts in forty-six states over the period 1972 to 1992. During this period, eleven of the states studied implemented court-mandated education aid reforms. Murray and her colleagues find that these reforms significantly reduced spending inequality across districts.[63] The precise results vary with the measure of inequality they use, but all measures suggest large reductions in inequality—on the order of 20 to 30 percent. They also find that these reductions in inequality reflect an increase in spending by the districts that spent the least before the reforms combined with no change in spending in the highest-spending districts. Finally, they find that state aid reform is always accompanied by a significant increase in the share of education spending that is financed by the state government.

Evans, Murray, and Schwab (1997, 1999) explore the impact of court-ordered reform on the sources of revenue in various types of school districts. They find that the lowest-income districts (and the districts with the lowest levels of local revenue before reform) raised less money for education after reform but that the cuts in their local revenue were more than offset by their increased state aid.[64] These results imply that the typical reform did not impose a high minimum tax rate on all school districts.

An alternative approach to the impact of state aid reform on spending equity is provided by Hoxby (2001). Instead of treating state aid reform as an event, she develops a framework for classifying state aid systems, using equations similar to (1.1) and (1.2), and determines the parameters of the aid systems in every state in 1990. Many other studies have used a similar approach for a single state, but no other study has attempted it for all the states in the nation. This approach allows her to determine how the spending in a school district is affected by the parameters of the state aid system, which differ across states and sometimes across districts within a state, instead of assuming that all state aid reforms have the same effect.

Hoxby finds that per-pupil spending in a school district responds as expected to the parameters of a foundation aid program, and specifically, that it increases with the foundation amount and decreases with the required minimum tax rate.[65] She also finds that spending decreases with the tax price, which is defined as the amount of money a district must raise itself to obtain another dollar of spending per pupil.[66] A standard GTB program lowers the tax price in low-wealth districts, because, as shown earlier, it shifts a share of any spending increase onto the state. Moreover, a GTB program with recapture raises the tax price in high-wealth districts. This result implies, therefore, that a GTB program with recapture will decrease spending where wealth is high and increase it where wealth is low.

Hoxby summarizes these results by showing the impact of each state's education aid system on various measures of spending equality across districts (compared to a system of local finance alone). She finds that the state aid system increases equality in every state. The magnitude of this increase is particularly large in states with dramatic equalization programs.[67] In other words, state aid reform can increase across-district equity in per-pupil spending, but existing state aid systems also promote such equity, even if they do not reflect a major reform.

Overall, there appears to be a broad consensus that state aid reform can reduce across-district inequality in spending per pupil. As discussed earlier in the chapter, however, different aid reforms are linked to different notions of equity. A reform that raises the foundation spending level, for example, promotes an adequacy objective, and adjusting this spending level for educational costs provides a way to express this objective in performance terms. Moreover, the evidence in Hoxby (2001) suggests that all states engage in some equalization. The key issue for policymakers and courts, therefore, is not whether the state should use education aid to make education spending more equitable; instead, the issue is how it should equalize—and how much.

1.4.3   Effects on Equality of Performance

As discussed earlier, the emphasis in the debate about state aid reform has gradually shifted from spending to student performance. Another key question, therefore, is whether state aid reform leads to an increase in student performance, particularly for districts in which performance is relatively low. This question has proven to be difficult to study, however, and no consensus on the answer has yet emerged. Some insight into the complexity of the topic is provided by the chapters in part II of this book, each of which investigates, using the best available evidence, the impact of a particular state aid reform on student performance. Although some of the evidence indicates that state aid reform can boost student performance, none of the findings are definitive, and some of them are quite ambiguous. In Texas, for example, evidence from state-designed tests indicates that aid reform boosted the performance of poor students and students from minority groups, but this result is not confirmed by the evidence from national tests (Imazeki and Reschovsky, chapter 8).

As discussed by Figlio (chapter 3), the main problems confronting any national study of the impact of state aid reform on student performance are (1) the enormous diversity in the nature of state aid reform plans and (2) the paucity of national-level student performance data. One study that addresses the first of these problems is Hoxby 2001.[68] Following the methodology she developed to study the impact of state aid reform on spending equality, Hoxby estimates the impact of various state aid parameters on the dropout rate, which is one dimension of student performance. She finds that a higher foundation spending level is associated with a lower dropout rate. A typical foundation program does not, of course, raise spending in high-spending districts. Thus, Hoxby concludes, "equalization improves student achievement the most (perhaps only) in schools that would have very low spending if left to their own devices" (1228).[69]

Overall, the available evidence suggests that complicated reform plans that involve GTB formulas and recapture have complicated impacts on student performance that are difficult to sort out and that may not always correspond to the effects that were expected when the plans were formulated. This is, in effect, another application of the insight provided by Feldstein (1975) many years ago, namely, that one cannot predict the outcomes of a state aid reform without understanding the incentives it creates for school districts and estimating how the districts will respond to those incentives. In contrast, the available evidence is also consistent with the view that foundation plans can boost student performance in low-performing districts. Nevertheless, the precise nature of this impact is still unclear, and more research is needed to determine the impact on performance of various state decisions, such as the foundation spending level, whether districts are required to impose a tax that does not fall below a certain minimum rate, and whether the foundation level is adjusted for educational costs.

1.4.4 Effects on School District Efficiency

School district inefficiency is defined by scholars as a situation in which a school district spends more than necessary to achieve a given student performance. School districts are inefficient when they provide services that make minimal contributions to student performance or when they use outmoded management or teaching techniques.[70] Unlike student performance or school spending, however, school district inefficiency cannot be directly measured, and scholars are just beginning to devise methods for studying it. All existing methods have important limitations, and scholars have not reached a consensus on the best method to use (see Bifulco and Bretschneider 2001; McCarty and Yaisawarng 1993).

Using data for New York state, Duncombe and Yinger (1997, 2001a) estimate the impact of state aid on school district efficiency and then simulate the impact on efficiency of various state aid reform proposals. They measure efficiency using a technique called "data envelopment analysis," which determines the extent to which each district spends more per pupil than other districts with the same student performance.[71] They also control for education costs; as noted earlier, a district should not be called inefficient if spends more than other districts due to the characteristics of its students or other factors beyond its control.

Duncombe and Yinger (2001a) find that a school district's efficiency increases when it receives less aid than districts with which it is likely to compare itself, namely, those that are similar to it in terms of property values and student enrollment, or when it is in a class of districts that receives less aid than other classes. These results suggest that low-aid districts make extra efforts to keep up with other, similar districts. In addition, the higher the tax price in a district, that is, the higher the property tax increment voters in the district must pay to increase public services, the higher is district efficiency. This result suggests that voters monitor school districts more carefully when more of their own funds are at stake.

On the basis of these results, Duncombe and Yinger estimate that introducing a foundation aid program with an adjustment for educational costs, which corresponds to the program type described in the top right corner of table 1.3, would lower the efficiency of the neediest districts, which are, of course, the districts that receive the biggest increment in aid under such a program.[72] In other words, some of the aid provided to these districts "leaks out" in the form of lower managerial efficiency. In some cases, this leakage is substantial, but it never eliminates the benefits from increased aid. Under the current aid system, the efficiency level is 62.2 percent in New York City, about 53 percent in the downstate small cities and suburbs, 72.5 percent in the upstate "big-three" cities, and about 68 percent in the upstate small cities and suburbs.[73] A cost-adjusted foundation program that set the foundation level at the amount of spending required to reach the median of the current performance distribution and doubled the state aid budget would reduce the efficiency index in New York City, which receives the largest increase in aid under such a reform program, to 49.8 percent, and would reduce the efficiency index in the upstate big-three cities to 62.4 percent. Suburbs and small cities in the state, which would receive aid cuts under such a reform program, would experience small increases in efficiency. Even after the reform, however, the average large city would still be more efficient than the average small city or suburb.

Despite these few attempts to study the link between state aid reform and school district efficiency, the gap between policymakers and academics on this issue is still huge. As noted earlier, policymakers formulating education finance reform programs in Kentucky, Michigan, and Texas took the position that state aid reform needs to be accompanied by programs to boost school district efficiency, especially in high-need districts. Many other states are adopting accountability programs without any explicit link to state aid reform. As also noted earlier in the chapter, however, there is virtually no evidence that accountability programs can boost performance without raising costs, which is the same thing as boosting efficiency. Moreover, no study exists to help policymakers design a state aid reform that will minimize negative impacts on school district efficiency, particularly in the neediest school districts. More research on these topics is urgently needed.

1.4.5   Unintended Consequences

Major state aid reform can influence many outcomes other than school spending and student performance. In other words, state aid reform can have many unintended consequences. Three different types of unintended consequence have been stressed in the literature and are discussed in several of the chapters in this book: changes in property values, movement to private schools, and increased funding from private educational foundations.

1.4.5.1   Impacts on Property Values   As many scholars have pointed out, state aid reform can affect property values. More specifically, property values are likely to rise in school districts that receive more state aid because of the reform and to fall in districts that receive less aid. These property value changes may reflect property tax rate cuts that are made possible by reform or reform-induced increases in educational performance, either of which increases the amount people are willing to pay for housing in a given school district. Clear evidence that state aid reform affects property values is provided by Dee (2000) and Hoxby (2001), and Nechyba (chapter 4) simulates the impact of various aid reform plans on property values.[74] Dee finds, for example, that state aid reform has a large, positive, statistically significant impact on property values in school districts with relatively low local school revenues, that is, in the districts most likely to be aided by the reform.[75] Dee also finds that state aid reform boosts apartment rents in these districts.

The impact of property tax rates and school quality on house values, which is known as capitalization, is of interest to policymakers because, as emphasized by Wyckoff (1995, 2001), it alters the distribution of gains and losses from state aid reform. People who own property in districts that gain from reform are winners, and people who own property in districts that lose from reform are losers. People who move into either type of district in the future, however, are likely to be unaffected by the reform. If they move into a district that gained from reform, for example, they will have to pay for access to this gain in the form of a higher housing price (or a higher rent). As a result, the winners and losers are a very specific set of people, namely, those who owned property at the time the reform was announced.

Although the primary purpose of state aid reform is to alter educational outcomes, a few state supreme courts have also expressed tax equity objectives for the education finance system. Indeed, the notion of access equality can be thought of as a form of tax equity. However, the tax equity standards expressed by courts and policymakers have to do with tax rates and revenue-raising ability, not with capital gains and losses. One could argue, following Wyckoff, that capitalization should be considered in any analysis of tax equity, but it seems unlikely that it actually will be.

Nevertheless, capitalization is an important unintended consequence of state aid reform, even if the reform does not have any expressed tax equity objectives. The capital gains and losses potentially generated by a particular reform plan are likely to influence political support for the plan, and they have real fairness consequences that scholars should continue to investigate.[76]

1.4.5.2 Movement to Private Schools School aid reform also might have the unintended consequence of encouraging some parents to send their children to private schools.[77] This issue is examined in detail by Nechyba (chapter 4). This type of consequence is, of course, particularly relevant for state aid reform plans that limit supplementation in wealthy districts. Hoxby (2001) estimates that the most extreme reform plans in this category could boost private schooling in the wealthiest districts by as much as three percentage points. Because the national average private school attendance is about 11 percent, this is a fairly large effect. In contrast, Sonstelie, Brunner, and Ardon (2000) do not find a significant increase in private school attendance in California, one of the states with an extremely equalizing aid system.

The potential for increases in private school enrollment as a result of school finance reform is obviously of great interest to policymakers, because it can place a limit on their ability to achieve certain educational equity objectives. If attempts to achieve educational equity through leveling down drive many children from high-income families into private schools, then more equality within the public education system may be attained at the cost of less equality in the elementary and secondary education system taken as a whole. Unfortunately, however, the available evidence on the impact of aid reform on private school attendance is ambiguous, and this topic is certainly worthy of further investigation.

1.4.5.3 New Funding through Private Educational Foundations Another unintended consequence of state aid reform might be the creation of private education foundations in wealthy districts. Because these foundations are private organizations, they are not subject to the same constraints as public schools, and they can, in principle, replace some of the funds that are eliminated in wealthy districts by restrictions on supplementation. On the surface, this appears to be exactly what happened in California. In 1971, the year of the *Serrano I* decision, California had only 6 education foundations; now it has over 500 (Sonstelie, Brunner, and Ardon 2000). A careful look at these foundations reveals, however, that they have a relatively small impact on education finance in the state. In 1994 they raised only $45 per pupil, on average, and over 90 percent of the students in the state were in districts in which annual contributions were less than $100 per pupil (Sonstelie, Brunner, and Ardon 2000).

As in the case of increased recourse to private schooling, the creation of private foundations is of concern to policymakers because these foundations can, in principle, undermine educational-equity outcomes. Some educational-equity goals cannot be achieved if restrictions on supplementation through tax revenue are offset by supplementation through private foundations. The available evidence indicates, however, that so far, at least, this type of response to education finance reform has not been large enough to warrant serious concern.

1.4.6   General Equilibrium Effects

Finally, a state aid reform can have complex consequences and feedback effects that are relevant for the reform's objectives. This type of feedback, called a general equilibrium effect by economists, is explored by Nechyba (chapter 4).

As Nechyba makes clear, the most basic type of general equilibrium effect arises from the link between school quality and residential location. Under most circumstances, the only children eligible to attend a particular public school are children who live in the school district in which the school is located. As a result, households compete for housing in desirable school districts, and high-income households generally outbid low-income households for housing in the districts that have the best schools. State aid reform can have a direct impact on this sorting process. By improving schools in low-wealth or high-cost districts or by limiting supplementation in high-wealth or low-cost districts, state aid reform can alter the relative attractiveness of various districts and alter the type of households each district contains. If more high-income households are attracted to a high-poverty district, for example, the poverty concentration in that district will decline, thereby lowering the cost of education. This decrease in educational costs will magnify the initial impact of state aid reform. Nechyba also shows that movement to private schools can have a similar type of feedback effect: By altering the mix of students in public schools, such movement can alter educational costs.

One important example of a general equilibrium effect, which was first pointed out by Inman (1978) and Inman and Rubinfeld (1979) and which is simulated by Nechyba (chapter 4), arises in the case of a GTB program. Under this type of aid formula, the aid a district receives depends on its tax base, but its tax base, that is, the value of its property, depends on the aid it receives. Low-wealth districts, which receive a large increase in aid when this type of aid formula is implemented, experience a property value increase, which leads, in turn, to a decrease in their aid, thereby undermining the reform effort. The opposite outcome, which also undermines the reform, occurs in high-wealth districts.[78]

Stricker and Yinger (2003) point out that this type of negative feedback does not arise with a foundation aid program, at least not if the foundation level is set high enough. A foundation plan is insulated from this type of effect because it specifies the amount a district must spend on education. Moreover, under some foundation program designs, capitalization can actually enhance the equalizing impact of the program. This type of enhancement occurs when property value increases in low-wealth districts result in higher local revenues and thereby allow the state to boost the foundation level with no increase in the state aid budget. Stricker and Yinger also show that the impact of foundation aid on school district efficiency could result in feedback effects that either enhance or undermine a reform plan's equity objectives.

The general equilibrium issues raised by Nechyba in chapter 4, particularly the link between school quality and residential location, are also important for understanding the impacts of vouchers, which, as pointed out earlier, might be included in future school finance reforms. As Nechyba carefully explains, voucher programs make it possible for many students to attend public or private schools in districts other than the one in which they live. This mobility weakens the link between school quality and property values and alters the way households are sorted across school districts. For example, the introduction of a voucher program might encourage some wealthy families that send their children to private schools to move to previously low-wealth school districts, thereby boosting those districts' school tax revenue and school performance.

Nechyba uses simulation techniques in chapter 4 to build a strong case for the view that policymakers and academics need to pay more attention to the general equilibrium effects of state aid reform. Unfortunately, however, there is virtually no empirical evidence on the magnitude of these effects. More work on this topic is clearly needed.

1.5   Conclusions

State supreme courts, policymakers, and scholars appear to have reached a consensus that a foundation plan with a foundation level based on a generous notion of educational adequacy, a required minimum tax rate, and some kind of educational cost adjustment that provides extra funds for high-need districts forms the core of an acceptable reform of state education finance.[79] This emerging consensus still leaves a lot of room for debate, of course. Exactly how high should the foundation level be? What is a reasonable minimum tax rate? Should the tax required for funding the reform be a state tax (to facilitate recapture) or a local tax (to facilitate local control)? What type of cost adjustment is appropriate? Nevertheless, this consensus regarding the centrality of a foundation plan narrows the debate considerably, and a great deal has been learned in recent years about some of these unresolved issues, such as the features of various approaches to cost adjustments.

Beyond this emerging consensus on the use of a foundation plan, however, there is little sign of agreement. Perhaps the most contentious question is whether a foundation plan is sufficient to achieve educational equity, particularly in the eyes of state supreme courts. The answer would appear to be affirmative if a state's supreme court decides that the state can meet its constitutional obligations simply by providing an adequate education in every district. In fact, however, few courts have issued a clear-cut ruling of this type. Instead, many courts have hinted at broader equity objectives without being clear, or, in some cases, even consistent.[80] Moreover, a foundation plan could be sufficient to meet a strong equality objective if its foundation level were set high enough. The problem, of course, is that such a high foundation level would require an enormous increase in state aid, and hence in state taxes, or else an extremely high required minimum local tax rate. No state has yet been willing to follow either of these routes.

Hence, many states have decided to move beyond an adequacy standard, usually by turning to limits on local property tax revenues, a GTB formula with recapture, or some other active method to reduce supplementation by high-wealth districts.[81] Although reducing supplementation may cut the increase in state taxes necessary to achieve a strong equality objective, it also may impose a cost on society in the form of poorer education performance in high-wealth districts. The more stringent the limits on supplementation, the higher this cost will be. The challenge facing policymakers is to design a reform plan in which the equity gains resulting from the reform outweigh these costs. Moreover, programs that limit supplementation may push parents in high-wealth districts to send their children to private schools or to set up private educational foundations that provide the supplementation that is not allowed through property taxes. Although the size of such responses does not appear to have been large in the case of existing reforms, they do have the potential to undermine the equity objectives of future aid reform efforts.

A consensus on the reforms that should accompany a new foundation aid program might be easier to achieve through a shift away from the question of how to reduce supplementation to the question of how to share the financial and other burdens imposed by school finance reform. Regardless of the constitutional and/or policy objectives it is designed to achieve, any school finance reform imposes burdens on some state residents. Reforms that raise the minimum required local property tax rate impose a burden on the low-wealth or high-cost districts the plan is presumably most designed to help. A reform plan can also impose a burden on high-wealth or low-cost districts if it includes cuts in their state aid, recapture provisions, state takeover of the property tax, or limitations on their ability to raise local school taxes. And of course, any reform plan that raises state taxes to pay for an increase in state aid imposes burdens on state taxpayers in all school districts; the distribution of these burdens depends on the incidence of the new taxes. Every state needs to find a way for these three (overlapping) groups to share the burden that is perceived to be fair and that meets the state's constitutional requirements.

A related issue is the considerable confusion that still appears to exist about the access equality standard. Some state supreme courts have endorsed access equality, but many of these courts also appear to believe that access equality is the same thing as wealth neutrality or even the same thing as equal outcomes. This is clearly not the case.

Access equality refers to the nature of a district's budget constraint, not to any educational outcome. The same type of confusion arises when aid programs add (or scholars recommend) a GTB program as a second tier on top of a foundation plan, then justify this as a way to promote an outcome-based equity standard. In fact, such an approach appears to be a poor tool for promoting any standard of this type, at least in its current forms.

All of the participants in the school aid debate, including courts and policymakers and scholars, appreciate the value of a simple formula, and GTB programs undoubtedly linger because they are based on a simple formula with considerable intuitive appeal. In fact, however, standard GTB programs do not fit with the performance focus of current education policy, revised GTB programs that account for the link between spending and performance are rare, and revised GTB programs that account for the behavioral responses of school districts to the programs are too complicated to be adopted. Thus, GTB programs helped to focus attention on the possibility for state aid reform in the years right after the *Serrano I* decision, but it is not clear what role they can or should play today.

Finally, a key emerging issue is whether to combine state aid reform with an accountability program. Such an approach has great intuitive appeal; the available evidence indicates that state aid increases lead to greater school district inefficiency, and state policymakers want to take steps to ensure that new aid funds are well spent. Unfortunately, however, the available evidence also indicates that existing types of accountability programs are likely to undermine, not enhance, the equity objectives of state aid reform. Programs that set high student performance standards without giving high-cost, low-wealth districts the resources they need to meet these standards are a recipe for these districts to fail. Programs that reward districts on the basis of student test scores without formally and explicitly accounting for the impact on these scores of student characteristics and wage costs, which are not the product of school district actions, inevitably penalize those districts that need help the most. Basing rewards on test score gains appears to be a step in the right direction, but these gains may also be influenced by factors that are outside a district's control. States that are serious about improving the performance of students in high-cost districts should move cautiously on accountability programs until these programs can distinguish between managerial inefficiency and high spending caused by a concentration of disadvantaged students or a high-wage environment.[82]

Federal legislation passed in 2001 declares, through its title, that no child should be left behind. This legislation notwithstanding, the sad truth is that many children are being left behind, particularly in large, poor urban school districts. How can states help these children? Some state policymakers, usually spurred on by state courts, have made considerable progress in reforming the education finance system that contributed to the educational disparities that exist in their state, but many other states, including some that have passed so-called reforms, have not made much progress at all. The chapters in this book are designed to build on past experience as a guide to help all states move toward more equitable education finance systems.

Notes

This chapter has benefited greatly from the presentations and comments made by the participants in the Conference on State Aid to Education, which was held at the Maxwell School, Syracuse University, in April 2002. Indeed, many of the ideas expressed in this chapter are based on something I learned at this conference, and I am very grateful to the people who participated, including the authors of the other chapters in this volume. I would particularly like to single out the discussants at this conference, Katharine Bradbury, Timothy Gronberg, Robert Inman, Therese McCarty, Robert Schwab, David Sjoquist, Leanna Stiefel, and Robert Strauss, who did a wonderful job of highlighting important issues in the papers presented at the conference and identifying themes that appeared in several of the state reform plans. Moreover, the discussants ran a very informative wrap-up session designed to bring out the key themes of the conference. Other participants, many of whom also made helpful remarks during the conference discussion, are listed in the preface. In addition, I received helpful comments on earlier drafts of this chapter from Julie Cullen, Tom Dee, Bill Duncombe, Peg Goertz, Anna Lukemeyer, Therese McCarty, Jerry Miner, Dick Murnane, and Allan Odden. Although my debt to all of these people is large, none of them should be held responsible for anything I say.

1. Strictly speaking, the California Supreme Court was responding to a trial court's ruling that even if the facts alleged by the plaintiffs in *Serrano* were true, they did not establish that California's school financing system was unconstitutional. The 1971 *Serrano* decision, referred to as *Serrano I*, overturned this ruling and sent the case back to the trial court for further discussion of the facts. The facts were compelling, however, so the legislature interpreted this ruling as a rejection of the existing system and passed Senate Bill 90, which set up a new system, in 1972. This new system was definitively rejected by the California Supreme Court in 1977 in a decision referred to as *Serrano II* (see Sonstelie, Brunner, and Ardon 2000). The 1971 decision was based on both the U.S. Constitution and the California constitution. A 1973 U.S. Supreme Court decision in *San Antonio Independent School District v. Rodriguez* effectively overturned that portion of *Serrano I* that was based on the U.S. Constitution but left standing the conclusions based on the state constitution (see chapter 2). Because of this U.S. Supreme Court decision, educational-finance equity is now debated exclusively in state courts.

2. All significant state court decisions on education finance, including these supreme court decisions and the decisions discussed in the following paragraphs, are summarized in appendix A (with full legal citations).

3. The North Carolina case is back before the state supreme court.

4. Before the most recent litigation in Kansas, the state supreme court there also upheld an education finance reform stimulated by a lower-court decision. See chapter 5 and appendix table A.2.

5. The figures presented in tables 1.1 and 1.2 include all the big-city school districts in Casserly 2002 that have data on the share of students that passed the reading and math tests required by the state in which they are located. These figures understate the difference in test scores between big cities and the rest of their states because the big cities' results are included in the state averages.

6. Fischel (2001), for example, concludes that "court-ordered centralization of school finance and the supposed fiscal disparities that have driven it are largely wrongheaded" (161).

7. The remaining two states, Iowa and Nebraska, require tests in these two subject areas but allow each district to decide which tests to administer. See Goertz and Duffy 2001.

8. See also Meyer et al. 2002, which provides up-to-date details about states' accountability systems.

9. This approach has been picked up at the federal level, too. The No Child Left Behind Act of 2001 includes rewards and sanctions for individual school districts based on changes in student performance in the district. See Robelen 2002.

10. Wages also vary across districts because of variation in districts' generosity and in teachers' negotiating skills. It obviously is inappropriate for state to reflect wage variation from either of these sources, so state aid formulas should make use of wage cost indexes, not actual teacher wages.

11. Evidence that class size affects performance is provided by Krueger (1999, 2002) and Krueger and Whitmore (2001). Evidence that prekindergarten programs can boost performance in later grades for children who are poor or otherwise at risk is provided by Karoly et al. (1998).

12. In addition, Hawaii has a state-run education system, which at least suggests educational equality, and as noted previously, the recent constitutional amendment in Florida explicitly requires "uniform" schools. It is not clear, however, how Florida courts will interpret this requirement.

13. Hoxby (2001) contrasts "school finance equalization" (SFE) programs, which are defined as programs that link aid to property values, with "categorical" aid programs, which are defined as programs that link aid to student characteristics or other school district characteristics. For example, she specifically defines foundation aid to be a scheme that "is like flat categorical aid *except* that it redistributes among districts based on per-pupil property values, not on sociodemographic characteristics of households" (1194–1195, emphasis in original). She also argues that "categorical aid has been almost entirely replaced by SFE for major redistribution" (1193). As shown in this chapter and as illustrated by the reforms in Kansas, Kentucky, and Texas, however, student characteristics can easily be incorporated in an SFE program, such as foundation aid.

14. I say "in principle" because many states use pupil weights that are ad hoc and not associated with an attempt to estimate an educational cost index. As shown by Duncombe and Yinger (2003), however, the empirical procedures used to obtain a comprehensive cost index can also be used to determine per-pupil weights that result in approximately the same adjustment for the cost impact of student characteristics as does the cost index.

15. Scholars do agree on several issues regarding cost indexes, however. For example, there is widespread agreement that a cost index should not give districts an incentive to place students in a "special-needs" category (see chapter 3). Similarly, it is generally agreed that a cost index should not reward a district for paying overly generous wages (see Duncombe and Yinger 1997, 1998).

16. One qualification to this statement is that relatively inefficient districts might not meet a performance target. See Duncombe and Yinger 1998. I return to the link between aid and efficiency in section 1.4.4.

17. This approach would not literally ensure equality by any of the definitions of education, because district budgets can be supplemented with private contributions, which cannot be prohibited by the state. As discussed in section 1.4.5.3, such private supplementation has appeared in many districts in California.

18. State aid that is funded through state taxes other than the property tax also involves redistribution across districts and may also influence supplementation. I return to this issue in section 1.3.3.

19. Many studies have demonstrated that school districts respond to this type of price incentive. For a recent review see Fisher and Papke 2000.

20. Feldstein also demonstrated, no doubt inadvertently, that such behavioral responses are difficult to estimate; in fact, his estimates differ significantly from others in the literature. See Fisher and Papke 2000 and Duncombe and Yinger 1998.

21. An alternative, earlier classification effort came to a similar conclusion, namely, that 80 percent of the states at the time of the study used a foundation formula (Gold, Smith, and Lawton 1995).

22. In Texas, for example, the GTB matching aid is capped at a specified local tax rate, which turns out to be the maximum allowable rate under the state's property tax limitation measure. See chapter 8.

23. This may not occur in all cases, of course; that is, some second-tier GTB programs may increase educational equity. The ability of these programs to promote equity is quite limited, however, because, as explained earlier in the chapter, they have little power to influence educational spending in high-need districts unless the required minimum tax rate is set below the rate high-need districts would otherwise select. Note that this limit on equalizing effectiveness does not arise with a stand-alone GTB program, which always increases spending by low-wealth districts. As noted earlier in the chapter, however, this increase in spending is generally not sufficient to bring all low-wealth districts up to any reasonable adequacy standard. Indiana and Missouri address this issue by combining a GTB program with a minimum required local property tax rate. See appendix B.

24. This explanation for Odden's simulation result is mine, not his. He presents the simulation results with no explanation.

25. A large literature shows that increases in state aid go partly toward reductions in local taxes. See Fisher and Papke 2000. The simulations by Nechyba (chapter 4) show the impact of such a response on the outcomes of state aid reform, and evidence on this issue for New York is provided by Duncombe and Yinger (1998, 2000).

26. For more on the Tennessee Supreme Court decision and the reforms it generated, see Cohen-Vogel and Cohen-Vogel 2001.

27. The New Jersey court made its first pronouncement on this issue in 1973 when it said, "Although we have dealt with the constitutional problem in terms of dollar input per pupil, we should not be understood to mean that the State may not recognize differences in area costs, or a need for additional dollar input to equip classes of disadvantaged children for the educational opportunity" (*Robinson v. Cahill* [1973], 72). In its 1995 decision, *Campbell County School District v. State*, the Wyoming Supreme Court also explicitly required extra spending for disadvantaged students. See Lukemeyer (chapter 2).

28. A 2000 trial court decision in North Carolina (*Hoke County v. State*), which is being appealed by the state, also called upon the state to fund prekindergarten programs for all at-risk four-year-olds (ACCESS 2003). (Recall that the benefits of prekindergarten programs are reviewed in Karoly et al. 1998.) Whole-school reform programs, which attempt to alter many aspect of school life, such as curriculum, management techniques, and parental involvement, are widely used, but evidence concerning their effectiveness in improving educational outcomes is quite mixed. See Ladd and Hansen 1999 and Berends, Bodilly, and Kirby 2002. The New Jersey Supreme Court actually required a particular whole-school reform plan, Success for All, with its extension, Roots and Wings (Goertz and Edwards 1999). This plan has shown signs of effectiveness in some studies, but few of them were conducted by independent scholars. One recent independent study (Bifulco et al. 2002) finds, for example, that Success for All actually lowers elementary math performance in New York City schools while having no impact on reading. As the National Research Council's Committee on Education Finance puts it, some whole-school reform "[d]esigns have achieved popularity in spite rather than because of strong evidence of effectiveness and replicability" (Ladd and Hansen 1999, 213). Moreover, whole-school reform programs appear not to work very well when they are imposed on a school instead of being selected by the teachers and administrators at the school (Berends, Bodilly, and Kirby 2002). Indeed, there is some evidence of this outcome in New Jersey (Hendrie 2001).

29. This argument is echoed by New York's highest court in *CFE v. New York* (2003), in which the court says, "[W]e cannot accept the premise that children come to the New York City schools ineducable, unfit to learn" (slip op. at 42–43).

30. Gold, Smith, and Lawton (1995) estimate that two-thirds of U.S. states use an aid formula that contains some form of extra compensation for low-income students. A few states also have cost adjustments in their building aid formula. See appendix table C.4.

31. See appendix table B.4 and Carey 2002, table 1b. One troubling feature of the aid formulas in nine states is that they give more aid to districts with lower student test scores, presumably on the grounds that low test scores reflect a concentration of disadvantaged students (appendix table B.6). Test scores also reflect the quality of education the district provides, however, and such provisions serve to reward incompetent districts. These provisions clearly should be replaced with educational-cost adjustments based on factors outside district control.

32. No state currently uses a statistically based adjustment for educational costs. Moreover, the share of the state aid budget that goes to categorical aid programs for economically disadvantaged students (for handicapped students) is only 3.9 percent (6.6 percent) in states with such programs. Only four states spend more than 5 percent of their aid budgets on categorical programs for at-risk students (appendix table B.2).

33. Carey cites Maryland Commission on Education Finance, Equity, and Excellence 2002; Reschovsky and Imazeki 1998; and Duncombe 2002. In these studies the cost of educating a poor student is between 97 and 159 percent higher than the cost of educating a nonpoor student.

34. Categorical aid programs serve a similar purpose and face a similar restriction in California. See Kramer 2002. See also Carey 2002 and appendix B.

35. An alternative analysis of educational costs in Texas is provided by Alexander et al. (2000).

36. This statement implicitly holds educational quality constant; that is, the issue is whether a consolidation lowers per-pupil costs without cutting educational quality.

37. As shown in appendix B, several states also give more aid to districts that have more highly qualified teachers. This provision is presumably designed to encourage districts to raise their teachers' qualifications. This type of aid never covers the full cost of hiring more qualified teachers, however, and in practice it serves to reward wealthy districts, which can afford to hire highly qualified teachers. In other words, this is another type of antiequalizing aid program.

38. An example of court signals on supplementation is provided by the New Jersey Supreme Court's first education finance decision: "Nor do we say that if the State assumes the cost of providing the constitutionally mandated education, it may not authorize local government to go further and to tax to that further end, provided that such authorization does not become a device for diluting the State's mandated responsibility" (*Robinson v. Cahill* [1973], 72–73).

39. As indicated in appendix table B.4, twenty-eight states restrict supplementation through an explicit tax or expenditure limit, a recapture provision, or some other provision stronger than simply requiring voter approval.

40. Many scholars have argued in favor of an equality standard, which generally requires restrictions on supplementation. See Kramer 2002 for a recent example.

41. Evidence from Massachusetts (Cutler, Elmendorf, and Zeckhauser 1999) indicates that the voters most affected by tax limitations are the most likely to take advantage of overrides, if they are available.

42. Fischel (2001) claims that school finance equalization leads to tax limitations. Evans, Murray, and Schwab (2001) show that this is not the case. Specifically, they identify seven states other than Vermont that have an education finance system reformed in response to a court order but no property tax limitation and nine states that have a tax limitation but have not reformed their school finance systems.

43. McCarty and Brazer (1990) recommended building recapture into a GTB program. A GTB program can also be designed to recapture funds from districts with a high ratio of wealth to educational costs.

44. By refusing to use state funds for this provision, Vermont shifted the budgetary uncertainty from the state to the school districts. However, the state is in a much better

position to handle this uncertainty. After all, state officials cannot make a budget without forecasting the revenue from each source, after accounting for the relevant behavioral responses to the tax. The only difference between the GTB revenue source and others is that the forecast must consider the behavioral responses of school districts, instead of the behavioral responses of individuals or firms.

45. These reforms apply only to a few districts because V^* in the Texas version of equation (1.2) is set not far below the property value per pupil in the state's richest district. In Vermont, V^* is set near the property value per pupil in the average district.

46. One possibility is to set V^* in the GTB formula at the wealth level at which foundation aid falls to zero and to use the GTB formula solely to determine recapture from districts with wealth above V^*, not to determine aid for districts with wealth below V^*, all of which receive aid through the foundation program.

47. This difference is known as the flypaper effect; money given directly to a school district is more likely to remain in a school district's budget than is a change in income that has exactly the same impact on voters' budget constraints. For a review of the literature on this topic, see Hines and Thaler 1995.

48. As shown by Flanagan and Murray (chapter 6), this combination of policies resulted in virtually no change in the state's share of education spending.

49. Even this approach limits supplementation by districts that received foundation aid under the original plan but do not under the revised plan.

50. For further evidence on this debate, see Downes and Shah 1995; Manwaring and Sheffrin 1995; and Silva and Sonstelie 1995.

51. Moreover, the long-run consequences of supplementation are poorly understood. Loeb (2001) shows that unlimited supplementation might undermine state voters' support for a high state-funded foundation level. In other words, some limits on supplementation might be needed to sustain adequacy. Even with limits on supplementation, however, the high cost of sustaining a generous foundation aid program may result in waning voter support for state education spending over time. This appears to be the case in Kansas (see Duncombe and Johnston, chapter 5).

52. As emphasized by Fischel (2001), a school district's wealth also might be influenced by its ability to attract or retain various types of property, a factor that does not reflect decisions by the state.

53. More formally, a district will not use its own resources for education unless the marginal benefits of doing so exceed the marginal costs. As a result, limits on supplementation impose a net cost whenever they prevent supplementation using local taxes that a district would otherwise choose. Measures of this type of loss are not available for school finance reform, but they are documented for property tax limitations. See Bradbury, Mayer, and Case 2001. Transferring state aid from wealthy to poor districts also lowers educational benefits in wealthy districts, but these losses are presumably offset by increased educational benefits in poor districts.

54. One particularly troubling feature of the STAR program is that it gives a higher property tax exemption to taxpayers in high-wealth counties. I know of no equity standard that can justify this provision. In addition, the STAR program is accompanied by a state-funded credit on the New York City income tax, which goes to both renters and owners. Other cities in the state, however, which also have relatively large renter populations, do not receive any extra payments. See Duncombe and Yinger 2001a.

55. In 1999, New Jersey passed a property tax exemption modeled on the New York plan that used $1 billion in state funds that could have been used to meet the New Jersey Supreme Court's mandate to improve educational equity. See Gray 1999. The New Jersey case is discussed in more detail later in the chapter.

56. With a GTB formula, the state's contribution is determined largely by the value of the V^* parameter and by whether the formula includes a recapture provision.

57. This sentence refers, of course, to the debate about whether money matters. For an argument that it does not, see Hanushek 1996 and Hanushek 1997; for arguments that it does, see Ferguson 1991; Ferguson and Ladd 1996; Krueger 1999; Krueger 2002; and Krueger and Whitmore 2001.

58. Even programs that base rewards and punishments on *changes* in average student scores (instead of on levels) run into serious problems. See Ladd and Walsh 2002. Among other things, these programs, which include the federal No Child Left Behind Act of 2001, punish schools that were efficient in the past and therefore have less room for improvement. Moreover, schools with high costs must spend more than other schools to obtain the same *increase* in student scores, just as they must spend more to attain the same performance target.

59. As the New Jersey Court put it in 1973: "The State's obligation includes as well the capital expenditures without which the required educational opportunity could not be provided" (*Robinson v. Cahill* [1973], 72).

60. The saga in Ohio recently took a strange new twist. In December 2002, the Ohio State Supreme Court upheld earlier decisions overturning the state's reliance on the property tax, but then in May 2003, it prohibited the trial court from enforcing those decisions. See ACCESS 2003 and appendix table A.2.

61. The battle hasn't quite ended. The New Jersey Supreme Court responded to the state's budget crisis of 2002 by granting a one-year delay in the requirement for full implementation of its programmatic requirements. Then, in April 2003, the court required both parties in the suit to participate in mediation concerning state-requested changes in the programmatic requirements imposed by the court. See appendix A and ACCESS 2003.

62. Kramer (2002) provides an alternative look at the impact of state aid reform on spending equity in two of these states, Kentucky and Texas, and in California.

63. Murray and her colleagues measure "reform" either with a dummy variable that equals one in a year after a court-ordered reform has been implemented or with a variable to measure the number of years since the last implementation of this type. These two approaches yield qualitatively similar results. The text discussion is based on the first approach.

64. Using national data for 1990 alone, Dee (2000) essentially replicates a key finding of Evans, Murray, and Schwab (1997). To be specific, he finds that court-mandated reform raises spending in low-spending districts but has little impact on high-spending districts.

65. Although her theoretical discussion (as well as equation (1.1)) implies that school district behavior is affected by net aid (the foundation amount minus the required minimum tax rate multiplied by the local tax base), Hoxby estimates separately the effects of the foundation amount and of the required minimum tax rate (and does not, as called for by her theory, interact the tax rate with the local tax base). This approach leads to the following misleading statement: "The introduction of a stringent FA [foundation aid] scheme might increase the foundation tax rate by 30 mills, or 0.030. The coefficient

indicates that a 30 mill increase would generate a 6.4 percent fall in per-pupil spending" (1216). In fact, however, a scheme that raises the foundation tax rate without also raising the foundation amount is *antiequalizing*; any scheme that raises net aid will raise spending.

66. This definition leaves out the voter's tax share, usually measured as the ratio of the median to the mean property value, which is included as part of the price of education in most studies. See Inman 1979; Ladd and Yinger 1991; and Fisher and Papke 2000.

67. Hoxby also finds, however, that state aid makes a majority of the poorest districts (those with mean household income or with per-pupil property values below the 20th percentile) worse off in the two states with the most dramatic equalization programs in 1990 (California and New Mexico).

68. Other relevant studies include Card and Payne 2002; Downes 1992; and Downes and Figlio 2000. These studies and others are reviewed in Evans, Murray, and Schwab 1999.

69. Hoxby also estimates another model in which the dropout rate is a function of per-pupil spending, and the foundation amount and other state aid parameters are used as instruments to deal with the simultaneity of spending and performance. Because spending is not statistically significant in this model, Hoxby claims that the evidence linking the foundation amount to the dropout rate is "mixed" (1228). However, this alternative model, which she calls an "education production function," is not compelling. In an education production function, performance is a function of inputs and student characteristics (often called "fixed inputs"). Hoxby's approach relies on the strong assumption that spending is a good proxy for inputs purchased by the school, such as teachers, after controlling for student characteristics. Several other variables in the model, including income and the share of the district population over sixty-five years old, are often considered demand variables, and some scholars argue that they do not belong in the regression (Dewey, Husted, and Kenny 1999). In my view, however, these are efficiency variables, which should be included.

70. For example, Strauss et al. (2000) discuss the efficiency consequences of outmoded procedures for hiring teachers.

71. The results of this analysis obviously depend on the definition of student performance. Duncombe and Yinger measure performance using the share of students meeting state-determined standards on elementary math and English tests, high school graduation rates, and the share of students that graduate from high school with a Regents diploma, which requires them to pass certain state tests.

72. Duncombe and Yinger (1998) present simulations of GTB programs that account for the impact of these programs on tax prices and hence on school district efficiency. With a standard GTB program, for example, a low-wealth district receives a high matching rate, which corresponds to a large reduction in its tax price, and therefore becomes much less efficient.

73. Note that efficiency is lower in the small cities and suburbs than in the large cities. This result reflects the fact that small cities and suburbs provide a wider range of educational programs, some of which, such as music and art programs, make only minimal contributions to the performance objectives specified in note 71. This efficiency result undoubtedly would be different if student performance in these programs were included in the performance standards. To the best of my knowledge, however, all existing state accountability systems use performance standards similar to the ones used in Duncombe and Yinger's analysis.

74. There is also a large literature on the capitalization of property tax rates and school performance without reference to state aid reform. This literature is reviewed in Ross and Yinger 1999. For a recent contribution see Downes and Zabel 2002.

75. Dee (2000) claims that studies of capitalization provide insight into the impact of state aid reform on school quality. Under the assumption that aid reform does not result in property tax reductions in poor districts, he interprets reform-induced property value increases as a sign of an improvement in student performance or in some other dimension of education that homeowners care about. Unfortunately, however, Dee does not test this assumption, and the evidence in support of it is mixed, at best. Evans, Murray, and Schwab (1997, 26) conclude, for example, that "successful litigation will lead the state government to provide the lowest revenue districts additional state aid of $700 per student 10 years after reform. These districts reduced local revenue by $190, and thus total revenue rose by $510." Dee's approach cannot rule out the possibility that property value increases are due solely to the $190 cut in local revenue. His approach does work, however, for a foundation-based reform plan that requires a minimum tax rate at or above the rate used by high-need districts before the reform—as do the reforms implemented in several states.

76. As noted in section 1.3.4, a state aid reform plan must select a method of funding, and the choice of a funding method also has fairness consequences. A few studies investigate the impact of state aid reform on tax incidence. See Cullen and Loeb (chapter 7).

77. Of course, state aid reform also lowers the incentive of parents in needy districts to send their children to private school. See chapter 4. This type of response is not as important, however, because few parents in needy districts send their children to private schools to begin with.

78. Hoxby (2001) also mentions this type of feedback, along with two others. First, the parameters of an aid reform program are sometimes functions of behavioral outcomes, such as mean per-pupil spending in the state. Second, movement to private schools could lower voter support for state aid or for local property taxes in high-spending districts.

79. For an analysis of this consensus in court cases, see Minorini and Sugarman 1999a; Rebell 2002; and chapter 2; for a view on the scholarly consensus, see Odden 1999 or Guthrie and Rothstein 1999.

80. Perhaps the clearest ruling of this type comes from the 1976 *Serrano II* decision by the California Supreme Court, which affirmed a lower court's ruling that wealth-related spending could not be more than $100 higher per pupil in any one district than another. This approach obviously requires severe limits on supplementation. It also does not recognize variation across districts in the cost of providing education; however, categorical aid is not wealth related, so it could, in principle, still be used to offset educational cost differences across districts.

81. Recall that any increase in state taxes to pay for a higher foundation level reduces supplementation in wealthy districts to some degree. The point here is that many states have selected policies that go beyond this minimal reduction in supplementation. See appendix B.

82. The caution also applies to federal legislation, but it obviously was not heeded by the people who wrote the No Child Left Behind Act of 2001. This act devised rewards and penalties that do not account for student characteristics or wage costs.

2   Financing a Constitutional Education: Views from the Bench

Anna Lukemeyer

2.1   Introduction

In the United States, education reformers have long been troubled by the differences in money and resources available to different school districts and by the resulting differences in the educational opportunities that these districts can offer their students. These disparities are due, at least in part, to the fact that school districts in many states rely on local property tax revenues for a significant portion of their budgets and that local districts often vary dramatically in property wealth per pupil. State aid systems, even when they are designed to equalize the resources available to different school districts, rarely do so completely. Sometimes (or in some part), state aid systems may exacerbate the inequalities.

In response, reformers in many states have brought suits, arguing that, because of these disparities, property tax–based school funding systems violate federal and state constitutions. Over forty states have now faced court challenges to their school funding systems, and plaintiffs have prevailed (in full or in part and at some level of court) in more than half.[1] And there is convincing evidence that the distribution of school spending is more equal in states that have undergone judicially mandated reforms (Murray, Evans, and Schwab 1998; Evans, Murray, and Schwab 1997).

Courts and court interpretations of what the U.S. Constitution and state constitutions require have thus played an important role in the development of school finance systems. The possibility, if not the reality, of a court challenge must be considered in designing a state aid system. This chapter provides an overview of school finance reform suits.[2]

2.2 History and Underlying Legal Theories

Legal scholars (Thro 1990; Levine 1991) have categorized school finance reform suits in terms of three "waves."[3] Each wave differs from the others in terms of the rates of plaintiffs' victories and the primary legal basis for those victories.

2.2.1 Wave I

The first wave of cases extended from the late 1960s until 1973. These cases focused on claims that school funding systems violated the equal protection clause of the Fourteenth Amendment to the U.S. Constitution. Wave I began with cases brought in federal district courts, but plaintiffs achieved their most influential victory in a state court: the California supreme court's 1971 decision in *Serrano v. Priest*. In that decision, the court found that claimed disparities in California school funding and resources violated both federal and state equal protection clauses.[4] Less than two years later, however, in *San Antonio Independent School District v. Rodriguez* (1973), a five-justice majority of the U.S. Supreme Court concluded that very similar disparities in the Texas school system did *not* violate the federal equal protection clause. Although some plaintiffs have continued to bring federal equal protection challenges to school finance systems, *Rodriguez* essentially foreclosed federal equal protection claims as a viable route to reform.

2.2.2 Wave II

After *Rodriguez*, plaintiffs in the second wave brought suits in state rather than federal courts, arguing that school finance systems violated state constitutional provisions. These claims took two forms. First, most state constitutions contain provisions guaranteeing protections similar to those of the federal equal protection clause (Enrich 1995). In interpreting state constitutions, state supreme courts are not bound by federal court interpretations of even identically worded federal constitutional clauses. They can thus interpret clauses in state constitutions as providing protections that the U.S. Constitution does not. Therefore, plaintiffs continued to bring claims based on state equal protection clauses.[5]

In addition, all state constitutions contain provisions addressing public education (Enrich 1995). These provisions, commonly termed "education clauses," provided a second basis for plaintiffs' claims. In the case inaugurating wave II, *Robinson v. Cahill* (1973), the New Jersey

Supreme Court found that that state's school funding system violated the state's education clause. Wave II lasted from 1973 to 1989 and resulted in relatively few reformers' victories. Both equal protection and education clause claims provided a basis for plaintiffs' victories (Levine 1991; Thro 1994).

2.2.3 Wave III

Wave III began in 1989, when three state supreme court victories provided renewed momentum to school finance reform litigation. That year, courts in Montana, Kentucky, and Texas held that their states' school finance systems violated their states' education clauses. Although state equal protection clauses have continued to play a role in some reformers' victories,[6] most wave III courts overturning school finance systems have relied primarily on education clauses (Thro 1994).

2.3   Application of Legal Theories to School Finance Claims

2.3.1   Education Clause Claims

In most civil suits, plaintiffs bear the burden of both pleading a claim that the law recognizes and proving their claim to the court. First, they must state a legally recognizable claim. That is, they must allege that a violation has occurred of an obligation that the law recognizes and that the court can remedy. Second, if they have stated a recognizable claim, then they must produce evidence and prove that the defendant did, in fact, breach the obligation as they claim.

To prevail on an education clause claim, plaintiffs must successfully meet both burdens. First, they must persuade the court that the education clause requires the state to meet a judicially definable and enforceable obligation, such as, for example, equal per-pupil educational spending or equal access to educational resources. Second, they must prove that, in fact, the state is not meeting that obligation (see Thro 1994).

Two cases, one in which plaintiffs were successful and one in which they were not, illustrate common patterns in courts' analysis of education clause claims. *Board of Education, Levittown Union Free School District v. Nyquist* (1982), a wave II case, provides a good example of a case in which plaintiffs did not succeed on their education clause claim. In *Levittown*, property-poor school districts and their students claimed that the New York school finance system, which provided grossly different levels of funding and, therefore, grossly different levels of educational resources across districts, violated the state constitutional provision requiring the legislature to provide "a system of free common schools, wherein all the children of this state may be educated" (*Levittown*, 439 N.E.2d at 368).

Although plaintiffs experienced some victories in the trial and intermediate appellate courts, New York's highest court ruled against them.[7] The high court acknowledged that there were substantial inequalities in resources and educational opportunities across school districts. Because the state's education clause made "no reference to any requirement that the education to be made available be equal or substantially equivalent in every district," however, the court determined that the clause did *not* require equal educational opportunities, as the plaintiffs claimed. Instead, the clause required only a school system that "assur[ed] minimal acceptable facilities and services" throughout the state and that provided statewide access to a "sound basic education" (*Levittown*, 439 N.E.2d at 368–369). In this case, the plaintiffs had failed to claim or prove that their school districts were not providing an education meeting the state's minimum requirements. Observing that the state's average expenditure per pupil was among the highest in the country and that New York was an acknowledged leader in public schooling, the court concluded that the current system met the education clause standard as it had defined it and denied plaintiffs' claim.

The Kentucky Supreme Court's opinion in *Rose v. Council for Better Education, Inc.* (Kentucky 1989), one of the leading cases of the third wave and one of the cases discussed in this volume, provides an example of a plaintiff's victory. In *Rose*, school districts, students, and a nonprofit corporation of school districts claimed that the state's school finance system placed too much emphasis on locally generated revenue, resulting in inadequacies and inequalities throughout the state, in violation of section 183 of Kentucky's constitution, which required the Kentucky General Assembly to provide "an efficient system of common schools throughout the state."[8] After reviewing records of constitutional debates and judicial opinions from Kentucky and other states, the court concluded that section 183 required a school funding system that provided every child, rich or poor, with "an equal opportunity to have an adequate education" (*Rose*, 790 S.W.2d at 211). Further, the court defined the level of education that the state must provide its students as a high one:

[A]n efficient system of education must have as its goal to provide each and every child with at least the seven following capacities: (i) sufficient oral and written communication skills to enable students to function in a complex and rapidly changing civilization; (ii) sufficient knowledge of economic, social, and political systems to enable the student to make informed choices; (iii) sufficient understanding of governmental processes to enable the student to understand the issues that affect his or her community, state, and nation; (iv) sufficient self-knowledge and knowledge of his or her mental and physical wellness; (v) sufficient grounding in the arts to enable each student to appreciate his or her cultural and historical heritage; (vi) sufficient training or preparation for advanced training in either academic or vocational fields so as to enable each child to choose and pursue life work intelligently; and (vii) sufficient levels of academic or vocational skills to enable public school students to compete favorably with their counterparts in surrounding states, in academics or in the job market. (*Rose*, 790 S.W.2d at 212)

The court interpreted the evidence as a "virtual concession" that Kentucky's school system was not only unequal but also underfunded and inadequate throughout the state (*Rose*, 790 S.W.2d at 197) and concluded that the state had failed to meet its constitutional obligations under the education clause.

2.3.2   Equal Protection Clause Claims

In contrast to those adjudicating education clause claims, courts evaluating equal protection claims traditionally follow a different and more formal structure.[9] Plaintiffs bringing equal protection claims argue that the law unjustifiably discriminates against them, treating them less favorably than others. Under traditional equal protection doctrine, the degree of legal tolerance for such unequal treatment depends on the level of scrutiny applicable to the challenged law or government action. Most laws—such as, for instance, laws that govern most business and economic matters—are subject only to "rational-basis" scrutiny. Rational-basis scrutiny is very deferential to the validity of the challenged law: laws survive this test so long as the unequal treatment is rationally related to a legitimate state interest. Courts apply this test liberally in favor of the challenged legislation, and most laws easily satisfy it.

Courts use heightened, less deferential scrutiny only under specified circumstances. They employ the very rigorous "strict" scrutiny only if the challenged unequal treatment is based on a "suspect" classification, such as race, or if the challenged law burdens a fundamental right, such as freedom of speech. To survive strict scrutiny, a law must serve a compelling state interest.[10] Few laws meet this test.[11]

Plaintiffs bringing an equal protection claim usually attempt to per-suade the court that it must apply strict scrutiny to the school finance system. They typically contend that the school funding structure fails to treat similarly situated students equally because the quality of the education offered to them depends on the property wealth of their school district,[12] that education is a fundamental right, and that district property wealth (or district residents' wealth) represents a suspect class. Consequently, the plaintiffs argue, the court must evaluate the school finance structure using strict scrutiny.[13] Defendants, on the other hand, commonly contend that school finance involves neither fundamental rights nor suspect classes. Therefore, they assert, the court should apply only rational-basis scrutiny. Because the property tax–based school finance structure is rationally related to a legitimate state interest in local control of education and educational funding, defend-ants contend, the current system should be upheld.[14]

2.4   Judicial Definitions of Constitutional Obligations

Not all courts have interpreted their state's equal protection or educa-tion clauses as imposing an obligation on the state that is subject to effective judicial enforcement. Courts that do not interpret their con-stitutions as imposing such an obligation often view education finance issues as committed to the discretion of the legislative branch and sub-ject to no or very limited judicial education clause review[15] and only rational-basis equal protection review. In these states, of course, judi-cial mandates based on these clauses may play little or no role in school finance reform.[16] Of the five states examined in this volume, only in Michigan was school finance reform undertaken outside of a judicially defined context.[17]

This part of the chapter and the part that follows concentrate on cases in which courts have interpreted the education or equal protec-tion clauses in their state constitutions as imposing a judicially en-forceable obligation. Of course, as the previous discussion of *Levittown* shows, the mere fact that the court interprets the constitution as im-posing an enforceable standard is not, in itself, sufficient for a plain-tiff's victory: The court may find that the current finance system meets the standard or simply that plaintiffs have failed to show that it does not. Even so, the court's interpretation (at least until it is overruled or modified) provides a constitutional minimum below which the school finance system may not fall. This section discusses the major ways in which courts have defined the constitutional standard that a state's school finance system must meet. Section 2.5 presents trends on related issues of interest to those attempting to design a school finance system.

2.4.1   Framework for Analysis

As Figlio observes in chapter 3, different people may define school finance equity differently, and different definitions of an equitable school finance system can imply very different distributions of school spending, school resources, and student outcomes. Drawing particularly on the work of Duncombe and Yinger (1996) and Levine (1991),[18] the current chapter presents a typology for categorizing courts' definitions of the characteristics of a constitutional school funding system.[19] This typology characterizes constitutional requirements in terms of two dimensions: equity objects and equity standards.

Equity objects describe what is being distributed according to an equality or some other standard of fairness or equity. Three categories of equity objects appear relevant to this litigation:

1. spending per pupil

2. school resources and services (such as teachers, curricular offerings, laboratory equipment, and counseling programs)

3. student outcomes or achievement.

When defining a state's constitutional obligation, a court's choice of equity object matters because different equity objects imply different distributions of funds. Because some districts face higher input costs than others, equalizing spending across districts is unlikely to result in equalizing school resources and services. Districts in urban areas may, for instance, have to pay higher salaries to attract teachers. Similarly, because of differences in student and family characteristics, equality in school resources or services may not substantially reduce disparities in student outcomes. Districts with higher concentrations of students needing special services, disadvantaged students, or students whose native language is not English, for example, may need to provide additional resources (and thus may face additional costs) to bring their students to a given level of achievement.[20]

Further, there is evidence that the impact of these factors in central-city schools is significant (Duncombe and Yinger 1997; Reschovsky and Imazeki 1998, 2001; Yinger 2001). For instance, Reschovsky and Imazeki (1998) estimated that Milwaukee school districts with high concentrations of low-income students required two and one-half times as much money as the average district to achieve a given level of student performance. This represented an increase of $8,080 (per low-income student) over the average spending of $5,082 per student. Yinger (2001) reached a similar conclusion with respect to New York City schools. Focusing on per-pupil spending, then, can hurt schools with high input costs or high concentrations of disadvantaged students or other students needing special help.

The second dimension of the typology involves the standards used to assess equity or fairness in the distribution of the chosen object. Four standards appear useful for analysis of school finance reform litigation:

1. *Minimum adequacy.* All schools must provide some minimum level of spending per pupil (or resources or other equity object). The required level may be high or low. Schools are free to spend above this level without limit but may not fall below it.

2. *Equality.* Expenditures per pupil (or other equity object)[21] must be equal across school districts. Alone, an equality standard implies no absolute minimum. It is satisfied so long as all districts spend equally, regardless of the spending level.

3. *Access equality.*[22] Access equality attempts to counter differences in tax bases across school districts and to equalize revenue-raising ability. This standard is met when each school district can produce equal amounts of the chosen equity object with a given tax effort.

4. *Wealth neutrality.* The selected equity object may not vary systematically with district property tax base. This standard allows different districts to provide widely different levels of resources (or other equity objects), so long as the level of object is not systematically related to district tax wealth.

Access equality, as a goal or standard for school finance reform, is not the same as either equality or wealth neutrality, and achieving access equality is unlikely to result in equal educational spending across districts or even in wealth neutrality (Feldstein 1975; Friedman and Wiseman 1978). Taxpayer choices (and voting) with respect to spending for local government services are affected by, among other variables, taxpayer income and taxpayer preferences. Because of differences in income and preferences, even with equalized tax bases across districts, taxpayers in some districts may choose lower rates of taxes and of educational expenditure (Feldstein 1975; Clune 1992; Odden 1992; Reschovsky 1994; Ladd and Yinger 1994). Therefore, even with full access equality, districts with large concentrations of families facing the constraints of a lower income may choose lower school tax rates. Thus, access equality may well reproduce a pattern that reformers oppose: lower school spending in lower-income districts.

Clearly, then, the combinations of equity standards and equity objects that reformers seek and that judges choose to enforce have implications for the school finance system that results. An equal-spending standard implies a different distribution of funds than a minimum-adequacy standard. Equalizing outcomes—or even resources—may require a very different distribution of funds than equalizing spending.

2.4.2   Courts' Definitions of Equity Objects

The essential issues in this case are quality and equality of education. The issue is not, as insisted by defendants and intervenors, equality of funding.

—*Tennessee Small Schools*, 851 S.W.2d at 156

As the epigraph demonstrates, despite the fact that these school finance reform suits were brought as challenges to school funding systems, most courts who have interpreted their state's education or equal protection clauses as imposing an obligation on the state have defined that obligation primarily in terms of a substantive object (resources or outcomes) rather than dollars.[23] The courts do not, however, clearly distinguish between school resources and student outcomes in their definitions of the state's constitutional duty. Although the courts' definitions have almost always clearly encompassed resource objects (such as school programs and curricula), the courts have often defined the equity object in ways that could, but need not necessarily, encompass a role for outcomes. "Educational opportunity" or "quality of education" have been particularly common terms. To evaluate whether the school system provides an "educational opportunity" or an "education" meeting the constitutional standards, courts have considered a wide variety of evidence, such as spending per pupil; breadth and depth of curricular offerings; student-teacher ratios; availability of computers, up-to-date textbooks, and laboratories; condition of school facilities; various indicators of student achievement; and testimony of educators and other expert witnesses.

2.4.3   Courts' Definitions of Equity Standards

The majority of state supreme courts who have interpreted the constitutions in their states as imposing some enforceable obligation on the state have defined the state's duty in terms of a minimum-adequacy standard, either alone or in combination with one of the other standards. The level of education that these courts have defined as adequate has varied considerably, however. Some courts, such as the Kentucky court in *Rose*, have defined their constitutions as requiring a high level of competence in a broad range of subjects.[24] The New Jersey court, in *Abbott v. Burke* (1990), provides another example of a high standard:

Thorough and efficient means more than teaching the skills needed to compete in the labor market, as critically important as that may be. It means being able to fulfill one's role as a citizen, a role that encompasses far more than merely registering to vote. It means the ability to participate fully in society, in the life of one's community, the ability to appreciate music, art, and literature, and the ability to share all of that with friends. (*Abbott II*, 575 A.2d at 397)

Other courts have set the level fairly low. For instance, in *Olsen v. Oregon* (1976), the Oregon court concluded that the state's education clause required it to provide only "a minimum of educational opportunities" (*Olsen*, 554 P.2d at 148). Similarly, the Oklahoma court interpreted the state's constitution as requiring a "basic, adequate" education (*Fair School Finance Council v. Oklahoma* [1987], 746 P.2d at 1149).

In most cases in which the courts have defined the state's duty in terms of a minimum-adequacy standard, they have interpreted the constitution as clearly imposing only that standard. The New York court's opinion in *Levittown*, discussed in section 2.3.1, provides an example of a court defining the constitution in its state as imposing solely an adequacy standard, without elements of any of the other standards. In some cases, however, the courts have clearly adopted an adequacy standard but also used language that might, but need not necessarily, incorporate a relaxed equality standard. These cases include *Rose v. Council for Better Education, Inc.* (Kentucky 1989) (discussed in section 2.3.1), in which the Kentucky court articulated the constitutional standard as follows:

Each child, *every child*, in this Commonwealth must be provided with an equal opportunity to have an adequate education. Equality is the key word here. The children of the poor and the children of the rich, the children who live in the poor districts and the children who live in the rich districts must be given the same opportunity and access to an adequate education. (790 S.W.2d at 211)

Although the court emphasized equality and equal opportunity ("Equality is the key word here"), it apparently qualified that equality of opportunity as one of access to an *adequate* education.[25] Later in the opinion, the court made it clear that once the state provided an adequate education to all children, local districts could provide supplemental resources (790 S.W.2d at 212).

State supreme courts in a few cases have interpreted the constitutions in their states as *clearly* imposing *both* an adequacy *and* an equality standard. The majority of these courts have relied on both education and equal protection clauses to develop this combination of standards.[26] In *Abbott v. Burke* (New Jersey 1990, 1994), however, the New Jersey court found both standards in the state's education clause.

In Texas, another of the states discussed in this volume, the court also interpreted the state's education clause in terms of a combination of two standards. The Texas court, however, interpreted the clause as combining an adequacy standard with an access equality (rather than an equality) standard. In *Edgewood Independent School District v. Meno* (1995), the Texas court required that each district have substantially equal ability to raise the funds necessary to provide an adequate education as defined by the legislature through accreditation standards.

Finally, a small group of courts have interpreted the constitutions in their states as imposing primarily an equality, access equality, or wealth neutrality standard.[27] Perhaps the most distinctive feature of this group is that many of the courts appear not to distinguish among the three standards. Instead, they use language invoking one or another of them at different places in the opinion. The reforms in Vermont, also discussed in this volume, resulted from a decision falling into this group. In *Brigham v. Vermont*, the Vermont Supreme Court interpreted the education and equal protection clauses of the state's constitution as providing a "right to equal educational opportunities" (692 A.2d at 397). Although the Vermont court seemed to emphasize an equality standard, like many of the courts in this group, it sometimes used language invoking an access equality or wealth neutrality standard:

Equal opportunity ... does not allow a system in which educational opportunity is necessarily a function of district wealth [suggesting wealth neutrality]. Equal educational opportunity cannot be achieved when property-rich school districts may tax low and property-poor districts must tax high to achieve even minimum standards [suggesting access equality]. Children who live in property-poor districts and children who live in property-rich districts should be afforded a substantially equal opportunity to have access to similar educational revenues [suggesting access equality]. Thus, as other state courts have done, we hold only that to fulfill its constitutional obligation the state must ensure substantial equality of educational opportunity throughout Vermont [suggesting equality]. (692 A.2d at 397)

The role of an adequacy standard in school finance litigation has been the subject of some debate. Some argue that a high minimum-adequacy standard can be a particularly effective route to school finance reform (Jensen 1997). Others point out that a court's interpretation of the constitution in its state as imposing an adequacy standard can sometimes play a conservative role in school finance litigation, allowing the court to uphold the existing school funding system, despite substantial inequalities, on the basis that all districts can provide their students with an education meeting some (perhaps low) standard of adequacy (Lukemeyer 2003). Courts in the states examined in this volume provide some support for each view.

The Kentucky court's opinion in *Rose* represents a court's use of an adequacy standard as a strong lever for reform. As the discussion in section 2.3.1 shows, that court defined the Kentucky constitution as imposing a very high minimum-adequacy standard and found that the entire educational system failed to meet that standard. Thus, in Kentucky, a decision interpreting the constitution as requiring a high minimum-adequacy standard stimulated extensive reforms. Further, *Rose* has been a particularly influential decision, and adequacy standards have been the ground for overturning school finance systems in a number of states (Jensen 1997).[28]

In contrast, in the Texas litigation, an adequacy standard played a conservative role. In Article VII, section 1, the Texas constitution states: "A general diffusion of knowledge being essential to the preservation of the liberties and rights of the people, it shall be the duty of the Legislature of the State to establish and make suitable provision for the support and maintenance of an efficient system of public free schools." In 1989, in *Edgewood Independent School District v. Kirby*, the Texas Supreme Court interpreted this clause as requiring access equality:[29]

There must be a direct and close correlation between a district's tax effort and the educational resources available to it; in other words, districts must have substantially equal access to similar revenues per pupil at similar levels of tax effort. Children who live in poor districts and children who live in rich districts must be afforded a substantially equal opportunity to have access to educational funds. (*Edgewood I*, 777 S.W.2d at 397)

Observing that the hundred richest school districts in Texas spent an average of $7,233 per pupil whereas the hundred poorest, despite a substantially higher property tax rate, spent only $2,978 per pupil, the court concluded that the existing school system was not "efficient" within the meaning of the clause (*Edgewood I*, 777 S.W.2d at 393, 397). In a suit that reached the Texas supreme court in 1991 (*Edgewood Independent School District v. Kirby*), plaintiffs challenged the reform legislation enacted in response to *Edgewood I*, arguing that it did not sufficiently mitigate access inequality across school districts. The court agreed, striking down the reform legislation.

Several years later, property-poor school districts were back in the Texas supreme court, arguing once again that reform legislation enacted shortly before (Senate Bill 7) did not go far enough to eliminate access inequalities. This time, however, the court upheld the reform legislation (*Edgewood Independent School District v. Meno* [Texas 1995] [*Edgewood IV*]). To do so, it added an adequacy standard to its previous definition of education clause requirements. Specifically, the court stated that, in *Edgewood I* and *II*, it had interpreted the education clause's efficiency requirement in terms of a financial standard (access equality). Drawing on the "general diffusion of knowledge" language in the state's education clause, the court in *Edgewood IV* concluded, however, that this clause also contained a "qualitative" component and that an efficient system required equality of access to revenues, *but only up to the amount necessary to provide an education meeting the qualitative standard*. The court found that in Senate Bill 7 the legislature had "equate[d] the provision of 'a general diffusion of knowledge' with the provision of an accredited education" and that the accountability provisions in Senate Bill 7 satisfied the constitutional obligation to provide for a general diffusion of knowledge statewide (*Edgewood IV*, 893 S.W.2d at 463). Finding that Senate Bill 7 provided "substantially equal access to the funding up to the legislatively defined level that achieves the constitutional mandate of a general diffusion of knowledge," the court held that the school finance system met education clause requirements (*Edgewood IV*, 893 S.W.2d at 464). In essence, then, in *Edgewood IV*, the court used a newly defined adequacy standard (the qualitative component) to limit the reach of its previously defined access equality standard and upheld the reform legislation as meeting this newly limited standard.[30]

In contrast to its Texas counterpart, the Vermont Supreme Court expressly rejected the use of an adequacy standard as a boundary on the state's constitutional obligation. The court stated that, even if the state's foundation aid program achieved its purpose of ensuring that every district had the funds to provide at least a minimum quality education,[31] this alone did not satisfy the state's obligation to provide substantially equal educational opportunities for all students in the state: "We find no authority for the proposition that discrimination in the distribution of a constitutionally mandated right such as education may be excused merely because a 'minimal' level of opportunity is provided to all" (*Brigham v. Vermont*, 692 A.2d at 397). The court shied away from requiring absolute equality of education opportunity, however, defining the state's obligation in terms of "substantial equality of educational opportunity" (692 A.2d at 397). And it left open the possibility of some unequalized spending, stating that the constitution did not "necessarily" prevent some districts from "spending more on education if they chose" (692 A.2d at 397).

2.5   Related Issues and Themes

In addition to their definitions of constitutional obligations, the courts in school finance reform suits have addressed several related issues that are relevant to the design of school finance systems. This section examines these issues.

2.5.1   State-Local Distribution of Responsibility for Providing an Education Meeting Constitutional Standards

Among courts concluding that the education clause in their state's constitution imposes a judicially enforceable obligation, almost all that have addressed the issue have held that the ultimate responsibility for providing a constitutionally adequate educational system rests with the state rather than with local governments.[32] The state may delegate to local governments some responsibility for implementing the school system and for funding it, but the state must see that local governments provide a constitutional education system, and it must carry the fiscal burden of such provision if local governments cannot.[33] Once the state has established a constitutionally adequate system, local governments can raise additional funds for supplemental educational resources.[34]

2.5.2   The Role of Standards for Funding in Relationship to the State's Constitutional Obligation

Even though the vast majority of courts have defined the obligation imposed by the constitution in their state in terms of substantive educational criteria, school finance reform suits come to the court primarily as challenges to the school funding structure. Therefore, the courts must, at least implicitly, identify a standard against which to measure the funding structure. For most courts, though, the measure of the constitutionality of the funding structure has been simply whether it allows schools to provide an educational program meeting whatever substantive standards the state's constitution requires. Beyond this, most courts have viewed designing a particular funding structure as a legislative task. Other than placing ultimate responsibility at the state level, the courts have been reluctant to interpret state education or equal protection clauses[35] as mandating any particular funding structure or distribution of the school tax burden.[36]

Courts in a few cases have articulated specific requirements for school spending or for the school finance structure in the state. The majority of these courts appear to have imposed a standard for spending as a means of attaining a substantive educational object for students rather than out of concern about the finance structure as such or the distribution of the school tax burden. A small number, however, have identified a standard for the distribution of the school tax burden.

Two states, New Jersey and Washington, provide examples of different ways in which courts falling in the first, student-centered group have used a standard for spending as a means to achieve a substantive goal. Throughout two rounds of school finance litigation—*Robinson v. Cahill* (1973–1976) and *Abbott v. Burke* (1985–present)—the New Jersey court has consistently defined the education clause in the state's constitution as imposing a substantive obligation on the state to provide "that educational opportunity which is needed in the contemporary setting to equip a child for his role as a citizen and as a competitor in the labor market" (*Robinson v. Cahill* [1973], 303 A.2d at 295). Nevertheless, after repeated legislative failures to design a constitutional funding system, the court imposed an explicit dollar standard for poorer urban districts with high concentrations of disadvantaged students: Per-pupil spending in these districts must be equal to that of the wealthy suburban districts, and sufficient additional dollars must be made available to fund the programs and services needed to meet the students' special needs (*Abbott v. Burke* [1990], 575 A.2d at 388).[37] In Washington, the genesis of the spending requirement was much simpler. In *Seattle School District No. 1 v. Washington* (1978), plaintiffs complained that the school finance system made provision of even basic educational services dependent, in part, on special levies requiring voter approval and that voter approval of such levies was often not forthcoming. In response to this situation, the court ruled that the state's education clause required the state to make ample provision for a constitutionally adequate educational system through regular and dependable tax sources.

In short, for the New Jersey court, the funding standard was simply an enforceable interim step. In Washington, the funding standard played a slightly different role, that of necessary support for the substantive standard. In both of these cases and in most of the cases in which the courts have identified an explicit standard for funding,[38] the standard has served primarily as an aid to meeting the state's substantive constitutional obligation.

In a small number of cases, however, the courts have articulated a standard for funding as a means of equitably distributing the school tax burden. The leading cases here are *Edgewood I, II*, and *IV*, in which the Texas court developed a taxpayer equity standard first (access equality) and then bounded it by substantive adequacy standard. Kentucky and Wyoming have also included a taxpayer equality standard as one part of the state's obligation under the education and/or equal protection clauses. In all of these cases, however, the taxpayer equity standards represented just a part (and for all states but Texas, a subordinate part) of the state's obligation under the education clause in the state constitution.[39]

2.5.3 Legislative Definition of an Adequate Education as a Standard for Funding

A number of courts have emphasized that the legislature is the appropriate party in their state to define the particular substantive content of a constitutionally adequate education.[40] Although the courts show varying amounts of deference when reviewing whether legislative definitions meet constitutional standards,[41] if a particular legislative definition passes constitutional muster, it often becomes the standard against which the school finance system in the state is judged. For instance, as the discussion in section 2.4.3 shows, in *Edgewood IV*, the Texas court interpreted school finance reform legislation as equating provision of a constitutional level of education with provision of an accredited education. Then the court apparently found that the legislative definition met education clause standards and approved the finance legislation challenged in that case on the ground that it provided all districts with reasonably equal access to the funds necessary to provide this level of education (*Edgewood IV*, 893 S.W.2d at 464). Similarly, the Kansas Supreme Court used the legislatively defined goals and accreditation standards "as a base" for evaluating whether finance reform legislation met education clause requirements. Since the evidence showed that all school districts could meet these standards, the court upheld the finance system (*USD No. 229*, 885 P.2d at 1182–1184, 1186).[42]

A court's deference to legislative authority to define the particularities of a constitutionally adequate education can also be viewed as imposing an obligation or duty on the legislature. In fact, in *Robinson v. Cahill I*, the state's failure to define specifically the substance of a constitutional education was a major factor in the New Jersey court's finding that the state had not fulfilled its duty under the state's education clause. For that court, this definition was a necessary first step to crafting a constitutionally adequate finance system.[43]

2.5.4 Rational versus Political Determination of School Funding Amount

Further, in some cases, the courts have required the state not only to identify the specifics of a constitutionally adequate education but also to determine rationally the cost of providing that education and to ensure that it is funded. Two of the courts that have been the most aggressive in this regard have been those in New Jersey and Wyoming.[44] These two courts are among the most aggressive in other respects as well, defining the constitutional obligation in their states in terms of both a high minimum-adequacy and an equality standard and requiring the state to fund additional resources and services necessary to allow disadvantaged students to compete on an equal footing with their more advantaged peers.

2.5.5 Providing Additional Resources for At-Risk Students

A factor motivating many school finance reformers is concern that schools with many disadvantaged or at-risk students do not have sufficient resources to educate their students successfully. Nevertheless, relatively few courts in school finance reform litigation have expressly

specified that the school finance system *must* provide additional resources for compensatory programs for at-risk or disadvantaged
students (Lukemeyer 2001, 2003).[45] Instead, most courts that have
addressed the issue have said simply that school finance systems *may*
adjust funding to take into account the needs of at-risk students, but
few have explicitly required them to do so. None of the courts in the
states studied in this book has explicitly interpreted the education or
equal protection clauses in its state as requiring school finance systems
to adjust funding in this way.[46] Decisions from courts in Texas, Kansas,
and Vermont indicate that these courts do not see their states' education or equal protection clauses as prohibiting such additional funding,
however. Texas and Vermont have expressly stated that the school finance system may provide additional funding for high-cost students.[47]
In *USD No. 229*, the Kansas Supreme Court upheld, against an equal
protection challenge, school finance reforms that included adjustments
for higher costs associated with educating some types of students.[48]
The Kentucky court did not explicitly addressed the issue in *Rose*, but
given its emphasis on providing rich and poor children with equal access to an adequate education, it seems very unlikely that the court
would interpret the Kentucky constitution as precluding adjustment
for costs of educating certain types of students.

2.6   Conclusion

Clearly, state courts have played an important role in defining a constitutional structure for financing education. Several commonalities
stand out across most of these school finance reform cases. First, state
courts have consistently defined the state's constitutional obligation in
substantive terms such as providing an educational opportunity or an
education that meets a broadly specified standard. Although some
courts have supplemented this substantive standard with a specific
standard for funding, for many, any finance structure is acceptable,
so long as it allows the state to meet the substantive constitutional
requirements. Second, the courts are almost unanimous in placing
the responsibility for devising and enforcing a constitutional school
system at the state rather than local level. Finally, a number of
courts have emphasized that the legislature must identify the specific
content and processes of education in the state that will meet this substantive standard.

The courts' emphasis on substantive obligations seems to have two opposing implications for the effectiveness of judicially mandated school finance reforms. To the extent that court rulings require legislators to determine educational funding on the basis of the cost of providing school resources and services that meet a specifically defined substantive standard, the emphasis on substantive rather than financial standards seems likely to rationalize the process of determining the amount of funds needed in school districts and, perhaps, to result in a finance system that more accurately accounts for differences in the costs among districts.

An alternative outcome seems plausible, however. Those courts defining only a substantive standard leave the legislature considerable leeway to enact school funding systems that "might" result in attainment of the courts' definition of educational equity but that are not well designed for that purpose. If this is the case, then judicial reforms are likely to be less effective and are less likely actually to result in an education system whose characteristics match those of the courts' definitions. Thus, for a substantive definition of educational equity to be effective, courts must be willing, as some courts have been, to enforce a rational (rather than a political) process for calculating school aid.

Beyond their emphasis on distribution of educational opportunity rather than funding, courts vary in their definition of what the constitution in their states requires with respect to educational equity. The majority of courts interpret the constitutions in their states as requiring primarily that the state provide an education in all schools that meets certain standards of adequacy. A minority of courts enforce one of the other types of standards—equality, access equality, or wealth neutrality—either alone or in combination with an adequacy standard. The courts' definitions of states' educational obligations tend to be vague in several ways that make it difficult to use them as templates for crafting a school finance system, however. First, whereas some courts' definitions of the requirements imposed by the constitutions in their states are clear in terms of the type of standard to be used to measure equity, others are not. Some use phrasing that suggests that they may (or may not) be supplementing an adequacy standard with an equality standard. In addition, courts' articulations of what constitutes an adequate education tend to be abstract and open to a considerable range of interpretation. A final area of confusion appears in courts' defining the constitutional obligation primarily in terms of equality, access equality, and wealth neutrality. Although finance systems designed to meet one of these types of obligations need not meet another, a number of courts seem to treat these obligations and the standards they imply as interchangeable. Again, all this vagueness of standards leaves legislatures considerable leeway (or room for error and repeated litigation) in designing a constitutional finance system.

We have good evidence that, overall, plaintiffs' victories in court cases that challenge a state's existing school finance system result in a more equal distribution of school funding and an increase in the state's share of total school funding (Evans, Murray, and Schwab 1997; Murray, Evans, and Schwab 1998). Whether the particular type of standard for educational equity that a particular state court articulates consistently affects the distribution of school funding or resources in that state remains a question for further research.

Notes

Revised version of paper prepared for the Conference on State Aid to Education sponsored by the Education Finance and Accountability Project, Syracuse University, April 5–6, 2002. The author wishes to thank Rebecca Raper for her excellent assistance with research and analysis of recent cases.

1. Numbers calculated from information presented in ACCESS 2003.

2. This chapter presents, in a condensed format, information and findings presented in earlier works by the author. The conclusions presented here, unless otherwise noted, are based on state supreme court decisions and may not be applicable to lower-court decisions. For a more detailed discussion of the themes in this chapter, see Lukemeyer 2003. For additional perspectives on this litigation, see Enrich 1995; Minorini and Sugarman 1999a; and Minorini and Sugarman 1999b.

3. McMillan (1998) argues that school finance litigation is entering a fourth wave in which courts' concerns about the legitimacy of their involvement in school finance issues and doubts about their competence to effect reforms are leading to fewer plaintiffs' victories. In addition, McMillan suggests that fourth-wave cases, unlike earlier cases, are characterized by a combination of school finance with racial and ethnic discrimination claims. An analysis of claims based on racial or ethnic discrimination is beyond the scope of this chapter.

4. The California Supreme Court was reviewing the lower court's decision to dismiss the plaintiffs' claims without hearing evidence. Under these circumstances, a reviewing court normally assumes that the facts as alleged by plaintiff are actually true. If the reviewing court finds that these facts describe a condition that violates the law as plaintiffs claim and that the courts can remedy the condition, then the reviewing court will remand the case to the trial court to provide plaintiffs with an opportunity to prove the facts. Alternatively, if the court concludes that what plaintiffs allege, even if true, violates no judicially enforceable law or obligation, then it will uphold the trial court's dismissal, and plaintiffs lose. In *Serrano I*, the court ultimately concluded that the facts that plaintiffs

alleged, if true, violated the federal and state constitutions. In a later (1976) case (*Serrano v. Priest II*), the court upheld the trial court's conclusion that plaintiffs had proven facts showing that the finance system was unconstitutional.

5. Because *Serrano I* was decided on the basis of both the federal and the California state equal protection clauses, the California court's decision was not necessarily overturned by *Rodriguez*, and the California court subsequently (1976) affirmed its decision on the basis of the state clause (*Serrano II*).

6. After wave II, state equal protection clauses formed a basis, in whole or in part, for plaintiffs' victories at the state supreme court level in *Tennessee Small School Systems v. McWherter* (1993), *Claremont School District v. Governor* (New Hampshire 1993) (reviewing decision to dismiss plaintiffs' claim without hearing evidence—see note 4), *Campbell County School District v. Wyoming* (1995), *Brigham v. Vermont* (1997), *Leandro v. North Carolina* (1997) (reviewing decision to dismiss plaintiffs' claim without hearing evidence—see note 4), and *Lake View School District No. 25 v. Huckabee* (Arkansas 2002).

7. These plaintiffs also made state and federal equal protection clause claims, which the high court denied. Upstate big-city school districts intervened as plaintiffs in this suit, also bringing state education clause and state and federal equal protection clause claims. The upstate big-city school districts alleged that, although they were not property poor, they were in a position similar to that of property-poor school districts because of the impact of "municipal overburden." The New York high court rejected their claims as well.

8. Plaintiffs also brought state and federal equal protection clause claims. Because the court was able to decide the case on the basis of the education clause claims, it did not have to decide the federal or state equal protection clause claims and it apparently did not do so.

9. Not all courts use the traditional form of analysis described here. Some, for instance, combine education clause claims and equal protection clause claims in an analysis more like that described for education clause claims.

10. Courts in different cases describe the strict-scrutiny test somewhat differently. The court in *San Antonio Independent School District v. Rodriguez* (1973) required the state to show a compelling state interest underlying the law.

11. Nowak and Rotunda (2000) provide a more detailed explanation of equal protection law.

12. See, e.g., *Kukor v. Grover* (Wisconsin 1989).

13. The court accepted this reasoning in *Serrano v. Priest* (1971, 1976), plaintiffs' first equal protection clause victory.

14. This argument carried the day in *San Antonio Independent School District v. Rodriguez* (1973). Some state courts, however, have concluded that their states' school funding systems result in inequalities that do not survive even rational-basis scrutiny (*DuPree v. Alma School District No. 30* [Arkansas 1983]; *Tennessee Small School Systems v. McWherter* [1993]).

15. Recent opinions from the Florida and Illinois Supreme Courts exemplify this deference: *Coalition for Adequacy and Fairness in School Funding, Inc. v. Chiles* (Florida 1996) (plurality concluding that to decide whether legislative appropriation for education is adequate would be to usurp legislative powers); *Committee for Educational Rights v. Edgar*

(Illinois 1996) (observing that education policy is almost exclusively within the province of the legislative branch and holding that questions relating to the quality of education are solely for the legislative branch); and *Lewis v. Spagnolo* (Illinois 1996) (reaffirming that questions of education quality are solely for the legislative branch even if plaintiffs allege a "virtual absence" of education within a district [710 N.E.2d at 816]).

16. There is some evidence, however, that litigation affects school funding even when plaintiffs lose (Hickrod et al. 1992). Although Kansas is not a state in which plaintiffs lost, that state's recent school finance reforms illustrate the complexities that can occur as legislators respond to the filing of a suit. As Duncombe and Johnston point out in chapter 5, Kansas's 1992 school finance reforms took place within the context of lawsuits brought by a number of school districts challenging the constitutionality of the school funding system existing at the time. The document that provided the legal context for the reform legislation, "Opinion of the Court on Questions of Law Presented in Advance of Trial," was an opinion on questions of law issued by the trial court judge before the case actually went to trial. This document, which interpreted the state's constitutional obligation rigorously as requiring equal educational opportunity for each child, set out the legal framework that the judge would use to evaluate the existing school finance system if the case came to trial and was part of an aggressive effort by the trial court judge to facilitate a settlement of the case (Berger 1998). In fact, the parties were able to agree on school finance legislation (described in chapter 5), and the trial judge dismissed the suit. Thus, this set of reforms was guided by a trial court judge's interpretation of the law that was never reviewed by a higher court (Berger 1998).

The resulting reform legislation was, of course, immediately challenged on various grounds by a number of wealthier school districts who were disadvantaged by the new finance scheme. A smaller group of poorer districts also challenged the reform legislation as not going far enough (Berger 1998). These suits reached the Kansas Supreme Court in *Unified School District No. 229 v. Kansas* (1994). That court defined the state's constitution as imposing an adequacy requirement and found that the current system met that requirement (*USD No. 229*, 855 P.2d at 1185–1187). It evaluated the parties' equal protection claims using a rational-basis test and, showing considerable deference to legislative judgment, upheld the finance system (*USD No. 229*, 855 P.2d at 1190–1193). Because the supreme court was addressing primarily claims brought by comparatively wealthy districts, the opinion leaves many questions unanswered with respect to the extent to which the Kansas constitution *requires* (rather than allows) equalizing aid for the poorer districts (Berger 1998). Overall, however, the supreme court's opinion seems to interpret the state's education clause and equal protection clause obligations less rigorously and with more deference to legislative judgment than the trial court's. In short, the interpretation of constitutional requirements driving the legislation appears different from the interpretation later articulated by the state's highest court. (For a fuller analysis of the interaction of judiciary and legislature in the Kansas reforms, see Berger 1998.)

17. Michigan experienced an early school finance reform suit, and at the end of 1972, the Michigan Supreme Court ruled that the existing funding system violated that state's equal protection guarantee. After the U.S. Supreme Court's opinion in *Rodriguez*, however, the Michigan court withdrew its earlier opinion and dismissed the finance reform suit without issuing a majority opinion (*Millikin v. Green*, 1973). A later suit was also dismissed (ACCESS 2003).

18. Many scholars have developed frameworks for characterizing different definitions of an equitable school funding system, including Berne and Stiefel (1984, 1999), Monk (1990), Levine (1991), Clune (1992), Reschovsky (1994), and Duncombe and Yinger (1996).

19. For a more thorough explanation of this framework and use of it in analyzing cases, see Lukemeyer 2003.

20. Of course, administrative judgment, school efficiency, knowledge of effective teaching techniques, and a host of other factors also affect the translation of spending into school resources and services and of school resources and services into student outcomes. Analysts disagree about the role and likely effectiveness of finance reform as a means of improving student achievement. For various perspectives on this issue, see Burtless 1996. Courts addressing school finance reform issues have often been aware of this controversy, but they have responded to it in different ways. For a review of courts' responses to this controversy, see Dayton 1993.

21. A definition that requires equality of student outcomes across school districts need not require that all students achieve at the same level. The definition might be met, for instance, if the proportions of students performing well, in the midrange, and less well were equal across districts.

22. The term "access equality" was first used by Levine (1991).

23. This is true of many early cases as well as more recent ones. See, e.g., *Robinson v. Cahill* (New Jersey 1973); *Horton v. Meskill* (Connecticut 1977).

24. The *Rose* court's standard is discussed in section 2.3.1. Other recent decisions setting a high standard include *McDuffy v. Secretary of the Office of Executive Education* (1993), in which the Massachusetts court adopted the Kentucky court's seven goals, and *Campbell County School District v. Wyoming* (1995), in which the Wyoming court described the necessary level as "well beyond . . . a minimal level of elementary and secondary education" and "the best that we can do" (907 P.2d at 1279).

25. In a later list of nine "essential" or "minimal" characteristics of a school system meeting education clause requirements, the court again emphasized both equality and adequacy standards. It required Kentucky schools to be "substantially uniform" throughout the state; to "provide equal educational opportunities to all Kentucky children, regardless of place of residence or economic circumstances"; and to "provide funding which is sufficient to provide each child in Kentucky an adequate education" (*Rose*, 790 S.W.2d at 212–213). It defined an adequate education as "one which has as its goal the development of the seven capacities recited previously" (*Rose*, 790 S.W.2d at 213).

26. *Tennessee Small School Systems v. McWherter* (1993); *Campbell County School District v. Wyoming* (1995); *Lake View School District No. 25 v. Huckabee* (Arkansas 2002). The Tennessee court interpreted Tennessee's education clause as imposing an adequacy standard that required the General Assembly to "maintain and support a system of free public schools that provides, at least, the opportunity to acquire general knowledge, develop the powers of reasoning and judgment, and generally prepare students intellectually for a mature life" (851 S.W.2d at 150–151). It interpreted the state's equal protection provisions separately as requiring equality: "The provisions of the constitution guaranteeing equal protection of the law to all citizens, require that the educational opportunities provided by the system of free public schools be substantially equal" (851 S.W.2d at 140). The Arkansas court also appeared to rely primarily on its education clause for the adequacy requirement and on its equal protection provisions for the equality requirement. In contrast, the Wyoming court interpreted its equal protection and education clauses together, finding the combination of standards in the combined interpretation of both clauses.

27. In addition to *Brigham*, discussed in the text, these cases include *Helena Elementary School District No. 1 v. Montana* (1989) (education clause only); *Horton v. Meskill*

(Connecticut 1977, 1985) (combined interpretation of education and equal protection clause); *DuPree v. Alma School District No. 30* (Arkansas 1983) (combined interpretation of education and equal protection clauses); *Washakie County School District No. 1 v. Herschler* (Wyoming 1980); and *Serrano v. Priest* (California 1971, 1976) (equal protection clause).

28. The Massachusetts court, for instance, adopted the Kentucky court's seven goals verbatim in defining the education clause obligation in that state (*McDuffy v. Secretary of the Office of Executive Education* [Massachusetts 1993]).

29. Although it emphasized access equality, the decision also included some language suggesting an equality standard:

We conclude that, in mandating "efficiency," the constitutional framers and ratifiers did not intend a system with such vast disparities as now exist. Instead, they stated clearly that the purpose of an efficient system was to provide for a "*general* diffusion of knowledge." (Emphasis added.) The present system, by contrast, provides not for a diffusion that is general, but for one that is limited and unbalanced. The resultant inequalities are thus directly contrary to the constitutional vision of efficiency. (*Edgewood I*, 777 S.W.2d at 396)

In later opinions, the court seems to have settled fairly clearly on an access equality interpretation of the "efficiency" requirement.

30. This does not, of course, render the efficiency requirement toothless. Its equalizing power diminishes, however, to the extent that the court allows the legislature to define the education necessary for "a general diffusion of knowledge" at a low level. The court warned that the legislature's discretion to define the constitutional level was not beyond judicial review, but the court gave no clear lower limit: "This is not to say that the Legislature may define what constitutes a general diffusion of knowledge so low as to avoid its obligation to make suitable provision imposed by article VII, section 1. While the Legislature certainly has broad discretion to make the myriad policy decisions concerning education, that discretion is not without bounds" (*Edgewood IV*, 893 S.W.2d at 463, n.8).

31. Under the school aid system reviewed by the court, this was the per-pupil amount necessary for an elementary student to receive an education meeting school approval standards (*Brigham v. Vermont* 692 A.2d at 388).

32. Among the states reviewed in this book, Kentucky, Texas, and Vermont have all explicitly placed the ultimate responsibility for providing and funding a school system at the state level (*Rose v. Council for Better Education, Inc.* [Kentucky 1989]; *Edgewood Independent School District v. Kirby* [Texas 1989, 1991]; *Edgewood Independent School District v. Meno* [Texas 1995]; *Brigham v. Vermont* [1997]). The Kansas constitution charges both the state and school districts with responsibilities for local schools. In *USD No. 229*, the Kansas Supreme Court interpreted this as putting some limits on state authority over school boards but concluded that the spending limits in that state's reform legislation did not unduly encroach on the local school district's power. Other cases in which the court has placed ultimate responsibility at the state level include *Robinson v. Cahill* (New Jersey 1973, 1975, 1976); *Pauley v. Kelly* (West Virginia 1979); *DuPree v. Alma School District No. 30* (Arkansas 1983); *Abbott v. Burke* (New Jersey 1990, 1994); *McDuffy v. Secretary of the Office of Executive Education* (Massachusetts 1993); *Roosevelt Elementary School District Number 66 v. Bishop* (Arizona 1994); *Campbell County School District v. Wyoming* (1995). So far as I know, only Maine's high court has indicated that the primary obligation for supporting education in that state rests with local rather than state government. The case in Maine that prompted that observation involved an equal protection (but not an educa-

tion clause) challenge to the state's distribution of cuts in state aid (*School Administrative District No. 1 v. Commissioner* [Maine 1995]).

33. *Brigham v. Vermont* (1997), 692 A.2d at 395 ("The state may delegate to local towns and cities the authority to finance and administer the schools within their borders; it cannot, however, abdicate the basic responsibility for education by passing it on to local governments, which are themselves creations of the state"); see also *Robinson v. Cahill* (New Jersey 1973, 1975, 1976); *Pauley v. Kelly* (West Virginia 1979); *DuPree v. Alma School District No. 30* (Arkansas 1983); *Horton v. Meskill* (Connecticut 1985); *Abbott v. Burke* (New Jersey 1990, 1994); *McDuffy v. Secretary of the Office of Executive Education* (Massachusetts 1993); *Campbell County School District v. Wyoming* (1995); *Hull v. Albrecht* (Arizona 1997) (legislation improperly delegates responsibility for constitutional school system to local districts because it allows them to opt against bonds necessary to finance adequate capital facilities); and *Lake View School District No. 25 v. Huckabee* (Arkansas 2002).

34. Among the states examined in this book, both Kentucky and Texas have explicitly stated that local governments may provide supplemental school funds or resources, and the Kansas Supreme Court approved that state's reform legislation even though it included the local-option budget provisions described by Duncombe and Johnston in chapter 5 (*Rose v. Council for Better Education, Inc.* [Kentucky 1989]; *Edgewood Independent School District v. Kirby* [Texas 1989, 1991]; *Edgewood Independent School District v. Meno* [Texas 1995]; *Unified School District No. 229 v. Kansas* [1994]). Of course, adequacy standards, which inherently allow some districts to provide additional school resources, have played a prominent role in these three courts' definitions of the obligations imposed by the education clauses of the constitutions in their states. The Vermont court, on the other hand, has explicitly refused to allow an adequacy standard to limit the state's equalizing obligation. Nevertheless, even that court has not ruled out local supplementation (*Brigham*, 692 A.2d at 397 ["Equal opportunity does not necessarily require precisely equal per-capita expenditures, nor does it necessarily prohibit cities and towns from spending more on education if they choose, but it does not allow a system in which educational opportunity is necessarily a function of district wealth"]). Other cases in which the courts have expressly stated that local governments may provide additional funding or resources include *Robinson v. Cahill* (New Jersey 1973, 1975, 1976); *Olsen v. Oregon* (1976); *Seattle School District No. 1 v. Washington* (1978); *McDaniel v. Thomas* (Georgia 1981); *Lujan v. Colorado State Board of Education* (1982); *Horton v. Meskill* (Connecticut 1985); *Kukor v. Grover* (Wisconsin 1989); *Skeen v. Minnesota* (1993); and *Roosevelt Elementary School District Number 66 v. Bishop* (Arizona 1994). Only a very few courts have expressed doubts about whether some local supplementation might be constitutional (*Abbott v. Burke* [New Jersey 1990]; *Campbell County School District v. Wyoming* [1995]).

35. Courts have interpreted other constitutional clauses, for instance, those specifically addressing taxation, as limiting structures that states can use to fund schools. See, e.g., *Buse v. Smith* (Wisconsin 1976); *Carrollton–Farmers Branch Independent School District v. Edgewood Independent School District* (Texas 1992); *Claremont School District v. Governor* (New Hampshire 1997).

36. See, e.g., *Brigham v. Vermont* (1997) (constitution does not mandate local property tax or any other structure as a required method of financing education); *Robinson v. Cahill* (New Jersey 1973) ("In light of the foregoing, it cannot be said that [certain amendments to the education article] were intended to insure statewide equality among taxpayers. But we do not doubt that an equal educational opportunity for children was precisely in mind" [303 A.2d at 294]); *DuPree v. Alma School District No. 30* (Arkansas 1983) ("[T]his court is not now engaged in—nor is it about to undertake—the 'search for tax equity'

which defendants prefigure.... [I]t is the legislature which by virtue of institutional competency as well as constitutional function is assigned that difficult and perilous quest" [651 S.W.2d at 95, quoting *Serrano II*]); *Horton v. Meskill* (Connecticut 1985) (declining as unsound plaintiff's request to fix a specified percentage of school funding that must come from state rather than local taxes); and *Olsen v.* Oregon (1976) (rejecting plaintiff's claim that the state may not impose minimum educational standards on local districts without also providing funding from state sources sufficient to meet those standards). In a few recent opinions, however, the courts have been more willing to impose specific funding obligations at the state rather than the local level (*Abbott v. Burke* [New Jersey 2000] [interpreting an earlier order as requiring the state to fund the entire cost of capital facilities]; and *Opinion of the Justices* [*Reformed Public School Financing System*] [New Hampshire 2000] ["First, the New Hampshire Constitution imposes solely upon the State the obligation to provide sufficient funds for each school district to furnish a constitutionally adequate education to every educable child" 765 A.2d at 677]).

37. By 1998, the New Jersey court had imposed specific programmatic requirements for the poor urban districts (*Abbott v. Burke* [1998]).

38. In addition to the *Abbott* cases and *Seattle SD*, cases in which the courts have articulated a spending standard whose primary function appears to be to support a substantive standard include *Serrano v. Priest* (California 1976) (California high court upholds trial court order requiring wealth-related disparities in spending—other than categorical aids—to be "considerably less than $100.00 per pupil" [557 P.2d at 940 n.1]); *Washakie County School District No. 1 v. Herschler* (Wyoming 1980) (court articulates a standard for spending because level of spending is directly related to quality of education, spending is judicially manageable, and equality of spending is a necessary precursor to equality of quality); *Campbell County School District v. Wyoming* (1995) (court defines obligation in substantive terms but takes equal spending, adjusted for differences in input costs and student needs, as its baseline); *Hull v. Albrecht* (Arizona 1997) (to satisfy constitution with respect to capital funding, state must establish minimum adequate facility standards and provide funding to ensure that no district falls below them, and the funding mechanism may not itself cause substantial disparities between districts).

39. *Rose v. Council for Better Education, Inc.* (Kentucky 1989) (if state uses property tax dollars to finance a constitutionally adequate education, it must assess and tax at a uniform rate); *Campbell County School District v. Wyoming* (2001) (state must fund necessary facilities through a statewide tax or other revenue-raising mechanism imposed equally on all taxpayers).

40. The courts through 1996 provided mostly very general guidelines of the sort illustrated by the Kentucky court's opinion in *Rose*. In a 1998 opinion, however, the New Jersey court, stymied by the legislature's apparent inability to implement a constitutional education system, prescribed very specific educational programs for implementation in poor urban school districts (*Abbott v. Burke* [1998]).

41. See, e.g., *City of Pawtucket v. Sundlun* (Rhode Island 1995) (court suggests that legislature's definition is basically unreviewable); *Board of Education v. Walter* (Ohio 1979) (court reviews whether legislative definition meets constitutional requirements with great circumspection); *Robinson v. Cahill V* (New Jersey 1976).

42. In a more recent suit, brought by two large school districts and minority and disabled students, the Kansas Supreme Court made it clear that, although in *USD No. 229* it used the legislative standards as a base, "the ultimate question on suitability must be one for the court" (*Montoy v. Kansas* [2003], 62 P.3d at 234).

43. Similarly, in a recent opinion, the New Hampshire court concluded that the legislative and executive branches had a duty to define the specifics of a constitutionally adequate education and to adopt standards of accountability to ensure its delivery (*Claremont School District v. Governor* [New Hampshire 2002]).

44. As the previous section shows, New Jersey required its legislature to specify the content of a constitutionally adequate education as early as 1973. And the New Jersey legislature has been relatively successful in setting out content and related substantive standards that meet the constitutional requirement of a "thorough and efficient" education (*Robinson v. Cahill* [1976]; *Abbott v. Burke* [1997]). In *Abbott IV*, however, the New Jersey court also concluded that, because the school finance legislation did not "in any concrete way attempt to link the content standards to the actual funding needed to deliver that content," it was "clearly inadequate and thus unconstitutional as applied to [plaintiffs'] districts" (693 A.2d at 429).

In *Campbell County School District v. Wyoming* (1995), the court required the legislature to "first design the best educational system by identifying the 'proper' educational package each Wyoming student is entitled to have whether she lives in Laramie or in Sundance. The cost of that educational package must then be determined and the legislature must then take the necessary action to fund that package" (907 P.2d at 1279). In *Campbell County II* (2001), the court reviewed in detail the legislative efforts to develop a cost-based model with adjustments for district and student differences.

See also *Leandro v. North Carolina* (1997) ("a funding system that distributed state funds to the districts in an arbitrary and capricious manner unrelated to such educational objectives simply would not be a valid exercise of that constitutional authority and could result in a denial of equal protection or due process" [488 S.E.2d at 258]).

45. *Abbott v. Burke* (New Jersey 1990), *Campbell County School District v. Wyoming* (1995); *Leandro v. North Carolina* (1997).

46. This statement excludes claims based on racial or ethnic discrimination.

47. *Edgewood Independent School District v. Kirby* (Texas 1989) ("This does not mean that the state may not recognize differences in area costs or in costs associated with providing an equalized educational opportunity to atypical students or disadvantaged students" [777 S.W.2d at 398]); *Brigham v. Vermont* (1977) ("In so holding, we emphasize that absolute equality of funding is neither a necessary nor a practical requirement to satisfy the constitutional command of equal educational opportunity. As plaintiffs readily concede, differences among school districts in terms of size, special educational needs, transportation costs, and other factors will invariably create unavoidable differences in per-pupil expenditures" [692 A.2d at 397]).

48. The equal protection clause challenge in USD No. 229, discussed in the text, was brought by the Blue Valley School District, which included "some of the wealthiest suburbs of Kansas City" (Berger 1998, 36).

3   Funding and Accountability: Some Conceptual and Technical Issues in State Aid Reform

David N. Figlio

3.1   Background

The past decade has witnessed the acceleration of twin movements in school reform in the United States. One of these movements, school finance reform, has touched nearly every state in some shape or form. The complementary movement toward school accountability has also exploded recently, with three-quarters of states explicitly grading their schools in some manner, and the recent passage of the No Child Left Behind Act of 2001 underscores the current importance of school accountability. State aid reform and school accountability are inherently interrelated. In some states, state aid is directly linked to school performance. In other states, the relationship between aid and performance is more subtle, but still potentially profound. In every case, school finance is likely to be affected by school accountability, and the converse is true as well. It is therefore clear that any discussion of state aid reform at the dawn of the twenty-first century must view state aid through the lens of the school accountability movement.

The purpose of this chapter is to reflect on some of the key conceptual and technical issues associated with the design of state aid systems. Central issues in such design involve defining equity and adequacy, determining the degree to which different schools' financial situations can be appropriately compared (and how to compare "apples to apples"), identifying the role of special education in school finance, and measuring school performance appropriately for use in school finance systems. Each of these issues, as well as many other conceptual and technical issues, has been discussed in detail by other researchers in other outlets. A specific goal of this chapter, however, is to discuss some of these issues in the context of school accountability.

3.2   Equity, Adequacy, and Accountability: Normative Questions

The school finance reforms that have taken place over the past quarter century have been influenced by concepts of adequacy and equity. The specific nature of these concepts, however, is normative and subject to debate. Therefore, before one explores any of the key conceptual and technical issues associated with state aid reform, one must first determine the goals of such reform. This section provides a brief overview of many of the central issues involved in defining equity and adequacy in school finance.

Throughout American history, there have existed great disparities in school spending. Large differences have existed between states, but differences were typically at least as great within states as well. These differences came about because education finance was decentralized, and because localities differed greatly in wealth and preferences. One outcome of these differences in spending was that some types of schools (e.g., those serving rural, low-income, and minority populations) often faced much bleaker funding circumstances than those serving more affluent, urban, and white populations.

In the second half of the twentieth century, Americans became considerably more concerned with these inequities in school finance and often sought to make school finance more equitable. Individual definitions of equity vary widely, however, as do perceptions about the objectives of increasing equity. Fundamental disagreements exist as to whether equity implies equality (see, e.g., Putterman, Roemer, and Silvestre 1990), and for those who believe that it does, there exists a conflict between those who would seek equality of *inputs* (revenues per pupil, for instance) and those who would seek equality of *outcomes* (such as, perhaps, test scores or graduation rates). These two interpretations of equality may have dramatically different implications for school funding if there exists substantial heterogeneity in costs across schools and groups. Whereas a state aid reform predicated on the first interpretation (equality of school inputs) should necessarily lead to reductions in funding disparities across school districts, one based on the second interpretation (equality of student outcomes) may well lead to increased inequality in resources and spending.

It is apparent that normative decisions must be made to develop a working definition of equity. Berne and Stiefel (1999) raise five questions that are important when analyzing equity in school finance:

1. Equity for whom? Two groups' equity concerns are often considered: school-aged children and taxpayers. Equity concerns regarding children often focus on questions such as whether different groups of children receive similar levels of services. Taxpayer equity viewed through a school finance lens (the approach to taxpayer equity almost universally considered in equity debates) implies that any given tax rate relates to the same level of per-pupil spending independent of the taxpayer's residential location. A public finance perspective on taxpayer equity, on the other hand, would focus on, for instance, making taxation related to the value of the services generated by the tax. On occasion, concerns regarding equity for school-aged children and those regarding taxpayer equity are aligned with one another, but this is often not the case.

2. What is the unit of analysis? Different levels of aggregations of students have been considered when thinking about equity. Are we interested in comparing states, or districts within states, or schools, or students grouped by various characteristics? Perceptions of equity may vary considerably depending on the unit of analysis considered.

3. Which stage of "education production" is considered? Some discussions of equity suggest that raw materials (inputs) in the production of education should be distributed equitably. Other analyses look at equity in the "process" of education production. Still other conceptions of equity focus on equity in outputs, such as test scores and graduation rates, or in longer-term labor market or other outcomes.

4. Are specific groups of special interest? Often, certain groups, such as low-income, minority, or disabled students, are specifically targeted in equity discussions. On the taxpayer side, low-income and low-wealth taxpayers and districts are often considered more closely than are other groups.

5. Is school finance equity to be evaluated ex ante or ex post? Ex ante evaluation of equity focuses on statutory design (e.g., how does the formula for distributing school aid in a state provide for different groups of students or schools in that state?) Ex post evaluation of equity, on the other hand, considers the actual outcomes realized in the system. Ex ante and ex post evaluation concepts can differ considerably as a result of a number of factors, most notably because the design of the state aid system can introduce unintended behavioral incentives for schools and students. For instance, Cullen

(2003) and Cullen and Figlio (1998) find that school districts respond to fiscal incentives within their state aid systems by classifying students as disabled. In practice, courts, when overturning school finance systems, have adopted ex post standards, but in principle ex ante standards could have been used in legislatures' designs of state aid systems.

There are no obvious answers to these questions, but the conceptual and technical issues associated with implementing a state aid system differ depending on those answers. Over the past decade, however (particularly following the Kentucky Supreme Court decision *Rose v. Council for Better Education, Inc.* in 1989), there has been a general trend toward attention to the adequacy of educational resources rather than the distribution of those resources. But adequacy may be even more difficult to define than is equity, because of the uncertainty as to how to determine what constitute an "adequate" level of school quality or outcomes. (The issue of how actually to measure outcomes is, of course, of central importance for defining equity as well.) Movement from an equity to an adequacy standard eliminates the need to ask some of the questions posed above. For instance, adequacy definitions are entirely child-centered, rather than taxpayer-focused, and adequacy notions tend to focus much more on outcomes and outputs than do equity notions. Berne and Stiefel (1999) note that legal arguments tend to distinguish equity as input-based and adequacy as output-based, but in reality it is certainly reasonable to describe the adequacy of inputs or the equity of outputs.

Adequacy concerns, however, raise several new normative questions that must be addressed. The two major questions that must be answered involve what exactly needs to be adequate, and how much of it is adequate. The first question—what needs to be adequate?—is often answered in terms of test scores in core curricular areas. Indeed, the move toward school accountability mirrors this tendency: Schools are identified in many state accountability systems, as well as the new federal accountability system, as adequately acceptable (though the particular term "adequacy" is never employed in the school accountability context) based on the fraction of students deemed to be proficient in reading and mathematics (and in some states, writing, or occasionally science and social studies). And just as school accountability systems often evaluate schools on different outcomes besides test scores— prominent alternative outcomes include graduation rates or measures of "citizenship," such as delinquency or attendance—or alternatively, different programs and curricular offerings, definitions of educational adequacy can and do take into account different outcomes of interest. This raises an important point: The notion of accountability makes sense only when tied to specific performance objectives. In this regard, accountability must be defined through the lens of educational adequacy. Adequacy standards, either explicit or implied, define the level of performance (either measured in terms of test scores or otherwise) that schools are being held accountable for producing.

The school accountability parallel is useful for discussing the second main question associated with defining adequacy as well. In the federal accountability law, states have the ability to set their own definitions of proficiency, both in terms of metrics as well as in terms of requirements to be deemed proficient. States today vary considerably in the proficiency rates required to achieve a passing score on their state-administered exams, and these differences are almost surely due (at least in part) to differences in standards across states. Similar differences also can and do exist when one examines what is considered to be an adequate level of achievement. In principle, the adequate level of spending necessary to generate target achievement levels is the foundation level of foundation grant state aid programs, by far the most common form of state education aid program in the United States. However, certainly foundation levels have often been set without regard to the adequacy issues described above but rather have been determined through political processes.

A related normative question involves whether to tie accountability directly to school finance—that is, whether to link state aid to performance standards. The rationale for doing so is that by linking state aid to some concept of school efficiency, states are targeting their resources for schools that use them most efficiently. There are many different measures of school performance, however, and the type of measure used is normatively determined and has potentially large distributional consequences. Many states have taken to evaluating their schools based on the fraction of students in the school who attain proficiency in academic subjects—indeed, this is the fundamental measure of school quality described in the federal education reforms. But this type of school evaluation is highly related to student and family attributes, leading many to argue that an accountability system based on evaluation of this type grades schools on the basis of student socioeconomic status rather than school performance. The flip side of this argument, raised by proponents of this type of accountability system, is that all schools should be expected to bring students to minimum proficiency levels, regardless of background. The likely outcome of tying state aid to this type of accountability system, however, is increased inequality in inputs (and presumably, outcomes as well).

An alternative way of introducing school accountability into state aid formulas would involve more approximately measuring the school's so-called value added, or contribution to student outcomes. A closer pass to this than the performance measures described in the preceding paragraph would be to control for student background characteristics, or as Duncombe and Yinger (1999) and others have suggested, to account formally for cross-school cost differentials when incorporating performance indicators into state aid formulas. (Measuring costs is an analytical question described in section 3.3.) The benefit of this type of accountability system is that schools are less likely to be rewarded or punished for factors arguably beyond their control. This type of system does have costs, however, in terms of reduced transparency and the introduction of a new set of political concerns. It is arguable that controlling for student background characteristics (or adjusting for cost indexes) results in inadequate measurement of a school's value added, and that some measure or transformation of student-specific change in test scores from one year to the next is the best indicator of a school's contribution to student outcomes. An approach of the latter type has the benefit of being scientifically rigorous, but at the same time is even less transparent than the cost-control approach mentioned above. But regardless of the concept of value added employed, the sets of schools identified for rewards or sanctions will likely differ dramatically from those based on "raw" performance indicators. Figlio and Page (2003), for instance, show that there is little correlation (and sometimes even a negative correlation) between school rankings in any type of levels-based school accountability system and those resulting from any conception of a value-added-based school accountability system. This implies that the outcomes of any policy linking state funding (or school choice) to school accountability systems will depend directly on the nature of the performance standards identified by the state.

There exists debate as to whether value-added measures of school performance are really to be preferred to raw measures of levels of performance. Some opponents of value-added measures argue that schools and students should be held accountable to a given standard, regardless of background characteristics or children's starting values.

This argument has a certain appeal, because it does not prescribe different standards for different groups of students (or schools), but given the high correlation between test performance and the background characteristics of those taking the tests, especially in aggregate, evaluating schools solely on performance levels, with rewards and sanctions associated with said performance, does not seem fair to schools with large numbers of students predicted to perform poorly based on background characteristics. Although some of these correlations may be explainable by factors within the control of the school system (e.g., different expectations for low-income and minority students than for higher-income and white students), it still defies reason to suggest that all of these differences are due to controllable factors, suggesting that equity concerns with evaluating schools solely on the basis of test-performance levels are valid.

There are, however, other reasons to believe that value-added measures of evaluating schools may not be a panacea. Gains in test scores within a particular student cohort may reflect school contributions to the educational attainment of the students within that cohort but may also reflect unmeasured characteristics of the students and their families. Student background characteristics are often found to be correlated with gains in test scores as well as test score levels, though this is not a universal finding, and schools that have high starting values do not necessarily experience high gains. Still, these correlations may be due to differential school selection by families of different types, but they may also point to different family inputs, either independently of or jointly with the school's efforts. They may also indicate that schools serving high-socioeconomic-status families may be better able to find resources to boost instruction and outcomes in tested subjects. These correlations suggest that value-added measures of school productivity should be taken with a grain of salt.

Another potential problem with some forms of value-added measures is that they may invite gaming of the system. If schools are rewarded on the basis of cross-cohort changes in test scores (for instance, comparing fourth graders in 2002 to fourth graders in 2001, rather than comparing the same students from year to year), schools may have an incentive to underperform in one year to facilitate greater gains the next. But even if school gaming does not generate problems with this type of system, measurement error might: Kane and Staiger (2002), for instance, show that schools that show poor gains in one year tend to show high gains the next, and vice versa. Measuring value added based on following the same students, rather than different groups of students, relieves some of these problems, but only partially. In sum, although value-added systems of measuring school performance are likely better than most systems, they are no "silver bullet."

Measuring school performance is relevant for standard questions concerning state school aid as well as for school accountability. Obviously if adequacy is to be measured using some performance standard, the same measurement issues that arise with regard to school accountability also come up when one is determining what constitutes an adequate level of performance (and, reasoning back, of spending). Questions regarding the measurement of performance are also important when one is asking questions regarding equity. If the goal of measuring equity is equality of outcomes, for instance, then the measurement issues with respect to accountability are the same as those relevant for equity determination. If the goal of measuring equity is equality of opportunity, one must still determine which outcomes are relevant and important and must seek to determine how much of the variation in value added (or student-level performance) is due to school productivity differences and how much is due to factors outside the school's control. Other parallels between state aid and school accountability issues exist as well.

Programs working toward advancing accountability and equity goals sometimes complement one another, but sometimes they work at cross-purposes. One of the principal arguments for school accountability programs is, in essence, an equity argument: The schools that may be most in need of accountability pressure are the schools that face the least competition or parental oversight. Presumably, these schools are those that serve families that are either liquidity constrained or members of minority groups. Given that these types of schools generally constitute the bottom of the equity distribution, so to speak, accountability systems could lead to differential improvements in the performance of these schools compared to other schools, which might in turn narrow the gap between the richest and poorest schools or members of society. On the other hand, it need not happen that way: If schools serving low-socioeconomic-status students are more able to "game the system" because they lack parental oversight, accountability systems could lead to no change in the distribution of school performance, or perhaps even a widening of the gap between the education received by the "haves" and that received by the "have nots." Moreover, if school accountability systems base financial rewards and punishments on student test performance, as those in a number of states do, then the gaps between education "haves" and "have nots" could grow as well. School accountability systems that base rewards and punishments on the levels of test performance are particularly likely to lead to increased inequality (unless corrections are made, such as those in California and South Carolina, for family background characteristics), though even accountability systems that base rewards and sanctions on value-added measures of student performance may be vulnerable if these measures of value added, or student test score gains in general, are correlated with socioeconomic or other student background characteristics. Likewise, programs aimed at increasing educational equity across school districts may have the consequence of undermining accountability objectives. Duncombe and Yinger (2001b), for instance, find that, by their measures, block grants and matching aid lead to reductions in school efficiency.

3.3   Some Analytical Issues

There are many more analytical issues involved in state aid system development and reform than could possibly be described in this setting. This section identifies several of the most important of these issues (identifying and measuring performance of schools, and describing and quantifying cost differences) and provides a general discussion of their importance and implications. I first discuss technical issues associated with measuring school performance (which are, of course, relevant regardless of whether school accountability systems are incorporated into state aid formulas, because adequacy standards should take performance into account as well). I then describe some of the issues associated with measuring cost differences across schools.

3.3.1   Measuring School Performance

The conceptual issues involved with measuring school performance fall into both the normative and the analytical categories. Normative issues include which performance indicators to use and what levels of performance to expect. Questions arising from these types of issues ultimately have political answers, though Duncombe and Yinger (1997) have, for example, attempted to infer empirically the performance indicators society values by looking at the capitalization of those indicators into real estate values when they constructed their index of educational performance. In this chapter, however, I assume that normative decisions have been made and focus solely on some of the key technical issues.

3.3.1.1 Aggregation Issues Three types of aggregation issues are relevant for state aid systems and school accountability systems. The first type involves aggregation across time. In different settings and different contexts, Kane and Staiger (2002) and Figlio (2002) demonstrate how unstable school rankings based on test performance are from one year to the next. The fundamental problem here involves measurement error: Tests have large stochastic components to them, and schools deemed improving at one point in time could (almost necessarily) be found to be declining at another point. Such measurement error has implications for rewards and sanctions in state aid systems and school accountability systems: Should schools be punished or rewarded on the basis of a single "good draw" or "bad draw"? Problems raised by this question are particularly exacerbated when performance is measured as changes in proficiency from one year to the next across different cohorts (as is the case in the federal school accountability law). When two successive years' average test scores are each measured with error (not least because the compositions of students in the classrooms change dramatically, though this is not the only reason), it is unclear what, if anything, is being uncovered by an accountability system that rewards (penalizes) improvements (declines) in fractions of students passing the test from one cohort to the next. Both Kane and Staiger (2002) and Figlio (2002) illustrate that taking moving averages across several years considerably reduces the likelihood that measurement error will lead to dramatic instability in measured school performance, although this does remain a problem.

A second type of aggregation issue involves aggregation across types of tests (or other performance indicators). Although scores on mathematics and reading tests, for instance, tend to trend together within a school, Figlio (2002) shows that the correlation between changes from one year to the next in scores on one test and changes across the same time period in scores on another test is quite weak. Therefore, performance standards that require meeting particular criteria on multiple outputs may be overly difficult to attain (if the standards are set appropriately high), and those that require cross-cohort improvements on these criteria along multiple dimensions may merely reward schools with good luck and punish those with bad luck. Potential fixes to this problem include aggregating multiple outcomes into a single indicator (as in, for example, the approach described above by Duncombe and Yinger [1997]) or evaluating schools on multiple criteria separately without requiring standards to be met (or improvements to be realized) in every year.

A third type of aggregation issue involves how multiple subgroups in a school should be considered. Disaggregating students into subgroups (say, along racial, ethnic, or socioeconomic lines, or based on prior performance levels) exacerbates the measurement error problems described in the preceding paragraphs. On the other hand, for normative reasons, one might wish to pay special attention to the performance of certain subgroups, and indeed, many equity and adequacy discussions have centered on the performance of minorities, low-income students, and low achievers. The prescriptions for improvement of measurement described above are particularly relevant when students are divided up and the scores of the resulting subgroups, rather than those of the group as a whole, are examined. Kane and Staiger (2002) demonstrate that measurement error problems are most acute for small schools; the same is true for smaller subgroups within schools.

3.3.1.2 Identifying Value Added How exactly to quantify a school's value added is up for debate. At the very least, however, accounting for value added requires some control for circumstances such as student and family background characteristics. Typically, however, student background characteristics (or more specifically, the background characteristics available in administrative data) explain only a small portion of the observed variation in individual test scores. (Student information aggregated to the school level does a better, though still extremely incomplete, job of explaining aggregate test scores.) Therefore, it seems important to go beyond observed background attributes of a school's when one is measuring the school's value added.

Measures that aggregate changes in student test scores from year to year are arguably closer indicators of a school's contribution to student outcomes than are those that consider only test-score levels. Such measures range in complexity from the extremely simple and transparent (for instance, simply averaging year-to-year test score gains) to very complicated models that impose considerable structure on the relationships between inputs and outputs. All models of value added require annual (or at least extremely frequent) testing of students, using tests that can be vertically equated (that is, the test scores for one grade can be compared to those of the next) and are administered uniformly across schools. Moreover, and even more fundamentally, the system for collecting, storing, and reporting administrative data must be able to follow students reliably from year to year.

As mentioned earlier in the chapter, value-added measures of school performance, regardless of how the measurements are made, are still imperfect indicators of a school's contribution to student gains. Given the correlations often found in the data between student test score gains and background characteristics, empirically controlling for student body attributes may be warranted. Whether such a correction is warranted is not obvious, however, and depends in part on what the particular accountability system in question seeks to measure.

All measures of school performance based on scores on standardized tests must also address the question of which students should be included in the test pool for the purposes of enforcing standards and accountability. This is inherently a normative and political question, rather than a scientific one, though it derives from a positive debate. Key decisions must be made with regard to whether mobile populations are counted in the accountability testing pool, as well as whether disabled students should be considered for school reporting purposes. Florida, for instance, has taken two very different tacks with regard to student mobility. In the first iteration of the state's A+ Plan for Education, Governor Jeb Bush's education reform enacted in 1999, school evaluations were based not only on the performance of stable students, but also on that of students who had recently arrived in the school. But the next year, those evaluations were based only on students present in the school for the entire school year up to the testing date. These rule changes had substantial implications for schools and students, and the sets of schools identified as low-quality or high-quality changed considerably when only the more stable set of students was included. States also vary with respect to how they answer the question of which disabled students should remain in the test pool for the purposes of constructing performance measures. Whereas Florida, for example, excludes all disabled students, even test-taking students, from the school-level aggregates used to measure productivity, Virginia goes to the other extreme, including all disabled students in the accountability pool, except for the rather small fraction whose individualized education plans explicitly exclude them from testing.

These issues pose substantial trade-offs for policymakers seeking to develop state aid systems. A policymaker deciding which students to include or exclude in assessments of school performance, for example, may wish to exclude mobile and disabled students, out of a concern for fairness: Schools with large fractions of mobile and disabled students could argue, with validity, that they are being judged on factors well outside their control. On the other hand, excluding students on the basis of *classification* provides schools with an incentive to reclassify or move students selectively to look better against performance metrics. Special education offers schools a margin that may be worked for these purposes. Cullen (2003) and Cullen and Figlio (1998) have demonstrated that schools tend to reclassify students who are on the margin of special education classification in response to *fiscal* incentives, and Garing (2002) demonstrates that schools' classifications of students are responsive to *parental* fiscal incentives as well. Three recent papers, Cullen and Reback 2002, Figlio and Getzler 2002, and Jacob 2002, show that special education classification responds to *accountability* incentives too. For instance, Figlio and Getzler (2002) find that when Florida introduced high-stakes testing for the purposes of school accountability (and ultimately school finance), schools tended with increased regularity to reclassify students with poor previous test performance as disabled. These incentives, of course, also have a different type of implication for school finance, as the increased classification of marginal students as special education students increases total education costs for school districts and states.

The same types of trade-offs are relevant with the decision to move from levels-based assessment of schools for accountability and school finance to a more value-added-based assessment. The argument for basing assessment on value added is very much the same as the argument for excluding disabled and mobile students from the high-stakes (for schools) testing pool: Schools with certain populations that tend to fare worse on standardized examinations argue that their quality is masked by the poor outcomes of students starting at a low level. On the other hand, introducing value added (or even controlling for background factors) raises political concerns, both because it becomes more difficult, when value added is introduced, for the lay public to interpret the assessment of schools, and (according to an argument currently popular) explicitly controlling for the different student compositions in schools is seen by some as making excuses for poor performance, or alternatively, holding different types of students (and hence, schools) to different standards. It is possible that including background characteristics as part of a cost correction, à la Duncombe and Yinger (1997), might be a politically palatable way to control in part for student attributes in an environment in which it would be difficult to do so otherwise.

School accountability and school finance systems may each provide different incentives for schools to reclassify, move, or hold back students. Whereas school accountability systems tend to encourage schools to classify students as disabled, for instance, school finance systems may either encourage or discourage this practice, depending on the financial incentive structure imbedded in the finance system. For instance, some states compensate school districts for disabled students on the basis on predicted disability caseloads, rather than actual disability counts. In such a case, reclassifying a student as disabled to avoid that student's being counted in an accountability system will be costly to the district, which must now provide special services for the student without additional compensation from the state. On the other hand, other states provide compensation to districts for marginal students that exceeds the additional cost required to educate if they are classified as disabled. In these states, school accountability incentives may exacerbate the incentives to overclassify students as disabled that are provided by the finance system. Similarly, moving students from school to school across years may lead to increased costs to school districts, but school accountability systems that exclude mobile students may provide sufficient incentives to make these moves worthwhile for school districts.

3.3.1.3 What Is Adequate? Establishing what constitutes an adequate level of school funding (and student performance) is inherently a political question, rather than one that can be answered definitively by researchers. But the brief discussion above regarding measuring adequacy suggests that there exists extraordinary heterogeneity across schools and school districts within states, and it is therefore also likely that one cannot expect the same performance from the same amount of funding from two schools with very different student compositions, even when the schools have the same degree of efficiency.

3.3.2 Measuring Costs of Education
Many of the same issues that arise in the determination of school performance appear in different contexts in the determination of cost differences across schools. The rationale for adjusting for cost differences is very similar, theoretically, to the rationale for measuring the value

added of schools in educational production: When two schools face very different circumstances, the schools have varying difficulties in meeting any type of performance goal. Duncombe and Yinger (1999) provide the nice metaphor of a "temperature standard" for schools: It takes fewer resources to heat a school in the wintertime to 72 degrees Fahrenheit in Florida than it does in Wisconsin. Providing the same heating budget to both schools would lead to dramatic differences in measured productivity along one dimension (in terms of actual comfort level attained), but this would not separate factors that are in the control of school officials from those that are outside of their control. The purpose of cost adjustments is to guarantee, as much as is possible, that two schools facing very different circumstances have the same potential, after adjustment, to generate a specified level of student outcomes. The word "potential" is important here because it highlights one of the conceptual questions raised in section 3.2—that of ex ante versus ex post realization of the goal. An ex ante view of this issue would be that cost adjustments should be made to the amount of aid awarded to schools without regard to differences in productivity—two schools, after appropriate cost adjustments are made to the amount of aid they receive, would have an "equal chance" of success. An ex post view of this issue would be that differential productivity should possibly be taken into account and that perhaps further adjustments to costs should be made to account for differences in school productivity. There are technical and normative concerns in both views; these are not discussed in this chapter.

I turn now to some of the analytical issues involved in the measurement of cost differentials. Any researcher or practitioner involved in school finance can attest to the fact that school districts face substantial differences in the costs of educating their student populations. These differences come about for numerous reasons, not least because student populations vary considerably in their needs. Special education population differences, described to an extent in section 3.3.1 are but one of the sources of these cost differences; other cost differences arise because of varying needs for remediation and other types of educational services.

Moreover, these same characteristics associated with increased basic costs of services may also influence input prices. Hanushek, Kain, and Rivkin (1998), among others, show that teachers are more likely to select employment in more affluent and majority-white schools, when they have the opportunity, and Figlio (1997b) shows that high-paying (generally suburban) school districts can attract high-quality teachers away from their lower-paying neighbors, even independent of school and student body attributes. Furthermore, numerous authors, such as Ferguson (1991), Ferguson and Ladd (1996), Goldhaber and Brewer (1997), Hanushek, Kain, and Rivkin (1998), and Wright, Horn, and Sanders (1997), have shown that teacher quality (though not the types of attributes typically rewarded by teacher salary structures) significantly improves student outcomes. It is therefore reasonable to expect that teacher dollars at some schools do not go as far as they do in other schools. Given the widespread recognition that costs differ substantially across school districts, it is somewhat surprising that states rarely attempt to systematically adjust the amounts of education funding they award for costs. Often cost adjustments are made in very ad hoc ways, with potentially deleterious consequences that could become even more apparent in an era of adequacy standards and school accountability. Cost adjustments that do not take into account both the direct and indirect cost differences associated with educating different types of students will likely lead to systematic underprovision of school services for low-income and minority students, relative to their high-income white counterparts.

There have been several serious attempts to address the issue of adjusting for input costs across school districts. These approaches generally consist of adjusting costs either for geographic differences or for background characteristics of student populations, though occasionally both cost factors are accounted for simultaneously (Duncombe and Yinger 1997). Cost adjustments based on geography are predicated on the notion that personnel costs vary considerably from place to place. Since personnel costs account for the vast majority of costs borne by school districts, geography-based cost adjustments are personnel cost indices.

3.3.2.1 Adjusting for Geographic Characteristics The best-known and most sophisticated of the personnel-based measures is Chambers's (1995) Teacher Cost Index. This index is regression based and adjusts for regional differences in amenities and the general cost of living in an attempt to distinguish the true cost to a school district of doing business from factors that are discretionary to the district. Within-state variation in the Chambers model is accounted for by utilizing district characteristics arguably outside of the district's control. A drawback of the Teacher Cost Index, however, is that its complicated structure and reliance on regression makes it somewhat challenging to implement and explain politically.

Alternatives to the Teacher Cost Index include Barro's (1992) index, based on average teacher salaries, and the cost-of-living index utilized by McMahon and Chang (1991). The Barro index creates a measure of average teacher salaries independent of teacher experience and education levels. This approach can be manipulated, however, by school districts that could respond to its implementation by changing their teacher skill mix, say, by hiring only teachers with graduate degrees or more highly experienced teachers. The McMahon and Chang index captures simple differences across districts in housing costs and income, as well as population growth. Whereas the Barro index is likely to overstate true cost differences from district to district, the McMahon and Chang index seems likely to understate those cost differences. In practice, states tend to adjust cost estimates for geographic differences by applying local consumer price indexes or differences in local wages. Regardless of which measure is used, it seems certain that any adjustment for differences in costs based on geographic characteristics will improve the fairness of the distribution of state aid (Mishel and Rothstein 1997).

Yinger (2001) points out several key problems with using cost indexes like the Teacher Cost Index and the Barro and McMahon and Chang indexes for the purpose of calculating within-state differences in costs. One concern is that these indexes are generated from national-level regressions and might not reflect cost differences unique to a given state. A second concern is that these cost indexes do not directly control for private wages and hence may be biased. In addition, these indexes generally include in their regressions only a small number of indicators of classroom environment. The essence of these concerns indicates that although this type of index can be quite useful for adjusting for cost differentials, it makes sense to construct an index more specifically designed for the state in question, and using current data.

A related issue involves the treatment of district size in cost measurement. Unusually large or unusually small school districts are likely to have higher per-pupil costs than otherwise similar districts of a more average size. Very large school districts require infrastructural features not necessary in smaller school districts. On the other hand, very small school districts and schools may not have reached an efficient scale, and fixed costs account for a larger fraction of the school costs in these districts and schools. Duncombe and Yinger (2001a), studying consolidation of rural school districts in New York, show that consolidation of small districts leads to significantly reduced total costs. On the other hand, they find little or no effect of consolidation of larger rural districts, which enjoy modestly reduced operating costs after consolidation but increased postconsolidation capital costs.

3.3.2.2 Adjusting for Student Characteristics The majority of states include some adjustment in their state aid formulas to reflect the different costs associated with special student populations, either for at-risk children or for specific education programs or grade levels. Most notable are adjustments made for special education populations and students with limited English proficiency. State aid formulas (particularly those that are foundation-based) generally provide additional multiples of the base aid amount for students with special needs. For instance, different broad special education classifications (e.g., specific learning disability, educable mentally handicapped) typically generate different specific multipliers based on disability identification *per se*, rather than the level of service provided disable students. Chambers et al. (2002) provide evidence that these broad special education classifications explain only a very small portion of the variation in true special education costs incurred by school districts. Some states, concerned about districts' overclassification of students as disabled because of fiscal incentives to do so (Cullen and Figlio 1998), have moved to a "census-based" system of special education finance in which allocations of state aid to school districts for special education are based on predicted numbers of students in the various classifications (and predicted costs) generated from student body characteristics, rather than actual costs. (And as mentioned earlier in the chapter, there may be incentives for school districts to "game the system" by over- or under-classifying students as qualifying for special education services, and there also exists some evidence that such gaming actually takes place.)

In practice, it is not obvious which approach to adjusting school aid amounts for special-needs populations—providing state aid for predicted populations of students with special needs or providing state aid based on actual numbers of students in various classifications—is fairer for districts with reasonably large student populations. Small school districts are more at risk, if the first of the two methods is used, of "prediction error" (that is, of enrolling a significantly larger special education population than "predicted" by the state's model). For such districts, an unusually large number of extremely costly students could, if uncompensated for, seriously affect school district finances.

As challenging as it is to identify school districts' special education populations and compensate those districts for those populations fairly, these tasks pale in comparison to that of identifying at-risk students, of whom there is no clinical definition. The best indicator of one aspect of risk likelihood is child poverty, and participation in the federal school lunch program is the closest approximation to poverty available to state aid administrators. But participation in this program often carries a stigma, and it drops off so substantially from elementary to secondary school that it is difficult to view free and reduced price lunch participant counts as more than an extremely crude measure of socioeconomic status at the secondary level. At the elementary level, this stigma is less apparent, and participation in the program is quite a bit higher, but sizable differences in participation rates across schools serving geographical areas with similar low-income populations suggest that school and district policy (and salesmanship) may determine at least in part differences in participation and therefore, measured school socioeconomic status. This problem is borne out in the data: in Florida, school- and district-level correlations between neighborhood or school district poverty, as measured by the Census, and federal school lunch program participation rates are almost twice as high for elementary schools than for secondary schools. Hence, aggregating elementary students to secondary school or district catchment areas is likely to be a better indicator of the socioeconomic status of secondary students than would be directly counting secondary school free- and reduced-price-lunch caseloads.

Measures of other factors that put students at risk for poor academic performance are even less likely to be available to policymakers, but recent advances in the matching of birth records and student information systems may improve prediction in this area. Roth et al. (2002), matching vital statistics at birth to student records in Florida, show that perinatal conditions such as low birth weight, congenital anomalies, and labor and delivery complications are by far the strongest predictors of early-elementary-aged disability status and academic problems (and attendant costs to school districts and states), and Chaikind and Corman (1991), using survey data, suggest that birth weight affects elementary school costs.

Even if the at-risk student population in a particular district could be identified, the challenge would remain of attempting to determine the appropriate cost adjustments to make to aid awards to compensate the district for the costs of educating its at-risk population. There exist very few studies of the "typical" costs associated with educating low-income and other at-risk students. The most common multiplier considered by researchers for at-risk students is 1.2, calculated by Levin (1989) based largely on Title I allocations per student in 1987. But basing cost estimates on federal budgetary decisions, although a handy rule of thumb in many research contexts, is not an ideal way to implement policy. Moreover, this figure is unlikely to capture the increased teacher salaries necessary to attract equal-quality teachers to work in impoverished schools and districts.

3.3.2.3 Simultaneous Adjustment for Student and Geographic Characteristics Recent researchers (most notably, Duncombe and Yinger [1997] and Reschovsky and Imazeki [1998]) have developed models that adjust cost estimates for both geographic differences in input costs and for the additional costs associated with special-needs students. Of these, Duncombe and Yinger (1997) present the most thorough example of such a strategy. In addition, several cost indexes have been developed that indirectly control for school performance. Examples of this type of approach include Bradbury et al. 1984 and Ratcliffe, Riddle, and Yinger 1990.

Duncombe and Yinger (1997) argue that school spending, education production, and school outcomes are all simultaneously determined, and using data from New York, they estimate the relationships between school district spending and numerous cost factors arguably outside of the direct control of school district officials, including district size, measures of the socioeconomic and English proficiency status of children in the district, input prices, and disability rate in the district. The outcome of this analysis is a relative cost index for each district in the state, representing the relative challenges presented to different districts in educating students. Some of the assumptions embedded in this model are controversial, and the model has several features that could make it less desirable than simpler models for policy applications. For instance, in the Duncombe and Yinger model, extreme cost outliers (most notably, New York City) can have very large swings in estimated relative costs depending on the particular specification of the model. In Duncombe and Yinger 1999, for example, the model's calculated direct cost index for New York City when efficiency is treated as endogenous is nearly twice its calculated index when efficiency is modeled as exogenous. But the most striking feature of Duncombe and Yinger's research is its highlighting of the extraordinary differences in costs that exist across school districts in New York. Reschovsky and Imazeki (1998) also describe very large differences in their calculated cost index across school districts in Wisconsin. Thus the simultaneous treatment of input prices and the cost of educating students with special needs in models for adjusting school aid amounts to localities is quite important and promising, but more work remains before this type of approach is fully ready for translation to public policy.

3.3.2.4 Accountability, Costs, and Equity Introducing school accountability and performance standards, even if they are not incorporated directly into the state aid formula, can have significant consequences for cost adjustments. Increased school choice that is tied to school accountability, for instance, may exacerbate school district cost differentials if students from already high-cost, low-socioeconomic-status districts are provided with an "exit option," and particularly if the most motivated families are the most likely to select out of their existing school. Along similar lines, some high-achieving students attending schools branded as low performing may also select into the private sector and leave the public sector altogether. These types of potential student responses to school accountability suggest that cost adjustments may need to be updated even more frequently in a regime of school accountability than in one with less accountability-driven choice. As mentioned earlier in the chapter, school accountability systems may provide schools with an incentive to overclassify students as disabled or to retain low-performing students in grade with higher frequency; these types of responses to increased accountability, and the fact that they are likely to occur differentially from district to district, suggest that the relative costs of districts are likely to change as schools are held more accountable.

The historical experience with *fiscal* accountability suggests that input prices may change as well with increased *academic performance* accountability. As one example, Figlio and Rueben (2001) show that one consequence of the so-called tax revolt of the late 1970s and 1980s was that many higher-quality potential teachers selected out of the teaching force and were replaced by lower-quality teachers (where quality is measured by potential teachers' test scores). Interestingly, Figlio and Rueben find that this response was in many cases due not to actual changes in resources as a result of the pared-down budgets that followed the revolt, but rather, apparently, to changes in teachers' perceptions of the education environment. Early evidence from Florida's experience with school accountability suggests that teachers, when they perceive that school grading is arbitrary or biased against their schools, are likely to contemplate leaving their schools. This may be one of the reasons why Downes and Figlio (2000) and Figlio (1997a) find evidence of much larger effects of tax limits than would be predicted by looking at the changes in actual school revenues and spending as a result of the tax limits. These pieces of evidence indicate that teacher input costs may increase with school accountability and that the increases in these costs may be differentially borne by low-socioeconomic-status school districts, precisely the districts that already face inflated teacher costs for any given unit of teacher quality. Although this last point is speculative, it does suggest that hasty design of a school accountability system or performance standards embedded within a state aid system might have unintended consequences that transcend the direct effects described earlier.

On a related point, there exists compelling evidence from Black (1999) and others that house prices reflect student test scores. Test scores have become well publicized in most states over the past decade, even in the absence of the federal accountability system. But ratings of schools may present additional information to the community, and this additional information may influence house prices, regardless of the quality of the signal presented in the school-grading mechanism.

Figlio and Lucas (2000) study the effects on the Gainesville, Florida, housing market of the introduction of Florida's A+ accountability system in 1999. Using a house-level fixed-effects specification and controlling for time-varying neighborhood effects, they show that although test scores remain capitalized in house prices following the introduction of school grading, the grades had an independent and large effect on the distribution of house prices, at least in the short term. Neighborhoods with schools that had unexpected positive shocks, captured by a favorable school grade holding constant all the variables used to construct the school grades, saw immediate increases in house values, whereas neighborhoods with schools experiencing unexpected negative shocks saw reductions in their house values. This finding has direct implications for school finance. School districts with large numbers of sanctioned schools may experience reductions, at least in the short run, in their tax bases, requiring either reductions in school spending above and beyond the amounts of the state and federal sanctions, or increases in local tax effort to maintain current levels of spending, or increased state effort (and potential taxation) to maintain local spending. School districts with few if any sanctioned schools would experience effects in the other direction. Although it is not yet known whether these responses will persist in the long term, Figlio and Lucas's results suggest that arbitrarily assigned school grades might have significant ripple effects in housing markets and on school finance in general.

It is as yet unknown whether the effects of school grading on house prices are entirely redistributive, or if there may be some net gain (or loss) in house prices generally as a result of an accountability system. On the one hand, if in general the perception of schools in an area improves, then this general increase in the perceived quality of schools should lead to an overall increase in house prices, much as would be the case with any other local amenity. Given that the goal of the No Child Left Behind Act is to effect positive change in school quality, this may be an expected outcome of the federal accountability policy. On the other hand, as described above, it is highly likely that a large number of schools will face sanctions under the federal system. This could have the effect of decreasing public impressions of overall school quality, which may depress general housing values. It is clearly too soon to know which of these outcomes is most likely to play out nationally.

Taken together, these indirect fiscal consequences of school accountability suggest that accountability systems may have the effect of reducing equity among school districts. In addition, specific design aspects of the federal No Child Left Behind Act likely will directly lead to increased inequality across school districts. Figlio (2003) uses data from Florida to forecast the school districts in that state likely to be sanctioned under the No Child Left Behind Act. He indicates that the direct fiscal impacts of the federal accountability reforms will likely be borne overwhelmingly by districts serving large numbers of low-income students, particularly in the early years of the program. This pattern is in large measure deterministic, as the federal accountability rules effectively sanction only low-income schools, since sanctions are tied to Title I allocations. Even among Title I schools, however, accountability sanctions will likely be imposed mainly on schools in particularly poor and heavily minority communities.

As a result, the federal accountability program will likely work to offset some of the school finance equalizations attempted by state legislatures or often ordered by state supreme courts. (Incidentally, this disequalization, if it occurs, will also counteract one of the goals of the federal Title I program itself, which provides additional Title I aid to schools in states that have more-equalized school finance systems.) Figlio (2003) shows that the school districts with the highest fractions of minority and low-income students, precisely the districts typically supported in school finance equalization scenarios, are the schools projected to lose the most under the federal accountability rules. To the extent to which this triggers further equalization aid from the state, it will lead to increased fiscal responsibility from the state. (On the other hand, a state bailout of this type would undermine the goals of the federal accountability system.) Alternatively, districts would either have less revenue with which to work or would need to raise revenues to replace the lost Title I grants.

3.4 Conclusion

This chapter discusses some of the important issues involved in state aid reform. Appropriate identification and determination of cost differences are key for developing state aid formulas, and in an era with increased focus on adequacy standards and school accountability embedded within state aid formulas, so is measurement of performance. But implementation of state aid reforms is challenging, not least because the design of state aid and school accountability programs may influence the outcomes of these programs, and the two types of programs may work at cross-purposes. Special care must be exercised when implementing new accountability systems or reforming state aid in an era of school accountability.

4

Prospects for Achieving Equity or Adequacy in Education: The Limits of State Aid in General Equilibrium

Thomas J. Nechyba

4.1 Introduction

When thinking about policy issues and giving advice to policymakers, economists often rely on intuitions emerging from partial equilibrium models. For many issues this seems perfectly appropriate, but sometimes the issues on which we are asked to provide advice are so fundamentally general equilibrium in nature that partial equilibrium thinking can yield misleading conclusions. Education policy is a prime example. State and local education policy does not simply affect the educational opportunities children in current schools will have. Because they are reflected in real estate markets and housing prices, educational policies alter the incentives that guide decisions parents make in terms of where to live, which school (public or private) to send their children to, and how to participate in the political process as it affects education. General equilibrium price effects can be large, as can the mobility effects that cause and support them. Furthermore, since it is now widely believed that the composition of the student (and parent) population in a school is an important determinant of the level of educational quality produced in that school, these general equilibrium decisions may have large impacts on school quality even if public school spending does not change appreciably.

This chapter therefore analyzes different types of state government aid to education within the context of a single general equilibrium model whose structural parameters are set to be consistent with important features of data on housing prices, income distributions across districts, school spending levels, and private school market activity. I argue that an understanding of general equilibrium effects of state education policy is important not only for predicting the impact of various policy options, but also for appreciating the economic root causes of the current inequities within public schools in the United States. Section 4.2 therefore begins with an overview of how local public finance models can help us understand what economic factors must be important in order for large inequities in public education to persist in equilibrium. Section 4.3 then provides a quick, nontechnical overview of a model (fully developed elsewhere) that incorporates these economic factors and successfully replicates important features of the data. This model is then offered as a tool capable of analyzing different types of state aid to education.

I begin the policy analysis in section 4.4 by reporting on results of simulations that compare the equilibrium outcomes under a fully decentralized, property tax–financed public education system to those under a fully centralized, equalized and state income tax–funded system. What is striking in those policy simulations is how far even a policy that fully equalizes public school spending remains from one that equalizes educational opportunities for children. This is because housing market conditions continue to lead to large levels of segregation that have an impact on nonfinancial inputs into local public schools. Similarly striking is the role played by private schools in the two extreme systems simulated. The comparison between these two extreme systems allows us to get a sense of the limits of state intervention in producing equality within public schools as they are currently set up.

Section 4.5 proceeds to an analysis of more traditional grants in aid to public school districts. Such grants may take the form of block or matching grants, and each of these types is analyzed in turn. Matching grants are in principle the better tool for raising either the overall level of school spending or the level in particular districts. One must consume this result with caution, however, given that the levels of matching undertaken by the state government must themselves ultimately be subject to voter consent, and it is difficult to imagine that state voters will allow the price incentives embedded in matching grants to raise overall spending levels much beyond what they desire. Block grants, on the other hand, have rather little impact on spending in a general equilibrium world unless they are large or require a high level of maintenance of local tax effort. Because they lack the substitution effects inherent in matching grants, block grants aim to increase spending solely through income effects. Given, however, that—in a general equilibrium world—taxpayers must also fund these block grants through their state income taxes, these income effects are much smaller than in a partial equilibrium context, and they may well be negative in high-income districts. The general equilibrium prediction, then, is that block grants to local school districts are unlikely to have major impacts on local education spending unless they are so large that local school budgets expand even if the local government reacts by reducing its own support for local schools to the minimum legally permitted level. Furthermore, simulations suggest that equalizing aid that is based on local fiscal capacity is likely to be considerably more effective at equalizing spending if based on a matching rather than a block grant formula. This is in part due to general equilibrium price effects that tend to undermine equalizing state formulas when state aid is structured to be inversely related to local property wealth.

Finally, section 4.6 concludes the chapter's analysis by focusing on a new proposal for state aid to education: giving state income tax revenues to parents in the form of a private school voucher rather than to school districts in the form of grants. Here I report on results that suggest large general equilibrium mobility and price effects for some types of vouchers and not for others. This links closely to the incentives of households with children attending private schools to settle in poor public school districts to take advantage of depressed housing values. Vouchers cause general equilibrium effects by uncoupling the decision of where to live from that of where to send children to school. Although the focus in the policy simulations conducted in this chapter is strictly on vouchers, similar general equilibrium forces are likely to be important in regard to other policies—such as charter and magnet schools—that move public education away from a model in which what school a child attends is determined solely by the residential choice of his or her parents.

4.2   Sources of Interjurisdictional Inequities

It is difficult to provide sound advice to state education policymakers without stepping back and first understanding the forces that have led to the current levels of inequities and inadequacies in state public school systems. One way to identify the causal channels through which such inequities and inadequacies emerge is to attempt to imagine a world in which, despite having different levels of income and child ability, all households have equal access to the same level of public school quality. In this attempt, one quickly discovers that so long as admittance into a public school is based on where a child lives (as it is in most U.S. states), and so long as we are open to the possibility that households will move if this improves their welfare, it is not at all easy to find realistic assumptions under which such perfect public school equity could in fact emerge as an equilibrium outcome.[1]

It is often assumed that local financing of public education is the primary culprit behind existing public school inequities. Conceptually, however, it is not immediate why this ought to be the case. Given that households can gain admittance to any public school by merely moving into that school's attendance area, how could inequities persist in equilibrium? Why do households not simply move until all public school quality differences disappear and equilibrium is reached? Is it merely the case that different households value education differently and therefore sort into different districts (much as some households like white bread and some like wheat), or is it possible to sustain high levels of inequality in public education even in a model in which all households agree on the value of education? If rich districts provide better public schools, why are the poor—assuming that they too value education—not "chasing the rich" by moving into their districts?

It is in the general equilibrium models of the local public finance literature that one finds answers to these questions. Simple models point to assumptions that must be made in order for strong notions of equity to emerge in equilibrium, and more complicated models introduce the real-world forces that generate and support inequity in public education as the expected outcome. Once a model is rich enough to capture the forces that lead to the observed levels of inequity, it can then be used to analyze the likelihood that different types of policy proposals might succeed in alleviating inequities or at least guaranteeing minimum levels of adequacy. Although one easy way to generate unequal levels of public education in a model is simply to assume that households sort based on different intensities of preferences for education, and particularly that the poor care less about education than the rich, my view is that it is not fruitful to begin with such an assumption. Rather, I begin in the next section by seeking out models that can explain the emergence of inequities as well as incentives that prevent the "poor chasing the rich" phenomenon under the assumption that underlying preferences are shared among all households.

4.2.1   Income Differences

Just as equity-based court challenges to local school financing became important in the 1970s, Westhoff (1977) presented a simple model in which equilibrium differences in public service levels emerged not from differences in tastes, but solely from differences in household incomes. Local jurisdictions were constrained to finance a particular public service through a proportional local income tax, and each jurisdiction could choose its most preferred tax rate (through majority-rule voting). Under certain conditions, in any stable equilibrium in this model, households segregate voluntarily into jurisdictions with different tax rates and different public service levels simply because high-income households demand more of the public service (and are willing to pay higher tax rates for it) than low-income households. Much is missing from this very simple model, but it makes the useful point that income differences alone can generate "voluntary" interjurisdictional differences in public services in the presence of local income tax financing of those services.

4.2.2   Local Taxes of a Housing Good

Of course, few local school districts rely heavily on local income taxes, and much of what is interesting about local public finance happens in the context of land and housing markets. It thus became natural to ask whether Westhoff's result can be sustained in a model in which housing plays an important role and is taxed to fund local services. Epple, Filimon, and Romer (1993) prove that it can. Modeling housing as a homogeneous consumption good that is supplied within each jurisdiction according to an exogenously specified supply schedule, they demonstrate that, under certain assumptions, differences in income are again sufficient to sustain an equilibrium in which public service levels differ across jurisdictions. Tax-inclusive housing prices are higher in districts that provide public services, and low-income households "voluntarily" choose not to chase the rich into these districts because of these higher housing prices. Whereas Westhoff requires local income taxes to support inequities in public service provision, Epple et al. demonstrate that equilibrium housing-good prices can do the same in the presence of local property taxes. Both obtain the equilibrium prediction that households will stratify perfectly into jurisdictions based on their income.[2]

4.2.3   Heterogenous Land and Housing Markets

Both Westhoff and Epple et al. rely on somewhat restrictive assumptions on preferences to ensure the existence of equilibria that exhibit inequities in public service provision. These assumptions become unnecessary when land and housing are modeled somewhat differently.

Epple et al. treat housing as a good similar to other goods in that it can be consumed in any quantity at any location (although its price varies along an exogenously specified, jurisdiction-specific supply schedule). Nechyba (1997a), on the other hand, models land and housing as already existing (rather than being built and torn down as demand changes). In that model, house and land quality differs within and across jurisdictions, and this quality distribution can be calibrated to give rise to house price patterns that reflect real-world patterns. This then generates jurisdictions that have different average land and house quality levels while at the same time allowing for overlaps in land and housing quality across districts. Equilibria with interjurisdictional differences in public service provision exist under much more general conditions in this model, and patterns of house prices and income levels within and across jurisdictions can more accurately reflect those observed in the real world (without resorting to the introduction of heterogeneous preferences).[3] The imperfect stratification that emerges is driven in large part by the inelastic housing market that is the foundation of the model, thus adding (to the previous explanation of household income differences) a new force that tends to produce inequities in public service provision: the existence of heterogeneous housing markets in different districts, with housing that is durable once built and thus difficult to alter.

Put differently, the only forces that cause households to segregate in the Westhoff and Epple et al. models are those connected with the local public sector: Households segregate because their different income levels cause them to desire different levels of public services and local taxes. While retaining this force, Nechyba's model adds a segregating force that has nothing at all to do with the public sector: heterogeneous housing and land markets that will cause the rich generally to locate in different areas than the poor. Therefore, were the public sector eliminated from the models, there would be no segregated equilibrium in the Westhoff and Epple et al. models, whereas segregation would still occur (albeit at different levels) in the Nechyba model. How this exogenously specified heterogeneous housing stock emerged in the first place is not something that can be explained in Nechyba's model. Given the durability of housing, however, whatever housing stock is present at the beginning of a policy simulation is likely to exist and be important for some time, regardless of whether it arose by some historical accident or through deliberate zoning rules.

4.2.4 School Production

Thus far, we have talked of the "local public service" as a mere abstract local good, and implicitly we have assumed that its quality level is solely related to total local public spending and the size of the local population. For many public services (roads, for instance) this may be a good assumption. In the area of primary and secondary education, however, the assumption is empirically invalid. Although disagreement persists regarding the degree of importance of financial resources in education production,[4] there is little disagreement that other inputs are at least as important and probably more so. These other inputs include teacher quality (which, because of union wage scales, is typically not correlated with teacher wages), peer abilities, parental monitoring, and targeted contributions by parents. There are good reasons to believe that their level of each of these inputs in any particular school would be correlated with parental income even if financial resources were fully equalized across all schools.[5] For purposes of this chapter, I refer to these effects together as "peer inputs," that is, inputs (other than financial resources in school budgets) that are correlated with peer household income.

Without the introduction of such nonpecuniary inputs into the local public service, interjurisdictional inequities in the provision of the public service can be eliminated in each of the general equilibrium models previously discussed simply by centralizing funding and distributing it on a per capita basis. Indeed, centralization of funding has been the main policy advocated by many who are concerned about equity within public education. This brief overview of general equilibrium modeling of local public finance forces, however, suggests that local funding itself is not the primary problem. Rather, local funding combined with the ability of households to move generates equilibria in which housing market conditions support segregation of households by income. This segregation results in differential funding of public services *and*, to the extent that inputs into services like public education are nonpecuniary but correlated with parental income, in differential nonpecuniary inputs into the pubic service. Moving from local to centralized funding may equalize financial inputs, but it does not eliminate the segregating forces present in housing markets, nor does it eliminate the incentive of high-income households to find ways to segregate in order to take advantage of nonpecuniary inputs into school production. General equilibrium theory therefore predicts that fundamental interjurisdictional inequities in public education will persist under full equalization of school funding so long as nonpecuniary inputs (peer inputs) are an important component of school production. Results from three decades of equalization suggest this prediction to be correct.[6]

4.2.5 Conditions for Perfect Interjurisdiction Equality in Public Education

I began this section by asking under what conditions we could envision a world in which, despite the reality of the existence of household income inequality and the tendency of households to move to improve their welfare, school quality could be equal across public schools that admit students through geographic districting. My reading of the local public finance literature suggests two such conditions: First, funding for public education must be centralized and equalized across schools; and second, financial inputs must be the only inputs that matter in producing school quality. The first of these conditions is a policy choice; the second is not. Given the empirical evidence in support of the proposition that, even if financial resources are important, other (nonpecuniary or peer) inputs into schools are substantially more important in the production of school quality, and given that these peer inputs are correlated with parental income, this second condition is empirically invalid. As a result, the geographic income segregation that arises in housing market equilibrium is certain to support continued large interjurisdictional inequities even as school funding is more equalized—thus pointing to a fundamental limit on how much equalization is likely to arise through the political process.

4.3 A Structural General Equilibrium Model

As suggested in its introduction, this chapter will attempt to use a single general equilibrium model to draw some conclusions on the general equilibrium impacts of different forms of state intervention in primary and secondary education. This model has been developed in a series of papers over the past several years, and many of the results pulled together in this chapter derive from this previous research. The strength of the structural model underlying the model presented here is that it allows us to replicate accurately a number of stylized features of public schools and local public finance in the real world. It therefore provides a benchmark model that includes the economic forces that have led to current inequities in public education, and it allows us to gauge the relative importance of competing general equilibrium effects as different policy simulations are conducted. The theoretical details of this model are fully spelled out in Nechyba 1997a and Nechyba 1999, and the details of data calibration for the model are given in Nechyba 2000, Nechyba 2003b, and Nechyba 2003c. I therefore provide in the following only a brief description of the main features of the computational version of the model used for the simulations in this chapter, noting that the model includes the very forces identified in the previous section as likely economic forces responsible for current inequities in public education.

The model begins with a continuum of households N in which each household is endowed with one house, a child with a given ability, an income level and preferences over private consumption, neighborhood and house quality, and school quality consumed by the household's child. Preferences of all households are assumed to be identical,[7] but incomes, house endowments and abilities differ across households (with income imperfectly correlated with child ability). Houses are divided exogenously into neighborhoods (within which all houses and neighborhood characteristics are of equal quality), and collections of neighborhoods form school districts.[8] Schools produce educational quality by combining per-pupil spending with peer inputs,[9] and all schools—public and private—face the same production technology. Per-pupil spending levels in public schools are determined through majority-rule voting over local property taxes in a locally financed system and through voting over state income taxes in a state-financed system. Spending in private schools, on the other hand, is set by each school so as to maximize profits (which are zero in competitive equilibrium). Eligibility for admission to the single public school in each district is determined solely based on whether a student lives within the district boundaries. Private schools, on the other hand, are allowed to set a minimum peer-quality level below which they will not accept any student. Thus, private schools have two competitive advantages over public schools: They can set a level of per-pupil spending (which is equal to tuition) that reflects the desire of parents more closely, and they can select among student applicants to determine the composition of their student body. At the same time, public schools have the advantage of being free to anyone living within the district boundaries.[10]

Table 4.1
Predictions versus data

	Representative school districts		
	Low income ($d = 1$)	Middle income ($d = 2$)	High income ($d = 3$)
Mean land value	$157,248	$192,867	$271,315
Predicted mean land value	$117,412	$205,629	$292,484
Median household income	$30,639	$45,248	$67,312
Predicted mean household income	$31,120	$46,216	$65,863
Per-pupil spending	$6,702	$7,841	$8,448
Predicted per-pupil spending	$6,652	$7,910	$8,621
Fraction choosing private school	0.21	0.23	0.20
Predicted fraction in private school	0.20	0.23	0.13
Fraction raised locally	0.52	0.77	0.87
Fraction raised locally in model	0.52	0.77	0.87

In calibrating this model to real-world data, the following stylized features are matched by the calibration algorithm: House and neighborhood quality parameters are set to replicate the distribution of house prices observed in the data; the income distribution is set to approximate the empirical distribution observed in the data; the utility weights placed on private consumption and school quality are set to replicate the actual levels of public school spending set through majority-rule voting; and the production function weights placed on per-pupil spending and peer-quality inputs are set to replicate the levels of private school attendance observed. Table 4.1 provides some stylized facts about the data and compares these to the predictions of the calibrated computer model.[11]

4.4 General Equilibrium under Local and State Financing

I begin my discussion of state aid to education by comparing two very opposite ways of financing public schools: (1) a fully decentralized, local property tax–financed system and (2) a fully centralized, equalized, and state income tax–financed system. I make this comparison in the context of the model described in section 4.3, with production and preference parameters calibrated to New Jersey data. In each of the systems I analyze, spending levels are determined through majority rule, with local residents voting on local spending (financed through proportional property taxes) under the first system and statewide majority-rule voting determining equalized spending levels under the second. Although few states are contemplating implementing either of these extreme alternatives, the analysis presented here can help establish a benchmark of just how much of an improvement in educational equity might be possible given the underlying economic differences faced by households residing in different geographic areas and facing different economic realities.

Table 4.2 begins by comparing the equilibrium outcomes under a fully decentralized system and those under a fully centralized system to the equilibrium observed under the hybrid New Jersey system. The second row of the table presents per-pupil spending figures that clearly follow the expected pattern: The highly unequal spending pattern under local property tax financing is ameliorated by state intervention under the New Jersey system and eliminated under a centralized state income tax system. If spending were all that mattered in schools, a centralized system (under the assumption that the political process would permit resources to be truly equalized) could thus eliminate all inequities in public education. As argued in previous sections of the chapter, however, the actual production process in public education differs substantially from one in which only per-pupil spending matters. The second row of table 4.2 therefore presents the level of peer inputs under the three systems of public school financing.[12] As expected, peer inputs are distributed unequally across the three districts, but no discernable amelioration of this unequal distribution arises from more centralized school spending. This then translates, in the third row of table 4.2, into continuing interjurisdictional differences in public school quality even as school spending is fully equalized under state funding.[13]

The next two rows in the table assess the average impact of different systems of public school financing on schools. Others, such as Silva and Sonstelie (1995), have pointed out that, in a stylized model in which school districts are composed of a single type of household, majority rule will result in less overall per-pupil spending under state financing than under local financing, so long as the income distribution is skewed such that the mean is above the median.[14] Given that the model uses the skewed income distribution in the data, a similar result is expected here and indeed appears, with spending under state equalization 7 percent lower than under both local funding and the New Jersey system. This lower overall investment in education under

Table 4.2
The limits of equalization

	Decentralized system plus NJ state formula			Decentralized local property tax			Centralized state income tax		
	District 1	District 2	District 3	District 1	District 2	District 3	District 1	District 2	District 3
Per-pupil spending	$6,652	$7,910	$8,621	$5,000	$7,326	$10,215	$7,195	$7,195	$7,195
Peer inputs	0.2684	0.4701	0.6521	0.2613	0.5142	0.6404	0.2826	0.5469	0.6470
School quality	0.4322	0.6178	0.7803	0.3674	0.6192	0.8183	0.4616	0.6316	0.6841
Average spending		$7,753			$7,731			$7,195	
Average quality		0.6152			0.6204			0.5960	
District income	$31,120	$46,216	$65,863	$29,725	$50,262	$63,212	$29,891	$51,309	$62,000
Property values	$117,412	$205,629	$292,484	$123,224	$211,729	$294,825	$118,486	$226,345	$316,308
% Private	20	22.5	12.5	30	20	10	22.5	17.5	15
Cost of same house*	—	—	—	$120,366	$199,721	$266,608	$129,957	$184,759	$207,950

Source: Tables 2, 3, 5a,b,c in Nechyba (2003a), table 3 in Nechyba 2003b and table 5 in Nechyba (2003c), as well as some calculations performed independently.
Notes: Property values reported in this table are converted here from annualized flows using a 5.5% discount rate.
*One house type (k_{dh} in the utility function) is available in all three districts.

centralization is almost fully responsible for the 4 percent lower school quality in the next row of table 4.2.

Finally, the remaining rows of the table provide some additional details of the three equilibria. Segregation persists at roughly similar levels under all three types of public school financing. Similarly, the level of private school attendance does not change dramatically, although the geographic pattern of private schools does change. The relationship between private school attendance and centralization of public school finance is treated thoroughly in Nechyba 2003c, in which the initially counterintuitive prediction of slightly lower private school attendance under equalized state financing is explained as the result of general equilibrium price effects. Although these effects are not readily apparent in the average district property values, they become more apparent when the opportunity cost of a house of equal quality but located in different districts is analyzed.

Note that the opportunity cost of a house under local property taxation includes both the price of the house as well as the tax payments owed on that house. The opportunity cost of the same house under centralized state income taxation, on the other hand, is simply the price of the house and does not include any tax payments, as these payments are now independent of the residential location choice of the household. The last row of table 4.2 gives the opportunity cost of a house of the same quality ($k_d = 0.93$) in all three districts under both local and state financing. Under local financing, the cost of the same house in district 1 is 45 percent of what it would be in district 3; under state financing, this percentage rises to 63 percent. Put differently, under state income tax financing of schools, the relative price of a house of the same quality in district 1 rises by over 70 percent. Parents who choose to send their children to private schools therefore have a substantially greater incentive to locate in district 1 under local property tax financing (even if housing options in that district are less than ideal) than they do under state tax financing. Thus, private school attendance is high in district 1 under local financing and declines under state financing not only because public schools are improving in district 1, but more importantly, because general equilibrium price effects make locating in district 1 much less attractive. Similarly, private school attendance in district 3 rises as a result of centralization not only because public schools are getting worse, but also because housing is getting relatively cheaper for those who previously located in poor districts and sent their children to private schools from there.[15]

Table 4.3
Centralization and residential segregation

Private schools allowed	Public school financing	Average district income			Average district property value		
		District 1	District 2	District 3	District 1	District 2	District 3
Yes	None	$25,700	$50,175	$67,325	$158,327	$227,189	$266,474
No	Local property tax	$17,628	$39,647	$85,925	$101,683	$204,075	$392,402
	State income tax	$19,875	$42,250	$81,075	$102,086	$220,725	$387,549
Yes	Local property tax	$29,725	$50,262	$63,212	$123,224	$211,729	$294,825
	State income tax	$29,891	$51,309	$67,325	$118,486	$226,345	$316,308

Source: Table 3 in Nechyba (2003b) and table 3 in Nechyba (2003a), with property values converted from annualized flows using a 5.5% discount rate.

However, not all of the households that previously sent their children to private schools that migrate to districts 2 and 3 under centralization continue to choose private schools, since public school quality in those districts is better than in district 1. This, then, accounts for the slight decline in overall private school attendance under centralization.

4.4.1 Segregation and Property Values under Local and State Financing

Table 4.3 investigates the link between school finance and residential segregation a bit further. The first row in the table assumes no public school sector and thus fully eliminates any distortion of residential location choices from public sector choices regarding taxes and school quality. Thus, this row provides a benchmark that gives the levels of income segregation that are expected simply from differences in housing quality across school districts. The remainder of the table then provides evidence on the degree to which the public and private school sectors contribute to changes in the level of segregation one would expect merely from housing markets.

Rows 2 and 3 eliminate the private sector and fully focus on distortions from public financing of schools. Spatial income segregation increases dramatically, and this effect is large regardless of whether public school funding is through local property taxes or is equalized through central state income taxes. As a crude measure of income segregation, one can compare the ratio of average incomes in district 3 to average incomes in district 1. This ratio increases by 86 percent and 56 percent under local and state public school funding (respectively) over what would be expected simply from interjurisdictional differences in housing quality. Rows 4 and 5 of the table then add the presence of a private school sector back into the model, and segregation levels decline dramatically as households that send their children to private schools take advantage of depressed housing values in poor school districts. In fact, comparing rows 4 and 5 to row 1 suggests that having a mix of private and public schools causes residential segregation (as measured by the ratio of district 3 to district 1 average income) to *decline* by almost 20 percent over what would be expected from interjurisdictional differences in housing quality, regardless of whether public sector is financed through state income taxes or local property taxes.

Thus, although public school financing introduces a residentially segregating force, it also causes house prices to be depressed in poor districts and inflated in rich districts as these prices capitalize local public school quality. Effects on house prices result in a desegregating force when private schools are added to the model, however, because households that send their children to private schools, which tend to have middle to high levels of income, take advantage of depressed housing prices in poor districts. This further results in an increase in house prices in poor districts and a decline in house prices in rich districts, implying corresponding increases and decreases in the tax bases of the respective districts (at least under local taxation). Thus, although households in poor districts with above-average incomes that send their children to private schools do not add to peer inputs into the public schools, their presence does add to local tax bases and to the fiscal capacity of poor districts to finance public schools.

4.5   State Grants-in-Aid

Section 4.4 presented a full general equilibrium comparison between two extremes: a fully centralized and a fully decentralized public school system. I now consider some hybrid systems that include a mix of income tax and local property tax funding. These hybrid systems assume local voting on property taxes under the assumption that voters know of the exogenously specified state aid formula composed of block and matching-grant components. A block grant program is simply a vector $\mathbf{b} = (b_1, b_2, b_3)$, where b_i is the per-pupil block grant from the state for each student in public schools in district i. Similarly, a matching grant program is defined by a vector $\mathbf{m} = (m_1, m_2, m_3)$, where m_i is the matching rate given to district i. This notation as well as the results reported in the following discussion are based on work first reported in Nechyba 2003c and Nechyba 1996a.

Table 4.4 begins by reporting equilibrium outcomes under block and matching grants that apply equally to all districts. Such universal grants are textbook responses of higher-level governments to aid in the internalization of local externalities, and their aim is typically to raise the overall level of spending on a particular local public good. This is in contrast to more-targeted grants that are analyzed in table 4.5, which are more likely a response to equity considerations that arise from "too little" spending on a public good in poor districts. Most real-world aid formulas, such as that for New Jersey, which was used to calibrate the model, clearly involve a combination of these two types of grants. The exercise in this section, however, is to isolate different effects of universal and targeted components of block and matching grants, which is why the tables report results from these more stylized versions of state aid.

4.5.1 Uniform Statewide Grants

It is well understood that block grants give rise only to income effects, whereas matching grants give rise also to substitution (or price) effects. Thus, one can demonstrate in a partial equilibrium setting that equally funded matching grants will typically result in higher levels of local spending than block grants (Oates 1972). In a general equilibrium setting, the income effects are smaller than in a partial equilibrium setting, because taxpayers have to pay for the state aid program through higher taxes.[16] Table 4.4 confirms this partial equilibrium intuition in a general equilibrium setting. The last column of the table provides the average cost of the state aid program per (public school and private school) family as an indication of state taxpayer burdens. The range of the state aid costs is similar for the block and matching programs on which the table focuses. At the same time, the average per-pupil spending on public schools changes little as the state introduces block grants, whereas average spending rises dramatically as matching grants become larger. Average school quality in the state follows a similar pattern.

Although universal matching grants are therefore substantially more effective at raising the overall level of spending on education, such universal grants have significantly worse equity properties than similarly funded block grants. The ratio of district 3 to district 1 spending on public education falls as block grants become large, whereas it rises for matching grants. Although spending increases in all districts under universal matching grants, it rises at a faster rate in the wealthier district, resulting in a progressively larger district 3 to district 1 spending ratio.[17] For block grants, on the other hand, districts essentially lower local per-student funding by roughly the amount of the per-pupil block grant, *unless the block grant is binding on local budgets.*[18] Such binding of local budgets may come about in two possible ways (and only one of these is modeled here): First, the size of the grant may simply be so large that spending will increase even if local governments lower their taxes for schools to zero; and second, grants may require a minimal local tax effort above zero. Unless states making block grants require local governments to continue contributing exactly as they did before the grant, low levels of block grants then have little impact on total statewide spending. In the simulations presented here, there is no

Table 4.4
Universal, income tax-financed state grants

	Percentage in private schools			Average per-pupil public state spending	District 3/ district 1 spending	Average public school quality*	District 3/ district 1 quality	State aid per family
	District 1	District 2	District 3					
a. Universal block grants								
$b_1 = b_2 = b_3$								
$0	30	20	10	$7,731	2.043	0.6204	2.229	$ 0
3,000	27.5	20	7.5	7,834	2.109	0.6508	2.394	2,450
5,000	27.5	20	7.5	7,409	2.002	0.6032	2.204	4,083
7,000	22.5	17.5	7.5	8,321	1.515	0.6571	1.887	5,892
b. Universal matching grants								
$m_1 = m_2 = m_3$								
0.0	30	20	10	$ 7,731	2.043	0.6204	2.229	$ 0
0.2	22.5	12.5	7.5	9,232	2.675	0.7214	3.037	1,320
0.4	12.5	10	5	9,944	2.613	0.7599	2.744	2,581
0.6	10	10	2.5	10,764	2.891	0.8175	3.097	3,734
0.8	0	5	0	12,107	3.348	0.9088	3.429	5,291

Source: Adapted from table 6 in Nechyba 2003c, with some additional calculations.
Note: *Average public school quality refers to a weighted measure of peer quality and spending (where the data suggest that these are weighted roughly equally by parents). It therefore represents parental perceptions of school quality. The actual values in these columns are properly viewed as an *index* of quality.

requirement that local governments contribute anything on their own, which implies that only as block grants become large ($7,000 in table 4.4) do they begin to bind on district 1's budget, thus forcing district 1 to spend more on education so long as negative local taxes are not permitted. This leads to a decline in the ratio of district 3 to district 1 spending as block grants become large.[19] Were the state grant systems in the simulations to require a minimum local tax contribution above zero, the grant size at which local budgets began to bind would, of course, be lower, and spending differences between rich and poor districts would begin to narrow with smaller universal grants.[20]

Although the results of these simulations suggest that statewide grants, particularly those relying on matching incentives, can be a powerful policy tool for eliciting higher overall spending on public education, these results must be consumed with some caution. The simulations in this section specify an *exogenous* institutional relationship between state and local spending (some combination of matching rates and block grants) and then proceed to investigate general equilibrium consequences of local voting behavior under that institutional arrangement. The model does not claim the institutional arrangement itself to be an endogenous result, which should lead us to question whether matching grants that result in the dramatic increases in overall spending found in the simulations could be politically feasible. The answer would seem to rest on whether there indeed are interdistrict spillovers that states can effectively internalize. If so, then the incentives embedded in matching grants could indeed represent a political solution to a prisoner's dilemma in which each jurisdiction commits to an efficiently higher level of spending. If, however, voters are unaware of such spillovers (or if such spillovers simply do not exist), it would be difficult to find a political-economy explanation of how any state grant system could survive politically and lead to large increases in overall spending.

4.5.2 Targeted State Grants

Whereas statewide grants of the type discussed in section 4.5.1 are motivated by a general desire to increase overall spending on education, targeted grants typically are motivated more by equity concerns. Table 4.5 reports on the equilibrium impact of block and matching grants targeted solely at district 1 (the poorest district in the model), and as in the case of universal grants, it is assumed that no local tax effort is required as a condition for receiving the state grant.

Table 4.5
Targeted, income tax–financed state grants

	Percentage in private schools			Average per-pupil state spending	District 3/district 1 spending	Average public school quality	District 3/district 1 quality	District 3/district 1 wealth
	District 1	District 2	District 3					
a. Targeted block grants								
$b_1 (b_2 = b_3 = 0)$								
$ 0	30	20	10	$7,731	2.043	0.6204	2.229	2.394
3,000	35	20	10	7,610	1.942	0.6126	2.360	1.909
5,000	40	17.5	10	7,891	2.036	0.6329	2.491	1.609
7,000	22.5	15	7.5	9,026	1.602	0.7048	2.101	1.531
b. Targeted matching grants								
$m_1 (m_2 = m_3 = 0)$								
0.0	30	20	10	$7,731	2.043	0.6204	2.229	2.394
0.2	32.5	20	10	7,723	2.047	0.6164	2.296	2.273
0.4	30	20	10	7,862	1.882	0.6275	2.207	2.064
0.6	25	15	10	8,121	1.720	0.6419	2.122	1.982
0.8	15.5	15	7.5	8,190	1.491	0.6336	1.780	1.871

Source: Adapted from table 7 in Nechyba 2003c, with some additional calculations.
Note: Average public school quality refers to a weighted measure of peer quality and spending (where the data suggest that these are weighted roughly equally by parents). It therefore represents parental perceptions of school quality. The actual values in these columns are properly viewed as an *index* of quality.

Although targeted block grants of the kind modeled here clearly do have welfare benefits for district 1 residents (in the sense that a portion of their funding for public schools now comes from other districts), they do not lead to appreciable increases in school spending in the district until the amount of the block grant becomes binding on local budgets. For low levels of the targeted grant, district 1 simply responds by lowering local property tax rates, and only once those rates have reached zero does education spending in the district increase dramatically. As a result, just as in the case of universal block grants, the ratio of district 3 to district 1 spending (and quality) does not fall dramatically unless block grants are large.[21] Targeted matching grants, on the other hand, are much more effective at lowering the difference in spending between rich and poor districts continuously as they are phased in from low matching rates to high ones.

4.5.3 District Power Equalizing

Thus far, we have assumed that block or matching programs are exogenously fixed. State aid may, however, be linked to key local fiscal variables that are thought to represent the local level of fiscal capacity or fiscal need. For instance, the notion of "district power equalization" favors linking matching grants inversely to local property values. This introduces an additional general equilibrium component to the policy discussion, because it opens the possibility that the very existence of a state aid program may alter property values in such a way as to undo the intended effects of the program (Inman and Rubinfeld 1979). More precisely, if districts with low average property values receive disproportionately larger matching rates, this in itself is likely to raise equilibrium property values, which in turn will reduce the matching rates of the state grant program.

Simulations with models of the type used in this chapter, however, suggest that there is a limit to the size of this general equilibrium effect, although it can still be large for certain types of district power–equalizing formulas. Essentially, the model used in this chapter differs from others in that large differences in house prices are built into the model, even in the absence of any public sector activity (as seen in the first row of table 4.3). These differences arise from interdistrict differences in existing housing stocks, which limit the extent to which district power–equalizing aid (based on local property wealth) can undermine its own formula through general equilibrium price effects. At the same time, the degree to which different forms of equalizing aid can affect demand for housing among households that send their children to private schools turns out to be important in regard to how much general equilibrium price effects may undo the equalizing impact of aid when aid is based on local property wealth.

Consider the last column of table 4.5, in which general equilibrium effects of grants targeted to district 1 are reported. This column gives the ratio of property wealth in district 3 to that in district 1. As expected, for both block aid and matching aid that is targeted to district 1, the difference in property values in the two districts narrows as aid levels increase. Despite the fact that per-pupil spending levels in district 1 rise much faster under matching aid (because of the substitution effects discussed above), and despite the fact that spending differences between the districts narrow considerably faster under matching aid than under block grants as a consequence, property values converge more rapidly under block aid. The reason for this is the role played by the private sector in the local economy.

Under targeted block aid, as the size of the block grant increases, an increasing fraction of local spending on public education is financed through state income taxes, which are paid regardless of where a household settles, and property taxes in district 1 therefore decline (to reflect the decreasing local contribution to the education bill). Thus, in terms of the incentives of households that send their children to private schools, district 1 becomes increasingly attractive as targeted, state-financed block aid replaces local property taxes. In addition to the upward pressure on property values in district 1 from the subsidy from taxpayers in other districts to households in district 1 that send their children to private schools, there is increasing demand for property in district 1 on the part of households that send their children to private schools as targeted block aid increases in district 1. Both of these effects are smaller under matching aid, in which local property taxes are a perquisite for receiving any state aid.

The general equilibrium forces that may undermine an equalizing state aid formula based on local property wealth are therefore substantially greater if the equalizing formula relies on block rather than matching aid. In fact, for similarly costly targeted state aid programs in table 4.5, differences between property values in the rich and poor districts narrow twice as quickly for block aid as for matching aid. Given that the aim of equalizing state aid is to narrow spending differences in education and not property value differences, it is therefore quite straightforward that equalizing state aid ought to rely solely on matching components and not on block aid unless state governments can find effective ways to link block aid to minimum levels of local tax contributions to education.

4.6 State Aid for Choice

Whereas most state aid has typically taken the form of grants to local governments, recent policy debates have increasingly included talk of using a portion of state aid to increase parental choice, particularly for those parents whose choices under the current system are limited. In this section, I therefore focus on a final set of policies that extend private school choice through the use of state income tax–funded vouchers. As in the case of grants to districts, these state-funded aid programs can be universal in nature or can be targeted to either low-income parents or parents whose children attend low-performing public schools. The argument in favor of a universally available voucher typically rests on the hypothesis that inefficiencies in public schools can be remedied through increased competition (Friedman 1962), whereas the argument for targeted vouchers arises from the same equity concerns that have fueled many of the court challenges to inequities in public education.[22]

The general equilibrium effects of this very different type of state aid to education have been investigated in Nechyba 1999, Nechyba 2000, and Nechyba 2003a and are linked closely to the previous discussion of the role of private schools in the absence of vouchers (see table 4.3). Within the context of a residence-based public school system that exhibits large differences in school quality across districts, housing prices are depressed in low-performing public school districts and inflated in high-performing districts. For parents who choose to have their children attend private schools (and who therefore can choose housing independent of schooling), this produces strong incentives to locate in underperforming public school districts. Thus, if state aid is used in part to fund private school vouchers, new private schools are likely to emerge in low-performing public school districts where housing for middle-income households is available. The resulting migration will tend to raise average incomes and tax bases in poor districts while lowering them in wealthy districts. Although this does not guarantee that public schools in poor districts themselves will improve in quality, it does provide fiscal benefits to homeowners in poor districts while providing additional options to parents. Furthermore, to the extent that the public school system declines in quality because of "cream skimming" by private schools, these mobility effects will tend to be spread across schools in all districts, not just in those in which new private schools are established. In fact, the simulations reported in the following discussion suggest that, for modest levels of vouchers, the adverse impact of vouchers on public schools tends to be greatest in wealthier districts.

Tables 4.6 and 4.7 provide general equilibrium results for three types of state-financed vouchers that differ in terms of who is eligible to use them. Panel (a) of each table represents outcomes from vouchers for which every resident of the state is eligible; panel (b) represents outcomes from vouchers restricted to residents of district 1, the low-performing district; and panel (c) represents the outcome of vouchers restricted to households earning less that $25,000 per year. Table 4.6 presents results assuming that all funding for public schools comes from local property taxes, whereas Table 4.7 assumes the New Jersey financing system for public schools.

The two tables provide fairly similar qualitative messages. For modest levels of vouchers (i.e., vouchers under $4,000), most of the increase in private school attendance occurs in the poorest district. Average per-pupil funding of public schools does not change dramatically, and the difference between the highest-spending and lowest-spending public school narrows for modest levels of vouchers except when they are targeted to low-income households (panel (c) of the tables). Average public school quality falls, but so do differences in school quality between rich and poor districts (again, for voucher amounts less than $4,000). The net cost of all vouchers in general equilibrium is negative because of the savings in public school spending from lower public school populations.

As first pointed out in Nechyba 1999 and Nechyba 2000, many of the effects observed in these tables is due to residential mobility. In response to depressed housing values in district 1, parents who move their children to private schools as a result of vouchers tend to migrate to the better neighborhoods in district 1, thus raising property values and average community income in that district. Households that have the most to gain from private schooling are those with high peer quality,[23] which implies that public schools suffer lower levels of peer input. Since much of the increase in private school attendance from vouchers results from households who move from living and attending public schools in districts 2 and 3 to attending private schools (re-

Table 4.6
State income tax–funded vouchers (under decentralized public school funding)

Voucher amount	Percentage in private schools			Average public school spending per pupil	District 3/ district 1 spending	Average public school quality	District 3/ district 1 quality	Net cost of voucher
	District 1	District 2	District 3					
a. Universal voucher eligibility								
$ 0	30	20	10	$7,731	2.043	0.6204	2.229	$ 0
1,000	40	27.5	10	7,774	1.954	0.6044	2.245	−161
2,500	62.5	40	12.5	8,012	1.911	0.5739	2.151	−286
4,000	87.5	82.5	30	8,072	1.878	0.4813	2.419	−828
5,000	100	100	37.5	9,696	***	0.5321	***	−206
b. Eligibility restricted to district 1 residents								
$ 0	30	20	10	$7,731	2.043	0.6204	2.229	$ 0
1,000	37.5	25	10	7,476	1.908	0.5453	2.110	−390
2,500	70	40	10	7,115	1.667	0.5271	2.003	−1,332
4,000	100	40	17.5	6,606	***	0.4607	***	−1,714
5,000	100	40	19.8	6,589	***	0.4653	***	−1,439
c. Eligibility restricted to low-income households								
$ 0	30	20	10	$7,731	2.043	0.6204	2.229	$ 0
1,000	30	20	10	7,731	2.043	0.6204	2.229	0
2,500	45	20	10	7,905	2.029	0.6194	2.460	−131
4,000	82.5	25	7.5	8,320	1.960	0.6456	3.330	−320
5,000	100	25	10	8,509	***	0.6761	***	−255

Source: Adapted from table 5a in Nechyba 2003c, with some additional calculations.
Note: Average public school quality refers to a weighted measure of peer quality and spending (where the data suggest that these are weighted roughly equally by parents). It therefore represents parental perceptions of school quality. The actual values in these columns are properly viewed as an *index* of quality.

Table 4.7
State income tax–funded vouchers (under New Jersey formula)

Voucher amount	Percentage in private schools			Average public state spending per pupil	District 3 / district 1 spending	Average public school quality	District 3 / district 1 quality	Net cost of voucher
	District 1	District 2	District 3					
a. Universal voucher eligibility								
$ 0	20	22.5	12.5	$7,753	1.296	0.6153	1.805	$ 0
1,000	32.5	22.5	15	7,725	1.207	0.6035	1.767	−175
2,500	40	27.5	22.5	7,502	1.150	0.5645	1.716	−330
4,000	67.5	40	30	6,914	1.556	0.4773	2.339	−753
5,000	100	82.5	32.5	7,385	***	0.4220	***	−656
b. Eligibility restricted to district 1 residents								
$ 0	20	22.5	12.5	$7,753	1.296	0.6153	1.805	$ 0
1,000	35	22.5	12.5	7,869	1.226	0.5971	1.698	−182
2,500	47.5	30	15	7,695	1.197	0.5534	1.616	−614
4,000	82.5	42.5	15	7,408	1.623	0.5019	2.460	−1,280
5,000	100	47.5	17.5	7,430	***	0.5093	***	−1,321
c. Eligibility restricted to low-income households								
$ 0	20	22.5	12.5	$7,753	1.296	0.6153	1.805	$ 0
1,000	20	22.5	12.5	7,753	1.296	0.6153	1.805	0
2,500	20	22.5	12.5	7,753	1.296	0.6153	1.805	0
4,000	40	22.5	12.5	7,899	1.264	0.6089	2.046	−140
5,000	67.5	20	10	7,698	1.710	0.6121	2.783	−427

Source: Adapted from table 5c in Nechyba 2003c, with some additional calculations.
Note: Average public school quality refers to a weighted measure of peer quality and spending (where the data suggest that these are weighted roughly equally by parents). It therefore represents parental perceptions of school quality. The actual values in these columns are properly viewed as an *index* of quality.

gardless of location) and living in district 1, however, high levels of peer input are drawn disproportionately from districts 2 and 3, thus causing disproportionately larger declines in school quality in those districts. Furthermore, since private school attendees tend to come from households that have higher incomes and thus demand higher levels of public school spending when their children are in the public system, districts 2 and 3 also suffer declines in per-pupil spending as the median voter in those districts shifts (as a result of the movement to district 1 of households that send their children to private schools). These migration-induced outcomes from vouchers are similar for universally available vouchers (panel (a) of the tables) and vouchers restricted to residents of district 1 (panel (b) of the tables), because—even when eligibility for vouchers is not restricted to residents of district 1—most of the parents who want to move their children to private schools move to the cheaper houses available in that district. Only when vouchers are targeted to low-income households does general equilibrium migration cease to be an important economic force.

When voucher levels become high (i.e. $4,000 and above), public schools in district 1 begin to suffer dramatic declines in quality as both spending and—more importantly—levels of peer input become very low and few children remain in the public schools. At that point, the simulations suggest a dramatic widening in the gap between public school quality in district 1 and 3, which had been shrinking as lower levels of vouchers were introduced. These results suggest an important tipping point in terms of voucher size, a tipping point after which public schools in poor districts may suffer unacceptably large declines in quality under a voucher program.

Much of this analysis of vouchers is, however, subject to some major caveats. In particular, as suggested elsewhere (Nechyba 2003c), the results of these simulations can be viewed as worst-case scenarios because of the implicit assumptions built into the model. First, public schools are assumed to be using resources efficiently throughout these simulations; thus any positive competitive response to increased competition from the private sector is assumed away. Second, the model assumes no gains from the less heterogeneous student population that tends to take shape in especially poor public schools as voucher levels increase; thus any potential gains from greater curriculum targeting to particular peer groups are also assumed away. And third, the model assumes a perfectly inelastic supply of housing, which requires that each immigrant to a district replaces a current resident in that district. As a result, the immigrant households into district 1 that send their children to private schools replace relatively high-peer-input households in that district that previously attended the local public schools, thus lowering peer inputs in local public schools. In many real-world cities, immigrant households that send their children to private schools may, however, end up occupying previously vacant land and therefore cause less of this type of pressure on local public schools. Each of these assumptions tends to bias the results of the simulations in favor of declines in overall public school quality, increases in inequality within the public school system, or both. Nechyba (2003a) demonstrates that, under empirically plausible extensions of the model, modest levels of private school vouchers may in fact cause increases in public school quality at the same time as the overall variance in public school quality declines. Nechyba (2003a, 2003b), however, demonstrates that the general equilibrium and migration effects identified in this chapter remain largely unchanged when assumption about school competitiveness or curriculum targeting are added to the model. The only difference that emerges as school competitiveness and curriculum targeting assumptions are added to the model is that overall public school quality falls less (or rises) under vouchers.

4.7 Conclusion

Viewing state aid to primary and secondary education through the lens of a general equilibrium model that is capable of replicating the status quo gives no clear answers as to how exactly state education aid ought to be structured. Although state financing of public education can indeed cause spending differences from district to district within the state to disappear, this is not likely to produce anything close to an elimination of school quality differences in a system in which public school admissions are based on residential districting. State aid in the form of grants can most effectively generate increases in spending on public education if the aid is based on a matching rather than a block aid formula or if a block aid formula includes relatively high levels of required minimum local tax efforts, and equalizing aid based on local property wealth (or fiscal capacity) is less likely to be undermined by general equilibrium adjustments in local wealth if it is based on matching aid. Alternatively, state aid to parents to enable them to choose private alternatives to public schools more easily provides the advantage of allowing for a severing of the link between residential housing and school choices, but cream skimming by private schools may produce overall declines in public school quality. These declines, to the extent that they occur, are likely to be spread across all public schools in a general equilibrium world and are unlikely to be primarily focused on public schools in poor districts, in which private school vouchers are likely to have the greatest uptake. Other forms of state intervention to increase parental choice (through charter and magnet schools, for instance) may have similar general equilibrium effects.

Although the ideal state aid package is likely to contain elements of all these programs, all are limited by the general equilibrium forces that this chapter has explored, and discussion of all is informed by a better understanding of the role of general equilibrium forces in generating current public school inequities. Ultimately, as Inman and Rubinfeld (1979) suggested some time ago, inequities in public services have much to do with the link between residential location and service consumption, with the fact that households have vastly different resources at their disposal, with the rigidities in housing quality differences between political districts (whether this happened through benign historical forces or activist local zoning), and with the reality that households are willing to move to improve their welfare. When the public service we are concerned with is public education, there is the additional factor that quality schools are produced not primarily through financial inputs, but more importantly through other peer inputs that correlate with income. Although centralization of financing of public education can play a role in equalizing public school quality, the residential segregation of households seems unlikely to be eliminated by changes in public financing of schools. Furthermore, public education is different from other public services in that an active private school market plays an important role in the general equilibrium economy, and the private school market's response to state aid in some cases strengthens and in other cases weakens the intent of state policymakers. The general equilibrium nature of the issues involved in school finance debates and the link between the issues and local public finance issues further imply that other types of policies, such as housing vouchers for poor families, may have equally large impacts on education quality and may need to enter more explicitly into the education finance debate. Ultimately, state policymakers concerned with inequities in public school access and quality must look beyond mere spending difference to local incentives, housing markets, school district boundary setting, and new ways of admitting students to certain schools (like charter and magnet schools, and private schools supported through vouchers).

One concluding note of caution is perhaps in order. The results reported in the tables of this chapter are derived from simulations based on a model informed by real-world data—but the numbers themselves are not data from the real world. Rather, they are the best predictions I can offer using a single model capable of incorporating many of the important economic forces that real policies are likely to encounter. In the words of one of the commentators on the paper on which this chapter is based, simulation models can become "seductive" devices and create a false confidence that we know more after examining the simulation results than we actually know. Real policies will be introduced into worlds more complicated than the already complicated stylized world of the model used in this chapter, and impacts of real policies will likely be different in different contexts depending on the particulars of the affected area. The numbers generated in this chapter should therefore not be interpreted too literally. They can help guide our thinking; they can reveal effects and trends we may not have thought of in our partial equilibrium models; and they can even provide useful comparisons of policies and develop our intuitions with regard to likely magnitudes of policy effects. In all these ways, they can help guide the kinds of questions policymakers and empirical researchers should ask, but they cannot ultimately substitute for serious empirical analysis of policies as they unfold in more complicated settings.

Notes

This chapter was prepared as a paper for the education conference at Syracuse University, April 5–6, 2002. Funding for this research from the National Science Foundation (SBR-9905706) is gratefully acknowledged, as are comments from Robert Inman and Johnny Yinger, as well as participants at the conference.

1. For an early general equilibrium approach to this issue within an urban setting, see Inman and Rubinfeld 1979, which concludes that household income inequality and free residential mobility in the presence of zoning can fundamentally explain persistent inequality in the provision of public services.

2. Epple and Platt (1998) extend this model to include different preference types as well as different incomes. This extended model then produces two-dimensional stratification.

3. As in the previous studies, local tax rates are set in Nechyba's model by majority rule. The model allows either property or income taxes to serve as the local tax instrument,

although property taxes are shown to be a dominant local tax strategy when local governments consider general equilibrium consequences of switching even partially to local income taxes (Nechyba 1997b).

4. A long series of studies continues to investigate this, with an example of different positions taken by various authors in Burtless 1996.

5. Loeb and Page (2000) demonstrate empirically that, given that public school teacher wages are typically based on rigid wage scales, good teachers tend to be rewarded not by additional income but rather by being assigned to higher-income public schools. Ability is likely to be at least somewhat correlated with parental income (Solon 1992; Zimmerman 1992), and high-income parents are more likely to monitor the schools their children attend (McMillan 1999) and to give their own resources to those schools (Brunner and Sonstelie, forthcoming). A related way of putting it is that poor districts tend to have greater fiscal need (in addition to less fiscal capacity) (Ladd 1976).

6. We should note that Westhoff's model (which lacks a housing market) is the only of the three models discussed to predict full equalization of public service quality in the presence of centralized funding and nonpecuniary inputs. This is because high-income households have no way to keep low-income households out of their jurisdictions when there is no housing market to capitalize local conditions.

7. The functional form of the utility function is $u(d, h, c, s) = k_{dh} c^\alpha s^\beta$, where d indicates school district, h indicates house type or neighborhood, c indicates private consumption, and s indicates school quality. The parameter k_{dh} represents housing and land quality as well as neighborhood quality unrelated to schools. The parameters α and β are calibrated to replicate per-pupil spending levels in the data as those emerging from majority-rule voting. Any choice of utility function such as this necessarily introduces implicit assumptions about behavioral elasticities, with Cobb-Douglas forms such as this being no exception. As elasticities change, so will the magnitudes of the simulation results such as those reported in the tables in this chapter. In making benchmark functional-form assumptions, Cobb-Douglas functional forms represent typical starting points—and therefore they feature prominently on both the preference and the technology side of this model.

8. The computable version of the model has three districts and five neighborhoods in each district, with the house quality (k_{dh}) distribution across neighborhoods in each district calibrated to yield housing price distributions that replicate those observed in the data.

9. The school production function is $s = f(x, q) = x^\rho q^{(1-c)}$, where x is per-pupil spending and q is average peer inputs in the school. A minimum of $5,000 per-pupil expenditure is assumed to be necessary in order for a school to open. Peer input is a combination of child ability and parental income, with child ability weakly correlated with parental income. The parameter ρ is calibrated to replicate the private school attendance rates observed in the data.

10. In practice, the main advantage that is important for private schools is the ability to set peer inputs. Note that the specification of the private school sector implicitly assumes a perfectly elastic supply of private schools; that is, if a private school of particular characteristics is demanded and can make positive (or zero) profits, it will be supplied. The private school market modeled here therefore represents a long-run market, with short-run effects likely to include fewer private school market changes than predicted by the model.

11. One notable aspect missing from the model is an explicit labor market. This is not a large shortcoming within the static context of the current model, but it becomes important in models that attempt to link school finance explicitly to economic growth and future-generation income inequality (see, for example, Fernandez and Rogerson 1998).

12. Peer inputs at the school level are average peer quality levels of households attending the school. The household peer quality is distributed between 0 and 1 and is properly interpreted as an index of child ability and household contributions to the school.

13. It should be noted that the proper interpretation of "school quality" in this model is "parental perceptions of school quality." Parents may care about spending in schools for a variety of reasons having little to do with academic achievement, and thus spending can be an important factor entering into parental choices on education even if it has little correlation with SAT scores, graduation rates, and so on.

14. The logic behind this prediction is straightforward: If each district is composed of a single type of household, then that type's most preferred spending level will result in each district under decentralized majority rule. Thus, the average spending in the state is simply the average of the most preferred spending levels in the population, which is predicted by mean income. Under centralization, on the other hand, the median-income voter (assuming no private schools) determines the spending level. Thus, if the median is less than the mean, state financing results in less spending than local financing.

15. Nechyba (2003c) reports that roughly two-thirds of the change in the private school attendance pattern is in fact due to the general equilibrium price effects and not the change in public school quality.

16. In fact, for high-income districts, the income effects are negative, as these districts pay for a disproportionate share of the statewide block grant program.

17. As pointed out by one of the discussants of this chapter (when it was presented as a paper at the Syracuse University conference), this result hinges on the implicit elasticity assumptions embedded in a Cobb-Douglas preference framework.

18. This statement is not quite accurate, because the model does include a small flypaper effect resulting from a change in median voters as funding shifts from local property to state income taxes. In particular, the ratio of income to property holding in the data turns out to be skewed in such a way that local voters will indeed choose more local spending if part of the spending is covered by state income tax–funded block grants, even if no net resources have been added to the community. Furthermore, it should be pointed out that empirical studies have claimed to find larger flypaper effects than what this model predicts, and to the extent that these effects are real, this model underpredicts the effectiveness of block grants at raising per-pupil spending.

19. An interesting general equilibrium side effect of block grants is that relative property values in district 1 *decline* because of less demand from families that send their children to private schools. This is because as schools are increasingly funded through state income taxes that support the block grants, households that send their children to private schools that settle in districts that spend little on public education enjoy less of an advantage from doing so than under local funding of schools (since state income tax burdens are independent of residential location.) At the same time, the effects are different from a fully state funded (and equalized) system of the type discussed above. Despite the fact that block grants increasingly lead to a largely state-financed system, they also leave room for *local discretion* that is exercised by high-income districts in the form of supplemental (property tax–financed) spending. Although a move toward state financing through

block grants therefore leads to the same decrease in private school attendance in poor districts as a move toward an equalized state system would, it does not lead to a corresponding increase in private school attendance in the rich districts because of this added local discretion. (For more details on the relationship between different forms of centralization and private school attendance, see Nechyba 2003c).

20. A caveat to this observation is that, even with explicit requirements for local governments to maintain some local contribution to education, such governments may find other ways of shifting budget categories to make it appear that they are maintaining the level of local tax effort in order to obtain grants. For instance, spending on public parks may be shifted to local education budgets. The greater the required local tax effort and the greater the size of the grant, the more incentive the local governments have to be creative in this way. To the extent that this shifting of budget categories happens, the assumption of no required local tax effort is better for analytic purposes even if actual state grants have local tax effort requirements.

21. Ironically, overall state spending on public education actually rises faster under targeted rather than statewide grants, because there is less of a negative income effect on rich districts under targeted grants, given that the total income tax required is lower under targeting.

22. In fact, some have suggested that courts specifically mandate an immediate remedy of vouchers to plaintiffs from badly performing and badly funded public schools (Nechyba and Heise 2000).

23. A distribution of household peer quality between 0 and 1 is assumed in the model, where this peer quality is partially correlated with household income. This can be interpreted as reflecting both child ability and household contributions to the school environment.

II

Analysis of State Aid Reforms in Individual States

5 The Impacts of School Finance Reform in Kansas: Equity Is in the Eye of the Beholder

William Duncombe and
Jocelyn M. Johnston

In 1992, in response to a lawsuit alleging unequal educational opportunity in the state, the Kansas legislature reformed the state's education finance system. The reform placed most taxing and spending decisions in the hands of state government and greatly restricted local control over school budgets. This chapter describes the major features of that reform and revisits our earlier analysis of its impact on the state's school districts (Johnston and Duncombe 1998). More specifically, we analyze the equity impacts of the reform, focusing on the role of the weighting system designed to compensate for education cost differences, and on the effects of supplemental local-option budgets. We also identify characteristics associated with districts that have emerged as "winners" and "losers" subsequent to the reform.

The conclusions that can be drawn about relative equity improvements since the reform depend crucially on how cost differences are measured and whether the local-option budget is included in the evaluation. If the pupil weights adopted by Kansas lawmakers are used to adjust spending numbers and the base budget is used, then the reform has been completely successful, that is, all districts spend the same amount per weighted pupil. In addition, the correlation between spending per weighted pupil and property wealth (or fiscal health) has been substantially reduced. If all the local levies allowed under the reform are included in the evaluation, however, then the relative equity improvements are generally small, even using the state's pupil weights. These pupil weights reflect very large adjustments for low enrollments and almost no adjustment for at-risk students. Based on a cost function estimated for this study, we develop cost-adjusted spending estimates. Disparities in cost-adjusted spending have not generally been reduced since the reform. Although the data available on education outcomes are limited, we conduct a preliminary analysis of the impact of the reform on dropout rates and state assessment tests. Our results suggest no reduction in performance disparities in the postreform years.

5.1   School Aid Reform in Kansas

The 1992 Kansas reform is best viewed in the context of features specific to the state. Kansas is a large state geographically (the fifteenth largest in the nation) but is sparsely populated. In the western half of the state, population densities average fewer than fifteen persons per square mile, and populations there are declining. Western Kansas is dominated by agricultural economies, supplemented by natural gas deposits in the southwestern portion of the state. The two major urban areas (Wichita and the Kansas City metropolitan area) account for major portions (nearly 32 percent) of the school-aged population, and both are located in the eastern half of the state. The east-west and urban-rural political divisions had an impact on the 1992 reform. Western districts, still bitter about consolidations of districts in the 1960s and loath to consider additional consolidation, are represented by lawmakers who have threatened more than once to secede from the state.[1]

Despite the state's political and fiscal conservatism, the Kansas populist tradition supports moderate redistribution through public programs, including education. For most of the period since 1992, Kansas has been led by moderate Republican governor Bill Graves, who has had to devote much of his political capital to fending off the conservative wing of his own party. Substantial tax cuts enacted in the latter half of the 1990s reduced both local property taxes for public schools and state income and other taxes that provide funding for the reform.

The 1992 reform was the first major overhaul of the education financing system in Kansas in twenty years. In 1973, Kansas had adopted a power-equalizing school aid design, the School District Equalization Act (SDEA), which distributed aid through a matching formula that varied inversely with school district property wealth and income (Thompson, Honeyman, and Wood 1993).[2] The equalization promised by the reform never materialized for several reasons: (1) In addition to state aid distributed through the formula, the state also awarded each district a "rebate" of 24 percent of all state income tax revenues collected from that district, which by 1992 accounted for half of the state funds distributed to school districts (McCarthy Snyder

1995); (2) the formula by design reduced the local effort requirement for smaller school districts, which effectively allowed small districts with substantial property wealth to receive state aid;[3] and (3) the state instituted a cap on district spending growth that was higher for the smallest school districts (Kansas Association of School Boards 1994).

By 1991, local school district levies ranged from 9 to 98 mills, and per-pupil spending varied across districts from $2,725 to $10,428.[4] There were substantial disparities in per-pupil assessed property value: The lowest value in the state was $8,063 and the highest was $563,680 (in a district in which a nuclear power plant was located).[5] Clearly, the system was failing to achieve a reasonable level of relative equity among school districts. The old formula was "predicated on the initially tenuous and ultimately unfounded belief that equalizing the power to spend would inspire voters in poorer districts to adopt tax rates sufficient to equalize spending. Like similar plans in other states, the system was chronically underfunded, which magnified the effects of all these disequalizing features" (Baker and Imber 1999, 121).

In 1991, a number of school districts filed suit against the state, alleging that because the existing school funding system failed to provide equal educational opportunity for all Kansas students, the state's constitution had been violated (McCarthy Snyder 1995). Shawnee County District Judge Terry Bullock consolidated most of the lawsuits in the fall of 1991 and concurred that the finance system violated the state constitution (*Mock v. Kansas* [1991]). Instead of moving these cases to trial, Judge Bullock gave the state legislature one year to comply with ten "rules of law" that defined the constitutional requirements of the system. The key elements of this list include the following:

1. The state, not the local school districts, has the ultimate authority and responsibility to provide education.

2. All resources necessary to provide public education, including school facilities, should be provided equally to each child.

3. Some adjustment should be made in the finance system for the higher costs associated with educating some children.

Thus, the judge explicitly emphasized improving the relative equity among school districts in Kansas, and he defined relative equity in terms of resources. The judge implied that cost-adjusted resource equality was the standard by which he would judge the constitutionality of any reformed education financing system in the state.

5.1.1 The Original 1992 Reform

After intense debate, the Kansas legislature responded to the judge's ruling in the spring of 1992 by passing a major reform of the state's school finance system, which was to be implemented in 1992–93.[6] The School District Finance and Quality Performance Act dramatically changed the funding landscape for Kansas public schools. The reform incorporated new revenue and expenditure designs, as well as performance standards for state schools. The following is a summary of the major financial components in the original legislation.

5.1.2 General State Aid and Constraints on Local Control

One of the dominant elements of the reform was a mandated statewide *maximum* (and minimum) per-pupil base spending amount of $3,600 per pupil. With a few exceptions discussed below, the legislative response to the judge's ruling was to impose a strict relative equity standard that approached full equality of cost-adjusted resources. The "general state aid" formula for Kansas can be represented simply as

$$A_i = E^* \times WFTE - t^* \times AV,$$

where A_i is total aid to the district, E^* is the state-set base state aid per pupil (BSAPP), $WFTE$ is a measure of weighted pupils, t^* is the state-set millage rate, and AV is assessed property value. State aid is simply equal to the base general fund budget for a district minus what the district can raise with the state-set property tax rate. Initially, the state-set budget (E^*) was set at $3,600 per weighted pupil. For each district, the state general fund was responsible for filling the gap between the revenue raised through the state-set mill levy (t^* was initially set at 32 mills), and the budget required to fund the district's weighted full-time enrollment (FTE). In a handful of districts, the 32 mill levy generated excess revenues, which were subject to recapture by the state.[7] Local control over spending decisions was therefore strictly curtailed, with several exceptions (discussed in section 5.1.5).

These limits were sweetened to some extent by property tax reductions and enhanced state aid. For all but a handful of districts the 32 mill levy represented a significant reduction. In the first year of the reform, total public school spending in the state increased by roughly 10 percent, and local property tax relief totaled $262 million, or nearly half of the prereform level (Kansas Association of School Boards 1994; Tallman 1993). The legislative approach to funding new state school spending, sometimes referred to as "a-third, a-third, and a-third," was built on an assumption that state income taxes, state sales taxes, and local property taxes would each contribute roughly one-third of anticipated general fund revenue requirements.[8]

5.1.3 Weighted Pupils and Cost Adjustment

The prereform aid formula did allow some adjustments for low-enrollment districts in which education costs were higher because of diseconomies of scale, but the adjustments were complicated and somewhat arbitrary. Judge Bullock was clearly requiring a more rational cost adjustment. Addressing cost differences across districts is important because of the tremendous variation from district to district in enrollment size and socioeconomic background of students. For example, district enrollment size in 1991–92 varied from an FTE low of 77 to a high of 45,814. Roughly one-third of all state students were enrolled in the five largest districts (those with enrollments in excess of 10,000). In contrast, 32 percent of districts had enrollments under 400 and accounted for 6 percent of students (Bundt 1994; Tallman 1993). Table 5.1 demonstrates that per-pupil spending tended to be particularly high in these very small districts, but on average they also had higher property wealth and lower percentages of students qualifying for free lunch.

The Kansas reform, in response to concerns about the arbitrary nature of past cost adjustments, switched to using a weighted-pupil approach to account for student needs. The new funding system assigned higher weights to students in low-enrollment districts and for the first time assigned weights to those students considered at risk (for which qualification for free school lunch served as a proxy), and to those students requiring bilingual education, school transportation, or vocational education. The new basic aid formula increases the importance of determining accurately the appropriate pupil weights. The base state aid per pupil is multiplied by the weighted enrollment to determine the base, or general fund, budget of the district. The higher the weighted enrollment in a district relative to the actual enrollment, the more state aid the district will receive.

The weights assigned to various types of pupils should ideally reflect three types of cost factors: economies of size, student needs, and input costs. In a rural state, such as Kansas, adjustments for economies of size are important. Past research has indicated that there are significant economies of size up to an enrollment of approximately 2,000 students (Andrews, Duncombe, and Yinger 2002). States have

Table 5.1
Distribution of Kansas school district sizes, 1991–92

Enrollment category	Percentage of all districts	Percentage of all students	Average per-pupil spending	Average per-pupil assessed value	Percentage free-lunch students[b]
Old aid formula					
I Under 200 students	11.2	1.2	$8,483	$81,775	9.8
II 200–399 students	21.1	4.5	6,483	54,507	12.5
III 400–599 students	18.8	6.4	5,913	36,681	15.1
600–999 students	19.1	9.9	5,676	41,965	12.2
1,000–1,999 students	16.4	16.0	5,099	35,789	13.9
IV 2,000–9,999 students	11.5	30.4	4,510	23,788	12.1
V 10,000 or more students[a]	2.0	31.6	5,497	38,105	22.3
New aid formula					
I Under 100 students	1.0	0.1	$10,414	$105,612	8.6
II 100–299 students	21.1	3.0	7,414	65,929	11.8
III 300–999 students	48.0	18.9	5,917	42,858	13.0
1,000–1,725 students	13.5	12.2	5,236	39,002	13.8
IV Over 1,725 students	16.4	65.9	4,613	24,812	13.6

Notes:
a. The five largest districts, which comprised Category V, were Wichita, Shawnee Mission (suburban Kansas City), Kansas City, Olathe (suburban Kansas City), and Topeka. The total number of districts used in the calculations is 304; observations were missing for 17 other districts.
b. Data are for 1992–93.

attempted to deal with economies of size by accounting for district size and sparsity in the design of their aid formulas, encouraging districts to consolidate, or both (Duncombe and Yinger 2001b). The larger the adjustment for economies of size in a state's aid formula, the less incentives districts in that state have to consolidate. Given the present debate over the pros and cons of large schools and school districts, Kansas faces difficult choices regarding how to account for scale in the design of pupil weights.

Ever since the Coleman Report (Coleman et al. 1966), the importance of student, family, and peer characteristics for student performance have been confirmed through numerous studies. Student need factors such as child poverty, limited English proficiency, high special needs, parental education and income, and neighborhood safety and resources have been commonly found to affect student performance but are beyond of the control of school districts.

The third cost factor that should be reflected in assigned pupil weights, input prices, reflects the fact that the cost of doing business may vary across regions of the state. In general, both capital and personnel input costs are higher in large cities than in suburban and rural areas (Chambers 1997). In designing its pupil weights, Kansas has attempted to account for the first two factors, but not the third.

5.1.3.1 Pupil Weights for Size The heart of the pupil weights developed by the Kansas State Department of Education (KSDE) is adjustments for district size. In constructing these weights, the KSDE used information on actual district spending by district enrollment class for 1991–92 to construct median budget levels for three enrollment classes: under 100 students, 100–299 students, and 300–1,900 students. In subsequent adjustments to the aid formula, the ceiling of the third category was lowered several times and is now 1,725 (table 5.2). (Districts with more than 1,900 [1,725] students receive no pupil weighting for district size.) These three categories accounted for 1 percent, 21 percent, and 61.5 percent of all districts in the state, respectively (table 5.1). The median spending level in each class of district is used to construct an adjustment factor, which is multiplied by the actual enrollment in the district to determine its low-enrollment weight.[9]

5.1.3.2 Pupil Weights for Student Needs Kansas has adjusted for two types of student needs in its basic aid formula: students requiring

Table 5.2
Major legislative changes since enactment of 1992 reform

Statewide General Fund property mill rate[a]	1992–93	32 mills
	1993–94	33 mills
	1994–97	35 mills
	1997–98	27 mills
	1998–2002	20 mills
	1997–98: statewide school property tax exemption equal to $20,000 of appraised value	
Base state aid per pupil	1992–93	$3,600
	1995–96	$3,626
	1996–97	$3,648
	1997–98	$3,720
	1999–2000	$3,770
	2000–01	$3,820
	2001–02	$3,870
Local-option budget[b]	Beginning 1997–98, boards of districts with "below-average" combined general and local-option budget spending per pupil can enact local-option budgets without voter approval. Protest petitions apply only if new district per-pupil budgets exceed state average in schools of similar size.	
Low-enrollment weight threshold[c]	1992–93	1,900
	1995–96	1,875
	1996–97	1,850
	1997–98	1,800
	1998–99	1,750
	1999–2002	1,725

	Year	Threshold	Weight
Correlation weights and threshold[d]	1995–96	>1,875	.009031
	1996–97	1,850	.018062
	1997–98	1,800	.036121
	1998–99	1,750	.054183
	1999–2002	1,725	.063211

Declining enrollments[e]	Currently permits districts to use average of current and preceding two years' FTE for purposes of low-enrollment and correlation weights.
Ancillary facilities weight[f]	Restricted to districts spending at full 25 percent local-option budget authority. Revenues from state-approved special local levy are divided by base state aid per pupil. Result is new weight applied to pupils for first two years (only) in which new facility is operated.
Special education "weight"[g]	District categorical special education funds are converted to a pupil weight. The resulting revenue increment is temporarily deposited in the district general fund for purposes of calculating the LOB. District per-pupil weight is derived from ratio of categorical special education aid to base state aid per pupil.

Table 5.2
(continued)

At-risk weight[h]	1992–97	.05
	1997–98	.065
	1998–99	.08
	1999–2001	.09
	2001–02	.10

Source: Kansas Legislative Research Department 2001a.
Notes:
a. Property tax amendments enacted in 1994, 1996, 1997, and 1998. Property tax exemption amendment enacted in 1997.
b. This amendment does not preclude district authorization to adopt full 25 percent local-option budget authority subject to protest petition.
c. Amendment for new low-enrollment threshold schedule enacted in 1995.
d. Correlation weight amendments enacted in 1995, 1997, and 1998.
e. Declining-enrollment provisions enacted in 1993, 1997, and 1999.
f. Ancillary weight enacted in 1997.
g. Special education provision enacted in 2001.
h. At-risk weight increases enacted in 1997, 1998, 1999, and 2001. The most recent amendment requires districts to devote the most recent .01 weight addition to enhancing mastery of third-grade reading skills.

bilingual education and at-risk students. Students requiring special education services are considered in a separate aid program. Weights for students requiring bilingual education are estimated by determining the number of bilingual education hours approved by the state for the district, dividing that number by six, and then multiplying the result by a weight of 0.20 (Kansas Legislative Research Department 2001b). At-risk students are defined as students eligible for free lunch under the National School Lunch Program, administered by the U.S. Department of Agriculture, which is available to students with incomes below 130 percent of the federal poverty line.[10] The weight for at-risk students started as 5 percent in 1992–93 and grew to 9 percent for 2000–01 (table 5.2).[11]

5.1.3.3 Other Pupil Weights Pupil weights are also added for vocational education students and for students receiving transportation services to attend school. For the number of full-time equivalent students enrolled in vocational education, a pupil weight of 0.5 is used (Kansas Legislative Research Department 2001b). The calculation of transportation weights is based on actual district spending on transportation divided by the number of students transported more than 2.5 miles for the previous year.[12] The acceptable cost per transported student is divided by the state-set base budget ($3,600 in 1992–93), then multiplied by the number of transported students to determine the transportation weight (Kansas Legislative Research Department 2001b).

5.1.4 Accountability Provisions of the Reform
The reform also instituted a quality performance accreditation (QPA) process for the state's school districts, which was implemented in 1996. QPA, which is built on the principle of "continuous improvement" in student performance, requires the state board of education to establish "world-class" curriculum standards (State of Kansas Legislative Division of Post Audit 1996) and to assess student mastery of the curriculum standards by administering statewide tests in mathematics, science, reading, writing, and social studies.[13] Each year, the board must prepare and disseminate a public education "report card" to share information on the results of assessment tests and on other performance indicators.[14]

Each school district is required to participate in the QPA process through a five-year accreditation cycle that involves designing and submitting a school improvement plan. During the cycle, schools are evaluated by the state board for compliance with specific standards based on outcomes identified in their improvement plans. Potential sanctions for those districts ultimately denied accreditation include funding reductions and state assumption of responsibility for the local district (Kansas State Department of Education 2000).[15]

5.1.5 Concessions to Local Control and the Local-Option Budget
During the legislative debates that led to the 1992 reform, it became clear that the representatives of a number of districts would support the new system only if their districts could have access to some relief from the strict weighted per-pupil spending limits under consideration. The compromise crafted during the debates became known as the *local-option budget* (LOB). In addition to the LOB, the state agreed to provide aid for local bond and interest expense and to continue authorization for a local mill levy for "capital outlay" funds.

5.1.5.1 LOB Provisions The LOB, as originally envisioned, would permit districts to supplement their weighted FTE budgets by up to 25 percent, but these LOBs would be gradually phased out over time.

As it turned out, the phase-out provision was dropped from the final legislation. In essence, the legislature adopted a relative equity standard in which weighted pupil expenditure could vary by no more than 25 percent across districts. (Because of the weighted-pupil approach, actual per-pupil expenditures could vary by significantly more than 25 percent.)

Despite its success as a tool of political compromise, the LOB theoretically violates the strict relative equity standard required by the district court in the ruling that started the reform process. To compensate partly for this, the state provides supplemental aid to some needy districts using the LOB. The amount of state aid allocated for LOB purposes is equal to the district's LOB fund multiplied by one minus the ratio of the district's per-pupil assessed property value for the previous year divided by per-pupil assessed property value in the previous year for the district at the 75th percentile of the distribution of per-pupil property values. In essence, the state has set up a matching grant (very similar to a power-equalizing grant) to encourage local supplementation by low-wealth districts.

5.1.5.2 Capital Expenditures Under the reform, districts were permitted to issue general obligation bonds to support capital construction, and for the first time, state aid would be provided for principal and interest payments on these bonds. The principal and interest payment funds were not subject to a firm limit, although district voters have to approve local principal and interest expenditures in a bond levy election.[16] For debt issued after July 1, 1992, the state indicated it was willing to make 25 percent of bond payments for districts with the median assessed value per pupil and provided a one-percentage-point increase (decrease) for each $1,000 in district per-pupil assessed property value below (above) the median (Kansas Association of School Boards 1994). Since the median per-pupil property value in 1995 was $29,650, districts with assessed property values up to $54,000 per pupil would receive some aid. Given the unlimited nature of this provision and the fairly generous state support provided, this provision is one potential vehicle by which school districts are able to avoid the $3,600 weighted per-pupil spending cap.[17] The reform also provided a spending exemption for capital outlays,[18] and continued a policy that allowed districts to add up to four additional mills to the tax rate for capital expenditures financed through current revenue. No state assistance was made available to support this levy.

5.1.6   The Reform Revisited: Nine Years Later

The prevailing opinion among advocates for Kansas public schools is that during the eleven years since the implementation of the School District Finance and Quality Performance Act, the state has failed to live up to its funding responsibilities (Baker 2001b; Baker and Imber 1999; Tallman 2002). In addition, a series of changes in the state's financing formula for education have, in the eyes of many observers, either introduced new educational disparities or exacerbated flaws in the original formula. Many of these changes have resulted directly from low state spending growth. As complaints grew from lawmakers representing districts with no opportunity for increased education spending under the act—primarily in the urban and wealthy suburban Johnson County districts—the state legislature responded by making incremental changes to the finance system outlined in the act (and in effect in Kansas in some form ever since), some of which were designed to assist a handful of districts with specific needs. Over time, the state has turned increasingly to LOB revenues to fund growth in school budgets. The provisions of the act faced several legal challenges during the ensuing decade, but so far the act has survived intact.[19]

5.1.7   Changes to General State Aid and Local Tax Effort

Table 5.2 highlights legislative actions between 1992 and 2001. First, and perhaps most importantly, a series of amendments changed the required local property tax levy from the original rate of 32 mills. The property tax rate increased to 33 mills in 1993–94 and to 35 mills from 1994 to 1997. After this, however, the rate was dropped to 27 mills in 1997–98 and 20 mills since 1998–99. In addition, the 1997–98 legislative session generated a new school property tax exemption for the first $20,000 of a property's appraised value. The combination of these factors has dropped the uniform mandatory local property tax contribution for the basic budget from $2,500 per pupil in 1993 to less than $925 in 2001, a decrease of over 60 percent.

Although the state has increased its share of funding of the school finance system, legislative adjustments to base per-pupil spending have increased very slowly. From the initial budget level of $3,600, the budget per weighted pupil grew slowly to $3,870 in the 2001–02 school year, an increase of only 7.5 percent over a nine-year period. The Kansas Association of School Boards (2001) estimates that during this same period, the consumer price index increased by 19 percent and state personal income grew by nearly 46 percent. Figure 5.1 demon-

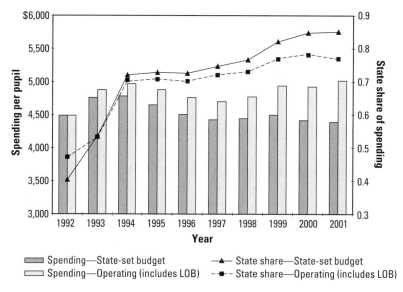

Figure 5.1
Spending trends and state share of spending with and without LOB. Spending is adjusted for inflation using the consumer price index for all urban consumers in the Kansas City metropolitan area (1989 = 100).

strates the slow growth in the state-set budget per pupil, especially when adjusted for inflation. When adjusted for inflation, state general fund budgets per pupil have actually declined over the period. Relief provided by increased LOB activity has filled some of the resulting funding gap. Inflation-adjusted operating expenditures increased 1.2 percent per year from 1992 to 2001, which is actually a faster growth rate than from 1989 to 1992; the latter period, however, encompasses the recession of the early 1990s. The annual growth rate in inflation-adjusted operating expenditure has been only 0.3 percent since 1993. A similar pattern is observed for total per-pupil expenditures, which incorporate capital outlay and debt service funds.

5.1.8 Changes to Pupil Weights

Most of the pupil weights originally assigned have not been altered significantly since the reform (see table 5.2). Changes to the low-enrollment weight included dropping the low-enrollment threshold gradually over a few years from 1,900 to 1,725. For all districts above this threshold, a weight of 6 percent was assigned for the first time.[20] Because of political pressure from growing districts, especially one fast-growing Johnson County suburban district, "ancillary school facilities" weighting was authorized beginning in the 1997–98 school year.[21] As noted earlier, the weight for at-risk students has been gradually doubled since 1992, from 0.05 to 0.10 (table 5.2). No change has occurred in the weighting for bilingual students, vocational students, or students transported more than 2.5 miles.

5.1.9   Changes to the LOB

By 2001, nine years after the reform, the LOB picture had changed substantially, partly because of what is widely viewed as inadequate rates of growth in state general fund allocations. Although the provision of the reform authorizing LOBs was initially supposed to expire by 1996–97, districts were authorized beginning in 1997–98 to adopt LOBs through board motion (without voter approval requirements) as long as combined general and LOB spending remained at or below the state average for schools of similar size. As a result, many districts that have adopted LOBs in response to this change actually use it to supplement the per-pupil amount far less than the statutory 25 percent authority. Nevertheless, this change has substantially increased LOB activity in the state, and it has provided a mechanism for local districts to compensate for lagging state funds. In addition, several other changes have extended local tax levy authority.[22]

5.2   Assessing the Reform

The Kansas school finance reform incorporates strict controls on local school funding decisions, but it also includes several measures designed to provide some relaxation of those controls. There is little doubt that the LOB is an effective political device, and that it may account for the political survival of the reform to date. By supplying matching aid to some needy LOB districts, Kansas effectively created a two-tiered aid system: a lump-sum grant to bring all districts up to the specified spending limit, and a matching grant to encourage additional tax effort by low-wealth districts. In this section, we examine the impacts of the weighting system and the LOB (and changes in capital spending) on relative equity across school districts in the state. We include an examination of the characteristics of the principal users of the LOB. We then analyze the reform in the context of several equity standards, including spending and student performance.

5.2.1 Evaluating Kansas's Pupil Weights

The amount of state education aid distributed to a school district in Kansas is driven almost exclusively by assessed property value in the district and the calculation of the weighted pupil count for the district. Given the array of pupil weights used by Kansas, it is important to examine how each affects different types of districts. We begin by examining the ratio of weighted pupils to FTE by district enrollment size class. The importance of the low-enrollment weight is clearly illustrated in the first column of table 5.3. Districts with under 100 students have a pupil weight of 1.40 compared to a weight of 0.065 in districts with an enrollment of 1,725 or higher. Thus, students in very small districts are expected to be 125 percent (2.399/1.065) more costly to educate than students in districts with at least 1,726 students. Students in districts with enrollments between 100 and 300 are estimated to cost 80 percent more on average than those in districts with more than 1,725 students and 40 percent more when enrollments are between 300 and 1,000. The transportation weights, although small by comparison, are also higher in small districts. None of the other enrollment weights averages more than 3 percent, and most do not show a distinct pattern by enrollment group.

Table 5.3 also includes a classification scheme we developed for a subsample of districts that considers district size, wealth, poverty rates, and geographic location.[23] Not surprisingly, the enrollment weights differ significantly across these district types.

Given the dominant role that low-enrollment weighting plays in cost adjustments to the Kansas basic aid formula, it is useful to ask whether there is evidence to support very high pupil weights for small districts. In a recent study of school consolidation in New York, Duncombe and Yinger (2001b) estimated the potential cost savings from consolidating small districts. Under the most extreme assumptions—consolidation of several equal-sized small districts into a district of 1,700 students—the potential cost savings are estimated to be similar to those imbedded in the pupil weights in Kansas.[24] The cutoff of 1,700 also appears consistent with much of the cost function research, which finds that most cost savings from consolidation are exhausted by an enrollment level of 1,500 to 2,000 students (Andrews, Duncombe, and Yinger 2002).

But compared to the low-enrollment weights, the weights for high-need students appears particularly low, even relative to other states. Alexander and Salmon (1995) found that most states had weights for

Table 5.3
Comparison of Kansas weighted pupil index:[a] Distribution by enrollment (FTE) and by district type (average in 2001)

Category	Low-enrollment weights	Transportation weights	Bilingual education weights	At-risk student weights	Other weights
Number of pupils (FTE)					
Under 100 students	1.398	0.112	0.000	0.022	0.012
100–299 students	0.909	0.100	0.003	0.025	0.013
300–999 students	0.506	0.080	0.002	0.019	0.018
1,000–1,725 students	0.239	0.061	0.000	0.016	0.022
1,726–9,999 students	0.065	0.035	0.004	0.021	0.019
10,000 or more students	0.064	0.019	0.005	0.025	0.022
District type[b]					
Large-city districts	0.064	0.019	0.009	0.046	0.016
Wealthy Kansas City suburbs	0.064	0.018	0.001	0.004	0.028
Other cities	0.064	0.026	0.022	0.030	0.013
Medium sized, East Kansas	0.166	0.040	0.001	0.017	0.040
Mineral wealth, West Kansas	0.512	0.061	0.018	0.027	0.013
Small, high-poverty	0.984	0.086	0.000	0.031	0.015
Very small, not high-poverty	1.219	0.111	0.005	0.025	0.004

Notes:
a. Weighted FTE for each category divided by regular FTE for each district in 2001 minus one (expressed in percent).
b. See chapter notes for list of districts in each category.

at-risk students and limited English proficiency (LEP) pupils of 0.25 or higher. In a recent study of the cost of adequacy in New York, Duncombe (2002) estimated pupil weights for free-lunch students and LEP students of approximately one. In other words, these students were estimated to be twice as expensive as regular students.

An alternative approach to estimating costs of scale and costs of at-risk students is to use regression estimates from cost models to construct education cost indexes (see Duncombe and Yinger 1999; Duncombe 2002). To examine how the regression approach might differ from the weighted-pupil method used by Kansas, we developed a cost model for Kansas school districts using 1997 data, which is reported in appendix table 5.A.1. Besides enrollment, other cost factors in the model include average teacher salaries (including fringe benefits), percentage of children in poverty in 1997, and bilingual hours per FTE.[25] In addition, we have included a measure of the child poverty rate in large districts (those with enrollments of 10,000 pupils or more) to reflect the potential for urban poverty to have a larger impact on education costs than rural poverty. Most of the coefficients on the cost variables have the expected relationship with per-pupil expenditures; only the enrollment variables, teacher salaries, and urban poverty measures, however, are statistically significant at the 5 percent level. The child poverty rate, and bilingual hours per FTE are significant at the 10 percent level. We constructed a cost index by holding the performance measures and efficiency factors at the state mean and allowing the cost factors to vary. The ratio of the predicted district spending to the state average spending (times 100) is the cost index.

While the cost index derived from appendix table 5.A.1 should be viewed with caution because of the marginal precision of some of the estimates, the results certainly are suggestive of the impact of these variables on costs in Kansas. In table 5.4, this cost index is compared with the cost index inferred by the weighted-pupil estimates produced by the state,[26] and with the cost of education index for Kansas districts (in 1993) produced by the National Center for Education Statistics (NCES). Average values for each index are compared by enrollment size, percentage of students receiving free lunch, and property wealth for Kansas districts. The importance of enrollment size for the Kansas weighted-pupil index is indicated clearly, with the index falling steadily as enrollment rises. The weighted-pupil index rises slightly with higher poverty (only in districts with very high poverty) and with property wealth. Not surprisingly, the districts with the highest index

Table 5.4
Comparison of Kansas weighted pupil index with other cost indices (state average = 100)

Category	Weighted-pupil index[a]	Regression cost index[b]	NCES cost of education index[c]
Number of pupils (FTE)			
Under 100 students	149.1	152.7	91.6
100–299 students	128.6	124.7	94.0
300–999 students	102.8	99.8	98.4
1,000–1,725 students	85.0	86.5	103.4
1,726–9,999 students	70.3	80.3	107.8
10,000 or more students	69.9	91.2	117.4
Poverty class percentile[d]			
0 to 25th	92.7	92.4	104.5
25th to 50th	100.0	98.4	99.6
50th to 75th	101.9	102.3	98.7
75th to 90th	102.4	103.6	97.6
Over 90th	114.8	119.4	95.4
Property value class percentile			
Under 5th	86.9	91.0	103.3
5th to 25th	91.3	92.8	102.2
25th to 50th	90.8	91.8	101.5
50th to 75th	102.5	101.5	99.1
75th to 90th	118.3	114.2	96.4
Over 90th	108.7	115.4	98.8
District type[e]			
Large-city districts	70.3	102.3	114.9
Wealthy Kansas City suburbs	69.6	80.1	120.0
Other cities	69.9	79.2	108.5
Medium sized, East Kansas	77.0	84.3	105.1
Mineral wealth, West Kansas	106.3	111.7	99.9
Small, high-poverty	126.3	129.5	92.6
Very small, not high-poverty	142.3	138.2	92.2

Notes:
a. Weighted FTE relative to regular FTE for each district in 1993 divided by the state average (times 100).
b. Index calculated by multiplying variables in cost model for 1997 by regression coefficients (see table 5.A.1). Dropout rate, math and reading test scores, and efficiency variables are held at the state average. Actual district values for cost variables are used to construct predicted spending, which is divided by state average spending (times 100) to get cost index.
c. Cost-of-education index for 1993. See Chambers 1997 for methodology.
d. Percentage of children in households with incomes below the poverty line.
e. See text for list of districts in each category.

values are small rural districts, and the lowest index values are in urban areas. The index in the smallest districts is more than twice what it is in districts with enrollment over 10,000. The cost index produced by the cost model is very similar to the weighted-pupil index for low-enrollment districts. Differences emerge, however, for larger districts and those with a higher percentage of students in poverty. Whereas the weighted-pupil index for the five districts with 10,000 or more students averages 70, the cost index for those same districts averages 91, and the index for the three large central cities is 102. According to the weighted-pupil index, districts with the highest poverty rates have 15 percent higher costs, while these costs are estimated to be 20 percent higher using the cost index. The NCES cost of education index, which attempts to measure differences in resource prices across a state, does not track closely with the other two indexes. Costs in larger cities are estimated to be 15 percent above average, but costs in the highest-poverty districts are estimated to be below average.

Given the importance of the low-enrollment weights to the distribution of aid, it is imperative that the state government study much more closely the cost impacts of scale. Simply using 1992 spending patterns to construct pupil weights is inadequate, because smaller districts in Kansas also have higher property wealth and lower poverty rates (Baker 2001b; Baker and Imber 1999). In addition to influencing aid distribution, these low-enrollment weights could discourage school district consolidations in those situations in which it may be feasible in terms of the potential cost savings.[27]

5.2.2 Use of the LOB (and Tax Levies for Capital Spending)

In the early years after the reform, less than half the districts adopted a local-option budget, and the total amounts of those budgets combined represented less than 10 percent of the base budget amount for the state. A number of districts were hesitant to use LOBs because of the opposition of local voters in a state with traditionally heavy reliance on property taxes (Fisher 1995). But by 1998 many districts were being squeezed by the slow growth in the state-set base budget level and state aid. The percentage of districts using LOBs jumped from 53 percent in 1997 to 76 percent in 1998 and approached 94 percent in 2001. For districts using an LOB in 2001, LOB revenues equaled 13 percent of the base budget and 10 percent of total district spending. The Kansas Association of School Boards (2001) estimates that property tax reductions attributable to the legislature's nine-year history of local mill levy cuts and the school property tax exemption total roughly $265 million. During the same period, district LOB spending has increased by nearly $223 million. In other words, the LOB has provided the only recourse to districts that feel compelled to use local revenues to substitute for stagnant state education spending.

It is clear that large urban districts were the heaviest LOB users, especially in the mid-1990s, along with the small wealthy districts of western Kansas (table 5.5). By contrast, very few of the poorer districts of western Kansas used LOBs, at least until the late 1990s. By 2001, the vast majority of districts used an LOB, and the majority had LOB spending of over 10 percent of the state-set budget.

Clearly, districts losing significant amounts of revenue after the reform were the main users of the LOB, particularly in the early years after the reform (table 5.6). Districts in 1997 not using the LOB had little change in their spending compared to 1992, whereas districts levying a tax to finance an LOB of at least 15 percent of their budgets had lost 20 percent of their budgets since the reform. Heavy users of LOBs in 1997 were generally in more urban areas with higher population, enrollment, property values, income, and percentage of minority students and a larger college-educated population. The same general pattern appeared in 2001, but generally with fewer stark contrasts. Districts that do not use LOBs were by then in the minority, and they were clearly small rural districts with very low enrollment, population, property values, minority population, and numbers of college graduates. In 2001, one-third of districts had LOBs that amounted to 15 percent of the state-set budget or more. The differences between heavy users and low to moderate users of the LOB were smaller by 2001 than they were in the mid-1990s. A number of districts of moderate size and wealth were heavy users of the LOB by 2001.

To examine this issue further, we ran several exploratory regressions on the determinants of LOB spending (table 5.7).[28] The dependent variable in the regressions is LOB spending as a percentage of general funding in 1992, which can be viewed as the difference between the desired level of spending and the state-set budget (relative to prereform desired level of spending). Demand for public education can be modeled as a function of income, state aid, the tax price, factors affecting preferences, and the constraint on local preferences resulting from the reform. Thus, this model is very similar in spirit to models of the impact of tax and expenditure limitations on local spending (Bradbury, Mayer, and Case 2001). To control for possible unobserved district

Table 5.5
Use of local-option budgets by district type: Local-option budget and supplemental state aid

Category	All districts	Large cities	Wealthy Kansas City suburbs	Other cities	Medium sized, East Kansas	Mineral wealth, West Kansas	Small, high-poverty	Very small, not high-poverty
Percentage using LOB								
1995	47	100	100	50	25	67	33	50
2001	94	100	100	100	100	100	78	83
Average LOB per FTE[a]								
1993	$115	$ 554	$ 815	$ 84	$ 87	$ 877	$315	$ 464
1997	305	1,109	1,132	245	282	929	414	855
2001	730	1,274	1,120	860	923	1,284	901	1,747
Annual rate of change (percent)								
1993–1997	27.6	19.0	8.6	30.7	34.3	1.4	7.1	16.5
1997–2001	24.4	3.5	-0.3	36.9	34.5	8.4	21.5	19.5
LOB as percentage of state-set budget								
1993	2.1	14.7	22.0	2.3	2.1	15.0	4.7	6.0
1997	5.4	27.8	28.7	6.2	6.5	15.4	5.8	10.6
2001	12.2	28.7	25.0	19.3	18.7	20.5	10.7	18.6
1993–1996 (average)	3.7	21.7	26.9	4.0	4.2	14.9	5.0	8.7
1997–2001 (average)	8.5	28.5	26.2	11.8	12.1	18.5	7.6	14.0

Note:
a. Average includes districts that did not use LOBs.

Table 5.6
Characteristics of districts using the LOB by percentage of use

LOB revenue as percentage of state-set budget	Number of districts	Percentage change in per-pupil budget since 1992	Enrollment (FTE)	Population (1997)	Median household income (1990)	Per-pupil assessed value	Percentage free-lunch students	Bilingual hours per FTE	Percentage of college grads (1990)	Percentage of minority pupils (1992)
1997										
Don't use LOB	142	20.07	944	5,331	$23,824	$36,295	2.3	13.0	4.2	4.1
0–5%	46	14.33	981	5,555	25,023	33,468	3.5	13.8	4.4	5.4
5–10%	54	14.72	1,056	5,621	25,124	37,454	6.3	13.9	5.2	4.3
10–15%	26	14.05	823	4,830	23,383	63,215	5.0	12.8	5.5	7.6
15–20%	10	8.30	6,118	52,460	28,069	76,213	3.6	14.4	10.2	20.5
Over 20%	26	−0.48	4,886	29,416	27,609	93,061	25.9	16.5	12.3	11.5
F-statistic (analysis of variance)[a]		19.66	10.00	8.73	2.45	8.17	0.52	4.23	2.45	5.60
2001										
Don't use LOB	19	20.60	365	1,693	$22,219	$39,264	26.6	2.3	11.5	5.0
0–5%	31	13.47	413	3,746	23,290	43,165	22.3	1.0	14.0	2.1
5–10%	77	9.18	606	3,305	22,725	41,718	22.1	6.6	11.7	3.6
10–15%	77	7.94	1,042	5,587	23,692	43,765	23.3	6.2	13.3	4.5
15–20%	47	−0.47	2,350	15,546	26,300	62,500	21.8	10.0	15.2	8.1
Over 20%	53	−7.59	3,563	20,847	29,156	69,449	21.5	12.7	15.9	8.7
F-statistic (analysis of variance)[a]		20.89	6.07	3.97	9.69	4.20	0.86	0.97	5.74	5.14

Note:
a. Tests the hypothesis that there is no difference in values across the groups. Critical F-statistic for 5 percent error is 4.4 ($df = 5, 297$).

variables, we estimated a first-differencing model by using percentage change variables for as many of the demand variables as possible. Level variables are also included in some of the models (see table 5.7).

As expected, the size of the LOB varies inversely with the magnitude of the spending constraint imposed by the finance reform. A 1 percent increase in state-set spending in 1997 relative to 1992 spending is associated with an 0.44 to 0.57 percentage point decrease in the size of the LOB in 1997, holding other demand factors constant. Thus, districts losing revenue after the finance reform appear, on average, to replace approximately half of it using the LOB. By 2001, only 20 percent of the lost revenue replaced by the LOB.

In addition, growth in enrollment and child poverty in a district is also negatively associated with LOB use, particularly in 1997. Increases in state aid and assessed value are positively associated with LOB use, particularly in 2001. Among the level variables, median household income has a statistically significant positive relationship to LOB use in 1997 (but not in 2001), and higher use of the LOB is positively related to the percentage of college graduates in a district and to district enrollment. To determine if the matching LOB aid offered by the state encouraged LOB use, we developed a tax price measure capturing the aid formula. If the grant stimulated LOB use, we would expect a significant negative relationship. The coefficient measuring this relationship is positive and insignificant in 1997 but is negative and significant at the 10 percent level in 2001. LOB aid may be beginning to encourage low-wealth districts to increase their LOB use since state aid for education has not kept up with inflation.

To examine the impacts of the reform on capital spending, we estimated a model of the determinants of change in capital spending per pupil for 1997 and 2001. If districts substituted capital spending for a loss in the state-set general fund budget, we would expect an increase in the state-set budget for a particular district after reform to be associated with a decrease in capital spending in that district. Instead, the coefficient for this relationship is positive and statistically significant in 2001.[29] If the 2001 coefficient is taken literally, it implies that a 1 percent increase in state-set general fund spending (compared to 1992) is associated with an increase of over 2 percent in capital spending, holding other factors constant. This result suggests that instead of serving as a substitute for funds lost through reductions in the state-set general fund budget, capital spending funded from tax levies is stimulated by increases in the budget amount.

Table 5.7
Factors associated with relative size of local-option budget as percentage of 1992 general fund spending (regression coefficients)[a]

	1997		
Variable	Model 1	Model 2	Model 3
Intercept	0.1071	−0.9437	−0.6145
Percentage change since 1992			
State-set spending[b]	−0.5681	−0.4988	−0.4440
Enrollment (FTE)	−0.2271	−0.2825	−0.2558
State aid per pupil	0.0093	0.0083	0.0054
Assessed value per pupil	0.0670	0.0517	0.0130
Child poverty rate	−0.0459	−0.0544	−0.0464
Level in 1992			
Median household income (1990)[c]		0.0981	0.1226
Percentage college graduates (1990)		0.1056	−0.0480
Percentage households with children		0.0099	−0.1369
Tax price associated with LOB aid[d]		0.0554	0.0660
Assessed value per pupil[c]			−0.0239
State aid per pupil[c]			−0.0454
Enrollment (FTE)[c]			0.0102
Child poverty rate (1990)			0.0997
Chi-square	87.31	101.75	114.51

5.2.3   Evaluation of the Relative Equity Effects of the Reform

The Kansas education reform focused explicitly on improving relative equity among school districts in the state.[30] Judge Bullock made it clear in his 1992 "rules of law" that the provision of education was ultimately the responsibility of the state, that resources must be provided equally to all children in Kansas, and that some adjustment should be made in the state's education finance system for high-need students. Given the inequities that existed among districts prior to the reform, we would expect to see a pattern wherein districts with lower fiscal capacity and higher student needs are the principal beneficiaries of the reform.

In table 5.8, we have identified major winners and losers from the reform, at least in terms of gains or losses in their general fund budgets from 1992 to 1995. Several distinct patterns emerge from the comparison presented in the table. First, the districts that experienced the largest gains in their budgets had the lowest spending in 1992, lower

Table 5.7
(continued)

	2001		
	Model 1	Model 2	Model 3
Intercept	0.1431	−0.8694	−0.9857
Percentage change since 1992			
State-set spending[b]	−0.2400	−0.2343	−0.1939
Enrollment (FTE)	−0.0780	−0.1380	−0.1123
State aid per pupil	0.0086	0.0083	0.0051
Assessed value per pupil	0.0871	0.0547	0.0173
Child poverty rate (1980)	−0.0090	−0.0160	−0.0094
Level in 1992			
Median household income (1990)[c]		−0.0192	−0.0010
Percentage college graduates (1990)		0.1035	0.1134
Percentage households with children		0.1818	−0.0175
Tax price associated with LOB aid[d]		−0.0912	−0.1763
Assessed value per pupil[c]			0.0013
State aid per pupil[c]			−0.0189
Enrollment (FTE)[c]			0.0275
Child poverty rate (1990)			0.0978
Chi-square	64.49	91.18	131.31

Notes:
a. Estimated with Tobit regression with lower limit of 0 ($n = 300$).
b. Defined as percentage change in state-set budget per pupil compared to the general fund.
c. Expressed as natural logarithm.
d. Equals one if property value per pupil is equal or greater than property values at 75th percentile.

enrollments and populations, lower income and property values, lower shares of college-educated population, and lower shares of bilingual and minority students. In most cases there was a monotonic change among these variables from districts experiencing the largest budget gains to those experiencing the largest budgetary declines. Not surprisingly, the use of the LOB was in direct proportion to the size of budgetary loss as a result of the reform. Once the LOB and other local levies are included in spending, relatively little difference is found between winners and losers in per-pupil operating costs and total spending.

To examine further the winners and losers from the reform and the potential effects of the reform on equity, we compared several different

Table 5.8
Characteristics of major winners and losers from the education finance reform, 1995

Change in budget from 1992 to 1995	Number of districts	Enrollment (FTE)	Per-pupil general fund budget (1992)	State-set per-pupil general fund budget (1995)	Per-pupil LOB (1995)	Per-pupil budget with LOB	Per-pupil total budget
Lose more than 30%	14	5091.71	$8,107	$4,978	$775	$5,806	$6,572
−30% to −20%	31	4278.25	6,811	5,142	638	5,860	6,265
−20% to −10%	60	1560.88	6,146	5,245	290	5,580	5,880
−10% to −5%	45	1037.23	5,782	5,338	222	5,611	5,866
−5% to 0	49	664.51	5,931	5,790	110	5,923	6,143
0 to 5%	39	698.09	5,664	5,793	113	5,937	6,465
5% to 10%	30	521.54	5,769	6,159	94	6,287	6,454
10% to 25%	31	622.23	5,015	5,745	43	5,800	6,017
Gain over 25%	5	344.98	4,969	6,467	0	6,467	6,580
F-statistic (analysis of variance)[a]		5.79	9.08	3.96	14.02	1.21	1.06

Table 5.8
(continued)

Change in budget from 1992 to 1995	Population (1990) (persons)	Median household income (1990)	Per-pupil assessed value	Bilingual hours per thousand FTE students	Percentage free-lunch students	Percentage college graduates (1990)	Percentage minority pupils (1992)
Lose more than 30%	26,541	$29,651	$145,809	85.7	17.43	18.56	7.12
−30% to −20%	28,174	24,715	71,896	49.9	26.44	15.17	13.74
−20% to −10%	8,131	25,869	43,923	44.6	22.27	15.20	6.84
−10% to −5%	5,343	25,378	38,715	4.8	20.47	13.47	4.94
−5% to 0	3,386	23,380	32,845	1.3	23.08	12.16	3.77
0 to 5%	3,577	23,300	31,383	10.1	20.12	12.67	2.86
5% to 10%	3,926	24,737	32,834	0.0	20.86	12.90	2.98
10% to 25%	3,035	23,240	27,102	7.3	23.98	11.40	2.51
Gain over 25%	1,796	20,836	29,568	0.0	20.50	11.87	1.50
F-statistic (analysis of variance)[a]	4.68	2.34	9.01	1.49	1.64	4.04	7.15

Note:
a. Tests hypothesis that there is no difference in values across the groups. Critical F-statistic for 5 percent error is 2.97 $(df = 8, 294)$.

measures of spending per pupil to the state average by type of district (table 5.9). When spending is calculated relative to the weighted-pupil counts developed by the state, the reform is found to have resulted in dramatic changes. The large urban districts and the mineral wealth districts in the western part of the state are estimated to have had above-average spending per weighted pupil prior to the reform, and the reform is found to have brought them down to the state average. In contrast, the other types of districts are estimated to have had spending levels 5 to 10 percent below average before the reform, and the reform is found to have increased spending per weighted pupil to bring them up to average. But if we examine spending adjusted by the cost index, the impacts of the reform appear to have been far less equalizing. Cost-adjusted spending in the large cities is estimated to have been far below the state average before the reform, and the reform is shown not to have brought them closer to the average. For very small districts with below-average poverty the spending adjusting for costs was above the state average in 1992 and remained above average after the reform. It is found that the reform did successfully bring the wealthy suburban districts around Kansas City and those in the western part of the state with mineral wealth from well above the state average down to or even below the state average by 2001. For the small, high poverty districts, the reform is found to have brought them from below the state average to slightly above it.

To evaluate more formally the success of school finance reform in Kansas, we have examined relative equity for school spending before (1990–91 and 1991–92) and after (1992–93 to 2000–01) the reform. A number of relative equity measures have been used in the education literature (Berne and Stiefel 1984), each with different strengths. We have selected two common equity measures: (1) the coefficient of variation (CV), which measures average variation around the mean (standard deviation divided by average), and (2) the Gini coefficient, which provides a more comprehensive measure of relative equity.[31] For both of these measures, pupil-weighted estimates were used to reflect the impacts of the reform on individual children rather than districts; a lower value for a particular measure indicates greater relative equity according to that measure.

Before evaluating relative equity, it is important to decide what it is that should be equalized, that is, relative equity in regard to what? Although most rhetoric (and court cases) on school finance equity focuses on per-pupil expenditure, this is an imperfect measure of the underlying factors in which parents and school officials are interested: either resources or outcomes. Equalization of resources across districts assures that all districts have the ability to buy the same quality teachers, equipment, and so on. Outcomes can be measured either directly or by adjusting spending for both resource costs and student needs. Kansas has taken the latter approach by using spending per weighted pupil, which we compare to spending adjusted by the cost index we developed. We have also examined equity for several student outcome measures.

5.2.4 Spending Equity Analysis

Table 5.10 presents several adjusted measures of education spending in Kansas that lead to an interesting set of contrasting conclusions about education equity in the state. When the state-set budget per weighted pupil is used, the equity improvements since reform are found to be dramatic. On all of the equity measures examined, the state is shown to have achieved close to perfect equality. This result, of course, is by definition, since the state sets spending to equalize the budget per weighted pupil. Thus, these results simply indicate that the reformed finance system has actually been implemented as intended. If we instead use the cost index prepared for this chapter, however, the equity story that emerges is very different. Using cost-adjusted spending, the pupil-weighted CV and Gini coefficients show only a small improvement in relative equity. Thus, the differences between the weighted-pupil count developed by the state and our cost index dramatically affect conclusions about the relative equity effects of the reform.

How do the conclusions change when the LOB is included in the spending estimates? Table 5.10 also presents relative equity results for operating expenditures, defined as the state-set budget plus revenue raised from the LOB and state aid provided to encourage poor districts to use the LOB. If the LOB has been used mainly by wealthy districts to avoid the per-pupil spending constraints imposed by the state, then including it in the spending estimates should worsen the relative equity measures. If, on the other hand, state aid to poor districts to encourage local supplementation is successful, the measures of relative equity should actually improve. Results for expenditures per weighted pupil with the LOB included, though they do not show perfect equality, clearly show that relative equity has improved significantly since the reform. For cost-adjusted expenditures, the relative equity measures for operating expenditures are actually better than

Table 5.9
District spending relative to state average by district type before and after 1992 education reform

Category		Large cities	Wealthy Kansas City suburbs	Other cities	Medium sized, East Kansas	Mineral wealth, West Kansas	Small, high-poverty	Very small, not high-poverty	State average spending
	Index relative to state average (average = 100)								
State-set general fund budget									
Expenditures per weighted FTE[a]									
Weighted-pupil index		70.3	69.6	69.9	77.0	106.3	126.3	142.3	
1989		105.9	124.2	97.7	94.9	116.6	89.7	97.8	$2,997
1992		105.9	126.2	95.4	92.4	118.0	89.1	101.0	3,415
1997		100.0	100.0	100.0	100.0	100.0	100.0	100.0	4,063
2001		100.0	100.0	100.0	100.0	99.9	100.0	100.0	4,508
Annual spending growth rate (percent)									
1989–1992		4.46	5.01	3.61	3.55	4.87	4.21	5.57	4.45
1992–2001		0.61	-1.34	1.79	2.14	-0.61	2.56	1.13	3.13
Cost-adjusted expenditures per FTE[b]									
Cost index		102.3	80.1	79.2	84.3	111.7	129.5	138.2	
1989		77.4	114.1	91.1	94.6	122.0	98.2	110.0	$4,204
1992		77.3	116.0	88.9	92.0	123.1	97.3	114.7	4,797
1997		74.9	94.2	95.9	98.7	104.5	106.0	111.1	5,231
2001		72.9	93.8	94.4	97.9	95.6	108.5	115.7	5,975
Annual spending growth rate (percent)									
1989–1992		4.45	5.07	3.64	3.56	4.81	4.17	5.95	4.50
1992–2001		1.81	0.08	3.16	3.17	-0.37	3.71	2.57	2.47

Table 5.9
(continued)

Operating spending

Expenditures per weighted FTE[a]

1989	105.9	124.2	97.7	94.9	116.6	89.7	97.8	$2,997
1992	105.9	126.2	95.4	92.4	118.0	89.1	101.0	3,415
1997	114.8	115.6	95.4	96.1	102.3	94.5	99.2	4,063
2001	109.0	105.9	101.1	101.0	101.4	93.1	100.4	4,508

Annual spending growth rate (percent)

1989–1992	4.46	5.01	3.61	3.55	4.87	4.21	5.57	4.45
1992–2001	3.47	1.14	3.81	4.15	1.41	3.64	3.07	3.13

Cost-adjusted expenditures per FTE[b]

1989	77.4	114.1	91.1	94.6	122.0	98.2	110.0	$4,204
1992	77.3	116.0	88.9	92.0	123.1	97.3	114.7	4,797
1997	86.5	109.8	92.2	95.3	107.3	100.7	109.6	5,780
2001	79.9	100.0	96.2	99.2	97.5	101.9	115.3	7,007

Annual spending growth rate (percent)

1989–1992	4.45	5.07	3.64	3.56	4.81	4.17	5.95	4.50
1992–2001	4.69	2.59	5.22	5.18	1.63	4.83	4.37	4.30

Notes:
a. Weighted FTE for 1993 is used for 1989 to 1992.
b. Expenditures are divided by a cost index constructed from a cost regression (appendix table 5.A.1).

Table 5.10
Relative equity measures for Kansas school districts before and after 1992 education reform

Category	State-set general fund budget[a]		Operating spending[b]		Estimated total spending[c]	
	Pupil coefficient of variation[d]	Gini coefficient	Pupil coefficient of variation[d]	Gini coefficient	Pupil coefficient of variation[d]	Gini coefficient
Expenditures per weighted FTE[e]						
1989	10.44	0.060	10.44	0.060		
1992	11.52	0.066	11.52	0.066	14.83	0.080
1993	2.97	0.010	8.73	0.052	11.52	0.066
1997	0.03	0.000	10.75	0.065	13.91	0.084
2001	0.04	0.000	6.67	0.039	11.49	0.069
Cost-adjusted expenditures per FTE[f]						
1989	14.27	0.075	14.27	0.075		
1992	14.48	0.076	14.48	0.076	17.84	0.090
1993	14.39	0.072	12.16	0.064	14.40	0.075
1997	13.39	0.067	12.03	0.064	15.39	0.082
2001	12.47	0.062	10.85	0.057	14.91	0.080

Notes:

a. State-set spending level multiplied by the weighted FTE in a district ($n = 301$). General fund spending used in 1989 and 1992.

b. State-set spending level plus local-option budget and state aid for LOB ($n = 301$). General fund spending used in 1989 and 1992.

c. Operating spending plus locally raised revenue for capital, debt service, and other categories ($n = 297$).

d. Pupil coefficient of variation is calculated by taking ratio of pupil-weighted average and pupil-weighted standard deviation.

e. Weighted FTE for 1993 is used for 1989 to 1992.

f. Expenditures are divided by a cost index constructed from a cost regression (appendix table 5.A.1).

those for state-set budgets, which showed significant improvement after the reform.

Finally, we include local property tax levies to support capital spending and debt service in the total spending estimates. When expenditures per weighted pupil with these tax levies included are analyzed, it becomes less clear that equity has improved since reform. Equity seems to have improved right after the reform in 1993 and 1994, to have worsened from 1995 to 1997, and then to have improved again after 1997. Overall, the improvement in relative equity in regard to total education spending is shown to have been modest at best, even using the pupil weights developed by the state. When cost-adjusted total spending per pupil is used as the measure of educational outcomes, some small equity improvement is evident right after the reform, but there is little evidence of change after this early improvement.

5.2.5   Outcome Equity Analysis

Although courts and legislatures are hesitant to make student outcomes formally the principal object of education finance reforms, the bottom line for most such reforms is whether they result in improvements in student performance and educational attainment. Kansas has traditionally had some of the highest performance on national tests in the country (Glasnapp and Poggio 2001). Prior to the reform of the state's education finance system, however, significant performance differences existed across students and districts. To examine the impacts of the finance reform on outcomes, we have looked at both dropout rates and measures of student achievement. Ideally an analysis of outcome equity in the state would be based on comparable test scores for students before and after the reform. Unfortunately, Kansas made major changes to the tests it uses for statewide assessments in 1995 and again in 2000. Thus, the only consistent series of scores we have for achievement tests are those for math and reading exams between 1995 and 1999. We first look at changes in performance by type of district before turning to an examination of overall relative equity effects.

Table 5.11 provides a view of how the reform affected student performance in different types of districts. Average district student performance levels on statewide tests and average district dropout rates are compared to the state average. Overall, dropout rates did not

Table 5.11
District performance measures relative to state average by district type before and after 1992 education reform

Category	Index relative to state average (average = 100)							
	Large cities	Wealthy Kansas City suburbs	Other cities	Medium sized, East Kansas	Mineral wealth, West Kansas	Small, high-poverty	Very small, not high-poverty	State average rate
Dropout rates								
1990	249.3	102.2	195.1	126.4	39.8	52.0	13.6	1.62
1992	208.1	62.5	149.8	99.0	104.5	71.5	56.2	2.91
1993	241.1	56.6	176.2	83.4	156.6	37.1	52.2	2.52
1997	290.5	58.3	160.5	57.2	82.1	41.4	90.5	2.44
1998	247.9	48.8	187.1	71.0	111.0	64.2	32.0	2.35
2000	236.7	57.4	150.9	75.3	112.6	67.0	61.7	2.07
Average rate (1989–1992)	5.06	1.74	3.77	2.47	1.85	1.46	0.93	2.27
Average rate (1993–2000)	5.96	1.29	3.96	1.68	2.72	1.21	1.39	2.34
Average percentage passing math test[b]								
1995	88.6	117.8	98.5	99.0	92.4	99.2	104.7	46.2
1999	88.6	121.8	101.9	107.0	99.1	93.9	97.4	48.4
Average rate (1995–1999)	41.9	56.7	47.4	48.8	45.3	45.6	47.7	47.3
Average percentage passing reading test[b]								
1996	90.6	107.8	98.7	101.9	102.3	96.7	105.6	63.8
1999	89.7	107.2	97.3	102.2	99.5	97.2	108.7	64.2
Average rate (1996–1999)	90.1	107.5	98.0	102.0	100.9	96.9	107.2	64.0

Notes:
a. Total dropouts divided by total enrollment in grades 7 to 12 ($n = 260$).
b. Percentage of students reaching proficiency as determined by the Kansas Department of Education ($n = 295$ for math, $n = 297$ for reading).

improve much after the reform either statewide or in any of the district groups (except the wealthy suburbs around Kansas City). The city districts had by far the highest dropout rates in the state, 1.5 to 2.5 times the state average. Relative to the state average, dropout rates in the city districts first worsened after the reform, but eventually returned to levels similar to those right before the reform. Dropout rates in the small rural districts remained well below the state average in the 1990s but did not improve. The districts showing the largest relative improvements in dropout rates in the 1990s were the Kansas City suburbs and medium-sized districts in eastern Kansas, in which rates are now well below the state average. Turning to test score results overall there was little improvement in the average passing rate in the state on the statewide reading and math tests from 1995 to 1999. Performance on the tests in the large city districts was 10 to 15 percent below the state average before the reform and has not improved. Performance has remained the highest in the wealthy Kansas City suburbs despite a relative reduction in education spending there since the reform.

Table 5.12 provides relative equity measures for dropout rates and for passing rates on the statewide math and reading exams. First, especially in comparison to those for spending, the equity measures for dropout rates indicate substantial inequity in educational attainment across Kansas students and school districts. In addition, the measures show that relative equity declined significantly after the reform, instead of getting better. These equity results may be affected, however, by the volatility of the dropout rate across years, particularly in small districts. To examine whether this volatility affected the results, we took averages of dropout rates for 1990–1992 and compared these averages to those for 1994–1996 and 1998–2000. The results still indicate a decline in relative equity after the reform.

Turning to student test performance measures, despite the fact that the only consistent data are postreform, we would nevertheless expect a pattern of improvement in these postreform data if the reform directed significant new resources to districts with poor test performance on average. The story that emerges from table 5.12 suggests little increase in equity at best, and possibly a significant decline in relative equity for tenth-grade math exams.

5.2.6 Other Equity Standards

Even if large improvements in relative equity in spending or outcomes have not resulted from the reform, it is still possible that the reform

Table 5.12
Relative equity measures for Kansas school districts after 1992 education reform: Student outcome measures

Cate-gory	Dropout rates[a]	Math exams: Percentage passing[b]			Reading exams: Percentage passing[b]		
		Fourth Grade	Seventh Grade	Tenth Grade	Fourth Grade	Seventh Grade	Tenth Grade
Pupil coefficient of variation[c]							
1992	59.61						
1995	63.10	11.75	12.57	11.60			
1996	65.73	11.45	13.38	12.85	8.12	7.55	6.14
1997	78.29	11.93	13.39	12.51	8.77	7.70	6.32
1998	69.16	12.27	14.52	13.69	8.83	7.97	6.58
1999	70.26	12.40	14.09	15.60	9.06	7.97	6.32
Gini coefficient							
	0.4844						
1995	0.4836	0.0658	0.0699	0.0648			
1996	0.5458	0.0640	0.0749	0.0709	0.0448	0.0419	0.0344
1997	0.5913	0.0666	0.0750	0.0698	0.0475	0.0421	0.0347
1998	0.5297	0.0685	0.0811	0.0756	0.0485	0.0435	0.0359
1999	0.5701	0.0702	0.0792	0.0846	0.0488	0.0436	0.0345

Notes:
a. Total dropouts divided by total enrollment in grades 7 to 12 ($n = 260$).
b. Percentage of students reaching proficiency as determined by the Kansas Department of Education ($n = 295$ for math, $n = 297$ for reading).
c. Coefficient of variation is calculated by taking pupil-weighted standard deviation and average.

could have led to improvements using other equity standards. One other standard that has been associated with relative equity is fiscal neutrality. Under this standard, equity has been achieved if the link between district resources (or student performance) and the fiscal capacity or fiscal health of a district has been broken. We calculated the correlation between several different spending measures and property wealth per pupil. An index of fiscal health was also correlated with the same spending measures. The fiscal health index we employed is calculated as the ratio of assessed property value in a district and our cost index. A ratio above one indicates a district with above-average fiscal health. The results reported in table 5.13 suggest that the reform has led to significant improvements in fiscal neutrality. The correlations we calculated have decreased from 0.3 and higher in the early 1990s to

Table 5.13
Fiscal neutrality analysis: Correlations of operating spending per FTE with district wealth

Year	Per-pupil assessed value		Fiscal health index[a]	
	Spending per weighted FTE	Cost-adjusted spending	Spending per weighted FTE	Cost-adjusted spending
1989	0.29*	0.25*	0.26*	0.23*
1992	0.48*	0.41*	0.42*	0.37*
1993	0.30*	0.21*	0.27*	0.18*
1995	0.28*	0.17*	0.25*	0.15*
1997	0.23*	0.17*	0.21*	0.14*
1999	0.21*	0.11*	0.23*	0.12*
2001	0.04	0.05	0.09	0.05

Notes:
a. Defined as assessed value per pupil relative to state average divided by cost index developed from cost regression (appendix table 5.A.1).
*Different from zero at 5 percent level of statistical significance.

below 0.1 by 2001 and are not different from zero at the 5 percent level of statistical significance. Thus, the reform does appear to have successfully broken the overall link between resources and district fiscal capacity and health.[32]

The equity standard most consistent with the standards movement of the last decade is performance adequacy. The goal of performance adequacy is to assure that students achieve a minimum level of student performance, not to limit high-performing students and districts. In our analysis of performance adequacy, we examine whether levels of student performance in the lowest-spending and lowest-performing districts have improved since the reform. In other words, did the reform help to bring up the bottom of the distribution? The focus on the lower half of the distribution is consistent with the emphasis on adequacy standards in most states. Ideally, we would examine how Kansas students are performing relative to state standards for achievement, but Kansas is still in the process of developing such standards. Instead, we will examine the size of the gaps between spending and student outcomes for certain districts and a certain standard.

One common equity measure of the lower half of a distribution is the McLoone index. This index is simply, in this particular application, the ratio of the pupil-weighted sum of spending (or performance) for districts below the median to the pupil-weighted sum of spending (or

Table 5.14
Closing of the operating spending gap for Kansas school districts before and after the education reform in 1992: McLoone index[a]

Year	Expenditures per weighted FTE[b]	Cost-adjusted budget[c]	Dropout rates[d]	Math exams (fourth Grade)	Percentage passing[e] (tenth Grade)
1989	0.94	0.89			
1990	0.94	0.89	0.60		
1991	0.94	0.89	0.65		
1992	0.94	0.88	0.56		
1993	0.95	0.89	0.48		
1994	0.94	0.89	0.58		
1995	0.93	0.89	0.52	0.90	0.92
1996	0.93	0.89	0.53	0.91	0.93
1997	0.92	0.90	0.43	0.90	0.91
1998	0.92	0.90	0.51	0.90	0.93
1999	0.92	0.92	0.51	0.90	0.89
2000	0.94	0.91	0.53		
2001	0.95	0.90			

Notes:
a. Sum of spending for districts below the median divided by the product of median per-pupil spending and the total number of students in these districts. One minus the McLoone index is interpreted as the spending gap between districts below the median and median spending ($n = 297$).
b. Weighted FTE for 1993 is used for 1989 to 1992.
c. Expenditures are divided by a cost index constructed from a cost regression (appendix table 5.A.1).
d. Total dropouts divided by total enrollment in grades 7 to 12 ($n = 260$).
e. Percentage of students reaching proficiency as determined by the Kansas Department of Education ($n = 295$ for math, $n = 297$ for reading).

performance) at the median. One minus the McLoone index measures the size (as a percentage of the median) of the gap that is still remaining between spending (or performance) in these districts and the median spending (or performance among districts in the state. We have calculated McLoone indexes for adjusted operating spending and student performance measures (table 5.14). The gaps between spending in these districts and median spending were quite small in 1992, typically 10 percent or less, and they have not been reduced since the reform. A similar story emerges when McLoone indexes are calculated for dropout rates and math exam performance.

5.3 Conclusions

With the impetus of pending court action, Kansas undertook a major reform of its school finance system in 1992 to increase relative educational equity in the state substantially. In terms of its magnitude and scope, the School District Finance and Quality Performance Act is one of most comprehensive school finance reforms attempted by a state. In contrast to reforms for similar purposes undertaken in Michigan and Vermont, the basic components of the Kansas reform are simple. The state sets a general fund budget for all districts, which is adjusted for each district for cost differences from district to district using pupil weights. The state also sets a basic property tax levy to be imposed by all districts. The difference between the pupil-weighted budget and the local tax effort is either provided in aid, if the difference is positive, or reverts to the state, if the difference is negative. In recognition of both political constraints and potential efficiency effects of imposing an absolute limit on education spending, the state includes a safety valve, the local-option budget, which each district can use, to supplement the pupil-weighted budget for the district up to 25 percent. In essence, the state thereby is permitting up to 25 percent variation around the absolute equity standard it has set. Although our original assessment of the Kansas reform raised questions about the potential impact of the LOB over time on relative equity, we suggested that the "local option budget could be viewed as a moderate price to pay for what it permits— political acceptance of a highly centralized, explicitly redistributive government initiative in a politically conservative state" (Johnston and Duncombe 1998, 155). Our updated evaluation of this reform provides a less optimistic assessment of the relative equity improvements resulting from the Kansas reform. Two factors have conspired to greatly limit the reform's equalizing impact.

First, the LOB has grown significantly in importance since the reform was implemented, in part because of the state's abandonment of its commitment to fund fully the more equitable financing system for its public schools that it had envisioned in formulating the reform. In assuming nearly two-thirds of total funding responsibility, and by curtailing most local budget control, the state assumed a powerful role in public education vis à vis local school districts, one that we argue is among the most powerful in the country. Instead of raising the basic general fund budget in line with growth of inflation and income, however, the state government increased the basic budget very slowly, with a rate of growth well below the rate of inflation. Although the state budget for education increased significantly, most of the growth was to fund a major decrease in the basic local school tax rate from 32 to 20 mills.

Districts have therefore relied on the LOB to fill the budget gaps created by the lack of full state financial support. Even with a state matching grant to encourage LOB use among poorer school districts, the heaviest LOB users are still primarily districts with higher income, property wealth, and lower shares of minority students. To compound the inequities caused by the LOB, the state has allowed districts to finance capital improvements using an additional local levy. The patterns of use of this levy mirror those of the LOB, in part because the state has added some provisions to the law to appease some of the wealthier suburban districts in the state.

The second component of the system that has greatly weakened relative equity improvements is the weighted-pupil counts constructed by the state to adjust for cost differences. The weighted-pupil measure is dominated by low-enrollment weights, and to a lesser extent transportation weights, both of which favor the rural districts of western Kansas. Whereas the low-enrollment weights for districts might have some basis in research, the very low weights assigned to at-risk and bilingual students are hard to justify. The resulting weighted-pupil counts greatly favor rural districts at the expense of urban districts, which have most of minority students living in the state. Some analysts and advocates indicate that the problems created by the low-enrollment weighting system could be reduced by recalibration of the weights for high-need students and by increased state funding (Baker 2001b; Baker and Imber 1999; Tallman 2002). Our own assessment of the costs of educating a high-need student indicates a significantly larger effect of poverty, especially in the large urban districts, than is reflected in the weighted-pupil measure.

The difference in the size of the at-risk pupil adjustment in the Kansas system and in ours accounts for the very different pictures that emerge from this study on the relative equity effects of the Kansas reform. Using the weighted-pupil measures developed by the state, the reform appears to have significantly improved relative equity in the state, even when the LOB is included. Using our cost-adjusted expenditures, however, the relative equity improvements seem to have been modest at best. For the three large city districts, where a quarter of the children in the state live, the reform has resulted in little closing of the resource or spending gap. The one bright spot in the equity assessment is fiscal neutrality. The reform appears to have broken the overall link between resources and outcomes and the fiscal capacity and health of school districts. Thus, the equity impacts of the reform are truly in the eye of the beholder. The state can claim success, whereas some needy districts feel, perhaps legitimately, that the reform has done little to help them reach academic standards.

One of our earlier conclusions was that the state's decision to diminish local control over district education spending might be unsupportable over time, even under the best of circumstances. This analysis suggests that during the past eleven years, many of which were among the most prosperous in decades, local districts have benefitted relatively little from the reform in terms of increased state education funding, and districts have become increasingly hostile over the suppression of local control. The stage has been set for a major conflict between the local interests that deal daily with education needs and the state policymakers who have, so far, refused to consider raising new revenues to meet their public school funding responsibilities. The current situation suggests that although the state originally intended, through the reform it introduced, to reduce disparities in public school funding, in actuality relative equity in the state may have increased very little, and the reform has not significantly increased resources and student performance for the students and districts with the greatest needs.

Appendix 5.A: Cost Model for Kansas School Districts

Table 5.A.1
Cost model for Kansas school districts (Regression results for 1997)

Variable	Coefficient	t-statistic
Intercept	4.1432	1.16
Performance measues		
Percentage passing: Math[a]	0.0134	1.99
Percentage passing: Reading[a]	−0.0055	−0.52
Dropout rates	−0.0340	−1.30
Cost factors		
Average teacher salary[b]	0.6678	1.98
Pupils (FTE)[b]	−0.6715	−7.56
Pupils squared[b]	0.0368	6.40
Percentage of children in poverty	0.2433	1.64
Child poverty rate in large districts[c]	0.9399	2.35
Bilingual hours per FTE	0.4445	1.79
Efficiency factors[d]		
Per-pupil property values	0.0000001	1.89
Per-pupil state aid	−0.0023300	−1.51
Median household income	0.0000046	1.59
Adj. R^2	0.73	
SSE	2.87	

Notes: The regression conducted was a two-stage least-squares regression with the dependent variable as actual operating expenditures per FTE ($n = 289$). Dropout rates, reading and math scores, and teacher salaries are treated as endogenous. See chapter text for details on instruments.

a. Average percentage of students passing exam in fourth, seventh, and tenth grades, except for reading, for which the test is given in third grade. Student performance for 1995 to 1997 was averaged to avoid possible cohort effects.

b. Variable is expressed as a natural logarithm.

c. Poverty rate in districts with enrollments of 10,000 students or more.

d. Measured in relation to the average for this variable in districts in same county and adjacent counties. See chapter text for details.

Notes

1. During the consolidation reforms of the 1960s, the number of Kansas school districts was reduced from over 1,600 to 306.

2. The formula can be expressed as

$$A_i = E_i - (W(E_i/E^*) \times t^*) - R = E_i(1 - (Wt^*/E^*)) - R,$$

where A_i is per-pupil aid to district i, E_i is per-pupil spending in district i, E^* is the state-set budget per pupil, W is a measure of district wealth that includes property wealth and income, t^* is the state-set local effort rate, and R is local revenue from other authorized sources. If the expected local tax effort, Wt^*, generates less than the state-set budget per pupil, E^*, then the district received positive aid (subtracting off other revenue); otherwise it received no aid (Kansas Legislative Research Department 1991).

3. The local effort rate was calculated as $E_i/E^* \times t^*$, where E^* is the "norm" operating spending for a particular enrollment group. Kansas tried several different enrollment class schemas over the years, but the norm spending level was always set substantially higher for districts with enrollment below 400 than for those with enrollments over 2,000.

4. These disparities were exacerbated by the state's income tax rebate to the districts. The lowest district rebate per pupil was $0 (some districts with relatively low mill levies received no rebate aid), and the highest was $1,413.

5. All residential real property in Kansas is assessed at 12 percent of market value. Agricultural, commercial, and industrial properties are assessed at 30 percent of market value. When the 1992 reform was enacted, the state was still reeling from a complete overhaul of property valuation implemented in the late 1980s.

6. For a detailed discussion of the legislative process involved in the adoption of the new school finance system, see Tallman 1993. Tallman, a lobbyist for the Kansas Association of School Boards, was a first-hand observer throughout much of the legislative session devoted to this topic.

7. Originally, the state-mandated property mill levy (32 mills, subsequently increased to 35 mills, then decreased to 20 mills) was to be imposed and collected directly by the state. In recognition of the psychological threat posed by such a system (i.e., state assumption of the local property tax base) legislators suggested an alternative (Tallman 1993). Counties would collect the property tax revenues and remit them to local school districts, as they had in the past. State aid would be used to fill the gap between those revenues and required spending. Balances remaining in local district budgets would then be returned to the state at the end of the fiscal year (with the exception of those funds in which some balance carryover was permitted). Despite the fact that local collection and retention was in fact only cosmetic—the state would continue to determine the level of taxing and spending—such an arrangement was viewed as more acceptable to local interests, including local banks and other traditional school fund depositories (Tallman 1993).

8. To fund the reform, the legislature raised the state retail sales tax rate from 4.25 to 4.9 percent, increased state income taxes by more than $100 million, and repealed sales tax exemptions for original construction, services, and utilities used in production (Kansas Association of School Boards 1994).

9. The actual process for determining the weighting factors for districts with more than 100 students involves five steps. Using the case of a district with 200 students the steps

involve (1) calculating an adjustment factor per pupil for each enrollment class ($9.655 for this class); (2) multiplying this adjustment factor by the difference between the district's enrollment and the lower enrollment limit for the class $(9.655 \times (200 - 100) = \$965.5)$; (3) subtracting this number from the median budget for the class before $(\$7,337 - \$965.5 = \$6,371.5)$; (4) taking the ratio of the result in step (3) to the median budget for districts with enrollment over 1,900 and subtracting 1 $(\$6,371.5/\$3,426 - 1 = 0.86)$; and (5) multiplying the result in (4) by the FTE to arrive at the additional "weighted" enrollment for low enrollment $(0.86 \times 200 = 171.9)$ (Kansas Legislative Research Department 2001b). Thus the district in this example would receive aid for 371.9 (200 + 171.9) students, even though its actual enrollment is 200.

10. Households receiving Food Stamps, Aid to Dependent Children, or Temporary Assistance to Needy Families, or those participating in the Food Distribution Program on Indian Reservations, are also eligible for free lunch. A description of the program and eligibility requirements is available on the Food and Nutrition Service website at ⟨http://www.fns.usda.gov/cnd/Lunch/AboutLunch/faqs.htm⟩.

11. The weight increased to 10 percent in 2001–02, with the additional 1 percent earmarked for use by the districts to promote mastery of third-grade reading skills.

12. Each year the KSDE determines the "best-fit curve" for the graph of transportation cost per transported student (over 2.5 miles) compared to transported pupil density (number of transported students divided by land area). For each district, the acceptable cost per transported student is determined by finding the point on the curve associated with the transported pupil density in that district.

13. Tests are administered in one elementary, and one junior high, and one high school grade (e.g., grades 4, 7, and 10 for math). The tests are criterion-referenced as opposed to norm-referenced, with the intent of measuring student performance against the Kansas curriculum standards and providing information to individual schools about whether their students are mastering skills outlined in the curriculum and are improving over time (State of Kansas Division of Legislative Post Audit 1996).

14. Performance indicators include graduation and dropout rates, enrollments in advanced math and science classes, and suspension and expulsion rates (Kansas Association of School Boards 1994).

15. As in many states, legislative debate in Kansas on the issue of curriculum standards evoked criticism from conservatives about the substance and influence of such topics as sex education; concerns centered on the notion of eroding parental control over education content (Tallman 1993). Subsequent state board of education curriculum debates included the now-famous (and temporary) addition of so-called creationism as a credible theory in science education. Although the state board of education never actually required modification of science curricula, it did put districts on notice that as a legitimate item in the new curriculum standards, creationism—and other alternatives to evolutionary theory—could be included in science assessment tests.

16. The new reform imposed no limit on the tax rate (mill levy) that can be used to finance principal and interest payments related to bonds. However, if bond indebtedness exceeds 14 percent of district assessed property valuation, state approval is required for the issuance of the additional debt. One of the potential problems with the bond and interest fund and the capital outlay fund is that they might encourage districts to use more capital-intensive teaching methods (computer aided instruction) that may not be cost-effective. Consequently, incentives may exist for districts to shift expenses into these

funds, which could have consequences for the equity effects of the reform and productive efficiency.

17. Other exemptions to the spending limits include the provision for a 2 percent contingency fund, the special education fund, and other programs supporting teacher training, parent education, and school innovations. Of these the special education fund is the most important, since spending in this area constituted over 15 percent of general fund budgets in 1994. Aid is provided to districts to cover a portion of the additional costs of these students (above the standard $3,600). Given the significant financial support provided for special education and the potential discretion districts have in classifying students as eligible for special education services, particularly those with limited disabilities (e.g., mild learning disabilities), special education has been one of the fastest-growing expenditure categories in education in many states (Lankford and Wyckoff 1996).

18. Permissible capital outlays include land, building acquisition and repair, and equipment purchase, including computers.

19. It only took two years for districts to realize that the LOB and low-enrollment weighting provisions had created winners and losers in the new system. Some of the "loser" districts, many of them only somewhat larger than low-enrollment districts, but saddled with far lower state-authorized per-pupil budgets, banded together with other districts and began to express dissatisfaction with the reform. In 1994, they sued the state, alleging that the new system was unfair and that it infringed on local control (*Unified School District No. 229 v. Kansas* 1994). The plaintiffs lost, and the court rebuffed their request for relief from the low-enrollment weighting provision of the reform. In 2000, the state was sued again, this time in federal district court, by a plaintiff alleging that the reform has "adverse disparate impacts" on districts with relatively high minority enrollments (*Robinson v. State of Kansas et al.* 2000), in violation of federal civil rights laws. The court refused the state's motion to dismiss, and the case has proceeded to the Federal Circuit Court of Appeals. Most recently, in November 2001, Judge Bullock dismissed a suit by plaintiffs alleging that under the reform, the state had failed to provide a "suitable" education to all districts because of funding disparities created by the LOB and other reform provisions (*Montoy v. Kansas* 2001). In this case, the judge invoked the quality performance accreditation portion of the reform, which created a body to review and accredit individual districts. Noting that the plaintiff districts had met accreditation standards, Judge Bullock suggested that the plaintiffs must therefore be providing a "suitable" education.

20. One legislator notes that rural lawmakers agreed to correlation weighting because they recognized the growing political and legal threat to the low-enrollment weighting system. They calculated that support of correlation weighting was preferable to reductions in their districts' budgets that might result from downward adjustments to the low-enrollment weights. Districts with decreasing enrollments were provided with relief through a declining-enrollment provision adopted in a 1993 amendment and subsequently altered in 1997 and 1999. Currently, the average district FTE level for the current and preceding two budget years is used as the current FTE level for purposes of the general fund per-pupil budget.

21. For all districts operating at full 25 percent LOB authority (i.e., those that are "maxed out"), an additional pupil weight may be added to the total weighted FTE for the first two years in which new facilities are operated. The State Board of Tax Appeals must approve the district's levy request for additional funds to cover new school operation. The weight is derived by dividing the amount generated from the levy by the district's base state aid per pupil.

22. Local levy authority for capital outlay purposes had been capped at 4 mills. This cap was recently suspended by the legislature, but increases in the local levy are subject to voter protest petition. In addition, a provision passed in 2001 was designed to maximize LOB revenue authority by altering the treatment of special education aid. This provision stipulates that the ratio of the special education categorical aid to the base state aid per pupil will serve as an additional number of weighted pupils. The state aid revenue generated from this calculation is deposited into the district's general fund in order to increase LOB revenues by temporarily inflating the district's general fund budget. Since the LOB is determined by multiplying a fixed percent (maximum of 25 percent) by state-set general fund budget, an increase in this budget will increase the LOB. The special education aid revenues are then deposited, as required, in the district's special education fund. It is possible that this provision could provide an additional incentive for districts to overclassify children as qualifying for special education services.

23. The district types were developed to provide a richer picture of how the reform affected selected districts in Kansas. Only a small sample (44 of the 304) of districts is accounted for in these classifications, but according to staff at the Kansas Association of School Boards, they are representative of distinct categories of districts in the state. The categories include (1) large cities (Kansas City, Wichita, and Topeka); (2) wealthy Kansas City suburbs (Blue Valley, Olathe, Shawnee Mission); (3) other cities (Lawrence, Salina, Manhattan, Garden City, Dodge City, and Liberal); (4) medium-sized districts in East Kansas (Ottawa, Pratt, Desoto, Hiawatha); (5) small districts with high property wealth because of natural gas, oil, or a nuclear power plant (Moscow, Hugoton, and Burlington); (6) districts with enrollments below 300 pupils and child poverty rates above 27 percent; and (7) very small districts with enrollments below 140 and poverty rates below 18 percent).

24. For example, if 17 districts of 100 pupils each are consolidated into a district of 1,700, the estimated cost savings are 65 percent (Duncombe and Yinger 2001b). The implied pupil weight of 1.86 $[(1/0.35) - 1]$ is higher than the weight in the Kansas formula. For eight districts of 200, the cost savings would be 45 percent, which is equivalent to a student weight of 0.82 $[(1/0.55) - 1]$.

25. Because spending per pupil in a district may also be higher because the district has more resources (leading to higher student performance), or because it uses its resources inefficiently, we have included several measures of student performance and efficiency. The cost model was estimated using two-stage least-squares regression. Three performance measures are included in the model: dropout rates and the average of student passing rates on examinations for math in fourth, seventh, and tenth grades and for reading in third, seventh, and tenth grades. The performance measures from 1995 to 1997 are averaged to remove large variation, particularly in very small districts, caused by cohort effects. Performance measures and average teacher salaries are treated as endogenous, because they can be determined as part of the budget process. Instruments were selected that were related to these performance measures but were not statistically significant when entered in the regression separately with performance. The instruments for a district are derived primarily from averages of other school districts in its county and in adjacent counties (enrollment, child poverty in 1990, bilingual student share, dropout rate, average math score, median house value in 1990, federal aid per pupil, population density, tax share, and average private wages in wholesale trade, retail trade, management services, and public services). Several efficiency variables were also included in the model. They were measured by averages of variables related to the fiscal capacity of a district (median household income in 1990, per-pupil property values, and per-pupil state aid) for districts in the same county or adjacent counties. These factors

have been found in other studies to relate to district efficiency (Duncombe and Yinger 2001b).

26. The weighted pupil index is constructed by taking the ratio of the weighted FTE to the regular FTE for each district and dividing this ratio by the state average for this ratio (then multiplying the result by 100). The simple average of this ratio for school districts is 1.54.

27. A recent study commissioned by the Kansas legislature (Augenblick et al. 2002) recommends changes in the current weighting system in the interests of adequacy (or a "suitable" education). Using both a "professional judgment" approach and a "successful school" approach, the study recommends differential funding levels for schools in four different size categories designed especially to compensate for higher costs in districts of small and moderate size. The professional judgment approach is based on the resource cost model and "market basket" models used in other studies. Educators are asked to specify resources they deem necessary for "prototype" schools to meet performance expectations. The successful school approach identifies schools that are currently meeting performance expectations and estimates costs based on their spending patterns (Augenblick et al. 2002).

28. A Tobit regression was employed, since over the half the districts in 1997 did not use the LOB (truncated at zero). For consistency we continued to use the Tobit for 2000, even though close to 90 percent of districts used a LOB.

29. Regression results for capital spending are available from the authors on request.

30. Tallman (2002) suggests that the reform politics focused more on tax equity than on spending equity, and much more on spending equity than outcome equity.

31. See Berne and Stiefel 1984 for a comprehensive review of education equity measures. The Gini coefficient is determined by ranking districts according to the per-pupil expenditure measure and the number of pupils. It measures the relative gap from district to district between actual spending by the district and equal per-pupil spending.

32. When correlations are calculated between per-pupil assessed value or the fiscal health index and measures of student performance, none of the correlations is statistically significant. It should be noted that with regard to the dropout rates, the correlations were negative and different at the 5 percent level of statistical significance from zero in 1991, but not in 1992. Thus, it is not possible to attribute the improvement in fiscal neutrality definitively to the reform.

6

A Decade of Reform: The Impact of School Reform in Kentucky

Ann E. Flanagan and Sheila E. Murray

6.1 Introduction

In 1989 the Kentucky Supreme Court ruled in *Rose v. Council for Better Education, Inc.* that the state's entire education system—governance, curriculum, and finance system—was unconstitutional. The court instructed the state to create an "efficient system of common schools" (1) and to create a system that had "substantial uniformity, substantial equality of financial resources, and substantial equal educational opportunity for all students" (191–192). The state responded by passing the Kentucky Education Reform Act of 1990 (KERA), which completely overhauled the financing, organization, and curriculum of K–12 education in Kentucky.

Rose has turned out to be a very influential case. The *Rose* decision inspired other courts to go well beyond equality in spending in their examinations of state education finance systems and instead focus on ensuring that all students in the state have equitable access to adequate educational opportunities. Indeed, the New Hampshire Supreme Court looked to the Kentucky case for "establishing general, aspirational guidelines for defining educational adequacy" (*Claremont School District et al. v. Governor et al.* [1997, 7]). The Ohio Supreme Court cites KERA as a guideline (see *DeRolph v. State*, 1997, first concurring opinion).

In addition, the reforms outlined in KERA to address educational adequacy were arguably the most comprehensive experiment in educational reform to date. Prior to KERA, state education systems were reformed incrementally: States typically introduced curriculum reforms and education finance reforms separately. Educators and policymakers both in and outside of Kentucky hailed the Kentucky reforms. The former governor referred to KERA as "the most important legislation enacted in the state since the adoption of its constitution" (Jennings 1990). The Kennedy School and Ford Foundation named KERA as one of the 1997 Innovations in American Government Award winners.

In the fourteen years since *Rose*, Kentucky has fully implemented a new education finance system, a revision and standardization of its curriculum, an accountability system, and a school-based governance structure. Our goal in this chapter is to examine the impact of changes in state education aid under KERA. Specifically, we investigate how inequality in educational resources has changed in Kentucky since KERA and what effect changes in school spending have had on student achievement in the state.

The remainder of this chapter has the following organization. In section 6.2 we describe the education finance system in Kentucky in the pre- and post-KERA years. Because curriculum and governance reforms were implemented in Kentucky alongside finance reforms, we describe Kentucky's experiences developing an assessment and accountability system and implementing school-based decision-making councils. In section 6.3 we discuss the impact of KERA on resource inequality in the state, and in section 6.4, we discuss the impact of KERA on educational outcomes. The final section presents a brief summary of the chapter.

6.2   Background and Overview of the Landmark *Rose* Decision in State Education Reform

6.2.1   Student Outcomes in Pre-KERA Kentucky
In the years prior to KERA, on almost every indicator of educational quality, Kentucky ranked in the lowest 25 percent of states. For example, high school completion rates in Kentucky were consistently the lowest in the nation. Only 68 percent of ninth graders were graduating from high school in four years. In a national survey of functional literacy, Kentucky residents were among the lowest; in the remote Appalachian counties of the state, about half of the population was functionally illiterate (Trimble and Forsaith 1995). Finally, only 11 percent of Kentucky high school students took the SAT, compared to 42 percent overall in the United States.

6.2.2   School Finance in Pre-KERA Kentucky
Local school districts in Kentucky relied heavily on the property tax to fund schools. For example, in 1986–87 approximately 73 percent

of local revenues were derived from the property tax; the remaining local revenues came from occupational taxes and taxes on motor vehicles, utilities, or both. Because of the wide variation in districts' fiscal capacities (for example, in the year prior to *Rose*, local average property values ranged from $29,807 to $244,305 per pupil), local spending per pupil varied widely. Historically, state aid to districts was essentially distributed as flat grants without regard to variation in tax bases across districts. As early as the 1930s, Kentucky was aware of and tried to remedy the inequality that resulted from variations in local tax bases. In 1952 the state implemented the Minimum Foundation Program (MPF), which established a minimum foundation amount to be spent on a per-classroom (as defined by the state) basis throughout the state. To participate in the program, districts were required to tax property in a district at a uniform rate applied to the assessed value of the property. The state then provided the difference between the foundation amount and the required local effort. The state aid formula used to calculate the foundation amount gave additional resources for rural school districts,[1] and aid amounts from the state were adjusted for additional costs such as vocational instruction, instruction for exceptional children, and instruction for children schooled in the home and hospital.[2] In 1976, the state no longer enforced the local effort the program became essentially a flat grant, given to all districts, funded by a state property tax.

To provide funds to help equalize the disparities in local fiscal capacity, in 1976 the state passed the Power Equalization Program (PEP). Under this program, the state provided funds to districts to supplement revenues raised through a local property tax at a state-set rate, so that those revenues would be equal to the revenue raised by taxing at that same rate in the county with the highest property values. In 1989–90, to participate in the program, school districts were required to levy a minimum tax rate of twenty-five cents per hundred dollars of valuation.

Through these programs, the state provided funding for the majority (63 percent) of school spending. Despite the MFP and the PEP, however, levels of education spending in Kentucky were still very low.[3] In the 1988–89 school year, the year prior to KERA, only six other states spent less per pupil than Kentucky. Moreover, the state's efforts to reduce large variances in tax bases across districts were not successful in reducing spending inequality. First, as noted previously, the state did not require the local effort component of the MFP. Second, local school boards were unwilling to tax themselves at a rate that took full advantage of the PEP. (Although districts were required to tax at the minimum rate to receive the full available PEP supplement that would bring them to parity with the wealthiest district, districts that taxed below this rate still received an amount equal to what they had received the previous year, so they did receive some power equalization funds.) Third, the state did not enforce uniform fair-market valuations on property throughout the state. Finally, the legislature had discretion in determining final appropriations to the programs and rarely fully funded them.

6.2.3   KERA Finance Reforms: Support for Education Excellence in Kentucky

In the 1990–91 school year, the state began implementing the reforms to its education finance system established under KERA. These reforms were phased in over a five-year period and have not been substantially revised since their inception.[4] The new education finance system, called Support Education Excellence in Kentucky (SEEK), relies on three levels of funding: a base guarantee, adjusted for specific factors, and two optional programs. The legislature determines the amount of the per-student base guarantee. The SEEK base in 1990–91 was $2,305, and it has been increased every year since then; in the 1997–98 school year, SEEK guaranteed districts $2,839 per pupil. This base guarantee is augmented in each district by weights for the percentage of students at risk (defined as students eligible for the federal free and reduced-price lunch program) and for the number of exceptional children with special needs, weighted according to the severity of the disability. In addition, the base guarantee is increased for pupil transportation based on the population density of a school district and the number of students who are receiving educational services in a home or hospital setting. The legislature has not changed the weights for these adjustments since SEEK was implemented.

The adjusted base guarantee is basically the MFP simply calculated on a per-pupil basis rather than on a classroom basis. Under SEEK, however, the local effort component of the program is actually enforced. Each district must levy a property tax of thirty cents per hundred dollars of assessed value or raise an equivalent amount through other taxes. If a district's locally raised revenues fall below the total required to fund the adjusted base guarantee, the difference is provided by the state.

Districts may exceed the minimum (as embodied in the adjusted base guarantee) by as much as 49.5 percent through a two-tier optional program. Tier I is a matching component provides incentives for low-property-wealth districts to contribute local revenues beyond the required minimum. If district per-pupil property wealth is less than 150 percent of the statewide average, the state will provide the difference between what the district wants to contribute and the maximum tier I component (15 percent above the adjusted base guarantee). The second component of the optional program (tier II) allows districts to generate, through local levies, up to 30 percent above the adjusted base guarantee and tier I funds. The tier II funds are not matched or supplemented by the state, and any tax levied to raise tier II funds must be approved by a vote of the district residents.

In addition to the funding in the SEEK formula, the state provides limited funding to school districts through a number of categorical programs such as those for gifted and talented, extended school services, state agency children, early childhood education, vocational education, textbooks, teacher testing and internships, staff development, family resource and youth service centers, and regional service centers. These programs are relatively small, representing less than 9 percent of total state aid in 1998–99 (Murray 2001).

The key differences between the Kentucky education finance system after the KERA reforms and the pre-KERA finance system are the increased amount of state aid available (through the matching provisions and the increased amount provided through the adjusted base guarantee) and the enforcement of local effort provisions and full market value property assessments. Most of the reforms were enacted immediately; however, the full market valuations were not fully enforced until the 1994–95 fiscal year.

6.2.4 Curriculum Reforms: The Kentucky Instruction Results Information System and the Commonwealth Accountability Testing System

Whereas the reforms to Kentucky's education finance system were largely in place a year after *Rose* and have remained relatively intact, the state struggled for a number of years to develop performance standards, align the curriculum with these standards, and implement an accountability system. *Rose* provided very general guidelines for a curriculum that would define an adequate education. (These guidelines are given in chapter 2.) From these guidelines, the state developed a set of performance standards that were also very general. For example, the *Rose* decision stated that students should have "[s]ufficient oral and written communication skills to enable students to function in a complex and rapidly changing civilization" (191). The legislature added mathematical skills to this definition, suggesting that "[s]tudents should be able to use basic communication and mathematics skills for purposes and situation they will encounter throughout their lives" (KERA, 1). Initially, the Kentucky Department of Education responded with a set of standards that were similarly broad, even for core academic subjects. For example, one of the mathematics standards developed stated that students understand mathematical change concepts and use them appropriately and accurately without specifying the specific concepts that should be mastered.

After several iterations, in 1996 the state published and distributed to schools a set of more detailed curriculum guidelines in the *Core Content for Assessment* (Kentucky Department of Education 1996). Under these guidelines, the mathematics standard given above was replaced by a set of standards that described the specific content and concepts to be mastered by students in the elementary, middle, and high school grades. For example, a high school student, according to the 1996 guidelines, should be able to "explain how a change in one quantity affects a change in another" (p. 92). The guidelines also suggested concepts related to those specified in the standards, gave sample teaching and assessment strategies, and offered ideas for incorporating community resources into instruction. Schools were expected to align their curricula fully with these standards in the same year they were issued.

The state arrived at the current version of its system to hold schools accountable for the state standards over a number of years. The first accountability system it implemented after KERA, the Kentucky Instruction Results Information System (KIRIS), was an interim system based on the very general content standards initially issued by the Kentucky Department of Education (described previously) and was put into place in the 1991–92 school year.[5] Under KIRIS, students in grades 4, 8, and 12 participated in a four-part assessment composed of multiple-choice items, open-ended paper-and-pencil responses, performance events (complex tasks involving both group and individual work), and a writing portfolio assessment.

KIRIS broke new ground in holding schools accountable by establishing financial rewards and penalties for schools on the basis of changes in a single accountability index. The index was determined by averaging the results of KIRIS assessments with a variety of noncognitive indicators of student outcomes such as the school's attendance, dropout, and retention rates, and the postgraduation experiences of its students. KIRIS and the accountability index were sources of intense controversy. Large gains in scores on the KIRIS assessments were reported early on, but education researchers suggested that the gains were inflated, because teachers tailored their teaching too closely to the assessments and students focused unduly on the specific content of the tests rather than focusing on the broad domains of achievement that the tests were intended to represent (Koretz and Barron 1998).

The assessment system used in Kentucky has since been modified substantially. In 1995 the state dropped multiple-choice items from KIRIS because of the desire to emphasize performance-based assessments. The decision to drop the multiple-choice items was widely criticized, however, because the results of the performance-based assessments could not be externally validated. In response to these criticisms, Kentucky reinstituted a new version of the standardized test it had used pre-KERA—the Comprehensive Test of Basic Skills (CTBS-5) for reading, language arts, and mathematics in grades 3, 6, and 9. The performance events were dropped from the assessment system.

In 1998 the state incorporated the new assessment system into a new accountability system, the Commonwealth Accountability Testing System (CATS). Aside from the changes made through the years in the assessments used, the accountability system has remained largely unchanged. It averages the school-level performance in the assessments with indicators of noncognitive skills to determine a single accountability index. Scores on this accountability index are reported annually, but schools are formally evaluated on the basis of changes over a two-year period. Each school is assigned a performance target, and schools that exceeded their targets are given cash rewards. Schools that fall below the target are provided with improvement funds and are subject to oversight by a distinguished educator.

Other curriculum reforms included the establishment of an ungraded primary program (grouping children in multiage, multiability groups for grades K–3), a preschool program for low-income children, tutoring programs, and family resource and youth service centers for schools with at least 20 percent of students in need, as well as increased teacher compensation and funding for professional development and technology assistance.

6.2.5 Governance

KERA required that by 1996, schools form and put into place school-based decision-making councils to set school policies, the idea being that the members of the councils (the school's principal, its teachers, and the parents of students who attend the school) can better decide how meet the needs of their students than can district administrators. The responsibilities of the councils are outlined in appendix 6.B. School districts with only one school and schools performing above the state accountability index are exempt, however, from the school-based decision-making requirement. As of 2002, 98 percent of schools had implemented the councils. Only eighteen schools in the state were exempt from the requirement based on their accountability indexes, and eight schools were exempt because they were the only school in their district.

Other governance reforms outlined in KERA included granting the Kentucky Department of Education the authority to take over failing schools (in the past, the department had only the authority to take over failing districts) and to enforce antinepotism regulations.

6.3 Impact of KERA on Resource Inequality

Although it was clearly the court's intention in the *Rose* decision that Kentucky should address the wide variations in tax bases and student performance across school districts, there may be some reason to suspect that the state's legislature may not have implemented finance reform to a degree sufficient to address these variations. Since the implementation of the KERA reforms, the legislature has rarely appropriated enough money to fund the aid programs or enforce the mandates for full market value assessments of property. In this section we investigate changes since KERA in the variations across school districts in per-pupil revenues and changes in the level of per pupil-spending. We also look at whether the state has been able to target resources to historically low-wealth school districts.

In table 6.1, we present some important background material on education resources in Kentucky. In the first panel, we describe the distribution of education revenues in the state according to their source: local, state, or federal. In the 1986–87 school year, on average, schools' real total revenues (in 2000 dollars) per pupil were $3,923. About 65 percent of school spending came from state sources, local governments on average contributed about 24 percent, and the remaining 11 percent

Table 6.1
Distribution of Kentucky education resources, SY 1987–97

	Pre-KERA	Post-KERA	
Revenues per student (2000 dollars)	1986–87	1991–92	1996–97
Local	935	1,276	1,763
State	2,532	3,735	3,876
Federal	455	562	570
Total	3,923	5,574	6,210
Measures of inequality			
Gini coefficient	9.0	6.9	6.0
Log 95th-to-5th percentile ratio	.470	.347	.331
Theil index ($\times 1000$)	13.2	7.5	6.1

Sources: NCES various (1994, 2000) years; U.S. Census Bureau (1987, 1992, 1997).

came from federal sources. Revenues dramatically increased 42 percent in real terms in the five years between the 1986–87 and 1991–92 school years and leveled off between 1991–92 and 1996–97. The state continued to be a significant funder of school resources, although local contributions grew to about 28 percent in 1997.

In the table's next panel, we present three commonly used measures of inequality to characterize the variation in educational resources across districts in Kentucky: the Gini coefficient, the Theil index, and the ratio of expenditures of the district at the 95th percentile of per-pupil spending to the district at the 5th percentile. Lower values on each measure are associated with less inequality.[6] The ratio of the 95th percentile in per-pupil spending to the 5th percentile is a simple ranking that treats transfers to the top or bottom of the distribution the same; changes in spending in the rest of the distribution do not change the 95th-to-5th ratio. Changes throughout the distribution of spending contribute to the values of the Theil index and the Gini coefficient. The Theil index gives more weight to changes in the tails of the distribution, and the Gini coefficient gives more weight to changes in the middle. In compiling the table, we used district-level data from the U.S. Census Bureau's Census of Governments: School System Finance (F-33) file. The F-33 data contain annual statistics on school districts' revenues by source and expenditures by type.

All of the inequality measures in table 6.1 follow a similar pattern. Across all measures, inequality in educational resources has fallen sharply in Kentucky since the passage of KERA. For example, the Gini coefficient fell from 9.0 in 1987 to 6.9 two years after the start of the finance reforms. The Theil index dropped considerably, from 13.2 in the pre-KERA years to 7.5 in the post-KERA time period. The 95th-to-5th ratio also declined during this time period. Since 1992, however, the reduction in inequality has tapered off: The reductions between 1992 and 1997 were significantly smaller than those immediately following the implementation of KERA. Picus, Odden, and Fermanich (2001), using similar measures, also find that inequality in Kentucky has declined in the ten years since the passage of KERA. They also find, however, that some of the reduction in inequality was reversed in the years between 1997 and 2000. For example, whereas the coefficient of variation, they find, declined steadily from 1990–91 to 1996–97, it increased slightly between the 1997–98 and 1999–2000 school years.

A reasonable interpretation of our finding that the within-state inequality in revenues declined after KERA and total revenues (as the table shows) increased is that the reductions in inequality were achieved as Kentucky directed more money to low-spending and property-poor districts. In table 6.2 we test this interpretation of the data.

We begin by identifying the districts at the 5th, 25th, 50th, 75th, and 95th percentiles of the distribution of pupil-weighted local resources in the 1989–90 school year. We use data on school district revenues and expenditures from the Kentucky Department of Education's *Annual Financial Reports* (1989–1990). (These data are discussed in appendix 6.A.) We then estimate the average per-pupil spending in those districts, according to the source of the revenue that funded the spending, in the pre- and post-KERA years. If KERA has targeted resources to low-spending districts, then we would expect the increase in district revenues to decline as we move up through the distribution of local revenues.

We find in table 6.2 that, following KERA, total per pupil-revenues rose in districts at all five percentile rankings in the distribution. For example, total spending for the districts at the 5th percentile of per-pupil revenues in 1990 was $4,300 and had increased to $6,586 per pupil in 1997–98. For districts at the 95th percentile of per-pupil spending in 1990, real total revenues increased from $5,208 to $7,301. For the lowest-spending districts, most of this increase came from the state. Local revenues did increase substantially, from $236 per pupil to $839 per pupil, but state revenues increased by almost 50 percent. For the wealthiest districts, however, almost all of the increase came from local resources, as revenues from the state actually declined slightly over the period, from $2,920 to $2,892. Thus, the state reduced the variation in district education spending by increasing aid (in real

Table 6.2
Mean per-pupil revenue and standard deviation by source of revenue and pre-KERA distribution of local revenues and property wealth

	Pre-KERA (SY 1989–90)				Post-KERA (SY 1997–98)			
	Local	State	Federal	Total	Local	State	Federal	Total
Percentile of local per-pupil revenue in 1990								
5th percentile	$ 236	$3,214	$849	$4,300	$ 839	$4,762	$ 985	$6,586
	(45)	(173)	(131)	(222)	(96)	(306)	(251)	(463)
25th percentile	379	3,018	652	4,049	1,199	4,253	758	6,210
	(65)	(147)	(189)	(250)	(97)	(339)	(187)	(455)
50th percentile	591	2,974	472	4,037	1,573	3,839	649	6,061
	(69)	(145)	(135)	(257)	(135)	(314)	(204)	(437)
75th percentile	1,083	2,877	358	4,318	2,275	3,349	537	6,161
	(223)	(179)	(166)	(322)	(293)	(450)	(265)	(594)
95th percentile	1,786	2,920	502	5,208	3,757	2,892	652	7,301
	(182)	(187)	(293)	(454)	(292)	(225)	(262)	(726)
Percentile of per-pupil property wealth in 1990								
5th percentile	$ 389	$3,140	$851	$4,379	$ 877	$4,899	$1,008	$6,784
	(396)	(237)	(275)	(366)	(183)	(311)	(315)	(526)
25th percentile	495	3,026	607	4,128	1,170	4,401	823	6,393
	(381)	(162)	(192)	(361)	(300)	(309)	(198)	(496)
50th percentile	670	2,999	493	4,162	1,538	3,958	687	6,183
	(282)	(155)	(149)	(344)	(281)	(200)	(186)	(472)
75th percentile	962	2,891	429	4,281	1,963	3,185	496	5,644
	(365)	(137)	(171)	(506)	(355)	(278)	(227)	(469)
95th percentile	2,397	2,803	346	5,547	3,468	2,754	618	6,839
	(665)	(130)	(102)	(665)	(446)	(164)	(227)	(669)

Source: Authors' calculations. Revenues are expressed in real 2000 dollars. Data sources are described in appendix 6.A.

terms) to the poorest districts in terms of local revenue and limiting the growth of (or actually decreasing) such aid to the wealthiest districts.

Local revenues, however, were only a part of the impetus for the *Rose* decision. The plaintiffs in the *Rose* case argued that low property values constrained local spending in some districts and that property wealth and student outcomes were highly correlated. We therefore repeated the exercise, this time using the districts at the 5th, 25th, 50th, 75th, and 95th percentiles of the distribution of pupil-weighted property wealth in 1990. These results are also presented in table 6.2. In terms of property wealth, the data show that Kentucky was able, through the KERA reforms, to target resources to low-wealth districts. In addition (not shown in the table), Kentucky was able to target resources to historically low-performing districts. In the next section, we consider the effect of these additional resources on student performance in Kentucky school districts.

6.4   The Impact of KERA on Schooling Outcomes

Rose declared the Kentucky school system inadequate largely because of the low level of educational achievement among Kentucky's students. In this section, we investigate the impact of the additional resources supplied to Kentucky school districts as a result of KERA on student achievement as measured by standardized exams.

Estimating the effect of finance reforms is problematic for many reasons. As discussed in section 6.2.4, how to assess student achievement was a source of intense controversy in the Kentucky curriculum reforms. Large gains in scores on the KIRIS assessments were reported soon after the reform was introduced but before any real curriculum guidelines were in place. In general, scores on state accountability exams are suspect because teachers may teach to the test. One solution would be to use standardized exams, such as the National Assessment of Educational Progress (NAEP), that are not part of an accountability system. Unfortunately, the sample of schools in the NAEP is representative of schools at the national and state level but not at the school district level. An alternative measure would be student outcomes related to the labor market, such as high school graduation rates, college matriculation rates, and wage rates. These outcomes, however, are more removed from the educational process than are test scores, and estimating the relationship between schooling earnings is also problematic. Although student test scores are only weakly correlated with labor market outcomes, when consistently measured over time, they are more closely correlated with schooling activities. Under the CATS accountability system, the state now has in place standardized exams that are comparable pre- and post-KERA for all Kentucky school districts.

Evaluating the effects of KERA's finance policies on student achievement is also complicated by the fact that KERA's finance reforms were introduced along with curriculum and governance reforms. Moreover, whether more resources improve student outcomes remains controversial largely because of an evaluation problem. That is, we are interested in comparing student achievement in a particular district, post-KERA, to what would have happened to student achievement in that district if districts were not exposed to the increased KERA spending. The problem is that cannot observe a hypothetical, that is, student achievement in the absence of KERA. We are left with relating changes in spending to changes in achievement, and in examining those relationships, there may be unobservable district preferences that account for higher district spending that are also related to student achievement. In this section, we use the change in the school finance *formulas* pre- and post-KERA to identify a reason why spending in some districts increased after KERA whereas spending in other districts did not. The key to this strategy is that whereas the change in the formula reflects the legislature's preferences for education spending, it may not reflect a given individual district's preferences.

Recently, several researchers have used changes in state education financing schemes in response to equalization efforts to help isolate a causal link between spending and district outcomes. For example, Barrow and Rouse (2000) take a market-based approach to examining whether increased expenditures on U.S. public schools are valued, at least by potential residents in a school district. A key to their approach is to use changes in state aid predict changes in state education expenditures. They find that, on average, additional state aid is valued by potential residents of a district: A one-dollar increase in state aid to a district increases aggregate housing values per pupil in that district between fifteen and seventeen dollars. Considering discontinuities in the Massachusetts aid formula following the Massachusetts Education Reform Act of 1993, Guryan (2000) compared student test scores in 1996 for districts that received state overburden aid and those that did not. Guryan found that increased spending improved fourth-grade test scores but had no effect on eighth-grade test scores. Clark 2002 uses an instrumental variables (IV) strategy to estimate the impact of changes in school spending on ACT scores in Kentucky relative to those in Tennessee. Clark does not find a statistically significant effect of KERA-induced spending on ACT scores.

6.4.1 Methodology and Data

To calculate changes in levels of state aid to districts due to finance reform, using data from the Kentucky Department of Education, we subtracted from the actual basic SEEK for each Kentucky school district in 1997–98 (adjusted base guarantee and state Tier I aid) the amount of aid the state would have given the district if the pre-KERA Minimum Foundation Program and the Power Equalization Program

Table 6.3
Means and standard deviations

Variable	Mean	Standard deviation
CTBS3 Spring 1990	52.91	5.46
CTBS3 Spring 1998	50.22	5.90
Per-pupil expenditure, 1989–90	3,359	416.21
Per-pupil expenditure, 1997–98	5,104	661.52
Percentage of district residents in poverty, 1989	27.98	12.56
Percentage of district residents in poverty, 1998	51.77	17.28
Per-pupil property assessment, 1990	172,240	74,074
Per-pupil property assessment, 1998	208,429	89,004
Percentage of nonwhite residents in district, 1990	5.75	7.60
Percentage of nonwhite residents in district, 1998	6.06	8.50

Source: Kentucky Department of Education (1990, 1998). There are 176 districts. Dollar amounts are in constant 2000 dollars.

had remained in place in 1997–98. The data used in determining school finance formulas, resources, and outcomes are described more fully in appendix 6.A.

In the first stage of our estimation strategy we used change in state aid, calculated as just described, to predict changes in real per-pupil expenditure between 1989–90 and 1997–98. Next, we used the predicted value of district per-pupil expenditure to estimate changes in third-grade math and reading composite test scores. Control variables included the percentage of district residents in poverty, per-pupil district property assessment, and the percentage of nonwhite residents in the district.

Means for characteristics of selected school district in school year 1989–90 and 1997–98 are presented in table 6.3. Unweighted test scores fell 1.31 percentage points over this time period, and real expenditures increased from $3,359 to $5,104 per pupil in 2000 dollars.

6.4.2 Results

In the first column of table 6.4, we present ordinary least squares (OLS) estimates of the relationship between the change in test scores in Kentucky after KERA and the change in per-pupil spending as a result of the KERA spending reform. The results from this estimation suggest that a one-dollar increase in per-pupil spending increases test scores by .0015 points. Because it is likely that the OLS coefficient estimates on spending per pupil are biased downward because of unobservable

Table 6.4
Estimates of the effect of change in education spending per pupil on change in test scores

Regressors	OLS	IV estimates	
		First stage	Second stage
	Dependent variables		
	Change in CTBS scores	Change in total education spending	Change in test scores
Change in total education spending	0.0015		0.0117
	0.0007		(0.009)
Predicted increase in state aid		0.126	
		(.0011)	
Adjusted R^2	0.01		
$F(4, 171)$		5.43	

Note: Standard errors are in parentheses. There are 176 school districts. All equations include a constant, change in nonwhite population, percentage in poverty, and district property wealth.

omitted variables that influence both changes in spending and test scores, we use changes in the school finance formula as an instrument for measuring changes in spending. The first-stage IV estimate of the relationship between observed changes in total spending per pupil and the predicted change in state aid is presented in the second column of table 6.4. The instrument is found to be significantly correlated with observed changes in state aid per pupil as reflected in the F-statistic (Bound, Jaeger, and Baker 1995; Staiger and Stock 1997). A one-dollar increase in predicted state aid per pupil is associated with a 12.5-cent increase in per-pupil total expenditure, controlling for changes in district characteristics. The second-stage IV estimate is presented in the third column of the table. Although this estimate is not statistically significant at standard levels, it suggests that KERA has had a positive impact on cognitive outcomes in the state. Our results should be interpreted with caution, however. For changes in state aid to be a valid instrument for measuring school spending, two assumptions must hold. First, expenditures per pupil must be correlated with changes in state aid. Second, the change in state aid must be uncorrelated with unobservable determinants of test scores. The first assumption holds, as the results from the first stage suggest. The second assumption would not hold, however, if the curriculum or governance reforms affected districts differentially and those effects were correlated with district spending, as is likely to be the case if poorer districts had more difficulty implementing the curriculum reform or implementing the school councils.

6.5   Summary

Kentucky is an excellent example of an important emerging pattern in school finance legal cases and educational reform in general. As it implements arguably one of the most comprehensive school reforms ever undertaken, the Kentucky experience provides insights for other states implementing accountability systems for their schools and school districts. In this chapter, we examined the impact of KERA on the variation in education resources across school districts in Kentucky and the effect of the additional resources provided as a result of KERA on student achievement. In terms of the variation in per-pupil spending, we found that inequality among Kentucky school districts fell dramatically in the years immediately following the passage of KERA. We also investigated how this reduction in inequality was achieved. Although spending increased in all Kentucky school districts after KERA was implemented, Kentucky reduced the variation in spending across districts by increasing aid (in real terms) more to the state's poorest districts (in both local revenue and property wealth) than to others and limiting the growth of spending in the wealthiest districts. We also investigated the impact of additional resources resulting from KERA using the change in school finance formula under KERA as an instrument for measuring the effect of district expenditures on test scores. Our results suggest this effect is small and statistically insignificant. A one-dollar increase in per-pupil spending may increase tests of basic skills by as much as 0.01 percentile point. Because of concerns about the validity of our instrument, however, these results should be interpreted with caution.

Appendix 6.A: Data

Estimating State Aid Using Pre-KERA School Finance Formula

The data we needed to construct our figures on state aid included the number of basic, vocational, special education, and administrative classroom units, tax rates, and assessed properties and SEEK funding in 1997–98. We constructed the number of classroom units according to the 1989–90 state aid formula. In 1990, one basic classroom unit was allotted to each district for every twenty-five kindergarten students in one-half-day average daily attendance (ADA), for every twenty-three students in ADA in grades 1 through 3, and for every twenty-seven students in ADA in grades 4 through 12. We used the grade specific October 1997 enrollment data to calculate basic classroom units, since ADA data were not available by grade level. The enrollment used in the basic classroom unit calculations was reduced by 9.6 students for each vocational teacher and 7.2 students for each exceptional-child teacher, as required by the school finance formulas. We used data from the Division of Data Policy Management and Research of the Kentucky Department of Education for certified staff in 1994, the latest year for which data were publicly available, to determine the number of vocational and exceptional-child teachers.

The Kentucky Department of Education's Office of District Support Services, Division of School Finance, reports SEEK funds by district in the *SEEK Bulletin* for every year from 1991–2000. The *SEEK Bulletins* report, by year and district, property value assessment; ADA for the current and previous school years and the two-month growth in ADA; base guarantees; adjustments to the base guarantees for at-risk students, exceptional students, and home and hospital schooling; adjustments for transportation; required local efforts; state and local tier I and local tier II proceeds; and finally total SEEK dollars (state effort) to districts.

District Expenditures and Revenues
The Office of District Support Services, Division of School Finance, also supplied data on school district revenues and expenditures through its *Annual Financial Reports*. The *Annual Financial Reports* provide data on receipts and expenditures of state, local, and federal revenues to school districts, current expenditures by district, and total expenditures by district. Detailed data from the *Annual Financial Reports* were provided for the academic years 1988–1994 and 1998–2001. These detailed data allowed current expenditures to be broken down by category: administration, instruction, attendance, health, pupil transportation, and operation and maintenance. Data on capital outlays, debt services, and fund transfers were also available in the detailed reports; these amounts are not included in current expenditures.

Student Outcomes
The Office of Assessment and Accountability, Division of Assessment Implementation, of the Kentucky Department of Education provided us with data on results from the CTBS for 1988–1990 and for 1997–2000.

Appendix 6.B: Responsibilities for School Councils.

Table 6.B.1
Responsibilities of school councils

---

1. To set school policy, consistent with district board policy, to provide an environment to enhance student achievement and to meet performance goals mandated by KERA.

2. To determine, within the parameters of available funds, the number of persons to be employed in each job classification.

3. To select textbooks.

4. To select instructional materials.

5. To determine student support services.

6. To consult with the principal to fill vacancies.

7. To select a new principal.

8. To determine the curriculum, including needs assessment and curriculum development.

9. To assign instructional and noninstructional staff time.

10. To assign students to classes and programs.

11. To set the schedule of the school day and week, subject to the calendar established by the school board.

12. To determine the use of school space during the school day.

13. To plan and resolve issues relating to instructional practice.

14. To select and implement discipline and classroom management techniques.

15. To select extracurricular programs and determine policies relating to student participation.

16. To develop procedures, consistent with local board policy, for determining alignment with state standards, technology utilization and program appraisal.

Source: Russo, Donelan, and Van Meter 1993.

Notes

This chapter originated in a paper presented at the Center for Education Research education conference, April 5–6, 2002. The authors wish to thank Lisa Barrow of Cornell University and the Federal Reserve Bank of Chicago, Bill Evans of the University of Maryland, and Susan Goins of the Kentucky Department of Education for helpful advice and data. The content of the chapter reflects the views of the authors and does not necessarily represent the policy of RAND.

1. The size of a basic classroom unit in the state's definition depended on whether a school was classified as isolated (basically, a rural one- or two-teacher school) or non-isolated. A basic classroom unit for an isolated school was allocated a basic classroom unit for every twelve students; a nonisolated school was allocated a classroom unit for every twenty-five kindergarteners, for every twenty-three students in first through third grades, and for every twenty-seven students in fourth through twelfth grades.

2. The state also supported districts through additional categorical programs for textbooks, school facilities, transportation, and other expenses.

3. Local revenues were also very low because tax assessments were very low and in 1965 the state enacted rollback laws to limit property tax rates.

4. The state provided several financial guarantees to districts during the implementation period. Each district was guaranteed to receive at least 8 percent more state funds in its 1990–91 budget than it had in the previous year and at least 5 percent more in the following year. The increase in state funds, however, was limited to 25 percent in either year. In the 1992 through 1994 budget years, the state included a hold-harmless provision, guaranteeing that no district would receive less funds per pupil than in the previous year.

5. The KIRIS assessments had been administered four times before specific curriculum guidelines were published.

6. See Berne and Stiefel 1984 for a thorough discussion of the properties of measures of equity in public school resources.

7 School Finance Reform in Michigan: Evaluating Proposal A

Julie Berry Cullen and
Susanna Loeb

7.1 Introduction

Michigan's Proposal A fits within the broad movement toward school finance equalization over the last decade or so in the United States. The reform, implemented in 1995,[1] stemmed from concerns about inequities in property tax burdens and expenditures across school districts in Michigan and radically changed the financing of public schools in the state. The primary source of school funding in Michigan shifted, as a result of the reform, from local property taxes to state sales taxes, and education finance became highly centralized at the state level. A modified foundation system replaced district power equalization as the mechanism for distributing basic aid to the state's school districts. Under the foundation system, spending per pupil was sharply increased in previously low-spending districts and was essentially frozen for higher-spending districts. This chapter describes the nature of these changes, their short-term results, and the tensions they have created that are likely to foster future change. We also briefly touch on the school choice and accountability reforms that Michigan implemented at approximately the same time as the school finance reform.

We begin by providing an overview of the condition of education in Michigan. Michigan currently has the eighth-largest public school enrollment among U.S. states. Between 1990 and 1998, Michigan's average daily attendance increased by 7 percent, which is about the median rate across states for the same time period (National Center for Education Statistics 2000, table 43). There have been no comparable shifts in the composition of Michigan's student body, at least with respect to race or ethnicity. In both 1986 and 1998, approximately three-quarters of Michigan's public school students were white, and about one-fifth were black (National Center for Education Statistics 2000, table 44). Michigan's population is concentrated in the southeast, in and around

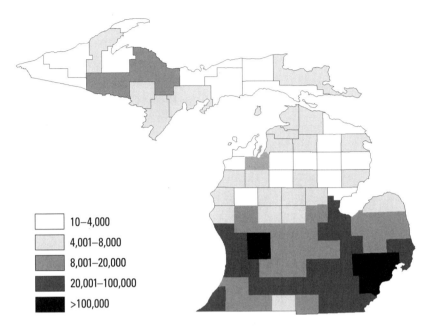

Figure 7.1
Total public school enrollment by county in Michigan in 2000.

the Detroit metropolitan area. Figure 7.1 shows public school enrollment by county in the state in 2000.

Despite the growth in enrollment, current expenditures per pupil
grew in real terms by 9.2 percent between 1990 and 1998.[2] In 1998,
Michigan's current expenditures per pupil were $7,717, 16 percent
more than the national average. Figure 7.2 plots these expenditures
over time. Since the 1960s, Michigan has spent more per pupil on average than the nation as a whole, and the gap between Michigan's per-
pupil spending and the national average increased during the 1990s.
This trend can partly be explained by the infusion of new state revenues associated with Proposal A.

Relative academic achievement for Michigan students also appears
to have improved (though unsteadily) in recent years. Across the nation, thirty-seven states participated in the NAEP for eighth-grade
mathematics in 1992, 1996, and 2000. Michigan ranked eighteenth in
1992, ninth in 1996, and thirteenth in 2000.[3] Figure 7.3 shows the percentage of fourth and eighth graders scoring at the basic level or above
in mathematics in 2000 for each of the participating states. Michigan is
at about the same place in the distribution at both grade levels. Figure

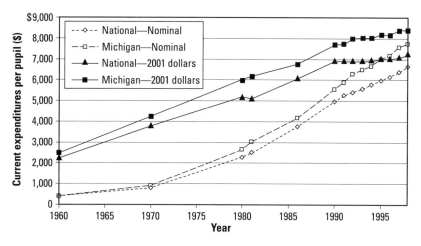

Figure 7.2
Current expenditures per pupil, 1960–1998.
Source: National Center for Education Statistics 2000, table 168.

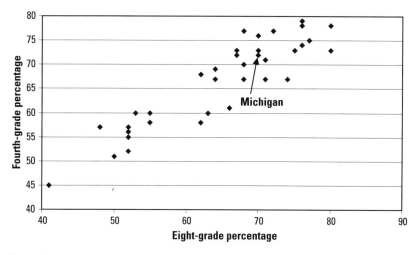

Figure 7.3
Percentage of fourth- and eighth-grade students in participating states scoring at the basic level or above on the NAEP mathematics exam, 2000.

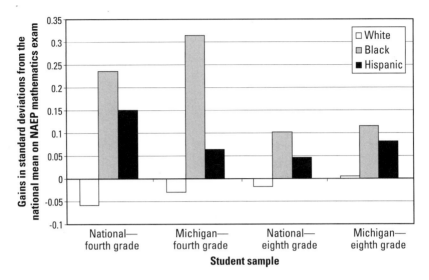

Figure 7.4
Gains (in standard deviations from the national mean) on the NAEP fourth- and eighth-grade mathematics exam, 1992–2000.

7.4 plots the gains in NAEP mathematics scores in Michigan between 1992 and 2000, relative to national average gains, by grade and race or ethnicity. For both grade levels, gains were slightly larger (or declines slightly less) in Michigan than nationally for black and white students, and they were larger for Hispanic students in the eighth grade.

Overall, Michigan's experience with public schooling in the 1990s appears to have been favorable for students, at least on average. Surveys suggest that voters as a whole strongly support Proposal A, though cracks in the system are beginning to show. In the next section, we describe the school financing system in Michigan that preceded the reform. Section 7.3 describes Proposal A in detail. Sections 7.4 through 7.6 explore the impact of the reform on tax burdens, expenditures, and student achievement. Section 7.7 discusses the interaction between Michigan's school finance reform and the state's school accountability and school choice reforms. The final section identifies tensions in the system and concludes with prospects for the future.

7.2   Before Proposal A

Prior to Proposal A, Michigan relied on a power equalization program to supplement revenues in districts with low property tax bases per pupil.[4] As described in chapter 1, power equalization plans (also know as guaranteed tax base plans or guaranteed yield plans) operate by setting a guaranteed tax base per pupil and allowing districts to choose local tax rates. State aid then supplements the revenues districts raise through local taxes by providing the difference between those revenues and what would have been raised with the same tax rate applied to the guaranteed base. Low-wealth districts are subsidized on the margin and face a reduced price of additional spending, proportional to their own tax base wealth divided by the guaranteed level. Districts with tax bases above the guaranteed level do not quality for subsidies since they raise more revenues locally than if the local tax rate were applied to the guaranteed base. In fact, if high-wealth districts are required to return excess revenues generated to the state, then these districts are taxed on the margin and must raise more than one dollar in local rev- enues to increase spending by one dollar. In addition to how responsive a district's demand for education is to the effective price, variations in the design of the program, such as the level of the guarantee and whether there are restrictions on the amount of local supplementation, will affect the degree to which spending is equalized across districts of differing wealth.

Michigan's power equalization program was not designed in a way that would have been expected to be strongly equalizing. Although there was no limit to the amount of local tax effort that the state would supplement for low-wealth districts, there was also no recapture of excess funds from high-wealth districts. Since districts with tax bases above the guaranteed base do not qualify for subsidies and are not required to surrender any local revenues, they are unaffected by the program and considered off formula. Over time, the guaranteed base did not rise as rapidly as property values, so that the share of districts that were off formula in the state rose throughout the 1970s and 1980s. By the late 1980s, more than three out of every ten districts were too wealthy to be affected by the system. At that time, the state implemented a weak recapture system, reclaiming a subset of categorical funds from districts with per-pupil wealth above the guaranteed base.

In 1994, the year prior to reform, the guaranteed tax base was set at $102,500 per pupil. If the per-pupil state-equalized value (SEV)[5] of properties in a district was below that amount, the district's tax levy was subsidized so that each mill (0.1 percent tax) levied raised $102.50 per pupil. In addition, these districts received a foundation grant of $400 per pupil. Districts with SEV per pupil greater than this had their foundation grants taxed until exhausted.[6] Therefore, basic per-pupil state aid for district i with state-equalized valuation per pupil V_i was given by $A_i = \text{Max}[0, \$400 + mills_i \times (\$102,500 - V_i)]$. In 1994, 34.2 percent of districts were off formula.[7] The median implicit price of raising an additional dollar in education funding across all on-formula districts was $0.70, ranging from a minimum of $0.32 to a maximum of $1.10. The price exceeded one dollar for the 3.4 percent of districts subject to recapture on the margin.

To provide a back-of-the-envelope sense of how equalizing this system would be expected to be. We evaluate the extent to which lowering the price of additional spending on education for low-wealth districts compensates for their lower income in determining the demand for education expenditures. To account readily for both the direct effect of higher resources on demand and the indirect effect higher resources have through a lower effective price of additional spending under the DPE system, we treat property wealth as equivalent to income. Median SEV per pupil in 1994 was $85,629 for on-formula districts and $177,481 for off-formula districts. The ratio between SEV per pupil in the high-wealth relative to the low-wealth communities was 2.08. The ratio of median prices was 1.43. We can combine these with reasonable estimates of price and income elasticities to predict, holding all else equal, how much more the median off-formula district would spend per pupil under the system than the median on-formula district. Using −0.25 for the price elasticity and 0.6 for the income elasticity, spending by the median high-wealth district is predicted to be 1.4 times as high as that by the median low-wealth district. In 1994, the actual ratio of the median current operating expenditures per pupil between the two types of districts was 1.25.[8]

Figure 7.5 plots the relationship between district SEV and district per-pupil revenues in 1994—including all local funds, unrestricted state funds from the power equalization mechanism, and those state categorical grants that were later included in the foundation program under the new system. The positive correlation between revenues and wealth is evident. The estimated coefficient on wealth from a regression of per-pupil revenues on per-pupil property wealth and a constant term reveals that each additional $10,000 of SEV per pupil increased district revenues by an average of approximately $90 (in 2001 dollars). This may overstate the tie between effective resources and wealth if educational costs are higher in high-wealth districts. Courant, Gramlich, and Loeb (1995) found that correcting for a subset

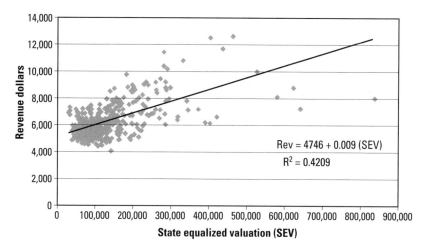

Figure 7.5
District 1994 base revenue per pupil prior to reform according to 1995 per-pupil state
equalized value (2001 dollars).

of cost factors lowered the estimated coefficient on wealth in a regression like the one above by between 12 and 23 percent, depending on the specification, though in all cases, the relationship between revenues and wealth remained highly statistically significant.

7.3 Policy Change through the Passage of Proposal A

Although there was some dissatisfaction with the power equalization plan, the driving force behind school finance reform in Michigan was the property tax. In 1993, the Michigan property tax burden was the seventh highest among the states (U.S. Census 1992); 61.4 percent of total local school revenues (including debt) came from local property taxes, compared to a national average of 44.7 percent (National Center for Education Statistics 1995, table 155). Michigan property taxes as a share of personal income had risen from 4.3 percent in 1978 to 5.0 percent in 1991, even though the national trend during the same period was toward reduced dependence on property taxes. There were many indications of Michigan voters' discontentment with the property tax. Eight referenda to reduce property taxes were held between 1972 and 1993, though all failed (Knittel and Haas 1998). Governor John Engler, who was elected in 1990, made a 20 percent reduction in property taxes one of his campaign promises.

On July 20, 1993, the state senate was debating Engler's latest proposal to reduce property taxes. Senator Debbie Stabenow proposed an amendment to eliminate the property tax as a source of local school finance, a move widely interpreted as an attempt to show how impractical it was to cut taxes without specifying new revenue sources for schools. Surprisingly, the senate passed the amended bill the same day, the house followed a day later, and the governor signed it into law. With little debate the state had eliminated $6.5 billion in school taxes for the 1994–95 school year. It took until March 1994 for the legislature and governor to present voters with two alternatives for the mix of revenues to be used to replace the local property tax: Proposal A and a "statutory plan" that would have been implemented had Proposal A failed. Proposal A primarily called for increases in the state sales tax, whereas the other plan would have increased state income taxes. Though the revenue sources differed, both plans would have centralized school finance decisions and increased spending per pupil in previously low-spending districts. Proposal A passed by a two-to-one margin, carrying all eighty-one counties in the state (Courant and Loeb 1997).

As shown in table 7.1, Proposal A fundamentally changed the system of taxation that raised revenues for schools, altering the local share of taxes and the types of taxes used.[9] Under Proposal A, earmarked revenues are deposited into the School Aid Fund to finance state education aid to districts. Revenues from a two-percentage-point increase in the sales and use tax under the proposal, a 50-cent-per-pack increase in the cigarette tax, and a new 0.75 percent real estate transfer tax, as well as 14.4 percent of individual income tax revenues (increased to 23.0 percent in 1997) are all directly deposited into this fund. Proposal A also included a new statewide uniform property tax levy of 6 mills on both homestead and nonhomestead property. Districts are required to levy an additional 18 mills on nonhomestead property to participate fully in the state school finance program.[10] Most districts are not allowed to levy additional mills to finance general operating expenditures. Average levies on both types of property were 34 mills before the reform, so these provisions represent significant property tax relief. With the dramatic centralization of education finance as a result of Proposal A, the state share of general funds for education rose from 31.3 percent in 1993 to 77.5 percent by 1997. Figure 7.6 shows the coinciding dramatic drop in the percentage of public school revenues coming from local sources subsequent to the passage of Proposal A. These

Table 7.1
Revenue sources for K–12 education in Michigan before and after reform

Tax	Prior to Reform	Proposal A
Sales tax	60 percent of proceeds from the 4 percent rate	60 percent from the 4 percent rate and 100 percent from the two-percentage-point increase
Use tax		All revenue from the two-percentage-point increase
Income tax		14.4 percent of collections from the 4.4 percent rate (down from 4.6 percent)
Real estate transfer tax		All revenue from the 0.75 percent tax
Cigarette tax (per pack)	$0.02 of the $0.25 tax	63.4 percent of proceeds from the $0.75 tax
Tax on other tobacco products		Proceeds of the 16 percent tax (on wholesale price)
Liquor excise tax	Revenue from the 4 percent tax	Revenue from the 4 percent tax
Lottery	Net revenue	Net revenue
State tax on all property		6 mills
Local homestead property tax	34 mills (average)	0
Local nonhomestead property tax	34 mills (average)	18 mills

Source: Adapted from Michigan House and Senate Fiscal Agencies 1994, tables 1 and 2.

changes in percentages actually understate the relative rise in the state role, since the local property tax levy became essentially state-controlled under Proposal A.

Proposal A also replaced the power equalization program with a modified foundation grant program. Under a foundation plan, a state chooses a foundation level of spending per pupil and a required local property tax rate (see chapter 1 for a more thorough discussion). Local districts receive the difference between what they raise through the required levy and the total foundation amount (the per-pupil foundation level multiplied by the number of pupils).

Foundation plans differ from one another in two important aspects. First, districts may or may not be allowed to levy additional local taxes to supplement the foundation level. Second, districts that raise more than the foundation level with the required local property tax rate may or may not be required to return the excess revenue to the state,

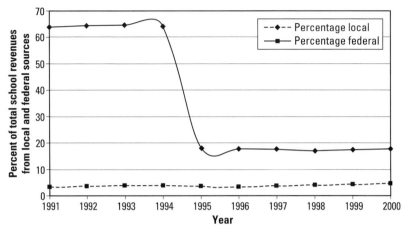

Figure 7.6
Percentage of total school revenues from local and federal sources, Michigan, 1991–2000.

though recapture of this form is uncommon. Although Michigan's foundation system does not have recapture, it does cap revenue in previously high-spending districts at 1994 levels. The system then improves equity across districts primarily by creating a spending floor that levels spending up in other districts. The required local contribution, under the Michigan foundation plan, is the amount raised by the 18 mill levy on nonhomestead property.

During the first year of reform (1995), districts were divided into three groups, each with different formulas for calculating district-specific spending limits (or allowances) and foundation grants. For the lowest-spending districts, those spending less than $3,950 per pupil in 1994, the foundation allowance was set at $4,200 for 1995.[11] Those districts spending between $3,950 and $6,500 per pupil in 1994 received foundation allowances of $160 to $250 more than their prior year's spending, with the increase based on a sliding scale and inversely related to prior spending. The per-pupil spending limit for districts spending above $6,500 per pupil in 1994 was set at $160 above their 1994 spending levels. The foundation grant, financed by the state uniform and the local nonhomestead property taxes, was set equal to the minimum of a district's allowance and the cap of $6,500. Districts with allowances above the maximum foundation grant are allowed to raise the additional funds for these allowances through local property taxes on homestead property, known as "hold-harmless mills."

Table 7.2
Foundation levels

	1995	1996	1997	1998	1999	2000	2001	2002	2003
Minimum	$4,200	$4,506	$4,816	$5,124	$5,170	$5,700	$6,000	$6,300	$6,700
Basic foundation	5,000	5,153	5,308	5,462	5,462	5,700	6,000	6,300	6,700
Academies, maximum	5,500	5,653	5,808	5,962	5,962	6,200	6,500	6,800	7,000
Hold harmless, maximum	6,500	6,653	6,808	6,962	6,962	7,200	7,500	7,800	8,000

Note: The hold-harmless maximum is $1,500 above the basic foundation through fiscal year 2002.

The state also established a benchmark level of per-pupil expenditure necessary to finance an adequate education known as the basic foundation level. Although the foundation grants for low-spending districts were set below the basic foundation level in the first year after Proposal A took effect, the goal was to steadily raise their grants to attain that level ($5000 in 1995) within a few years. Those districts receiving less than the basic foundation would see larger annual increases in their allowances. Districts with revenues at or above the basic foundation, which would include all districts by 2000, would receive the same annual increases in their foundation allowances. Thus, most of the nominal disparities in revenues at the time the system is fully phased in are held fixed by the system. Over time, continued equalization occurs as the value of the nominal differences between districts decreases.

The basic foundation level increases automatically each year by the ratio of current earmarked School Aid Fund revenues to 1995 revenues. In 2002, every district had a foundation grant of at least $6,300. The maximum foundation grant was $7,800, and there were forty-five districts with foundation allowances over $7,800 (ranging from $7,810 to $15,187). Table 7.2 shows the foundation levels for each year since the implementation of Proposal A. Annual funding increases have been below the inflation rate in the districts with the highest foundation allowances. Two-thirds of these districts are in southeast Michigan in the Detroit area. (Note that charter schools (academies) in Michigan have an alternative foundation level, discussed in more detail in section 7.7.)

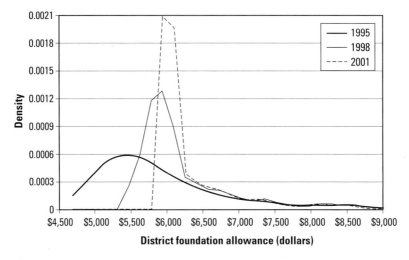

Figure 7.7
Probability density curves for district foundation levels. The curves shown are kernel density estimates of the probability density functions for district foundation levels for the years indicated (2001 dollars).

Figure 7.7 shows clearly how equalization through Michigan's basic aid formula operates. The distribution of the foundation allowance is shown for 1995, 1998, and 2001. Both the steady increase in the allowance at the bottom of the distribution and the stability at the top are evident.

In addition to the dramatic changes in its basic aid program, Michigan's system of categorical grants was revamped under Proposal A. More than thirty of the existing categorical grants, including contributions to teacher retirement, were eliminated and incorporated into the foundation allowance. Between 1994 and 1995, the share of state operating aid distributed through separate categorical grants fell from more than 40 percent to approximately 15 percent. This is an important point, since categorical funding is the only mechanism in place to account for differences in costs or resource needs across districts once most are pushed up to the basic foundation level. Other states with foundation systems tend to rely also on differential pupil weighting or district-specific adjustments to foundation levels to account for heterogeneity in student characteristics and or input costs across districts.

Appropriately accounting for differences in need from school district to school district, regardless of the method, is not straightforward. The difficulty arises because when two districts are observed with the same expenditures but different student outcomes, it is unclear whether the outcome differences result from differences in costs, in goals, or in efficiency. Because of this ambiguity, providing additional funds to districts that demonstrate higher need may lead to perverse behavior. For example, if a larger special education program is viewed by the state as increasing district costs, then districts may classify slow-learning students as disabled to appear more needy (Cullen 2003). Reliable measures of underlying need are based instead on characteristics of the student population that are not directly within the control of the school district.

Michigan's categorical grant program is subject to the design issues that result from these types of difficulties. One of the largest remaining categorical grant programs in the state is that for special education (which awarded about $400 million to school districts in 2001).[12] Though some special education funds are allocated through two smaller funds for low-incidence disabilities and regional service area support, most are allocated based on actual local special education expenditures, the majority of which are reimbursed at a rate of 28.6 percent (*Durant v. State of Michigan* [1997]). The danger involved in this form of reimbursement is that it weakens incentives for cost containment and may lead districts to classify an excessive number of students as disabled so that instructional spending for those students qualifies for reimbursement. The advantage is that it partially insures districts against the risk of serving a high-cost population.

The other dominant categorical grant program (which awarded $304 million to districts in 2001) is that for at-risk students, defined by low family income. The allocation for these students is 11.5 percent of the foundation allowance multiplied by the number of free-lunch-eligible students.[13] There are also categorical grants for early education, bilingual education, gifted education, and vocational education. There are no categorical programs to help districts with capital improvements.

7.4   Changes in Tax Burdens

In shifting from local to state taxes under Proposal A, Michigan shifted away from the property tax toward the sales tax. Prior to the reform of its education finance system, relative to other states, Michigan relied more heavily on property taxes and less heavily on sales taxes. Property taxes were 33 percent higher per capita than the national average, and sales taxes were 30 percent lower (Citizens Resource Council of Michigan 1991). Both taxes are now much closer to the national averages.

Taxes can be compared to one another along a number of dimensions, including equity, stability, and the extent to which they alter taxpayer behavior. The primary concern with the property tax in Michigan was that it was viewed to be inequitable, in part because property tax rates varied substantially across districts. In addition, the property tax is perceived as being a regressive tax. Fullerton and Rogers (1993) find that housing consumption as a fraction of income is higher than average at the lowest income levels and then becomes approximately proportional to income. This pattern is consistent with that found in earlier empirical work (Ihlanfeldt 1982). The elderly generally have higher property wealth for any given level of income and, as such, can bear a disproportionate share of the property tax. However, the prereform Michigan property tax had a circuit breaker to help low-income and elderly homeowners. Residents who were under sixty-five years old received a tax credit of 65 percent of taxes paid in excess of 3.5 percent of income. Residents sixty-five years and older received a 100 percent tax credit for taxes in excess of 3.5 percent of income. Credits were capped at $1,200 and phased out for incomes over $73,000 a year. Renters were allowed to claim 17 percent of their rent as property taxes.

The sales tax is regressive with respect to current income and approximately proportional with respect to lifetime income (Slemrod and Bakija 1996; Fullerton and Rogers 1993). The burden of the sales tax on low-income residents can be alleviated by the exclusion of food from the items taxed (Blume 1982). Because of the similar incidence of the two taxes, Proposal A should not have caused a substantial shift in tax burden among Michigan's taxpayers, except for in regard to two important aspects of the reform.[14] First, sales taxes increased to the same extent for renters and homeowners. The drop in the property tax on homestead property, however, was much greater than that on nonhomestead property. Thus, even if the lower costs to the owners of the rental properties due to reduced nonhomestead tax payments were fully passed on as lower rents to tenants, the decrease in rent would still be less than proportional to the decrease in property taxes for homeowners. Thus, renters pay an increased share of taxes as a result of the Michigan reforms, and more so the less changes in property taxes are reflected in rents. Second, the shift from the local to the state level and the uniform tax rates applied across the state altered the tax burden by geography; those districts with the highest property tax rates saw the biggest drops in their tax burdens after the reform.

Reductions in tax burdens for some districts could have a secondary impact on incidence by increasing their property values. Guilfoyle (1998) measures the capitalization of interjurisdictional differences in property taxes and school spending using Proposal A as a natural experiment. Using individual home sales data, he finds that a $1 tax differential between districts leads to a $5.20 home value differential (with home values higher where taxes are lower). He also finds significant effects of educational spending on home values (each $100 increase in per-pupil spending in a district raises home values in the district by 0.4 to 0.6 percent). These estimates imply that if a community were to raise education spending by increasing property taxation, the opposing effects of higher spending and higher taxes would come close to canceling one another. Since the tax cuts and spending increases due to Proposition A are reinforcing and both were partially capitalized into home prices, districts with low spending and high property tax rates before the reform particularly benefited. Capitalization is thus likely to have enhanced the equalization in revenues directly attributable to the change in school finance by raising property values in lower-wealth districts.

7.5 Changes in Patterns of Expenditures

Total school revenues increased in Michigan from a district average of $5,717 per pupil in 1991 to $7,231 per pupil in 2000 (2001 constant dollars). Figure 7.8 plots the changes in per-pupil revenues in Michigan over the last decade, highlighting the large jump between 1994 and 1995. Revenues across districts also became more equal in the 1990s. The coefficient of variation for school revenues in Michigan districts, which is the standard deviation divided by the mean, dropped from 0.22 in 1991 to 0.13 in 2000 (figure 7.8). Those districts with the highest initial total revenues experienced the least growth in revenues during the decade. The average revenue growth for the districts in the upper decile in 1991 was only 6 percent, whereas that for those in the lowest decile was 46.9 percent.[15]

Table 7.3 tracks changes in the foundation allowance and in current operating expenditures for districts in different quintiles based on their revenues prior to the reform. Real growth in both the foundation levels and expenditures is evident for most (though not all) years. The

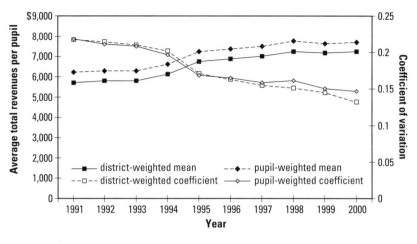

Figure 7.8
Average total revenues per pupil and coefficients of variation (standard deviation/mean) by year, 1991–2000 (2001 dollars).

lowest-spending districts (quintile 1) have consistently seen the greatest increases in their foundation levels, and the range between the minimum and maximum foundation levels decreased from $7,279 in 1995 to $5,598 in 2000. Note that the interquartile range ($480 in 2000) is much smaller than the range, indicating that the distribution has long tails. Figure 7.9 plots 1994 base per-pupil spending and 2000 foundation levels of Michigan school districts. The clustering of previously low-spending at the foundation floor of just under $6,000 clearly demonstrates the leveling up that took place between 1994 and 2000 at the bottom of the distribution. The sloped section falls slightly below the 45-degree line, since foundation levels fell slightly in real terms during the period for higher-wealth districts. Still, districts with higher base levels had higher foundation levels than other districts six years later.

Differences in current operating expenditures for Michigan school districts have also decreased over time. Figure 7.10 plots the 1994 and 2000 levels. Again the growth in expenditures at the upper end of the distribution does not appear as great as the growth at the lower end. The interquartile range decreased over the period, from $1,192 in 1994 to $963 in 2000. However, the changes over time follow a less consistent pattern than that found for foundation revenues, because many of the districts receiving increasing categorical grants are in middle of the

Table 7.3
Patterns in revenues and expenditures by year and quintile

	1994	1995	1996	1997	1998	1999	2000
Per-pupil foundation allowance							
Quintile 1	—	$5,017	$5,213 [0.039]	$5,429 [0.042]	$5,668 [0.044]	$5,540 [−0.023]	$5,851 [0.056]
Quintile 2	—	5,392	5,530 [0.026]	5,698 [0.031]	5,888 [0.033]	5,737 [−0.026]	5,851 [0.020]
Quintile 3	—	5,708	5,777 [0.012]	5,868 [0.016]	5,967 [0.016]	5,809 [−0.026]	5,859 [0.009]
Quintile 4	—	6,217	6,208 [−0.001]	6,249 [0.007]	6,325 [0.012]	6,163 [−0.026]	6,201 [0.006]
Quintile 5	—	7,879	7,822 [−0.007]	7,828 [0.001]	7,881 [0.007]	7,679 [−0.026]	7,668 [−0.001]
Range	—	7,279	6,893	6,577	6,313	6,102	5,598
75th minus 25th percentile	—	1,044	881	739	612	596	480
Current operating expenditures per pupil							
Quintile 1	$4,845 [0.057]	$5,242 [0.086]	$5,424 [0.034]	$5,642 [0.042]	$5,745 [0.020]	$5,908 [0.029]	$6,197 [0.049]
Quintile 2	5,159 [0.070]	5,575 [0.082]	5,693 [0.023]	5,911 [0.039]	5,997 [0.015]	6,153 [0.027]	6,284 [0.022]
Quintile 3	5,371 [0.064]	5,834 [0.087]	5,942 [0.019]	6,103 [0.028]	6,086 [−0.002]	6,158 [0.012]	6,287 [0.022]
Quintile 4	5,998 [0.064]	6,398 [0.069]	6,497 [0.016]	6,678 [0.029]	6,645 [−0.004]	6,753 [0.016]	6,855 [0.020]
Quintile 5	7,500 [0.044]	7,747 [0.038]	7,858 [0.016]	7,981 [0.017]	7,992 [0.001]	8,027 [0.008]	8,194 [0.022]
Range	8,555	6,895	7,074	7,182	9,664	6,226	6,271
75th minus 25th percentile	1,192	1,169	1,083	1,090	990	952	963

Note: Percentage change in revenues from previous year reported in brackets.

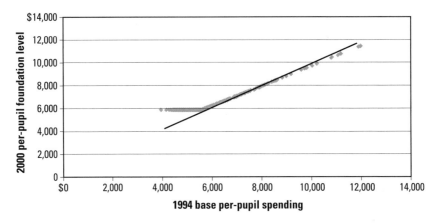

Figure 7.9
District foundation levels in 2000 as a function of base levels in 1994 (2001 dollars).
Though 1994 base per-pupil spending is not technically a foundation amount, the system
is built from systematic increases starting from this level.

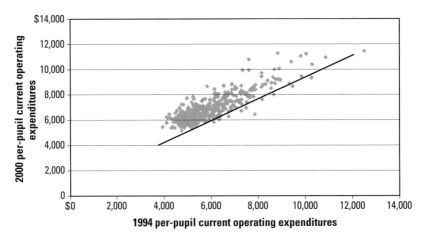

Figure 7.10
District per-pupil current operating expenditures as a function of 1994 levels (2001
dollars).
Source: Michigan Department of Education 1994 and 2000.

distribution of initial spending, not at the low end (see subsequent discussion in this section).

The revenue gains in Michigan districts under Proposal A have varied according to the demographic characteristics of the districts as well. Table 7.4 shows the correlations between percentage gains in total revenues from 1991 to 2000 and demographic characteristics of districts from the 1990 *School District Data Book* (National Center for Education Statistics 1994). Many of the expected relationships are evident. Districts with lower income per capita, lower state-equalized values for both homestead and nonhomestead property, and higher poverty rates had greater gains in total revenues after Proposal A. These gains were lower, however, in districts with high proportions of black and Hispanic students.

An important question is how the state's urban centers fared under reform. On average, the gains in revenues in Michigan's urban districts were lower (20.0 percent over the decade) than those in other districts (31.3 percent). Nevertheless, most of the large inner-city districts did see substantial revenue gains as a result of Proposal A. Detroit's revenues rose by 35.2 percent, Flint's by 41.2 percent, and Lansing's by 35.3 percent. Grand Rapids' revenues rose by 19.6 percent, which was the average increase of other urban districts. Figure 7.11 shows the percentile rank of these cities' school districts in the distribution of local and state revenues across districts over the decade, where the first percentile corresponds to the most resource-rich districts. The drop in percentile rankings over time for all cities but Grand Rapids indicates that these cities improved in terms of relative position over the 1990s. Interestingly, none of these city districts was in the group of districts that received the largest increases in foundation allowances. For example, Detroit's 1994 revenue, which served as the base for its foundation grants was $5,377. By 2001, the foundation grant in Detroit was $6,584, whereas its average total revenue per pupil was $8,842. The increased revenue over the foundation amount came largely from increases in categorical revenues directed to poor and low-performing students through the state's large compensatory education program. Revenues from categorical grants generally come with restrictions, and thus these additional funds may not be as valuable to districts as unrestricted revenues.

So far, we have ignored differences in costs that may affect the distribution of effective resources per pupil across districts. We apply two

Table 7.4
Correlations between revenue gains in the 1990s and district demographics

	Revenue gain	Percentage revenue gain	Income per capita	Homestead SEV	Nonhome- stead SEV	Percentage urban	Percentage poor	Percentage black/ Hispanic
Revenue gain	1.00							
Percentage revenue gain	0.95*	1.00						
Income per capita	−0.46*	−0.51*	1.00					
Homestead SEV	−0.43*	−0.48*	0.43*	1.00				
Nonhomestead SEV	−0.26*	−0.30*	−0.008	0.37*	1.00			
Percentage urban	−0.23*	−0.34*	0.47*	0.057	−0.046	1.00		
Percentage poor	0.48*	0.46*	−0.66*	−0.26*	−0.075	−0.15*	1.00	
Percentage black/Hisp	0.15*	0.027	−0.11*	−0.18	−0.03	0.37	0.47	1.00

Note: *Correlation is significant at the 1 percent level.

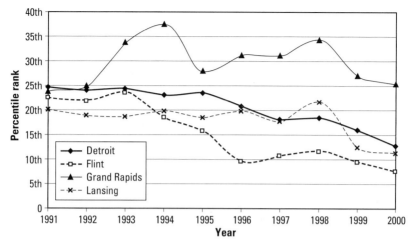

Figure 7.11
Percentile rank in local and state revenues per pupil for Michigan cities, 1991–2000. A
lower percentile rank indicates that revenues are relatively high.

cost adjustments to explore the extent to which the foundation program alone and the program including categorical aid target more
funds to higher-cost districts than to lower-cost districts. Recall that the
foundation allowance system essentially treats prior spending as a
measure of resource need, whereas the categorical programs incorporate student poverty and special-needs status into award amounts. The
first cost adjustment that we use is a district-specific index of local
nonpersonnel and personnel costs developed from a hedonic wage
model that isolates the impact of regional amenities and costs of living
from demand-driven differences in spending (Chambers 1998). The
second borrows estimates from Duncombe, Ruggiero, and Yinger 1996
(based on an analysis of New York) to incorporate differences in student characteristics that affect the costs of achieving given student performance outcomes.[16] The geographic index ranges from 0.80 to 1.19,
and the second, more comprehensive index ranges from 0.724 to 1.77.

Table 7.5 shows the coefficient of variation for three different district
spending variables in 2000. The first assigns all districts the state average foundation allowance in that year. The other two measures are the
actual district foundation allowances and operating expenditures per
pupil. (Variation in foundation allowances in 2000 was restricted to the
top two-fifths of districts, and all other districts were at the base foundation level.)

Table 7.5
Accounting for differences in cost factors across Michigan districts

	No cost adjustment	Geographic cost adjustment	Also accounting for student characteristics
State average allowance	0	0.078	0.116
Own foundation allowance	0.138	0.142	0.173
Own operating expenditures	0.151	0.158	0.167

Moving from row 2 to row 3 of the table without any cost adjustment leads to an increase in measured inequality. This means that categorical aid is not targeted to those districts with the lowest foundation allowances. This remains true when geographic costs are accounted for, but categorical aid actually reduces the disparity in effective resources relative to the foundation program alone once differences in student characteristics are also incorporated. This is not surprising, since categorical aid is explicitly targeted to two costly-to-educate populations: poor students and students with disabilities. What is surprising is that a system of equal per-pupil funding appears to distribute resources more equitably across districts than either the foundation system alone or the combined foundation and categorical programs. Also, the fact that successive adjustments for cost factors lead to larger coefficients of variation for both foundation allowances and operating expenditures implies that ignoring cost differences from district to district exaggerates the degree of effective equalization of resources. Therefore, any impact the reform has had on student outcomes would be expected to be somewhat muted relative to its impact on spending unadjusted for cost differences.

7.6   Proposal A and Student Outcomes

An important policy question is whether the sharp changes in the level and distribution of funds to Michigan school districts associated with Proposal A translate into changes in student outcomes. Evidence from other states' reforms does not reveal a close relationship between spending and outcomes. For example, Downes (1992) found that the nearly complete equalization of revenues in California after Proposition 13 did not significantly equalize student outcomes in the state. In practice, however, California's reform achieved equalization by leveling down spending in previously high-spending districts. The effects of

Michigan's reform could differ, since it operated primarily by leveling up resources.

Michigan has consistently reported mathematics test scores (a three-level measure of "low," "moderate," or "satisfactory") for fourth- and seventh-grade students since 1990–91.[17] We use the student-level data to create yearly district measures for the percentage of students passing (defined as not receiving a "low" score) and the percentage gaining the highest mark, "satisfactory" for the years 1991–2000. Figure 7.12a shows that there was an increase in both the average district pass rate and the average district satisfactory rate on this exam over the decade. In addition, as shown in figure 7.12b, the coefficient of variation on these two measures, as well as per-pupil expenditure, decreased substantially over the period. Part of the reason for the decrease in variation in scores, however, is an important ceiling effect, not only on the pass rate, but also on the satisfactory rate. Figure 7.12c plots the change in district pass rates on the fourth-grade mathematics examination

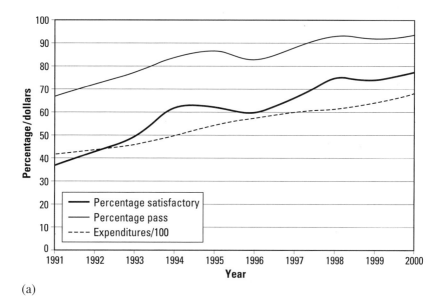

(a)

Figure 7.12
(a) Fourth-grade mathematics examination pass rates and satisfactory rates and per-pupil expenditures, 1991–2000; (b) Coefficients of variation in pass rates and satisfactory rates on fourth-grade mathematics examination and per-pupil expenditures, 1991–2000; (c) Change in the percentage passing fourth-grade mathematics examination by 1991 percentage passing; (d) Changes in expenditures per pupil and pass rates on fourth-grade mathematics examination, 1991–2000; (e) Change in per-pupil expenditures by 1991 pass rates on fourth-grade mathematics examination.

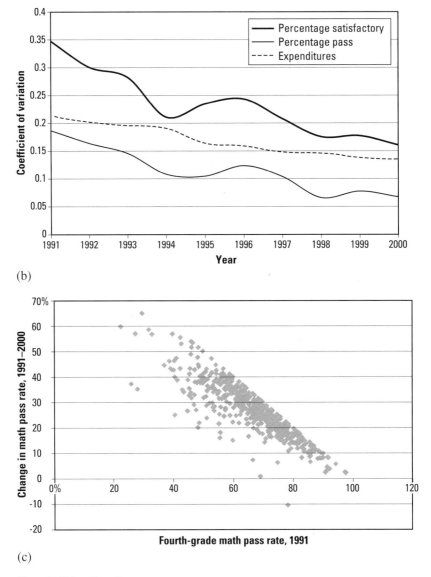

(b)

(c)

Figure 7.12 (continued)

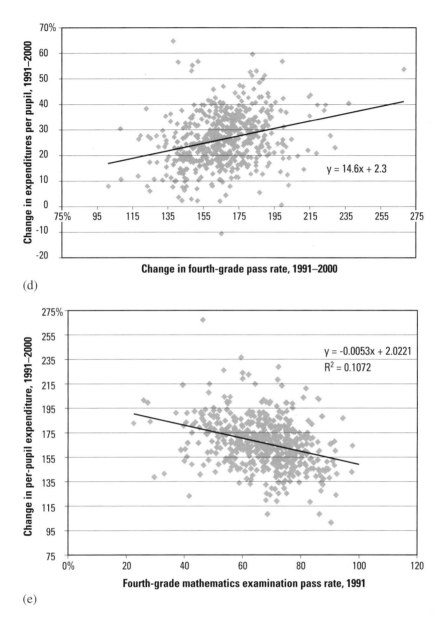

(d)

(e)

Figure 7.12 (continued)

from 1991 to 2000 according to the 1991 pass rate. Because the initial rate plus the change cannot sum to more than 100, there is a clear break in the distribution of gains. The ceiling effect for the satisfactory score is not quite as strong as for the pass rate, but it is still evident. Thus, when looking at the impact of the change in expenditures on student outcomes, it is important to take account of starting levels. We cannot expect districts with pass rates close to the ceiling at the beginning of the period to gain as much as districts that start with low pass rates.

A univariate regression of the change in the fourth-grade pass rate on the percentage change in total expenditures over the period indicates that a 10 percent increase in expenditures is associated with an approximately 1.5-percentage-point increase in the pass rate ($p < .001$), as illustrated in figure 7.12d. If the initial pass rate is included in the regression as a control variable, however, the relationship decreases to a 0.001-percentage-point increase in the fourth-grade pass rate for a 10 percent increase in expenditures (essentially zero) and is no longer statistically significant ($p = .995$). The same results hold for the seventh-grade scores. Without the control for initial level, a 10 percent increase in expenditures coincides with a 0.7-percentage-point increase in the pass rate ($p = .002$), but when the initial score is controlled for, the increase becomes 0.17 ($p = .452$).[18]

These models are clearly limited and may suffer from omitted-variables bias. Papke (2001) uses alternative methods and does find a positive and statistically significant relationship between increased spending and student outcomes as a result of Proposal A in a number of specifications, but not when lagged scores are included in the model. If initial scores and changes in expenditures are highly correlated, then it may simply be too difficult to parse out the effect of expenditures on gains. Figure 7.12e shows that there is variation in resource changes for each level of initial mathematics test score, though the correlations are -0.3 between the percentage change in expenditure and each of the initial student outcome measures (fourth- and seventh-grade pass and satisfactory rates). This is clear evidence that more resources were targeted to districts that were more likely to improve on test pass rate measures even in the absence of reform.

7.7   School Choice and Accountability Reforms

In addition to changing the way funds were raised for and delivered to Michigan school districts, Proposal A also included new school choice measures and led to a new accountability system for schools and school systems in the state. It is likely inevitable that such dramatic increases in the state role in education would be accompanied by increased state oversight and involvement. These two nonfinancial school initiatives can be viewed as complementary policy tools for encouraging the effective and efficient use of funds.

Proposal A expanded school choice in Michigan by allowing students to opt to attend public school academies (PSAs), known more widely as charter schools. PSAs are financed by state allocations based on the same per-pupil foundation formula that applies to other public schools, though charter schools do not have access to local revenue bases and have no required contribution. If a charter school is authorized by a school district, the charter school receives the minimum of the district's per-pupil foundation allowance or the state basic allowance plus $500 (see table 7.2). Since state per-pupil foundation aid follows students, it is presumed that public schools will compete to attract and retain students. However, charter-school entry has been fostered only at the elementary level, since per-pupil expenditures at the secondary level are higher than the average for grades K–12. There are no provisions for sources of capital funds for charter schools, so that site availability is a strong determinant of entry as well.

Only a few charter schools started up in the two years immediately following reform, but since then, the numbers have steadily increased: 78 in 1997, 108 in 1998, and rising to 196 in 2003. Despite the rapid growth in the numbers of charter schools in Michigan, only a small minority (1 percent) of students statewide attends PSAs. Unlike in other states, charter schools have tended to locate in more urban and disadvantaged areas and, for this reason, tend to have low average test scores. In a cross-cohort analysis, however, Bettinger (1999) does not find much evidence that these schools improve student achievement, even after initial student ability is accounted for. Nor does he find that nearby public schools are improving in response to competitive pressure from charter schools.

Options for choice have been further expanded in Michigan through "schools of choice" legislation that allows students to attend public schools outside their home district. Under the program that resulted from this legislation, a district that enrolls a pupil from outside the district receives, for that student, the minimum of its own and the sending district's per-pupil state foundation aid. A district does not have to accept transfer students, but if it does, it must admit students through a lottery if it is oversubscribed. Since operating revenues are now so closely tied to enrollment and there is little local leeway to raise additional funds, traditional public schools have realized that transfer students provide an opportunity to expand their budgets. By 2001, four out of every five school districts had signed on to participate in the program. Between 1997 and 2001, the number of students participating grew from 7,836 to 33,506. Student participation in schools of choice has largely been a Detroit phenomenon, with more than one-third of all transfers taking place within the Detroit metropolitan area, though there are other pockets of activity across Michigan as well. Urban districts that are losing students have been responding through marketing campaigns and, reportedly, by adding free full-day kindergarten (*Detroit News* 2001c). Some schools have closed due to insufficient enrollment (*Detroit News* 2001b). Where schools are aggressively competing for students, open enrollment has clearly had a tangible impact on school operations.

Michigan has also made changes to its school-level accountability system and has introduced an award system for both staff and students. Since 1993, the state has had a three-tiered accreditation system with such a broad middle tier that it did not distinguish between successful and failing schools. A proposal to replace the ineffectual system with a new performance-based accreditation system was approved in May 1999. More than 600 schools (one in five) were expected to lose accreditation, including nearly 40 percent of metropolitan Detroit high schools (*Detroit News* 2001a, 2001e). Because of public backlash when the state board moved to implement the system in the spring of 2001, however, the system was never implemented. School officials complained that the system's emphasis on test score levels did a better job of measuring student disadvantage than school effectiveness.

With additional impetus from Bush's No Child Left Behind bill, the state board approved another accreditation system, the Education Yes! Accreditation System, in March 2002. Once this system is phased in, schools will receive overall letter grades of A, B, C, D-Alert, or Unaccredited. Schools will not only receive an overall composite grade but also will be individually graded in six separate subareas: achievement level, change, and growth, as well as indicators of community engagement, instructional quality, and learning opportunities. Attendance and dropout rates are included among the student performance indicators to allay concerns about an overemphasis on test scores. The comprehensiveness of this new program promises to provide a better measure of what schools actually do than a system based primarily on test score levels.

Good performance in education is rewarded by Michigan at two levels. Since 2000, elementary schools that demonstrate sustained improvement on the achievement exams have been eligible for Golden Apple Awards. These are financial awards of $10,000 for use by the school's principal plus $1,000 for each full-time employee. Also, since 1999, high-achieving high school graduates are eligible to receive a $2,500 scholarship to attend an in-state college (and $1,000 to attend an out-of-state college) through the Michigan Merit Award Scholarship Program. One concern about this program is that it subsidizes students from more advantaged families because of the strong tie between family background and academic achievement. Whereas 34 percent of eligible white students qualified for the scholarships in the first year of the program, only 20 percent of Hispanic and 7 percent of black students did (*Detroit News* 2000). It is too early to judge whether these incentive programs have affected staff and/or student effort.[19]

7.8 Tensions and Prospects for the Future

School finance reform in Michigan has clearly equalized revenues across districts and increased the revenues of the lowest-spending districts. The reform may also have improved student outcomes. However, it has created a number of tensions, most the result of the reduced flexibility at the local level.

Prior to the reform, local districts had substantial control over the level of funding in their schools. Proposal A changed this, increasing funding (and thus spending) in previously low-spending districts and constraining revenues (and thus spending) in previously high-spending districts. It is likely that given the option, those districts with an influx of new monies would prefer to spend some of it on non-education goods, and those limited by the funding constraints would like to use other resources for schools.

Districts constrained from below or above may find ways around the restrictions by changing spending on unconstrained budget areas. For example, previously low-spending districts in Michigan may have an incentive to mask capital and other public expenditures as school operating expenditures. Preliminary analysis suggests that districts with low demand for education spending in Michigan are indeed less likely to raise additional revenues for capital than they would in the absence of the influx of new operating revenues (Cullen and Loeb 2002). Evidence from California supports the idea that districts subject to binding spending ceilings also engage in forms of fiscal substitution. Proposition 13 in that state imposes strict limits on noncategorical program expenditures while exempting from these limits programs such as vocational and special education. Increased disparity in spending on these programs across districts has apparently partly offset the reduced dispersion in general education spending per pupil (Sonstelie, Brunner and Ardon [2000]). Increased private contributions to schools that previously had access to high local property tax revenues have also partially offset the equalization (Brunner and Sonstelie, forthcoming).

Dissatisfied voters in high-demand districts in Michigan have also tried to get around the funding restrictions imposed by Proposal A directly, by changing the policy. For the three years immediately following Proposal A (1995–1997), districts had the option of levying up to an additional 3 mills for operating expenditures.[20] This option ended in the 1997–98 school year and was replaced with a funding mechanism that incorporated equalization. Starting in 1997–98, intermediate school districts (ISDs) could levy up to 3 mills to be distributed on a per-pupil basis across the member districts. A majority vote is needed across the member districts to levy these additional mills. Because ISDs combine districts with varied demand for school spending and property wealth, in only one have the voters approved these additional mills. Thus the policy has not successfully alleviated the constraints on districts that wish to spend more on education than the state's funding formula permits. A bill sponsored by state representatives in the summer of 2001 called for a revision to the law that would have allowed individual districts to raise up to 1 mill for school operating costs with voter approval. That bill did not pass, however, because of fears that it would undermine the initial reform and be a gateway to increasing property taxes and inequities.

Courant and Loeb (1997) noted that the loss of local control over education spending in Michigan should become increasingly noticeable over time. This prediction seems to be coming true.

Three other issues in regard to the reform of school financing in Michigan are worth noting:

• First, the current school finance program does nothing to equalize capital expenditures across districts (Theobald 2002). When left to local jurisdictions, the distribution of capital is likely to look much like the distribution of operating expenditures. Districts with high demand for schooling and high ability to pay will have better facilities. The difficulty comes in designing an equitable system that does not penalize districts for investments already made. The lack of state-provided capital funds is especially problematic for charter schools. Because charter schools have no taxing authority, it is difficult for potential academies to raise the revenues needed for startup costs.

• Second, the financing system under Proposal A imposes difficulties on districts that are losing enrollment (Theobald 2002). When a district loses a student, its costs do not necessarily decrease by the average per-pupil cost. Many costs are fixed, at least in the short run. Existing facilities need to be maintained; programs need to run while they are reorganized to fit the shrinking population (*Detroit News* 1995, 2001d). Even year-to-year fluctuations can be difficult to handle if fewer students than expected enroll, since teachers are hired on the basis of projected enrollment. This is especially true now that district revenues are tied so directly to enrollment and there is so little leeway to raise funds locally.

The current funding program for Michigan schools does attempt to mitigate the difficulties presented by time-varying district enrollments by basing part of district revenues on enrollment in February of the previous academic year and part on enrollment in September of the academic year in question. Prior to 2000, this split was 40 percent and 60 percent, respectively. In 2000, it changed to 25 percent and 75 percent, respectively, and currently it is 20 percent and 80 percent, respectively. Thus the trend has been moving away from adjusting for the previous year's enrollment, compounding the difficulties faced by districts with lower than expected enrollment.

School choice exacerbates these tensions by introducing further uncertainty into district budgets through added uncertainty about student enrollment. Moreover, if local students attending schools outside the home district have lower costs than those remaining, then that districts' costs are reduced by less than its revenue loss. There is strong evidence that charter school students do have lower costs than average students in their district, since new charter schools have concentrated in the lower grades. To address this, Horn and Miron (2000) recommend that foundation grants to districts be differentiated based on average costs by grade level. In general, the implicit assumption that the marginal student (in this case, the one who leaves the district) is as costly as the average student can create severe difficulties for districts.

It may, in fact, preclude the public-sector response to choice that is, in theory, the aspect of choice that will most improve education in the state.

• Third, the shift from local to state control of education funding means that such funding may be affected by a variety of state issues. At the state level, K–12 education has to compete with many other funding areas. The state's revenue surpluses, substantial at the time of reform, were used up by 1997. In that year, there were concerns about reductions in other state budget areas because of the guaranteed funding commitments for K–12 education (Harvey 1995). The concern could easily go the other way, however. The 1994 Proposal A legislation automated the yearly change in foundation levels based on the statewide revenues per pupil for taxes earmarked for the School Aid Fund. The legislature may feel pressure, however, to adjust the funding structure, and even within the framework included in the legislation, there is room for interpretation. Categorical programs, which are particularly important to districts with disadvantaged student populations, may be most at risk of losing funding, since their revenue levels are not tied to an index.

The state's ability to maintain these categorical funds may be limited because an increasing share of its revenues are earmarked for particular programs and thus restricted as to their use. Figure 7.13 plots the proportion of total direct revenues and of total tax revenues in the state that are restricted in this way. Prior to 1991 the proportion of total direct revenues that was restricted was approximately 55 percent. In 1991 it increased to 61 percent, where it remained until the passage of Proposal A in 1994. Since 1995, this percentage has climbed to 72 percent. The percentage of total tax revenue that is restricted has followed a similar trend. The Michigan legislature thus has less flexibility within the current system as to how it allocates its revenues.

Moreover, school revenues are now intricately tied to the network of state revenue-raising policies. Changes in any one of the state revenue instruments may reduce funds targeted to the School Aid Fund. Drake (2002) calculates that the series of changes made to the relevant revenue sources since the first year of the reform, such as increases in the income tax exemption level, reduced revenues earmarked for schooling by roughly $328 per pupil in 2002. School funding is now also more directly tied to economic conditions than previously, through the shift from the property to the sales tax. The instability of the sales tax combined with the indexing of the school aid formula to state taxes

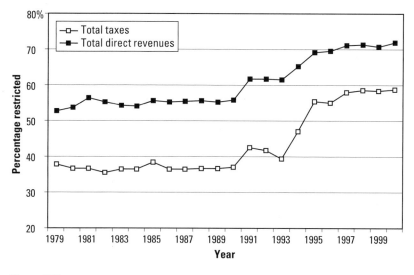

Figure 7.13
Restricted portion of Michigan state government revenues.

may become a problem for local districts that have no flexibility to raise additional funds.

In conclusion, Proposal A was a radical shift in school financing in Michigan along a number of dimensions. It equalized resources across districts by increasing revenues in the lowest-spending districts and essentially freezing the revenues of higher-spending districts; it shifted funding responsibilities to the state level and constrained the revenue-raising capacity of local jurisdictions; it decreased and equalized property tax rates and increased the sales tax; and it introduced school choice to Michigan in the form of charter schools and open enrollment. Each of these changes has created new challenges and opportunities. The tensions that have emerged most strongly so far as a result of the reform are dissatisfaction in high-demand districts that wish to increase their spending levels and financial difficulties in districts with shrinking enrollments and revenues. It is not yet clear whether these problems will be solved through tinkering with the current system or whether they will lead to more systemic change.

Notes

1. Here, and throughout the chapter we refer to school years by the fiscal year in which they fall. For example, 1995 refers to the school year 1994–95.

2. We use the consumer price index for all goods for September of each year to convert nominal values to values in constant 2001 dollars.

3. In keeping with its mathematics performance, Michigan scored slightly above the national average on all other NAEP tests, including fourth-grade reading in 1992 and 1998, fourth-grade science in 2000, and eighth-grade science in 1996 and 2000.

4. The state had moved from a modified foundation program to the district power equalization program in 1973.

5. SEV is constitutionally set at one-half of market value, but in practice tends to be slightly less than that.

6. For these high-wealth districts, categorical aid was also reduced by a percentage that varied directly with the yield from the local operating levy.

7. All calculations requiring district-level financial data are from Michigan Department of Education financial database files available for the years 1992–2002.

8. The difference between the actual and the predicted ratios may be partly due to district SEV being a noisy proxy for resident income, as well as to any systematic differences that may have existed between on- and off-formula districts other than wealth, such as the differences in costs described in section 7.5.

9. In addition to changing the relative importance of different taxes, Proposal A cut taxes overall. Local property taxes decreased by $5.258 billion following reform, though this was partially offset by a $1.258 billion increase in the state property tax (Courant and Loeb 1997). The sales tax increase added approximately $2.217 billion in revenues. Overall, state taxes fell by $844 million. The federal government took some of this tax break, however, since sales tax expenditures cannot be deducted from federal income tax, whereas property tax expenditures can. Courant and Loeb (1997) estimate the federal income tax cost to taxpayers of this shift from property tax to sales tax at $429 million.

10. A grandfather clause allows 13 (of the 524) K–12 districts that levied less than 18 mills on nonhomestead property prior to the reform to levy at their previous millage rate.

11. Revenue eligible to be counted in the base consisted of local school operating property tax revenue, state payments for formula aid and state payments for categorical programs that were "rolled up" into the foundation allowance. The base amount determines which group the district was placed in for calculating the foundation allowance. The allowance is then equal to the base amount plus a supplemental amount that varies across groups and is larger the smaller is the base amount.

12. The $746 million that the state labels as special education aid includes the full amount of the foundation grant for each special-needs student. This amount is really basic aid that has been relabeled, however, since the state attributes the entire required local levy to the local share of the foundation grant for general education students.

13. Prior to 2000, hold-harmless districts were not eligible for this aid. More recently these districts have been receiving aid, but at the lower rate of 5.75 percent.

14. Depending on the relative burden borne by business under property and sales taxes, which is hard to determine, the reform may have shifted toward or away from taxes on business.

15. This is in keeping with Prince 1996, which finds that revenues in the lowest-revenue districts increased by 30 percent in real terms between 1994 and 1997 whereas those in the highest-revenue districts declined by 4 percent.

16. Specifically, we use the coefficients on three demographic variables from model I in table 10-1 of Duncombe, Ruggiero, and Yinger 1996 and the actual values for districts in Michigan to predict the percentage increase in spending relative to a baseline (e.g., $1 + [0.8306 \times$ percentage in poverty$] + [2.1166 \times$ percentage in female-headed households$] + [0.3903 \times$ percentage of disabled students$]$). We then create a comprehensive cost index by normalizing the predicted values according to the average across all districts and then multiplying these values by the geographic cost index (which has also been normalized to equal one, on average).

17. Michigan also reports scores for reading in fourth and seventh grade and writing, science, and social studies in fifth and eighth grades, but the scoring has not been consistent over the relevant time period.

18. Similarly, a 10 percent increase in expenditures is associated with a 1.0-percentage-point ($p = 0.001$) increase in satisfactory rates in the fourth grade without the control for prior outcomes and a 0.2-percentage-point decrease ($p = 0.34$) with the control. The numbers for seventh-grade satisfactory rates are 0.2 ($p = 0.47$) and -0.4 ($p = 0.10$), respectively.

19. The grants rewarding good school and student performance may be leading to perverse behavior. Given that significant funds are redirected based on the high-stakes exams through both direct payments from the state and indirect student choice, it may not be surprising that seventy-one Michigan schools across twenty-two districts were involved in a cheating scandal in 2001.

20. Sixty-two of the 524 K–12 districts in Michigan approved these mills for 1996 (Prince 1996).

8 School Finance Reform in Texas: A Never-Ending Story?

Jennifer Imazeki and Andrew Reschovsky

8.1 Introduction

For over thirty years, Texas courts have been challenging the state's legislature to develop fairer and more equitable ways to finance public education within the state. On a more or less continuous basis, a stream of court cases has challenged the financing of K–12 education in Texas. This chapter reviews this judicial history, evaluates the success of the current system of school finance in Texas in achieving various school finance equity goals, and attempts to assess the ongoing school finance issues that Texas will face over the next few years.

With over four million students, the public school system in Texas is the second largest in the United States, currently educating nearly 10 percent of all public school students in the country.[1] Together the state's 1,036 regular school districts had $26.2 billion in revenue for the 2000–01 school year. Of this total, the federal government contributed 3.4 percent, the state government 43.6 percent, and local school districts the remaining 53 percent. In 1998–99, the latest year for which national data are available, current expenditures per pupil in Texas were $5,685, more than $800 per pupil below the national average, placing Texas thirty-fourth in per-pupil expenditures among the fifty states.

From a national perspective, Texas is a particularly interesting state to study. School finance in Texas has been largely shaped by a series of important court cases based on the full range of arguments used to challenge systems of public school finance in the United States, from equal protection cases, to well-articulated arguments for fiscal neutrality, and most recently, to arguments that the school system must provide all students with an *adequate* education. Texas is also interesting for the responses it has made to the court challenges. To achieve fiscal neutrality, it has implemented an innovative system of state aid that combines a foundation formula, a guaranteed tax base formula, and caps on the tax capacity of wealthy districts. In addition, Texas has recognized that certain characteristics of school districts and of students raise the costs of providing education. Its response has been to adjust its state aid formulas in ways that attempt to account for the full array of factors that have been found to be systematically related to the costs of education. Finally, Texas has been in the forefront in establishing student performance goals based on a set of standardized tests and using these tests to assess the performance of schools and school districts. Given the Texas background of the current president and the secretary of education, there can be little question that the early adoption of an accountability system in Texas influenced the focus on school accountability in the recently enacted No Child Left Behind Act (2001).

In the next section of the chapter, we review the history of school finance litigation in Texas and chart how the state legislature has responded to the various court rulings over the years. We then describe in detail the current system of school finance and explain how the state's rather complex multitiered system of state aid formulas works. In section 8.4, we assess how well the state responses have met the equity goals established by the courts. In section 8.5, we attempt to assess whether the current Texas school finance system allocates resources among school districts in a manner that will enable all school districts to meet the new state and federal accountability standards included in the No Child Left Behind Act. The system of school finance in Texas has changed dramatically over the past two decades. Although the current system of state aid to local school districts has passed constitutional muster, a number of recent developments suggest that a new school finance crisis may develop in the state over the next few years. In the final section of the chapter, we explore several factors that may contribute to this potential funding crisis. These include the growing opposition to a provision of the current state school aid system that requires a number of high-property-value school districts to contribute property tax revenues to poorer districts, the fact that an increasing number of school districts are reaching a state-imposed property tax rate limit, and the rising costs of meeting new accountability standards tied to student academic performance. We conclude the chapter by suggesting a reform to the current state aid system designed to address these problems.

8.2 The History of School Finance Litigation in Texas

In July 1968, Demetrio Rodriguez and a group of other parents jointly filed suit in federal district court in Texas challenging the Texas school funding system on behalf of children who resided in property-poor school districts. The plaintiffs claimed that the heavy reliance in the state on local property taxes for the funding of schools denied them equal protection as guaranteed under the Fourteenth Amendment of the U.S. Constitution. The legal argument was based on the assertion that public education is a fundamental interest that should not be conditioned on school district property wealth. The plaintiffs also argued that there was no compelling state purpose for utilizing a system of education finance that relied so heavily on the local property tax. The legal argument at the core of the *Rodriguez* case was based on the principle of fiscal neutrality. Based on the work of Coons, Clune, and Sugarman (1970), the plaintiffs argued that although individual school districts could choose how much they wanted to spend per pupil, these per-student amounts should not be a function of districts' property wealth.

The plaintiffs won in district court, and the case was appealed to the U.S. Supreme Court, which, in a 5–4 decision, reversed the district court's ruling (*San Antonio Independent School District v. Rodriguez* [1973]). The Court argued that despite its importance to society, education was not a fundamental interest, primarily because it is not a right explicitly guaranteed in the Constitution (Minorini and Sugarman 1999b). Furthermore, the Court argued that no convincing evidence had been presented that even property-poor school districts could not provide the basic skills necessary for participation in the political process. Because poverty and school district property wealth were not strongly correlated, the Court argued that the education financing system in Texas did not discriminate against poor children. The Court also argued that the preservation of local school district control over education provided a compelling reason for the state to maintain its system of funding education.

The *Rodriguez* decision had important implications for efforts to reform school finance throughout the country. The decision closed the door to future challenges of state school funding systems based on claims that those systems violated the equal protection clause of the U.S. Constitution. Ever since the *Rodriguez* ruling, all school finance cases, in Texas and throughout the country, have been argued on the basis of violations of state rather than of federal constitutional provisions.

Although eleven years passed until another suit was filed in Texas challenging the equity of the state's school funding system, the state's legislature during the intervening years took limited steps to reduce fiscal inequalities among school districts. Using revenues from a budget surplus, the legislature in 1975 increased state education funding allocated through an existing foundation formula and established a very small guaranteed tax yield formula (Johns 1976).

In 1984, the Mexican American Legal Defense and Education Fund filed a suit in Texas district court challenging the equity of the state's system of school finance. The plaintiffs in the case (*Edgewood Independent School District et al. v. Kirby et al.* [1989]) argued that Texas's heavy reliance on the property tax and the existence of a large variation in per-pupil property values led to a big disparity in spending per pupil across districts in the state. Even if they levied property taxes at high rates, school districts with relatively little property wealth per pupil were unable to raise sufficient revenue to finance education programs that met the state's minimum education requirements. The plaintiffs argued that the existing funding system in Texas violated both the equal protection clause and education clause of the Texas constitution. The education clause (Article 7, Section 1) requires that the state "make suitable provision for the state support and maintenance of an *efficient* system of free public schools" (emphasis added).

The trial court ruled in favor of the plaintiffs in a 1987 decision, declaring the state's school financing system unconstitutional. Although, on appeal, a state appeals court reversed the lower court ruling, in October 1989, the Texas Supreme Court affirmed the lower court's ruling in a unanimous decision and ordered the state legislature to develop an equitable system of school finance in time for the 1990–91 school year (Texas State Historical Association 2001). In its decision, the court took note of the large disparities in property wealth per pupil across districts. The poorest school district in the state had a property tax base per pupil of just $20,000, whereas the per-pupil property tax base in the richest school district was a whopping $14 million—a range of 700 to 1 (Texas Association of School Boards 1996). The court found that the state had not done enough to redress these differences in wealth, thereby resulting in a situation in which property-poor districts were unable to meet their constitutional obligation to provide students with an "efficient" education.

In response to the Texas Supreme Court decision, the Texas legislature enacted legislation (Senate Bill 1) in June 1990 that increased state funding for public schools by over $500 million. The plaintiffs in the *Edgewood* case were not satisfied with the new legislation, and they immediately brought suit to challenge its constitutionality. They argued that the new law left the basic structure of the state's school finance system in place and did not guarantee that the same tax effort would produce essentially the same amount of revenue in school districts with different amounts of per-pupil property wealth (Center for Public Policy Priorities 1998). In January 1991, the Texas Supreme Court, in a ruling generally referred to as *Edgewood II*, accepted the plaintiffs' argument and gave the legislature a couple of months to come up with a new funding system.

In response, the legislature passed Senate Bill 351. The new legislation combined the state's existing 1,058 independent school districts into 188 "county education districts" (CEDs). When fully phased in, these districts would levy a state-mandated property tax of $1 per $100 of property value on the first $280,000 of property value per pupil. The revenue raised ($2,800 per pupil) would be distributed on an equal per-pupil basis within each district. This new legislation was challenged by a group of wealthy school districts, and in January 1992, in a ruling referred to as *Edgewood III*, the Texas Supreme Court ruled that Senate Bill 351 was unconstitutional because it violated Article 7, Section 3, of the state's constitution, which required local voter approval of school property tax levies, and Article 7, Section 1-e, which prohibited a statewide property tax (Legislative Budget Board 2001).[2] The court gave the legislature a year to come up with a new system of school finance.

In May 1993, the legislature enacted Senate Bill 7, which it hoped would satisfy the mandate of the supreme court to develop a more equitable school finance system. The legislation was designed to achieve fiscal neutrality. A fiscally neutral system is one in which all school districts choosing the same property tax rate would have available approximately the same amount of revenue per student.[3] The legislation established a system of state aid to education that consisted of three major elements. The first element (tier I) was a foundation formula that provided school districts with a guaranteed amount of money per pupil if they agreed to levy a minimum property tax rate. The second element (tier II) was a guaranteed tax base formula that guaranteed all districts a certain amount of money for each extra cent of property tax effort. The third element, the so-called Chapter 41 recapture provision, involved capping the revenue-raising capacity of all school districts with property wealth above $280,000 per pupil. These high-wealth districts were given five options for implementing the revenue cap: (1) complete consolidation with a property-poor district, (2) ceding territory for purposes of taxable valuation, (3) purchasing "attendance credits" from the state, (4) contracting for the education of nonresident students, or (5) consolidating their tax bases with a property-poor district. The legislation included provisions that allowed for the phasing in of the recapture provisions over a number of years.

Senate Bill 7 also established a statewide accountability system for the state's schools. The basis of the accountability system was to be student performance on a series of standardized reading, writing, and mathematics tests. These tests, which were initiated in 1990, are known as the Texas Assessment of Academic Skills (TAAS). The legislation required that all schools in the state meet state standards for improving student performance on these tests. The standards were to be set not only for average student performance, but for the performance of students characterized by racial group and for that of economically disadvantaged students. School districts were required to provide extra instruction for students who did not meet the performance standards (Legislative Budget Board 2000).

In January 1995, the Texas Supreme Court, ruling in a case commonly referred to as *Edgewood IV*, declared that the school finance system established in Senate Bill 7 was constitutional.[4] Although there have been some revisions to the school funding formulas used in Texas since 1993, the basic system of state aid established in Senate Bill 7 remains in place today. It is described in considerably more detail in section 8.3.

In its ruling in *Edgewood IV*, the court expressed concern about inequities in the capital financing of school facilities in the state. Traditionally, the state had played a very limited role in providing funding for school buildings, leaving local school districts to bear most of the costs of capital facilities. The court suggested that if the legislature did not now deal with this issue, the entire school funding system might be deemed to be unconstitutional "in the very near future" (Legislative Budget Board 2001, 30). In response to this warning from the supreme court, the legislature did, in subsequent years, pass legislation that provided for additional state aid to school districts for instructional facilities and for debt financing. Funding for these two purposes was set at $1.45 billion for the 2002–03 biennium (Legislative Budget Board 2001).

In 1998, the equity of the Texas school finance system was again challenged in court. The suit, referred to as *Edgewood V*, charged that equity in education financing in the state was being eroded because of various provisions that allowed some property-rich school districts to escape in whole or in part the recapture provisions established in Senate Bill 7. The suit also claimed that no provisions for equalization existed with regard to the financing of certain old debt payments (Legislative Budget Board 2001). In part because the legislature in 1999 had addressed some of the issues raised in the suit and had increased both tier I and tier II funding, the suit has not been heard.

The long history of court challenges to the Texas school finance system has not ended. In the last section of the chapter we discuss the current challenges and issues related to school financing in Texas. Our discussion includes a review of two lawsuits that have recently been filed challenging the constitutionality of the state's school finance system.

8.3 Description of the School Funding System in Texas

Senate Bill 7 laid down the basic framework for the current system of school finance in Texas. In part because of the series of court cases and ensuing legislative reforms, the system is a complex assortment of formulas, adjustments, and weights, collectively known as the Foundation School Program (FSP). In this section, we briefly outline the basic components of the system.

The FSP distributes aid to districts under three tiers of funding. Tier I is based on a traditional foundation formula that guarantees a base level of funding to all districts that levy a minimum property tax rate. In 2001–02, the base funding level, called the basic allotment, was $2,537 per pupil in average daily attendance (ADA). This allotment, however, is adjusted in several ways. Districts with fewer than 1,600 and fewer than 5,000 students receive the small and mid-sized district adjustments, respectively. Districts that have low enrollments and are over 300 square miles in area qualify for the sparsity adjustment. Finally, a cost-of-education index is applied that is designed to reflect cost variations due to such factors as cost of living in the district and concentration of low-income students. Each of these adjustments increases the basic allotment for individual districts.

Additional adjustments to districts' tier I guaranteed level of revenue are made through the use of extra weights for certain categories of students. Within each district, each student in average daily attendance (ADA) is given a weight of one. Additional weights are assigned to students in special education, compensatory education, bilingual education, career and technology (vocational) education, or gifted and talented education, or in the public education grant program.[5] Once the basic allotment and ADA have been adjusted, a district's tier I guaranteed funding level is the adjusted allotment multiplied by the weighted ADA, plus a transportation allotment that is based on number of students and bus route miles.

To participate in the FSP, a district is required to levy a property tax at a rate of $0.86 per $100 of assessed valuation. A district's Local Fund assignment (LFA) is then calculated as the amount of revenue that the district can raise at the required tax rate. If the LFA is less than the tier I guaranteed level, the state makes up the difference. Thus, tier I aid is inversely related to district property wealth (i.e., the lower a district's wealth, the lower its LFA and the larger the difference between the LFA and the tier I guarantee). In keeping with the mandate of the courts, under tier I, all districts are able to raise the same amount of revenue at the required tax rate, regardless of property wealth.

Tier I also includes a per-pupil grant that is funded with money from the Available School Fund (ASF). The ASF per-pupil amount varies from year to year. In fiscal year 2002, it was $250. All school districts, including those not entitled to aid through the foundation formula (because they are able to fund their tier I guarantee fully through the local levy), are eligible for the ASF per-pupil amount.

For districts that choose to levy a tax rate higher than $0.86, tier II provides additional equalization funds, based on a guaranteed tax base formula. For the 2001–02 school year, districts were guaranteed $25.81 per weighted pupil in ADA for each penny increase in the tax rate over $0.86, up to a maximum tax rate of $1.50.[6] This means that for districts with property wealth of less than the guaranteed tax base of $258,100 per weighted pupil in ADA, the state makes up the difference between the amount of local property tax revenue at the chosen tax rate and the amount that would be raised if the district had the guaranteed tax base. Again, aid is inversely related to district property wealth, since the lower a district's wealth (below $258,100), the larger the difference between local revenue and the $25.81 per-pupil guarantee. Thus, all districts with property wealth below $258,100 are able to raise equal revenue at equal tax rates, regardless of property wealth. Districts with wealth greater than the guaranteed tax base will be able to generate more than the $25.81 for each penny of tax rate and thus will receive no tier II aid.

It should be noted that under tier II, districts with property wealth above $258,100 are able to generate more revenue with the same tax effort than lower-wealth districts. To further equalize revenues and increase fiscal neutrality, the Texas system required for the 2001–02 school year that districts with property wealth greater than $300,000 per weighted ADA reduce their wealth through one of the five recapture options presented in section 8.2. The most commonly chosen of these recapture options are the purchase of attendance credits from the state and paying for the cost of educating students in other districts. In 1999–2000, eighty-eight districts in Texas were subject to the recapture provision; all chose one (or some combination) of these two options (Texas Education Agency 2000). As we discuss in more detail in section 8.6, the recapture provision is perhaps the most controversial component of the state aid system and has been the impetus for the most recent court cases.

The Texas system also provides some equalization of debt service for capital facilities. The Instructional Facilities Allotment (IFA) Program involves a guaranteed yield formula, similar to that for tier II aid, that guarantees districts up to $35 per *unweighted* pupil in ADA for each penny of new debt service tax levied specifically for instructional facilities. In 1999–2000, an additional program was created to assist districts with existing debt. The Existing Debt Allotment (EDA) Program also guarantees districts, for eligible debt, up to $35 per unweighted pupil in ADA for each penny of debt service tax levied, up to a limit of twelve cents. These two facilities financing programs are referred to as tier III.

The FSP and the IFA were created to comply with court requirements that districts with similar tax efforts be able to raise similar amounts of revenue, regardless of property wealth in the districts. In the next section, we discuss whether the system has achieved this goal.

8.4 How Equitable Is the Texas School Funding System?

As discussed in section 8.2, the *Edgewood* litigation was motivated in large part by the disparity in spending per pupil that resulted from large variations in per-pupil property wealth across Texas districts.

Heavy reliance on the local property tax meant that low-wealth districts could not raise sufficient revenue to finance the level of education mandated by the state constitution, even when levying high tax rates. The current funding system thus attempts to provide equal revenues for equal tax effort. How well has the system done at meeting the original (*access equality*) objectives?

It should be noted that when the Texas Supreme Court upheld Senate Bill 7 as constitutional in 1995, it created three measures with which to assess the equity of the resulting financing system: (1) the percentage of total FSP revenue within the equalized funding system (with a target of 98 percent); (2) the percentage of students within the equalized funding system (with a target of 85 percent); and (3) the variation in revenue per weighted ADA between property-wealthy districts (i.e., districts subject to recapture) and districts with wealth below the tier II guaranteed wealth level (with a target of no more than $600). By these measures, the system has been equitable in each year since *Edgewood IV*.[7]

The third measure, variation in revenue between high- and low-wealth districts, is the only one of the three that actually gives an indication of the funding system's access or fiscal neutrality. In our analysis, we focus on measures of equity commonly found in the school finance literature. Specifically, following Berne and Stiefel (1984), we use the wealth elasticity of revenue per pupil as our measure of access neutrality. We also calculate the coefficient of variation and the Gini coefficient of school district revenue as measures of equality.

Table 8.1 shows summary and equity statistics for K–12 districts in Texas in 2000–01. The data are from the Texas Education Agency's *Snapshot* reports.[8] Large disparities in property wealth from district to district, which played such a prominent role in the *Edgewood* cases, are still evident. The wealthiest district in the state has an equalized property wealth per pupil that is 192 times the wealth of the poorest district (though this is down from the 700-to-1 ratio at the time of *Edgewood I*). The impact of the FSP grant system can be seen by looking at the distribution of total school district revenue per pupil displayed in the second column of the table. Despite large differences in property wealth per pupil across school districts, revenue per pupil appears to be fairly evenly distributed across districts, with a Gini coefficient of 0.102 and a coefficient of variation equal to 0.223.

Table 8.1
Equalized property value and revenue per pupil, Texas K–12 school districts, 2000–01

	Equalized property value per pupil	Revenue per pupil
Number of districts	958	958
Mean	$ 210,586	$ 7,214
Standard deviation	199,106	1,498
Range	2,156,904	15,881
Minimum	11,295	2,717
Maximum	2,168,199	18,598
Restricted range	311,474	2,901
10th percentile	79,907	5,940
90th percentile	391,381	8,841
Coefficient of variation	0.945	0.223
Gini coefficient	0.389	0.102
Wealth elasticity		0.125
Correlation between revenue per pupil and equalized property value per pupil	0.5849	

The equalizing effects of the FSP system can also be seen in table 8.2, which shows the coefficient of variation and Gini coefficient of revenue per pupil across K–12 districts in Texas in each year since 1987–88.[9] Both statistics have declined since the late 1980s, with the largest reduction occurring in 1994–95, after the enactment of Senate Bill 7. Since then the values of the two statistics have been relatively stable. The coefficient of variation peaked in 1991–92 with a value of 0.301 and declined to 0.210 for the 1999–2000 school year, whereas the Gini coefficient declined from 0.130 in 1988–89 to 0.099 in 1999–2000.

The FSP has also been quite successful at achieving access and wealth neutrality. Although the wealth elasticity of revenue per pupil is positive and statistically significant, its magnitude as of 2000–01 is a modest 0.125. This number implies that a 1 percent increase in property values per pupil (an increase of roughly $2,106 at the mean property value) is associated with a 0.125 percent increase in revenue per pupil, or an increase of $8.66 at the mean revenue per pupil. It is important to note, however, that for the 748 K–12 districts with per-pupil property wealth less than $246,000 (the tier II cutoff in 2000–01), the elasticity is only 0.02. This number implies that for two-thirds of all Texas public school pupils, namely, those living in these 748 districts,

Table 8.2
Distribution of revenue per pupil: Changes in school financing equity, 1987–88 to 2000–01, Texas K–12 school districts

School year	Average	Standard deviation	Coefficient of variation	Gini coefficient	Wealth elasticity
1987–88	$3,926	$1,082	0.276	0.129	0.199
1988–89	4,027	1,145	0.284	0.130	0.219
1989–90	4,262	1,171	0.275	0.127	0.217
1990–91	4,703	1,244	0.264	0.124	0.190
1991–92	5,100	1,537	0.301	0.127	0.167
1992–93	5,360	1,360	0.254	0.118	0.139
1993–94	5,397	1,533	0.284	0.121	0.156
1994–95	5,435	1,194	0.220	0.106	0.126
1995–96	5,831	1,314	0.225	0.107	0.108
1996–97	5,800	1,271	0.219	0.105	0.114
1997–98	6,225	1,525	0.245	0.111	0.134
1998–99	6,417	1,547	0.241	0.109	0.131
1999–2000	6,925	1,456	0.210	0.099	0.110
2000–01	7,233	1,611	0.223	0.102	0.125

the FSP has resulted in effective wealth neutrality.[10] The data in the last column of table 8.2 also demonstrate that the fiscal neutrality of the Texas school funding system has increased over time, as indicated by a quite sharp reduction in wealth elasticity since the late 1980s.

8.5 Does the Texas School Funding System Achieve Educational Adequacy?

The primary focus of school finance reform in Texas has been fiscal or access neutrality, breaking the connection between property wealth and dollars per pupil. As the analysis in the previous section suggests, Texas has been relatively successful at meeting this equity goal. Over the last several years, however, the focus of school finance reformers has been shifting from the distribution of school resources to school outcomes, namely, student academic performance. This shift is exemplified by the recently enacted federal education legislation, the No Child Left Behind Act of 2001, which emphasizes standards and accountability. Almost every state now has, or is considering, some kind of accountability policy in which districts, teachers, students, or some combination are assessed for their performance on specific outcome measures. Although these accountability programs may include monetary rewards or punishments, for individual teachers, schools, or school districts, there is generally little connection between school district performance and state aid formulas. For example, in Texas, a well-defined accountability system has been in place since 1993. Specifically, the state determines standards for two performance measures, test scores and dropout rate (and collects data on a number of other measures as well), then assigns each school an accountability rating (exemplary, recognized, acceptable, low-performing) based on performance relative to the standard.[11] Exemplary, recognized, and acceptable ratings are associated with increasing monetary rewards, whereas a district that receives a low-performing ranking may be subject to state intervention. As in most states, however, a district's accountability ranking is unrelated to the distribution of state (FSP) aid.

Nevertheless, the connection between resources and outcomes has been recognized by the courts for many years. In a number of states, for example, Kentucky, Wyoming, and New Hampshire, school finance systems were declared unconstitutional because they did not provide the opportunity for all students to receive an adequate education. In each of these cases, the courts explicitly stated that all students should be provided with the opportunity to acquire a certain set of skills. In several recent court rulings, for example, *Rose v. Council for Better Education* (1989) in Kentucky, or *Claremont School District v. Gregg* (1997) in New Hampshire, the courts have spelled out in great detail the skills that students must master to receive an adequate education.

Embedded in this adequacy movement is an understanding that equal dollars do not guarantee equal outcomes. Thus, states with finance systems that do very well at equalizing revenues or at maintaining fiscal neutrality may still exhibit large disparities in student outcomes, and thus there may still be students in those states who are not receiving an adequate education, because the amount of money necessary to achieve a particular performance standard may be different across districts as a result of variations in costs, for reasons that are outside the control of the districts. For example, some districts, because of their geographic location or the composition of their student bodies, may need to pay higher salaries than other districts to attract teachers of the same quality. Or a district with a high concentration of students from poor families or from families where English is not spoken in the home may need additional resources (in the form of smaller classes or specialized instructors) to reach a given achievement goal.

Some of these variations in cost have long been acknowledged and accounted for in state aid programs. For example, it is commonplace for districts to receive additional aid for each disabled student in a special education program. The ways in which states account for these cost differences in their aid formulas include pupil weights, add-on categorical aid, or cost-of-living adjustments. The FSP in Texas includes all of these. The tier I basic allotment is adjusted for district size and sparsity and then a geographic cost-of-living index is applied, while average daily attendance (in both tier I and tier II) is adjusted with weights for students in certain program categories.

Given that Texas has specific performance goals as part of its accountability system, and that sanctions are imposed on school districts in Texas that consistently do not meet the student performance standards, it is particularly important that the state ensure that districts have sufficient resources to allow them to achieve these goals. Without additional aid to compensate for higher costs, schools in high-cost districts may fail to meet the accountability standards, not because of their own inability to educate children, but because they have insufficient fiscal resources to do the job. Thus, the adjustments included in the FSP play a crucial role in helping districts increase academic performance.

The weights and adjustments used in Texas, however, may not be the most appropriate way to account for variations in school district costs. The origin of many of these weights is unclear. We suspect that the explicit and implicit weights used in the Texas school aid formulas are the result of political negotiations, rather than the product of the careful measurement of differences in the costs of educating various groups of students.[12] Because the accuracy of these adjustments and weights in reflecting the cost differences is unknown, it is possible that school districts with high concentrations of low-income or special education students may still not be receiving sufficient resources to meet the new accountability standards. Table 8.3 shows the distribution of revenue per pupil for K–12 districts in Texas, divided into quintiles by districts characterized in various ways, such as the percentage of poor students.[13] With the current FSP adjustments, districts with the highest proportion of English as a second language (ESL) students generally have *lower* revenue per pupil than districts with fewer such students. Small districts and districts with a high proportion of poor children and of special education students do, however, have higher levels of per-pupil revenues than larger districts and districts with relatively few poor and special education students.

Table 8.3
Distribution of revenue per pupil by pupil-weighted quintiles for selected districts, Texas
K–12 school districts, 2000–01

| Quintiles | Quintile statistics | | | | Revenue per pupil |
	Mean	Number of districts	Minimum value	Maximum value	
District size (number of students)					
1	1,040	765	56	3,745	$7,430
2	6,433	125	3,815	12,983	6,334
3	19,615	41	13,161	29,875	6,372
4	41,835	19	31,536	57,273	6,534
5	96,989	8	58,866	208,462	6,280
Percentage of students from poor families					
1	18.9	140	0.0	26.8	$6,853
2	36.2	268	26.9	43.6	7,121
3	49.3	244	43.7	55.2	7,133
4	63.0	219	55.3	74.4	7,527
5	83.9	87	74.5	97.3	7,522
Percentage of students enrolled in English as a Second Language (ESL)					
1	1.4	474	0.0	3.6	$7,378
2	5.2	197	3.7	7.1	6,955
3	9.7	161	7.2	12.8	7,202
4	17.4	82	13.0	27.0	7,182
5	40.7	44	27.2	61.3	6,709
Percentage of students in Special Education					
1	8.3	103	2.3	9.9	$7,172
2	10.5	74	10.0	11.0	7,401
3	11.7	121	11.1	12.2	6,753
4	13.3	223	12.3	14.2	6,856
5	17.6	437	14.3	41.3	7,502
Equalized property value per pupil					
1	$ 90,383	331	$ 11,295	$ 122,392	$6,850
2	141,339	184	122,555	163,194	6,840
3	185,352	170	163,208	211,513	6,815
4	246,168	114	211,735	292,214	7,471
5	542,426	159	292,831	2,168,199	8,649

The question that needs to be addressed is whether the additional revenue being targeted to certain groups of students is enough to cover the costs of educating those students to an acceptable level of academic performance? To begin answering this question, table 8.4 divides districts into quintiles according to a number of characteristics, such as their proportion of poor students, then displays data on several measures of average student performance in each quintile. Although the average passing rates on standardized tests do not vary much among districts with high and low values of property per pupil, these passing rates are generally lower in school districts with high rates of poverty and high concentrations of ESL students than in districts with lower concentrations of poor and ESL students.

One reason for the variation in student performance across school districts may be that the school funding system does not guarantee school districts with high concentrations of needy students enough money to educate their students to a level required by the state's accountability standards. In other words, the pupil weights and other cost adjustments currently in the FSP may not allocate an adequate amount of resources to certain school districts with high concentrations of students who are costly to educate.

In an attempt to provide an independent estimate of the amount of money school districts with various characteristics need to achieve state-mandated student performance goals, we have estimated a cost function for K–12 education in Texas. A cost function for education in a state quantifies the relationship between per-pupil spending for education, student performance, various student characteristics, and the economic, educational, and social characteristics of school districts. The "output" of public schools is measured by student performance and is assumed to be a function of school inputs (e.g., teachers and textbooks), characteristics of the student body, and the family and neighborhood environment in which students live. This relationship can be represented by equation (8.1), where S_{it} represents an index of school output, X_{it} is a vector of direct school inputs, Z_{it} is a vector of student characteristics, and F_{it} is a vector of family and neighborhood characteristics:

$$S_{it} = g(X_{it}, Z_{it}, F_{it}). \tag{8.1}$$

The subscript i refers to the school district, and the subscript t refers to the year.

The amount that a district will need to spend to produce a particular level of output is a function of school inputs and the prices of those inputs. This is shown in equation (8.2), where per-pupil expenditures, E_{it}, are considered as a function of school inputs, a vector of input prices, P_{it}, and ε_{it}, a vector of unobserved characteristics of the school district:

$$E_{it} = f(X_{it}, P_{it}, \varepsilon_{it}). \tag{8.2}$$

Finally, by solving equation (8.1) for X_{it} and plugging X_{it} into equation (8.2), we arrive at the cost function represented by equation (8.3), where u_{it} is a random-error term.

$$E_{it} = h(S_{it}, P_{it}, Z_{it}, F_{it}, \varepsilon_{it}, u_{it}) \tag{8.3}$$

Typically, equation (8.3) is assumed to be log-linear and estimated with district-level data for a given state. The resulting coefficients indicate the contribution of various district characteristics to the cost of education, holding constant the level of output. Table 8.5 shows the results of an estimate of equation (8.3) using 2000–01 data for K–12 school districts in Texas.[14] Reschovsky and Imazeki (2003) provide a full discussion of the data and estimation procedures used. Scores on TAAS and the percentage of students taking either the SAT I or the ACT exams and achieving a particular score (1,110 on the SAT I and 24 on the ACT) are used as measures of school output. The percentage of students in poverty is found to increase the cost of achieving a given level of output; however, the percentage of students with severe disabilities (i.e., autistic, deaf or deaf/blind) and the percentage of students with limited English proficiency are associated with lower costs.[15] We find that enrollment has a U-shaped relationship with spending per pupil: Costs start out high for small districts and fall as enrollment increases, until district enrollment reaches roughly 12,735 students, at which point costs begin to rise again.[16]

The results of our cost function estimates displayed in table 8.5 are quite similar to results from similar studies of education costs conducted for New York State (Duncombe and Yinger 1999, 2000), for Illinois (Reschovsky and Imazeki 2000), and for Wisconsin (Reschovsky and Imazeki 1998). A cost function for Texas schools was recently estimated by Timothy Gronberg as part of a large study completed by the Charles A. Dana Center (Alexander et al. 2000). Although he included some different variables in his study, his results are qualitatively similar to ours.

Table 8.4
Distribution of students by pupil-weighted quintiles for selected district characteristics, Texas K–12 school districts, 2000–01

Quintiles	Passing rate for TAAS exams				Dropout rate	Percentage taking College Board exams	Percentage passing College Board exams
	All students	African American	Hispanic	Poor students			
District size (number of students)							
1	84.22	73.66	78.53	78.51	0.71	61.43	19.76
2	83.56	76.23	78.34	75.98	1.02	61.07	24.99
3	83.41	78.19	78.58	76.30	1.20	57.53	26.00
4	84.63	77.91	77.73	75.28	0.86	70.23	31.45
5	77.03	70.65	71.40	69.03	1.81	61.46	27.91
Percentage of students from poor families							
1	89.68	79.56	82.76	80.64	0.55	69.08	30.84
2	86.37	74.96	79.32	79.20	0.59	62.31	23.11
3	84.92	74.66	79.06	79.04	0.79	61.41	20.29
4	80.80	70.11	76.43	75.86	0.90	57.89	17.90
5	73.61	76.49	72.23	71.91	1.39	54.59	7.45
Percentage of students enrolled in English as a Second Language (ESL)							
1	85.97	75.51	80.75	79.98	0.61	62.73	22.25
2	84.97	73.86	78.38	77.68	0.79	62.10	22.33
3	81.09	72.14	75.64	75.32	0.98	59.14	21.11
4	81.18	75.31	76.38	76.33	1.06	60.29	17.52
5	72.11	77.50	70.20	69.89	1.39	54.40	8.97

Percentage of students in Special Education

1	82.82	76.94	77.25	76.50	0.90	64.36	22.25
2	82.76	77.51	77.36	76.10	0.77	62.40	21.99
3	84.29	73.20	78.89	77.46	0.90	60.41	23.99
4	83.93	73.46	77.85	77.21	0.85	61.21	20.59
5	84.55	74.72	79.08	79.10	0.69	60.89	20.01

Equalized property value per pupil

1	83.13	76.15	78.14	78.22	0.85	58.31	17.30
2	83.57	73.84	77.35	77.39	0.83	59.13	20.59
3	83.77	72.48	77.64	76.42	0.76	62.39	23.31
4	84.14	73.85	78.34	77.15	0.81	66.19	24.44
5	86.75	75.39	81.30	80.21	0.59	66.12	24.68

Table 8.5
Education cost function, 2000–01, for 875 K–12 Texas school districts

Variable	Coefficient	t-statistic
Intercept	−2.53	−0.95
Log of composite exam score, 2000–01	9.19*	4.60
Log of lagged composite exam score, 1998–2000	−6.60	−4.54
Percentage passing College Board exams	0.98*	5.61
Teacher salary index	0.004*	5.84
Percentage of students eligible for free or reduced-price lunch	0.57*	5.84
Percentage of students with disabilities	−0.08	−0.29
Percentage of students with severe disabilities	−10.75*	−2.56
Percentage of students with limited English	−0.17*	−1.90
Percentage of students enrolled in high school	−0.37	−1.31
Log of student enrollment	−0.28*	−5.12
Square of log of student enrollment	0.015*	5.04
Indicator for Dallas or Houston	−0.259*	−4.65
SSE	8.265	

Notes:
*Statistically significant at the 5% level.
**Statistically significant at the 10% level.

The cost function estimation results can be used to build a cost index that summarizes all the information about costs in a single number for each district. By holding the output measures constant at some chosen level and allowing the cost factors to vary across districts, we can predict the level of spending required for each district to achieve the chosen output level. For example, if we assume that the policymakers in Texas define the minimum standard for an accountability system as the current average level of student performance, then a cost index can be constructed that will indicate, for any given district, how much that district must spend, relative to the district with average costs, in order for its students to meet the performance standard. Using the cost function estimates from table 8.5, and setting the performance standard equal to the Texas state average achievement on the TAAS and ACT exams, the district with average costs (i.e., each of the cost factors set equal to its mean) must spend $6,925 per pupil (in 2000–01) to achieve the performance standard. For any given school district, the product of this average spending level and its cost index (divided by 100) will indicate the minimum amount that district must spend to meet the performance goal. Thus, for example, a district whose cost index is 125 will need to spend $8,656 ($6,925 times 125/100, or 1.25) to reach the same performance standard.

Alternatively, the cost index can be used to gauge whether a district's actual revenue is sufficient to reach the performance goal. A district's cost-adjusted revenue per pupil can be calculated as current revenue per pupil divided by the district's cost index. If this amount is less than the state average, it indicates that the district does not have sufficient revenue to meet the performance goal.

Table 8.6 shows the distribution of current and cost-adjusted revenue per pupil in Texas school districts.[17] The table indicates that Texas does a mixed job at providing high-cost districts with sufficient resources to meet student achievement goals. The FSP does well at allocating resources to districts with high concentrations of special education students and districts that have high costs because of diseconomies of scale (i.e., low enrollments). The FSP is not, however, as successful at allocating sufficient resources to districts with high concentrations of poor and bilingual students.[18] For example, whereas average cost-adjusted revenue per pupil is over $500 per pupil higher in the quintile with the smallest school districts relative to the quintile with the largest school districts ($7,120 compared to $6,608), the cost-adjusted revenue per pupil in the quintile with the highest proportion of poor children is $2,200 per student *lower* than cost-adjusted revenue in the quintile with the smallest proportion of poor students ($5,852 compared to $8,095). The pattern of student performance illustrated in table 8.4 is consistent with the patterns illustrated in table 8.6 for the distribution of resources. Thus, TAAS passing rates are higher and dropout rates lower in the smallest district size quintile relative to the largest district size quintile, whereas, paralleling the pattern of resource availability, the TAAS passing rate is lowest and the dropout rate highest in the quintile with the highest proportion of poor children.

8.6   Funding Texas Schools: An Impending Crisis?

The past thirty years of Texas history have been characterized by almost continuous changes in the way the state has financed public education. Often forced to act by the courts, the state legislature has crafted a system of state aid to local school districts that is both innovative and complex. By most measures, Texas has made great strides

Table 8.6
Distribution of revenue per pupil by pupil-weighted quintiles for selected district characteristics, Texas K–12 school districts, 2000–01

Quintiles	Quintile statistics				Revenue per pupil	Cost-adjusted per pupil
	Mean	Number of districts	Minimum value	Maximum value		
District size (number of students)						
1	1,142	682	99	3,883	$7,226	$7,120
2	6,426	121	3,933	12,515	6,333	7,041
3	19,203	41	12,983	29,687	6,389	6,833
4	40,393	19	29,875	53,999	6,488	7,403
5	96,790	8	57,273	208,462	6,383	6,608
Percentage of students from poor families						
1	18.5	128	1.2	26.5	$6,843	$8,095
2	36.1	268	26.6	44.0	6,977	7,380
3	49.6	218	44.1	55.3	7,079	6,997
4	63.0	183	55.4	74.4	7,223	6,608
5	84.4	74	74.5	97.3	7,026	5,852
Percentage of students enrolled in English as a Second Language (ESL)						
1	1.5	419	0.0	3.6	$7,124	$7,371
2	5.2	184	3.7	7.1	6,891	7,116
3	9.6	146	7.2	12.5	7,021	6,884
4	17.3	82	12.7	27.2	7,175	6,660
5	41.1	40	28.0	60.5	6,605	5,811
Percentage of students in Special Education						
1	8.5	89	3.9	9.9	$7,012	$7,217
2	10.5	66	10.0	11.0	7,192	7,331
3	11.7	129	11.1	12.3	6,657	6,876
4	13.3	196	12.4	14.2	6,757	6,905
5	17.2	391	14.3	38.1	7,286	7,200
Equalized property value per pupil						
1	$ 89,969	307	$ 11,295	$ 122,392	$6,781	$6,603
2	140,996	170	122,555	162,905	6,711	6,701
3	183,380	148	163,134	208,702	6,706	7,026
4	242,796	112	208,870	292,831	7,153	7,370
5	524,200	134	293,547	1,340,059	8,314	8,581

over this period in increasing the equity of its school funding system and, more importantly, in improving the quality of education received by most Texas public school students. In recent years, student performance on state-mandated standardized tests has improved substantially, with the largest percentage gains being achieved by African American and Hispanic students and by students from disadvantaged backgrounds (Legislative Budget Board 2000).[19]

Even though state legislators, local school officials, and parents may all long for a period of stability in Texas education financing, for reasons to be explained below, the current system of school finance in the state is inherently unstable. Unless the legislature makes substantial changes to the current system within the next few years, a serious fiscal crisis is likely to develop, and there is a high probability that the supreme court will again declare the funding system unconstitutional. Complicating the search for a solution to its education funding problems is the overall fiscal climate of the state. Texas faced a budget deficit of nearly $10 billion in fiscal year 2004, and unless the economic recovery from the recession that began in 2001 is very strong, like most other states, it faces the prospect of future budget shortfalls.

Four elements of the school finance system in Texas will, unless further action is taken, in our view inevitably lead to a full-scale funding crisis: the continuously falling state share of public school revenues, the rising costs of meeting state and federal accountability standards, the fact that an increasing number of school districts are hitting the state's $1.50 tax rate cap, and the growing opposition to the state's Chapter 41 recapture provisions. In the following sections, we explain how these elements interact with one another and how each increases the probability that major changes will have to be made to the current system of public education finance in Texas.

8.6.1 The Falling State Share of Education Funding

Although there has been a steady increase in the amount of state money allocated to elementary and secondary education in Texas, over the past few years, the share of education spending through the Foundation School Program financed by the state has been declining. In 2000, the state share was 47 percent, and it fell to 44 percent in 2001 and to 40 percent in 2003 (Legislative Budget Board 2003).

The reasons for the falling state share of FSP financing are straightforward. Neither the state's foundation formula (tier I) nor its guaranteed tax base formula (tier II) is automatically adjusted for the rising costs of education. This means that as a school district's property tax base per pupil rises from one year to the next, both its tier I and tier II state aid allocations are reduced. Although increases in property values generate more property tax revenues for school districts, these same increases in value result in reductions in state aid allocations. As a result, school districts are forced to raise their property tax rates, both to make up for reductions in state aid and to meet rising education costs. Over the past decade, the state has on several occasions raised both the foundation level (called the basic allotment) and the tier II guaranteed tax base. Nevertheless, between the 1993–94 and 2001–02 academic years, the real (CPI-adjusted) basic allotment has fallen by over $200, whereas the guaranteed yield from the tier II formula has only barely kept up with inflation.[20]

8.6.2   The Rising Costs of Providing an Adequate Education

Texas has been requiring its public school students to take standardized tests since the mid-1980s. Beginning in the 1990–91 school year, students were required to pass the tenth-grade TAAS to graduate from high school. As indicated previously, the state rates the performance of every public school on the basis of student performance on the TAAS examinations and on the basis of several other criteria, such as dropout rates. Schools are expected to improve not only the average test scores of their students, but also the test scores and pass rates of each racial or ethnic group and the scores of students classified as economically disadvantaged. As explained in detail by Murnane and Levy (2001), there has been considerable controversy concerning the role that student testing in Texas has played in increasing student performance, especially among low-income and minority students. Regardless of the controversy, accountability standards both for students and for schools are being steadily raised. Meeting these new, higher standards will have important fiscal implications for all school districts.

Texas introduced a set of changes to its accountability system starting in the 2002–03 school year, including a new set of tests called the Texas Assessment of Knowledge and Skills (TAKS). New, tougher, promotion standards have been adopted covering promotion from the third, fifth, and eighth grades, and passage of a TAKS examination administered in the eleventh grade is now required for graduation from high school.[21] Texas will also have to comply with the new federal education legislation, which requires schools to test all students in grades 3 through 8 and make annual progress in meeting student performance goals for all students and for separate groups of students characterized by race, ethnicity, poverty, disability, and limited English proficiency (U.S. Department of Education 2002).

Our research on the costs of education in Texas (summarized in section 8.5) makes it clear that raising standards of student performance has a direct implication for the minimum amount of money necessary to meet those standards. For example, we estimate that raising test scores from the average (50th percentile) to the 75th percentile would raise expenditures per pupil in the district with average costs from $6,925 to $9,752. The cost implications of raising performance standards will be particularly striking in school districts with above-average concentrations of pupils with limited English proficiency and from economically disadvantaged households. Under current law, school districts are required to provide "intensive programs of instruction" for those students that fail to pass the standardized tests (Legislative Budget Board 2000). These programs are supposed to be designed to enable students to meet state-imposed standards of annual improvement in academic performance.

The Texas Education Agency (2002b) estimates that if the higher test standards that went into effect in 2002–03 had been in place for the spring 2002 TAAS tests, the percentage of students who would have met the minimum standard would have declined, with the impact falling particularly heavily on students characterized as at risk. For example, whereas 69 percent of at-risk students met current minimum standards for both the third-grade reading and mathematics tests administered in spring 2002, only 49 percent of these students would have met the new higher standards. This suggests that substantial amounts of additional resources will be needed first to maintain, and then to raise the performance of at-risk children to meet the higher standards.

Predictions by the National Center for Education Statistics (2001b) suggest that demographic trends in Texas will place further pressure on Texas school districts to increase spending over the next few years. For the nation as a whole, elementary and secondary public school enrollment is projected to be essentially unchanged between 2001 and 2011. During this same period, enrollment is projected to fall in the Northeast and Midwest by 4.8 and 3.0 percent, respectively. The picture is quite different in Texas, where enrollment is projected to rise by 5.4 percent over this period.

8.6.3   The $1.50 Property Tax Rate Cap

The combination of rising accountability standards and growth in enrollment creates substantial pressure on most Texas school districts to increase public school spending. Faced with these spending pressures and a declining share of FSP state aid, school districts will have no choice but to raise local property tax rates. A growing number of school districts are currently taxing at a rate of $1.50 per $100 of assessed valuation and thus do not have the option of raising property tax rates, as state law prohibits localities from levying a tax rate for "maintenance and operations" in excess of $1.50. Since the late nineteenth century, when the property tax was first introduced in the state as a source of school financing, Texas has placed either statutory or constitutional limits on the rate of property taxation. In the mid-1880s, property taxes were limited to $0.20 per $100 in rural areas and $0.50 per $100 in cities (Thomas and Walker 1982). Over time, these limits have been raised.

For the 2000–01 school year, approximately 19 percent of all school districts in Texas were taxing at the $1.50 per $100 limit. By the 2003–04 school year, nearly 40 percent of districts were at the limit. For those school districts, the existence of a binding tax limit means that they are completely unable to respond to the rising costs of education, whether those costs are rising because of the new accountability standards or increased enrollment or as a result of other factors. As more school districts hit the limit, there is a chance that the courts will argue that the current school finance system is unconstitutional because it prevents a sizable number of districts from providing their students with an *adequate* education, or in the words of Article 7, Section 1, of the Texas constitution, enough money to guarantee a "general diffusion of knowledge."

In April 2001, four Texas school districts used the tax rate cap as a basis for a suit filed in district court. In *West Orange–Cove Consolidated Independent School District v. Nelson* (2001), the plaintiff school districts claimed that because of the state's tax limit, a significant number of districts no longer had meaningful control over their school tax rates, and thus the local property tax had become a de facto state ad valorem property tax, something that is constitutionally prohibited in Texas. In July 2001, the district court ruled that not enough districts were at the tax rate limit to render the system unconstitutional. The judge suggested that the system wouldn't be unconstitutional until the tax rate limit was binding on something like half of all school districts in Texas.

In May 2003, the Texas Supreme Court reversed the district court ruling and sent the case back to the trial court for further consideration.

Preliminary data for the 2003–04 school year indicate that 39 percent of all districts will be at the $1.50 rate cap and another 34 percent will be within 10 cents of the cap.[22] This suggests to us that unless other aspects of the school finance system are changed, not many more years will pass before at least half of all school districts in the state are at the $1.50 limit.

8.6.4   Growing Opposition to Chapter 41 Recapture Provisions

In 2003, 118 Texas school districts with property wealth in excess of $305,000 contributed over $750 million to help finance education spending by poorer districts in the state under the recapture provision (Chapter 41) of Senate Bill 7, passed in 1993. Opposition to the recapture provisions appears to be growing, especially as an increasing number of Chapter 41 districts (as districts affected by the Chapter 41 recapture provisions are often called) are reaching the $1.50 tax cap. In April 2001, four taxpayers filed suit against the Dallas and the Highland Park Independent School Districts. The plaintiffs challenged the constitutionality of the recapture provision and are seeking to prohibit high-wealth school districts from collecting taxes for recapture (Legislative Budget Board 2001). The case has not yet been heard.

It is not surprising that residents of high-wealth districts are opposed to the recapture provisions of the state's education finance system. Not only are these school districts unable to increase their spending on education, but residents face a tax price for education that is greater than one. This implies that a dollar increase in per-pupil spending in the district will cost residents more than a dollar per pupil. Both Chapter 41 school districts and their residents have strong incentives to use both the political process and the courts to try to eliminate the financing system's recapture provision. In addition, Chapter 41 school districts have strong incentives to keep as much revenue as possible out of the state's equalization system by finding ways to shelter local tax revenue legally.

A strategy that appears to be growing in popularity among Chapter 41 school districts involves granting new business development long-term property tax abatements in return for the business's making voluntary "contributions" to the school district (Moak 2002). Alternatively, in return for a property tax abatement, a company can promise to construct a new school building and donate it to the school district. In both these cases, the school district secures cash or in-kind funding that is not subject to recapture.

The recapture provision also provides incentives for individual residents of high-wealth school districts to act in ways that may reduce the equity of the school finance system. Because residents of high-wealth districts receive very little direct benefit from the FSP state aid system, they have a strong incentive to try to influence the political process in a way that minimizes the level of state support for education. As the recapture provision limits the amount of financial support school districts subject to recapture can spend on the public education of their children, residents in those districts may choose to send their children to private school and to oppose proposed increases in both the tier I base allotment and the tier II guaranteed tax base.

8.6.5 The Way Forward

In the foregoing, we have argued that the current system of school finance in Texas is not sustainable in the long run. To meet ever tougher accountability standards, public spending on education in Texas must increase. Without changes, the current state aid system results in an increasing portion of total education revenue coming from local school district property taxes. As more Texas school districts run up against the state's $1.50 per $100 property tax rate limit, the probability increases that the state's system of education finance will yet again be declared unconstitutional. Finally, if successful, attempts to eliminate or subvert the system's recapture provisions will further reduce the amount of money that is available to finance equalization.

These developments suggest that within a few years, Texas will have to substantially increase the fiscal contributions it makes to the financing of education in the state. Without question, finding new sources of revenue to finance a major increase in state aid to education will prove to be very difficult politically, in light of the constitutional prohibition against a state property tax and the long-standing antipathy in Texas to the use of the individual income tax.

Although developing a full reform plan for state aid to education in Texas is well beyond the scope of this chapter, we conclude with a brief outline of a possible reform plan. We would leave intact most of the major elements of the existing state aid program. First, we would add inflation and cost adjustment provisions to the existing tier I foundation formula. The foundation amount (or base allotment) would be indexed for inflation and adjusted for differences across school districts in the costs of education. We propose replacing the existing system of pupil weights and other cost adjustments, either with a single cost index of the type described in section 8.5, or with a set of pupil weights in which the values of the weights are generated from a careful study of the costs of different groups of students reaching student performance goals. We would retain the tier II guaranteed tax base formula but would index the guaranteed tax base for annual increases in prices. Also, we would retain a property tax limit, although we would raise it to a level somewhat higher than $1.50 per $100. Finally, because they have become a lightning rod for opposition to the current system of school finance, we would eliminate the recapture provisions. However, to limit taxpayer inequity and to encourage residents of high-wealth school districts to maintain support for adequate funding of public education, we would limit the maximum allowable spending per student to a fixed dollar amount per student in excess of the tier I base (or foundation) amount.

By indexing tiers I and II and by making appropriate cost adjustments, the revised state aid system we propose would guarantee all Texas public school students an efficient education. Although eliminating the recapture provisions would allow somewhat higher spending per pupil in property-wealthy districts, in our view, accepting some degree of spending inequality and less than perfect fiscal neutrality is a quite reasonable price to pay for a system of school funding that would guarantee every student an adequate education.

Notes

The authors wish to acknowledge helpful comments by Timothy Gronberg, Allan Odden, and John Yinger and the very able research assistance of Heather Pries.

1. The total student count for the 2001–02 school year was 4,059,519 (Texas Education Agency 2002a). Data on the number of students relative to other states are for the 1998–99 school year (National Center for Education Statistics 2001a).

2. The official name of the *Edgewood III* case is *Carrollton–Farmers Branch School District v. Edgewood Independent School District* (1992). For a detailed and insightful treatment of the plaintiff's arguments and the court's rulings in *Edgewood III*, see Picus and Hertert 1993.

3. See chapter 1 for a full discussion of fiscal neutrality.

4. The official name of Edgewood IV is *Edgewood Independent School District v. Meno* (1995).

5. The extra weights for special education students range from 1.7 to 5.0 depending on the type of education program these students participate in; the weight is 0.20 for

compensatory education, 0.10 for bilingual education, 1.37 for career and technology education, and 0.12 for gifted and talented programs.

6. For the 2002–03 school year, this guaranteed yield per penny of tax rate was increased to $27.14. The pupil weightings used for tier II are identical to those used for tier I.

7. The tier II guaranteed yield and recapture wealth level have been increased in recent years to ensure that these equity targets are met.

8. Nine school districts were dropped because of missing or incorrect data.

9. To keep a consistent comparison sample over time, we use the set of K–12 districts in 2000–01. That is, only data for districts that existed in 2000–01 were retained in earlier years. A small number of districts were dropped in various years because of missing or incorrect data.

10. The Court-defined equity measures require that 85 percent of students in the state be within the FSP system. Our sample, however, excludes elementary and high school districts as well as charter schools.

11. For example, in order for a school to achieve a rating of acceptable, at least 50 percent of all students in the school, and at least 50 percent of each student group (African American, Hispanic, white, economically disadvantaged), must pass each section of the TAAS, and the dropout rate cannot exceed 6 percent for all students and for each student group.

12. We refer here to the pupil weights used for students in various programs (such as 0.2 for a student in compensatory education or 5.0 for a student in a speech therapy program) and the adjustments for district size. The cost-of-education index is the one component of the system whose construction has been transparent and well-documented (see Alexander et al. 2000).

13. Quintiles are weighted by student enrollment; that is, each quintile contains 20 percent of all students in Texas K–12 schools, not 20 percent of all K–12 districts. A similar analysis was conducted using expenditure per pupil. The qualitative results were the same.

14. To account for endogeneity of school output and input prices, the equation is estimated using two-stage least squares.

15. In contrast to the results of some other studies, our results show that costs appear to be lower when a district serves more limited English proficiency (LEP) or severely disabled students. These puzzling results can perhaps be explained by economies of scale: There are certainly fixed costs associated with having specialized programs for these students and thus, having more students in these programs could mean lower average costs per student. When a quadratic term for LEP students is included, there is some evidence that the relationship is U-shaped; the coefficient on the quadratic term is positive, though not highly statistically significant. In the case of severely disabled students, over a third of districts in Texas do not have any such students at all. When we include a dummy variable for simply having any severely disabled students, the coefficient on this variable is positive and statistically significant. Thus, the presence of these students does increase spending relative to districts that do not have any, but conditional on having any severely disabled students in a distract at all, having more can reduce costs.

16. To account for the large variance in district size in Texas, the regressions are weighted by district enrollment and a dummy variable is included for Dallas and Hous-

ton. If the indicator for Dallas and Houston is not included, the coefficients on the enrollment variables change so that average costs appear to fall for districts up to 53,565 students. The cost indexes (discussed below) generated from the two specifications are highly correlated with one another (a correlation coefficient equal to 0.98).

17. Note that because the cost function analysis did not include all K–12 districts in 2000–01, the distribution of current revenue per pupil in table 8.6 differs somewhat from the distribution shown in table 8.3. For ease of comparison, the distribution of revenue was recalculated only for those districts used in the cost analysis.

18. In Reschovsky and Imazeki 2003, we explicitly compare the distribution of a cost index generated from the estimation of a cost function with a cost index based on the pupil weights and other adjustments used in the Texas school aid formulas. This comparison allows us to quantify the changes in the distribution of state aid that would be needed to achieve educational adequacy.

19. The conclusion that the gap in achievement between white and minority students in Texas has been reduced is subject to some controversy. As reported by Murnane and Levy (2001), two studies conducted by different teams of researchers at the RAND Corporation compared the TAAS score results with the scores of Texas students on the NAEP and came to quite different conclusions. One study reported that the gap in mathematics test scores between racial groups was very large and was actually increasing. In contrast, the other study reported that nationwide the largest improvements in NAEP scores (in fourth-grade reading and mathematics tests) occurred in Texas and North Carolina.

20. In constant 1994 dollars, the basic allotment fell from $2,300 in 1993–94 to $2,094 in 2001–02. Also in 1994 dollars, the guaranteed yield in the tier II formula went from $20.55 in 1993–94 to $21.30 in 2001–02.

21. According to an article in the *New York Times*, fearing that too many students would fail the new tests, the state board of education voted in late 2002 to reduce the number of test questions students would need to answer correctly to pass the third-grade reading test (Dillon 2003).

22. These percentages were calculated from data available from the Texas Education Agency (2003).

9 School Finance Reform and School Quality: Lessons from Vermont

Thomas Downes

9.1 Introduction

In June 1997, the elected leaders of Vermont enacted the Equal Educational Opportunity Act (Act 60) in response to a state supreme court decision in *Brigham v. State* (1997). Act 60 may well have represented the most radical reform of a state's system of public school financing since the post-*Serrano*, post–Proposition 13 changes in California in the late 1970s. As a result, Act 60 could provide a unique opportunity to determine whether dramatic school finance reforms like those enacted in Vermont generate greater equality in measured student performance. This chapter represents an attempt to document the changes in the distributions of spending and of student performance that have occurred in Vermont in the post–Act 60 period.

The chapter begins with an overview of the institutional structure of educational finance and provision in Vermont. One purpose of this overview is to make the argument that the Vermont case is particularly interesting because there have not been dramatic demographic changes in the state since the enactment of Act 60 that could obscure the impact of finance reforms. With this context established, I review the research on the links between finance reforms and the distributions of education spending and of student performance. After briefly discussing the data utilized, I examine the extent to which there has been convergence across Vermont school districts in expenditures and in student performance.

All of the available data support the conclusion that the link between education spending and taxable resources in Vermont has been significantly weakened and that spending, however it is measured, is substantially more equal across school districts in the state. I also present evidence that the cross-district dispersion of performance of fourth graders on standardized test of mathematics has declined post–Act 60 and show that there is no evidence of increased cross-district dispersion of the test performances of second and eighth graders.

9.2   School Finance Reform in Vermont

In 1995 in Lamoille Superior Court, a group of plaintiffs that included Amanda Brigham, a nine-year-old student in the Whiting School District (Burkett 1998), filed suit against the state of Vermont. The goal of the suit was to force substantive reform of a system of school financing that the plaintiffs felt deprived students in property-poor school districts of equal educational opportunities and forced taxpayers in these property-poor districts to assume a disproportionate burden of the financing of public education. On February 5, 1997, the supreme court of Vermont ruled in favor of the plaintiffs, concluding that the existing system deprived "children of an equal educational opportunity in violation of the Vermont Constitution" (*Brigham v. State* (1997), 166 Vt. at 249). The court left it to the state's legislature to craft a new financing system that was consistent with the state constitution.

The focus in the plaintiffs' suit on both inequalities in educational spending and disparities in property tax burdens grew out of long-standing dissatisfaction in Vermont with the existing foundation system of education financing and the existing system of property taxation. Prior to Act 60, Vermont used a traditional foundation formula to determine the state aid a town received:

Total state aid $= [(Weighted\ average\ daily\ membership\ (ADM))$

$\times\ (Foundation\ amount)] - [(Foundation\ tax\ rate)$

$\times\ (Aggregate\ fair\ market\ value) \times 0.01],$ (9.1)

where the weighted ADM was determined by assigning weights of 1.25 to secondary students and to students from families receiving food stamps and weights of between 1.0385 and 1.0714 to students who must be transported to school and by averaging the weighted student counts from the previous two school years (Mathis 1995). Although the foundation amount was set with the intent of permitting districts spending that amount to meet state standards for students assigned a weight of one, fluctuations in the state's fiscal status led the state legislature to adjust the foundation tax rate to reduce the state's aid liability. As a result, the state share of basic educational expenditures fluctuated between 0.20 and 0.37, with the share declining when the state economy weakened (Mathis 2001). The period leading up to Act 60 was a period of decline in the state share.

The widespread dissatisfaction with the existing school financing system had not been ignored by elected officials. In both 1994 and 1995, the state house of the Vermont legislature approved legislation designed to overhaul education financing. Although this legislation failed to pass the state senate, the legislation contained key elements of the state's eventual response to the *Brigham* decision (McClaughry 2001).

The legislation, by highlighting concerns about education financing and property taxation, also influenced the dynamics of the state's 1996 elections. The state senate that was elected in 1996 was committed to property tax reform (Mathis 2001). The result was a state legislature that was ready to move on legislation that would comply with the *Brigham* decision and reduce the property tax burdens of poor individuals.

Given the political dynamic in Vermont, the speed with which Act 60, the legislation designed to comply with *Brigham* and to provide property tax relief, was passed surprised no one. Signed into law on June 26, 1997, Act 60 created a system of school financing that combined elements of foundation and power equalization plans. A statewide property tax was established, with revenues from the tax being used to finance a portion of foundation aid.[1] Under the act's provisions, if property tax revenues generated in a locality by levying the statewide rate exceed the amount needed to finance the foundation level of spending in that locality, the excess property tax revenues are recaptured by the state.

Under Act 60, localities are allowed to choose spending levels in excess of the foundation level. To weaken the link between property wealth and spending in excess of the foundation level, the act established a power equalization scheme that ensured that localities with the same nominal tax rates would have the same levels of education spending. The power equalization scheme also included a unique recapture element: All spending by local districts in excess of the foundation level is drawn from a sharing pool that consists of all the property tax revenues in the state generated by property tax rates in excess of the statewide rate. As a result, no revenues from statewide taxes are used to finance the power equalizing portion of the school finance system. Further, when the voters in a locality choose a nominal property tax rate above the statewide rate, they will not know how much in additional revenues will be available for that locality's schools with certainty until all other localities have made their taxing decisions and the size of the sharing pool is established.

Although the *Brigham* decision forced state policymakers to implement education finance reforms, the reality was that Act 60 was as much about property tax relief as it was about school finance reform. For taxpayers in many Vermont communities, the finance reforms by themselves would have dramatically reduced tax burdens by allowing localities to maintain or even increase education spending with substantially lower tax rates. At the same time, taxpayers in high-wealth communities, which have been labeled "gold towns," necessarily faced increases in their property tax payments under the act.[2] To lessen the burden on low-income residents of the gold towns, the drafters of Act 60 included in the legislation a provision that granted tax adjustments to certain homestead owners. These tax adjustments were explicitly linked to the taxpayer's income; the original legislation specified that all owners with incomes at or below $75,000 were eligible for adjustments.

All of these changes in the property tax were clearly designed to shift some of the burden of financing Vermont's schools away from state residents to corporations and nonresident owners of property in Vermont.[3] Thus, Act 60 continues the recent tradition of linking school finance reforms and tax relief that is exemplified by Michigan. For this reason, any complete evaluation of the success of Act 60 must consider both the changes in education provision and the changes in tax burdens that have resulted from it. Therefore, this chapter necessarily provides a partial view of the welfare implications of Act 60.[4]

The school finance reforms that were the central element of Act 60 were phased in over several years, with the new regime not fully in place until the 2000–01 academic year. Nevertheless, as was true in California in the aftermath of *Serrano* and Proposition 13, in some districts there were surprisingly rapid responses to Act 60. Not surprisingly, in the gold towns there was vocal opposition to Act 60. Also unsurprising, given the California experience, were the efforts in these towns to encourage residents to make voluntary contributions to the schools[5] and to shift to town governments responsibility for financing certain "school" functions. Another California parallel is the apparent growth in private school enrollments that have been mentioned in press reports (e.g., Norman 1998).

Care needs to be taken, however, to avoid making too much of the parallels between the California and Vermont cases. Act 60 gave Vermont school districts much more discretion over the level of expenditures than California districts have. The tax price of education spending has increased in the gold towns, but spending is not being forcibly leveled down as it was in California. Also, low-wealth towns were not required to maintain local effort; several such towns used the extra state aid they received as a result of Act 60 primarily to reduce nominal property tax rates. As a result, low-wealth towns were not necessarily leveled up. The reality is that Act 60 did not duplicate the California reforms, a fact on which section 9.3 expands.

Act 60 did not duplicate the California reforms in one other important way. The California reforms predated the nationwide push for accountability; Act 60 was passed at a time when most states were attempting to strengthen accountability and educational standards. As a result, several elements of the legislation built on the existing system of testing and standards in the state to strengthen accountability. For example, under Act 60 all districts were required to develop action plans to improve student performance on the tests that are part of the Vermont Comprehensive Assessment System. In addition, the act mandated that the state board of education take on a more active oversight role in monitoring the attainment of standards. Nevertheless, the central elements of the state's accountability system were unaffected by Act 60.

9.3 Why Study Vermont? A Review of Research on the Impact of School Finance Reforms

The school finance reforms implemented in California in the aftermath of that state's supreme court decision in *Serrano v. Priest* and of the nearly contemporaneous tax limits imposed by Proposition 13 represent a watershed both in the debate over the structure of school finance reforms and in the direction of research into the impact of those reforms. In the post-*Serrano* period, the California reforms and their supposed effects on the schools in that state have been discussed in every state in which school finance reforms have been implemented. Vermont is no exception; the perceived parallels between the California reforms and Act 60 have been mentioned repeatedly.[6]

The California reforms also shifted the focus of research on the impact of school finance. Prior to those reforms, the focus in the literature was almost exclusively on the impact of finance reforms on spending inequality. After *Serrano*, the scope of the analysis broadened to include the impact of finance reforms on the level and distribution of student achievement, on housing prices, on the supply of private schooling, and even on the composition of affected communities.[7] The California reforms also became the touchstone for theoretical work. Studies like Nechyba 1996b, Nechyba 2000, Bènabou 1996, Fernandez and Rogerson 1997, and Fernandez and Rogerson 1998 used a California-like system as the postreform case when trying to reach predictions about the likely effects of finance reform.

The problem with using the California case as a benchmark is that the case has proven to be the exception, not the rule. First, the limits imposed on local control over spending in California have not been duplicated in any other state. Even in Michigan and Vermont, the states in which the most extensive post-*Serrano* reforms have been implemented, some degree of local control over taxes and spending is permitted. Further, the population of students served by California schools has changed more dramatically over the last fifteen to twenty years than the population of students in any other state in the nation. From 1986 to 1997, the percentage of the California public school student population identified as minority increased from 46.3 to 61.2 percent. Nationally, the percentage of minority students grew far more slowly over the same period, from 29.6 to 36.5 percent.[8] As Downes (1992) notes, these demographic changes make it difficult to quantify the impact of the finance reforms in California on the cross-district inequality in student achievement.

The possibility that California might be the exception and not the rule in regard to the effect of reforming state education financing systems pushed a number of researchers to pursue national-level studies attempting to document the impact of finance reforms. On the spending side, Silva and Sonstelie (1995), Downes and Shah (1995), and Manwaring and Sheffrin (1997) all took slightly different approaches to quantifying the effect of finance reforms on mean per-pupil spending in a state. Because they used district-level data, Hoxby (2001), Evans, Murray, and Schwab (1997), and Murray, Evans, and Schwab (1998) were able to consider not only the effects of finance reforms on mean spending, but also the extent to which spending inequities were reduced by those reforms. As a result, these studies provide the most obvious sources for predictions of the long-run effects of Act 60. The problem is that these studies generate contradictory predictions.

Hoxby's results would lead us to expect leveling down, since Act 60 dramatically increases tax prices in towns with more property wealth. Murray, Evans, and Schwab, on the other hand, conclude that court-mandated reforms like Act 60 typically result in leveling up.

The same lack of a clear prediction would be apparent to the reader of national-level attempts to determine how the distribution of student performance in a state is affected by a reform of the state's system for financing education. Hoxby (2001) represents the first attempt to use national-level data to examine the effects of finance reforms on student performance. Hoxby finds that dropout rates increase about 8 percent, on average, in states that adopt state-level financing of the public schools. Although Hoxby's work does not explicitly address the effect of equalization on the within-state distribution of student performance, it seems likely that much of the growth in dropout rates occurred in those districts with relatively high dropout rates prior to equalization. In other words, these results imply that equalization could adversely affect both the level and the distribution of student performance in a state.

Although the dropout rate is an outcome measure of considerable interest, analyses of the quality of public education in the United States tend to focus on standardized test scores and other measures of student performance that provide some indication of how the general student population is faring. Husted and Kenny (2000) suggest that equalization may detrimentally affect student achievement. Using data on thirty-four states from 1976–77 to 1992–93, they find that the mean SAT score is higher for those states with greater intrastate spending variation. The period for which they have test score information, however (1987–88 to 1992–93), postdates the imposition of the first wave of finance reforms. Thus, the data do not permit direct examination of the effects of changes in education spending policies. In addition, because they use state-level data, Husted and Kenny cannot examine the degree to which equalization affects cross-district variation in test scores.[9] Finally, since only a select group of students take the SAT, Husted and Kenny are not able to consider how equalization affects the performance of all students in a state.

Card and Payne (2002) explore the effects of school finance equalizations on the within-state distributions of SAT scores. They characterize a school finance policy as more equalizing the more negative is the within-state relationship between state aid to a school district and school district income. They find that the SAT scores of students with poorly educated parents (their proxy for low income) increase in states that, under their definition, become more equalized. Data limitations, however, make it impossible for Card and Payne to examine the effects of policy changes on students residing in school districts in which the policy changes had the greatest impact. Moreover, although Card and Payne correct for differences from district to district in the fractions of the population taking the SAT test, it is still very likely that students who come from low-education backgrounds but take the SAT test are a very select group and are extremely unlikely to be representative of the low-income or low-education population as a whole.[10]

Downes and Figlio (2000) attempt to determine how the tax limits and finance reforms of the late 1970s and early 1980s affected the distribution of student performance in states in which limits were imposed and how student performance changed in these states relative to student performance in states in which no limits or no finance reforms were imposed. The core data used in the analysis were drawn from two national data sets, the National Longitudinal Study of the High School Class of 1972 (NLS-72) and the 1992 (senior-year) wave of the National Education Longitudinal Survey (NELS). The NELS data were collected a sufficient amount of time after the passage of most finance reforms to permit quantification of the long-run effects of these reforms by analyzing changes in the distributions of student performance between the NLS-72 cross-section and the NELS cross-section.

Downes and Figlio find that finance reforms in response to court decisions, like that in the *Brigham* case, result in small and frequently insignificant increases in the mean level of student performance on standardized tests of reading and mathematics. Further, they note that there is some indication that the postreform distribution of scores in mathematics may be less equal across school districts within a state than the prereform distribution. This latter result highlights one of the central points of this chapter: Any evaluation of finance reforms must control for the initial circumstances of districts affected by the reforms. The simple reality is that finance reforms are likely to have differential effects in initially high-spending and initially low-spending districts.

The fundamental reason for the absence of clear predictions of the impact of finance reforms has been mentioned by a number of authors (e.g., Downes and Shah [1995]; Hoxby [2001]; Evans, Murray, and Schwab [1997]): the tremendous diversity among the various school finance reforms that have been undertaken. In a national-level study, any attempt to classify finance reforms will be imperfect. So even though there is consensus that the key elements of a finance reform are the effects of the reform on local discretion and on local incentives and the change in state-level responsibilities in the aftermath of reform (Hoxby 2001; Courant and Loeb 1997), different authors take different approaches to account for the heterogeneity of the reforms. The result is variation in predictions generated by studies that are asking the same fundamental question. The answer, it seems, is not to try and improve the methods of classifying reforms but is instead to analyze certain canonical reforms carefully. Act 60 is likely to be just such a canonical reform.

In looking for guidance for an analysis of the Vermont education finance reforms, the first case to consider is that of Kentucky, where the reforms that followed a court decision invalidating the existing system of school finance may represent the most radical change to a state's system of public schooling provision. Flanagan and Murray (chapter 6 in this volume) document the effects of the reforms in Kentucky. Unfortunately, because the reforms in Kentucky were so extensive, any lessons from that case are probably not particularly relevant for those attempting to predict the effect of reforms that, like Act 60, primarily affect the system of school finance in a state.

Thus, the most direct antecedent in this case-study approach to analyzing finance reforms is Downes 1992, which showed that the extensive school finance reforms in California in the late 1970s generated greater equality across school districts in per-pupil spending but not greater equality in measured student performance. Duncombe and Johnston's (chapter 5 of this volume) work on Kansas offers an example of a recent case study of a canonical reform. This study of Vermont is another such example. Will the outcomes in Vermont duplicate those in California? What are the similarities in and differences between the results for Vermont, Kansas, and Kentucky? The data used to answer these questions are described in the next section.

9.4 Data

9.4.1 Sources
The majority of the data analyzed in this chapter are drawn from the *Vermont School Report* and from publications of the Vermont Department of Taxes. In addition, town-level data on school expenditures were drawn from Heaps and Woolf 2000 and from files created by the Vermont Department of Education and posted at ⟨http://www.

state.vt.us/educ/schfin/class/dist_class.html⟩. The Vermont Indicators Online database (http://maps.vcgi.org/indicators), maintained by
the Center for Rural Studies at the University of Vermont, was the
source of some pre-1999 information on income, demographics, and
property wealth at the town level. Finally, the Common Core of Data,
maintained by the National Center for Education Statistics, was the
source of school-level data on the racial and ethnic composition of each
school's student body.

The norm in Vermont is that towns and school districts are cotermi-
nous. There are, however, numerous deviations from the norm. Some
small towns do not operate elementary or secondary schools; the children from these towns are sent to public or even private schools in
neighboring communities, with tuition payments going from the sending towns to the receiving schools.[11] Many other towns do not have
their own high schools, choosing either to "tuition out" their high
school students or to participate in union high school districts.[12] Since
one of the goals of the research presented in this chapter was to quantify the impact of Act 60 on the inequality in services provided to the
schoolchildren of Vermont, the school district had to be the fundamental unit of analysis. Thus, several decisions had to be made to ensure
that what was presented was the most accurate picture of the impact of
Act 60 on the distributions of expenditures and student performance
across Vermont school districts. First, all towns that were not tuitioning out students at the elementary level were matched to the school
district serving elementary school students from that town. The same
matching process was completed for towns not tuitioning out high
school students.[13] Having made these town–school district matches,
it was possible to create school district–level versions of some variables that were only available in the existing data at the town level.
Second, districts were grouped into types based on the institutional
structure of elementary and secondary education in the overlying
towns. This made it possible to examine separately the impact of
Act 60 on school districts linked to towns with different institutional
structures.

Nevertheless, the reality in Vermont is that school spending levels
are voted on in town meetings, that state aid flows to towns and not
school districts, and that analyses of the impact of Act 60 have tended
to focus on variation across towns in expenditures. So even though
cross-town variation provides an imperfect indication of the variation
in expenditures across school districts (and thus across students) in

Vermont, results are presented in this chapter that use town-level data on expenditures. These results make it possible to compare the findings in this study to those in previous work. Further, the town-level data are such that it is possible to make a crude adjustment for the effect on expenditures of variation in institutional structure from town to town. In particular, the analysis in the chapter uses two alternative measures of expenditures, one of which is explicitly designed to adjust for variation in institutional structure from town to town.

9.4.2 Summary Statistics

One of the advantages of examining the impact of finance reforms in Vermont is the stability of the student population served by Vermont schools. For example, in the 1995–96 school year, 3.12 percent of the students attending public school in Vermont were identified as minority. This percentage fluctuated slightly over the next four academic years, from 2.73 percent in 1996–97 to 3.16 percent in 1999–2000.[14] Clearly, in Vermont, unlike in California, the schools were not trying to adjust to a dramatically changing population at the same time they were coping with the effects of finance reforms.

Other measures of the income and demographics of the Vermont student population were also relatively stable both immediately before and just after the implementation of Act 60. For each school year from 1994–95 to 2000–2001, table 9.1 provides summary statistics on certain key measures of the demographics and income of each school district in the state. Average adjusted gross income per exemption, a rough proxy for per capita income, did increase throughout the period, an unsurprising result given that all dollar figures in the table are nominal and that this was a period of strong economic expansion. What is more striking, however, is the stability across time of the poverty rate and the percentage of students eligible for free or reduced-price school lunches. The observable characteristics of the population of students being served by Vermont schools appear to have changed little over time.

This stability of measured attributes of the student population does not ensure that there have been no significant changes over time in critical unmeasured characteristics of the students served by the public schools in Vermont. In other words, in an event analysis of the impact of Act 60 on the distribution of student performance across school districts in the state, there will be no way to rule out the possibility that cross-time changes in the distribution are driven by cross-time changes

Table 9.1
Summary statistics: Selected characteristics of Vermont school districts

| | Pre-Act 60 | | | | | |
| | 1994–95 | | 1995–96 | | 1996–97 | |
Variable	Mean	Standard deviation	Mean	Standard deviation	Mean	Standard deviation
Current expenditure per pupil	5582.78	1546.03	5776.07	1502.84	5935.14	1012.70
Special education costs per eligible pupil	1202.85	628.48	1294.49	710.64	1363.33	654.22
Students per classroom teacher	17.96	11.34	17.53	3.87	17.28	3.28
Average teacher salary	32472.06	4249.53	33527.29	4520.34	33948.62	4495.41
Students per computer	—	—	—	—	14.16	11.86
Eligibility for free/reduced-price lunch (%)	—	—	—	—	27.66	17.90
Poverty rate	12.16	7.64	11.90	7.91	10.91	8.04
Average AGI per exempt (from tax returns)[1]	13581.38	2638.45	14220.30	2808.92	14894.31	3026.38
Grade 2 Reading: Pupils at/above standard (%)	—	—	—	—	—	—
Grade 4 Math: Pupils at/above standard (%)	—	—	17.41	14.62	—	—
Grade 4 Reading: Pupils at/above standard (%)	—	—	—	—	58.17	17.89
Grade 8 Math: Pupils at/above standard (%)	—	—	30.32	14.44	—	—
Grade 8 Reading: Pupils at/above standard (%)	—	—	—	—	73.03	13.15

Note: 1. In 1997–98 and 1998–99, average adjusted gross income per exemption is available for all school districts ($n = 248$). In the remaining years, average adjusted gross income per exemption is only available for those districts that correspond directly to towns ($n = 203$).

Table 9.1
(continued)

		Post-Act 60					
1997–98		1998–99		1999–00		2000–01	
Mean	Standard deviation	Mean	Standard deviation	Mean	Standard deviation	Mean	Standard deviation
6175.11	1105.13	6652.33	1294.00	7601.18	1330.29	8262.36	1491.91
1503.53	710.10	1693.59	839.70	—	—	—	—
16.86	3.04	16.57	3.56	15.70	2.97	15.09	2.91
—	—	34898.05	4889.94	35487.94	4857.72	36167.98	4821.56
8.04	4.65	7.35	4.84	6.76	4.44	—	—
29.20	17.99	29.42	18.12	28.82	17.41	28.04	16.87
11.59	7.40	10.74	7.50	11.85	7.70	10.68	7.04
15829.26	3194.75	16913.95	3401.20	17743.62	3573.72	18610.63	3799.96
75.70	13.62	71.89	15.34	75.63	14.60	78.01	14.22
32.47	19.10	37.94	17.88	38.14	18.84	42.05	18.99
79.19	13.22	86.12	11.00	83.04	12.70	79.30	13.23
37.98	18.16	31.75	16.56	32.08	15.65	35.76	18.65
61.38	16.70	63.02	13.82	58.62	15.27	63.27	14.21

in unobservables as opposed to by the effects of the finance reforms. That said, the Vermont context still provides researchers with the best opportunity to date to estimate the effects of finance reforms on the distribution of student performance.

The remaining rows in table 9.1 provide summary information on some of the expenditure and student performance measures available in the *Vermont School Report*. No obvious trends in student performance are apparent in table 9.1. Some performance measures improved after Act 60; others declined. For some of the measures of performance, dispersion fell after Act 60, but dispersion increased for other measures. Because the crude summary measures in table 9.1 give no indication of how post–Act 60 changes are linked to a district's pre–Act 60 status, however, no conclusions about the performance effects of Act 60 can be drawn on the basis of the evidence in table 9.1.

Table 9.1 also does not support any firm conclusions about the extent to which the link between local wealth and spending has been weakened by Act 60. That said, even the summary measures in table 9.1 provide some indication of the impact of Act 60 on the dispersion in expenditures across the state. The coefficient of variation of current expenditures per pupil increased from 3.61 in 1994–95 to 5.71 in 1999–2000. Although some of this increase predated Act 60, Act 60 has mattered, a fact that should be more evident when post-phase in expenditure measures are analyzed. It is to these measures that I turn in the next section.

9.5 Results

9.5.1 Distribution of Expenditures before and after Act 60
The starting point of any evaluation of the effects of Act 60 is the choice of a measure of per-pupil expenditures. When towns have been used as the unit of analysis, two measures of spending have been used in analyses of the extent of spending inequality and the effect of Act 60 on that inequality. Heaps and Woolf (2000) used budgeted expenditures per equalized pupil. (The concept of equalized pupils as it applies to Vermont, is discussed later in this section.) Because many towns send students to or receive students from other towns for whom tuition is being paid, however, inequality in budgeted expenditures may overstate true spending inequality. For example, overstatement of inequality could result because budgeted expenditures per equalized pupil are based on residential pupil counts that do not include tuitioned stu-

dents, resulting in artificially high per-pupil numbers for districts receiving tuitioned students. So as an alternative, other analysts, like Jimerson (2001) and Baker (2001a), use measures of spending based on the state's calculation of local education spending per equalized pupil. Local education spending is that portion of a school district budget paid by the general state support grant, local education tax revenues, and any aid from the sharing pool when applicable. Local education spending does not include federal aid or privately donated dollars.

In what follows, both measures of spending are considered, since neither is a perfect indicator of the educational opportunities available to students in a particular town. The argument for using budgeted expenditures is that this measure includes not only expenditures out of noncategorical state aid and property tax income, but also expenditures out of such diverse income sources as categorical aid for special education[15] and private donations to the schools. But because of the problems just discussed that are created by students for whom tuition payments are being made, local education spending per pupil must also be considered.

At the school district level, the choice of expenditure measures is somewhat more clear-cut. Current expenditures per pupil measures noncapital spending; total expenditures per pupil includes both current and capital spending. In the analysis that follows, both of these measures are examined. It is not possible, however, to examine the extent to which cost-adjusted spending has become more equal across districts. Both before and after Act 60, the state aid formula recognized the fact that certain students are more costly to educate and based aid amounts not on raw pupil counts but on equalized pupil counts, which are determined, in the post–Act 60 period, by assigning weights of 1.25 to secondary students and to students receiving food stamps and weights of 1.2 to students with limited English proficiency and by averaging the weighted counts across two school years (Mathis 2001). Since these weights are ad hoc and other critical determinants of cost are not taken into account in the calculation of weighted ADM, the cost adjustments in the basic state aid formula are imperfect (Downes and Pogue 1994). Categorical aid programs, like a small-schools grant program that was established by Act 60, may help to reduce inequality in cost-adjusted aid across districts. Nevertheless, any inequality measures presented in the subsequent discussion undoubtedly understate the extent of inequality in cost-adjusted spending across Vermont school districts, since high-cost districts are typically low-spending districts.

Although the circumstances cited by the plaintiffs in *Brigham v. State* had existed for many years, trends in school spending inequality in Vermont in the late 1980s and early 1990s undoubtedly contributed to the plaintiffs' decision to file suit. For example, from 1989–90 to 1994–95, current expenditures per pupil had grown at an annual rate of 3.77 percent at the top of the range. The annual growth rate at the bottom of the range was only 1.9 percent. The *Brigham* decision was handed down when the dispersion in expenditures across Vermont school districts was large and growing.

Standard inequality measures like the coefficient of variation and the Gini coefficient can both reflect the tail end of these trends and provide an initial indication of the impact of Act 60 on spending inequality in Vermont. When town-level measures of spending are used, the initial indication is that spending has become more equal post–Act 60. In particular, for budgeted expenditures in 1998–99, the coefficient of variation was 0.1508, and the Gini coefficient was 0.0851. In 2000–01, the coefficient of variation was 0.1305 and the Gini coefficient was 0.0731. These measures of inequality increased slightly from 2000–01 to 2001–02, to 0.1360 for the coefficient of variation and 0.0758 for the Gini coefficient, but both measures were still below their 1998–99 levels. Since Act 60 was already being phased-in in 1998–99, these numbers probably understate the extent to which inequality in education spending by towns has declined since the implementation of Act 60.

Inequality measures at the school district level tell much the same story as those at the town level. For example, for those school districts serving students in grades K–12, the coefficient of variation of current expenditures per pupil was 0.1482 in 1995–96. For these districts, the coefficient of variation fell to 0.1412 in 1996–97 but increased to 0.1488 in 1997–98, the last pre–Act 60 year. In the post–Act 60 period, the coefficient of variation for current expenditures per pupil in these school districts has consistently declined, falling to 0.1425 in 1998–99, to 0.1386 in 1999–2000, and to 0.1251 in 2000–01.[16]

For other types of school districts (i.e., those that serve only a portion of the K–12 population), the inequality measures tend to tell the same story: fluctuating inequality pre–Act 60 and declining inequality post–Act 60. The one exception to this pattern occurs for those elementary school districts located in towns that belong to union or joint high school districts.[17] For these districts, the coefficients of variation in current expenditures per pupil were 0.2760 in 1995–96, 0.1706 in 1996–97,

0.1837 in 1997–98, 0.1929 in 1998–99, 0.1889 in 1999–2000, and 0.2119 in 2000–01.[18] Whether this increase in inequality in spending in 2000–01 was an anomaly or a reflection of an increased ability of districts to circumvent Act 60 can only be determined as more years of data become available.

Even if this increase in inequality in elementary school districts located in towns that belong to union or joint high school districts proves not to be an anomaly, dispersion of expenditures does not necessarily imply unequal opportunities attributable to differences in taxable wealth, a reality that was recognized by the Vermont Supreme Court in the *Brigham* decision. For instance, dispersion in current expenditures per pupil could exist and be unrelated to property wealth if the state targeted categorical aid to districts with a greater proportion of disadvantaged students. What equalization of educational opportunities does require is elimination of the positive correlation between expenditures and taxable wealth. The *Brigham* decision makes this clear:

Equal educational opportunity cannot be achieved when property-rich school districts may tax low and property-poor districts must tax high to achieve even minimum standards. Children who live in property-poor districts and children who live in property-rich districts should be afforded a substantially equal opportunity to have access to similar educational revenues. (*Brigham v. State* (1997), 166 Vt. at 268)

Simple inequality measures do not tell us the extent to which Act 60 has produced a system of school financing in which the correlation between spending and wealth has been reduced. Thus, following the logic of Downes (1992), simple ordinary least squares regressions of spending measures on measures of local resources were used to determine the extent to which Act 60 has reduced this correlation. For towns, the results of these regressions are presented in tables 9.2a and 9.2b.

For the 246 towns in Vermont for which the relevant data are available, the first part of table 9.2a indicates that the correlation between budgeted expenditures per equalized pupil and equalized assessed valuation per pupil was 0.516,[19] clear evidence that districts with more real property wealth did have higher per-pupil expenditures prior to Act 60. Since Act 60 was already being phased-in in 1998–99, this correlation probably understates the actual strength of the relationship between school expenditures and property wealth in Vermont prior to the *Brigham* decision.

Table 9.2a
Relationships between expenditures and wealth measures for Vermont towns
Dependent variable: Budgeted expenditures per equalized pupil (robust standard errors
in parentheses)

Variable	1998–99	2001–02
Part 1		
Intercept	7099.495	9053.913
	(125.227)	(96.342)
Equalized assessed valuation per pupil	0.00093	0.00021
	(0.00027)	(0.00012)
R^2	0.266	0.019
Correlation coefficient	0.516	0.138
Part 2		
Intercept	5932.714	8204.978
	(357.866)	(403.246)
Median Family Income in 1989	0.04901	0.02973
	(0.01110)	(0.01160)
R^2	0.0873	0.0265
Correlation coefficient	0.295	0.163
Part 3		
Intercept	5781.257	8162.943
	(298.144)	(395.430)
Equalized assessed valuation per pupil	0.00088	0.00021
	(0.00024)	(0.00012)
Median family income	0.04102	0.02756
	(0.00910)	(0.01160)
R^2	0.326	0.0447
Correlation coefficient	0.571	0.211

The remainder of the first column of table 9.2a shows that, although the extent of the inequality found to have existed in educational opportunities varies across potential measures of taxable resources, the conclusion that opportunities were unequal before Act 60 does not depend on the measure of taxable resources used. For example, if permanent income is taken as the measure of taxable resources and median family income is used to proxy for permanent income, the correlation between budgeted expenditures per equalized pupil and taxable resources is 0.295, much less than the correlation between budgeted expenditures and equalized assessed valuation, but still strong.

As the discussion of table 9.1 indicated, after Act 60 dispersion in education expenditures across localities in Vermont was reduced, even in the phase-in years. Nevertheless, some degree of dispersion re-

Table 9.2b

Relationships between expenditures and wealth measures for Vermont towns
Dependent variable: Local expenditures per equalized pupil (robust standard errors in parentheses)

Variable	2000–01	2001–02
Part 1		
Intercept	6980.417	7520.317
	(75.355)	(80.534)
Equalized assessed valuation per pupil	−0.00036	−0.00029
	(0.00011)	(0.00009)
R^2	0.0613	0.0459
Correlation coefficient	0.248	0.214
Part 2		
Intercept	5419.094	6328.920
	(303.555)	(350.287)
Median family income	0.04200	0.03087
	(0.00941)	(0.01068)
R^2	0.0862	0.0362
Correlation coefficient	0.294	0.190
Part 3		
Intercept	5477.803	6398.556
	(278.514)	(339.070)
Equalized assessed valuation per pupil	−0.00042	−0.00035
	(0.00015)	(0.00013)
Median family income	0.04658	0.03446
	(0.00848)	(0.01013)
R^2	0.172	0.100
Correlation coefficient	0.415	0.316

mained. But the *Brigham* decision did not require equalization of expenditures; the decision required that the ability of a locality to fund public education be independent of (or negatively correlated with) its taxable wealth. The second column of table 9.2a and both columns of table 9.2b provide the evidence needed to determine whether Act 60 has resulted in an education financing system that satisfies the requirements set forth in the *Brigham* decision. From 1998–99 to 2001–02, the correlation between equalized assessed valuation per pupil and budgeted expenditures per equalized pupil in Vermont localities fell from 0.516 to 0.104 and, in the latter school year, was barely significant at the 10 percent level. Similar weakening in the relationship between this expenditure measure and other measures of taxable resources can be seen in table 9.2a. Further, in table 9.2b, which gives only post–Act 60

Table 9.3a
Relationships between expenditures and wealth measures for Vermont K–12 districts
Dependent variable: Current expenditures per equalized pupil (robust standard errors in parentheses)

Variable	1997–98	2000–01
Part 1		
Intercept	5551.390	7671.651
	(240.642)	(314.633)
Equalized assessed valuation per pupil in 1998	0.00208	0.00179
	(0.00065)	(0.00091)
R^2	0.200	0.120
Correlation coefficient	0.447	0.346
Part 2		
Intercept	4539.397	6690.965
	(779.732)	(733.089)
Adjusted gross income per exemption in 1995	0.11919	0.11254
	(0.05448)	(0.04636)
R^2	0.155	0.109
Correlation coefficient	0.394	0.330
Part 3		
Intercept	5131.453	7113.170
	(933.787)	(933.681)
Equalized assessed valuation per pupil in 1998	0.00153	0.00109
	(0.00091)	(0.00130)
Adjusted gross income per exemption in 1995	0.04390	0.05893
	(0.08008)	(0.08234)
R^2	0.219	0.135
Correlation coefficient	0.468	0.367

correlations between taxable resource measures and local expenditures per equalized pupil, the estimated relationship between equalized assessed valuation per pupil and local expenditures per equalized pupil is actually negative. Median family income continues to be positively related to local expenditures per equalized pupil, though this relationship does appear to be weakening over time.

In combination with the evidence on the simple distributions of expenditures, these results support the view that a good-faith effort has been made to satisfy the requirements of the *Brigham* decision. Although the correlation between taxable resources and the two expenditure measures considered here has not been reduced to zero, educational opportunities were more equal in 2001–02 than in 1998–99.[20]

Table 9.3b

Relationships between expenditures and wealth measures for Vermont K–12 districts
Dependent variable: Total expenditures per equalized pupil (robust standard errors in parentheses)

Variable	1997–98	2000–01
Part 1		
Intercept	6807.647	8886.544
	(478.282)	(444.865)
Equalized assessed valuation per pupil in 1998	0.00161	0.00133
	(0.00101)	(0.00110)
R^2	0.034	0.030
Correlation coefficient	0.184	0.173
Part 2		
Intercept	5464.105	7602.565
	(1577.796)	(840.889)
Adjusted gross income per exemption in 1995	0.12711	0.11493
	(0.10495)	(0.05254)
R^2	0.048	0.049
Correlation coefficient	0.219	0.221
Part 3		
Intercept	5455.199	7702.238
	(1614.335)	(857.560)
Equalized assessed valuation per pupil in 1998	−0.00007	0.00078
	(0.00097)	(0.00125)
Adjusted gross income per exemption in 1995	0.12948	0.08834
	(0.11663)	(0.05751)
R^2	0.048	0.059
Correlation coefficient	0.219	0.243

When we turn to school districts as the unit of analysis, the results do not provide quite as unequivocal a picture of the impact of Act 60 on the correlation between wealth measures and per pupil spending. In tables 9.3a and 9.3b, the results of regressions like those that generated the results in tables 9.2a and 9.2b are reported, with K–12 districts as the unit of analysis. In tables 9.4a and 9.4b, elementary school districts located in towns that belong to union or joint high school districts are the unit of analysis.[21]

When current expenditures per pupil are used as the spending measure, the correlations between spending and wealth decline for each wealth measure and both for K–12 districts and for elementary school districts located in towns that belong to union or joint high school districts. If, however, total expenditures per pupil are used as the

Table 9.4a
Relationships between expenditures and wealth measures for Vermont elementary districts located in towns that do not tuition-out high school students
Dependent variable: Current expenditures per equalized pupil (robust standard errors in parentheses)

Variable	1997–98	2000–01
Part 1		
Intercept	5489.755	7333.604
	(175.307)	(256.968)
Equalized assessed valuation per pupil in 1998	0.00098	0.00145
	(0.00024)	(0.00042)
R^2	0.170	0.155
Correlation coefficient	0.412	0.394
Part 2		
Intercept	5116.117	7112.060
	(505.333)	(733.717)
Adjusted gross income per exemption in 1995	0.07212	0.08422
	(0.03679)	(0.05340)
R^2	0.032	0.018
Correlation coefficient	0.179	0.134
Part 3		
Intercept	5187.736	7224.689
	(480.634)	(667.301)
Equalized assessed valuation per pupil in 1998	0.00088	0.00138
	(0.00024)	(0.00046)
Adjusted gross income per exemption in 1995	0.02655	0.01255
	(0.03745)	(0.05353)
R^2	0.161	0.147
Correlation coefficient	0.401	0.383

spending measure, there is not consistent evidence of a weakening in the relationship between spending and wealth. Only when K–12 districts are the unit of analysis and equalized assessed value per pupil is the wealth measure is the correlation found to have declined, from 0.184 in 1997–98 to 0.176 in 1998–99. For the other wealth measures, the correlation between total expenditures per pupil and wealth is found to have increased for the K–12 districts. And for each of the three wealth measures, the correlation between total expenditures per pupil and wealth is shown to have increased for elementary school districts located in towns that belong to union or joint high school districts. Explaining this strengthening of the correlation between total expenditures per pupil and wealth is a task for future work. What is apparent

Table 9.4b

Relationships between expenditures and wealth measures for Vermont elementary districts located in towns that do not tuition-out high school students

Dependent variable: Total expenditures per equalized pupil (robust standard errors in parentheses)

Variable	1997–98	2000–01
Part 1		
Intercept	6430.578	8294.678
	(231.805)	(318.056)
Equalized assessed valuation per pupil in 1998	0.00099	0.00156
	(0.00023)	(0.00047)
R^2	0.068	0.098
Correlation coefficient	0.261	0.313
Part 2		
Intercept	5635.405	7461.996
	(764.984)	(991.284)
Adjusted gross income per exemption in 1995	0.10323	0.13541
	(0.05418)	(0.07123)
R^2	0.024	0.025
Correlation coefficient	0.155	0.158
Part 3		
Intercept	5707.972	7578.357
	(735.322)	(939.968)
Equalized assessed valuation per pupil in 1998	0.00089	0.00143
	(0.00026)	(0.00052)
Adjusted gross income per exemption in 1995	0.05705	0.06137
	(0.05507)	(0.07464)
R^2	0.073	0.099
Correlation coefficient	0.270	0.315

now is that this correlation will be made stronger by recent legislation that excludes from the sharing pool property tax revenues that are raised to fund capital improvements.

9.5.2 Student Performance before and after Act 60

As the discussion in section 9.2 indicates, the *Brigham* decision focused on spending inequities. Further, the goals of Act 60 were to reduce spending inequities across school districts in Vermont and to provide property tax relief. Nevertheless, the justices of the Vermont Supreme Court made it clear in their decision that in their view, inequities in expenditures were likely to translate into inequities in outcome:

While we recognize that equal dollar resources do not necessarily translate equally in effect, there is no reasonable doubt that substantial funding differences significantly affect opportunities to learn. To be sure, some school districts may manage their money better than others, and circumstances extraneous to the educational system may substantially affect a child's performance. Money is clearly not the only variable affecting educational opportunity, but it is one that government can effectively equalize. (*Brigham v. State* (1997), 166 Vt. at 255–256).

Thus, how the distribution of student performance across districts changed after Act 60 is worth examining.

A crude indication of the impact of Act 60 on student performance is given by tables 9.5a and 9.5b, which present correlations in 1995–96 and 1999–2000 among some of the district characteristics summarized in table 9.1. The correlations between student performance and all available measures of the resources allocated toward education have weakened in the post–Act 60 period. The starkest example of the weakening of these correlations is the decline from 1994–95 to 2000–01 in the correlation between current expenditures per pupil and the percentage of fourth graders at or above the standard established by the state for the concepts portion of the New Standards Reference Exam (NSRE) in mathematics.[22] A more systematic assessment of the impact of Act 60 can be based on the results in table 9.6, which give a few typical event-analysis regressions that are similar in flavor to those in Downes and Figlio 2000.[23]

Because they include controls for district-specific effects and because they are based on a functional form that explicitly accounts for the reality that the proportion of students meeting the performance standard established by the state must range between zero and one, regressions like those whose results are presented in table 9.6 provide the most convincing estimates of the impact of Act 60. Further, because in these regressions the impact of Act 60 is allowed to vary with pre–Act 60 spending levels or pre–Act 60 property wealth, the regressions provide a direct indication of the extent to which the link between wealth and performance has changed post–Act 60. What is apparent from these regressions, and from a number of regressions in which other outcome measures are used as the dependent variable, is that there is some evidence that the gaps in performance between students in high-spending and those in low-spending districts and between students in high-wealth and those in low-wealth districts have, ceteris paribus, declined post–Act 60. In these regressions, the coefficient on the interaction be-

Table 9.5a
Correlations between selected characteristics for Vermont school districts, 1995–96

Variable	Current expenditure per pupil	Students per classroom teacher	Average teacher salary	Poverty rate	Average AGI per exemption (from tax returns)	Adults with college degree (1990) (%)	Grade 4 Math: Pupils at/above standard (%)	Grade 8 Math: Pupils at/above standard (%)
Current expenditure per pupil	1.0000							
Students per classroom teacher	−0.2011	1.0000						
Average teacher salary	0.2730	0.0023	1.0000					
Poverty rate	−0.0945	−0.0373	−0.1780	1.0000				
Average AGI per exemption (from tax returns)	0.2313	0.1337	0.5196	−0.5571	1.0000			
Adults with college degree (1990) (%)	0.1668	0.0813	0.3894	−0.5239	0.7964	1.0000		
Grade 4 Math: Pupils at/above standard (%)	0.1355	0.1817	0.1618	−0.2317	0.2211	0.2779	1.0000	
Grade 8 Math: Pupils at/above standard (%)	0.2058	0.0312	0.2371	−0.3380	0.3099	0.3741	0.1929	1.0000

Table 9.5b
Correlations between selected characteristics for Vermont school districts, 2000–01

Variable	Current expenditure per pupil	Students per classroom teacher	Average teacher salary	Poverty rate	Average AGI per exemption (from tax returns)	Adults with college degree (1990) (%)	Grade 4 Math: Pupils at/above standard (%)	Grade 8 Math: Pupils at/above standard (%)
Current expenditure per pupil	1.0000							
Students per classroom teacher	−0.3001	1.0000						
Average teacher salary	0.1822	0.3108	1.0000					
Poverty rate	−0.0933	−0.1774	−0.2763	1.0000				
Average AGI per exemption (from tax returns)	0.1781	0.3482	0.5772	−0.6019	1.0000			
Adults with college degree (1990) (%)	0.2464	0.2293	0.4617	−0.5707	0.8270	1.0000		
Grade 4 Math: Pupils at/above standard (%)	0.0640	0.0792	0.1303	−0.3028	0.3278	0.3107	1.0000	
Grade 8 Math: Pupils at/above standard (%)	0.2914	0.1394	0.1814	−0.3064	0.2986	0.3071	0.3257	1.0000

Table 9.6
GLM estimates of impact of Act 60 on student performance: Fixed effects estimates[1]
Dependent variable: Number of test-takers at or above standard in mathematical concepts (asymptotic standard errors robust to heteroskedasticity and within group correlation in parentheses)

Variable	Fourth Graders		Eighth Graders	
	Specification 1	Specification 2	Specification 1	Specification 2
Dummy variable indicating post-Act 60	-11.0842 (1.2278)	-11.4873 (1.2377)	-1.1104 (1.1417)	-0.7087 (1.1157)
Interaction of post-Act 60 dummy with per pupil equalized assessed valuation—1998	—	0.0000001 (0.0000010)	—	-0.0000013 (0.0000007)
Interaction of post-Act 60 dummy and current expenditure per pupil—1995	-0.00004 (0.00001)	—	-0.00004 (0.00002)	—
Poverty rate	0.0166 (0.0153)	0.0204 (0.0157)	0.0232 (0.0193)	0.0305 (0.0199)
Adjusted gross income per exemption	-0.00007 (0.00004)	-0.00007 (0.00005)	0.00005 (0.00004)	0.00003 (0.00004)
Dummy variable indicating 1995–96 school year	-12.6610 (1.1588)	-12.7888 (1.1904)	-1.2845 (1.0080)	-0.7463 (0.9941)
Dummy variable indicating 1997–98 school year	-11.6967 (1.1880)	-11.8655 (1.2138)	-1.0568 (1.0929)	-0.5050 (1.0742)
Dummy variable indicating 1999–2000 school year	0.0289 (0.0615)	0.0132 (0.0651)	-0.0443 (0.0601)	-0.0309 (0.0584)
Dummy variable indicating 2000–01 school year	0.3159 (0.1005)	0.3062 (0.1073)	0.1145 (0.1002)	0.1751 (0.1035)
Log of likelihood function	-2474.6375	-2522.3365	-1541.9252	-1591.7884
Number of observations	966	974	566	579

Note: 1. The constant is omitted from each specification. The omitted school year is 1998–99.

tween the Act 60 dummy and pre–Act 60 spending or pre–Act 60 wealth is never positive and significant. As can be seen in table 9.6, these coefficients are frequently negative and significant.

Care must be taken, however, not to make too much of the declines in inequality shown by these regressions. The coefficients on the inter-actions are not consistently negative and significant. Further, when these coefficients are significant, they are quantitatively small. For ex-ample, the coefficient in the first column of table 9.6 implies that, cete-ris paribus, the difference between the shares of fourth graders at or above the performance standard established by the state for a school district with spending one standard deviation below the mean in 1994 –95 and a school district with spending one standard deviation above the mean in 1994–95 would decline by 0.0021 if each district had the mean number of test-takers in 2000–01. It seems unlikely that such small declines in dispersion in performance justify a major policy in-tervention like Act 60.

9.6 Concluding Remarks

Act 60 represents a dramatic change in the system of education fi-nancing in a state with a history of a demographically stable student population. As a result, Act 60 may well provide an unparalleled op-portunity to assess the impact of a significant finance reform on a state's education system. This chapter represents a first effort at just such an assessment.

All of the evidence cited in the chapter supports the conclusion that Act 60 has dramatically reduced dispersion in education spending in Vermont and has done this by weakening the link between education spending and property wealth in the state. Further, the regressions presented in this chapter offer some evidence that student performance has become more equal across school districts in Vermont in the post–Act 60 period. And no results were obtained to support the conclusion that Act 60 has contributed to increased dispersion in student perfor-mance across Vermont's school districts.

By themselves, these results may provide useful information for pol-icymakers contemplating Act 60–style reforms. But the value of these results may well increase dramatically when taken together with the results of Duncombe and Johnston (chapter 5) and of Flanagan and Murray (chapter 6 in this volume). What is striking is the similarity across studies in the estimated effects of finance reform on student achievement. Prereform data on student test scores are not available to

Duncombe and Johnston; they find no evidence of a diminishment in the dispersion in performance when examining postreform test scores. They also document some recent relative improvement in dropout rates in high-poverty districts, though they also find increased dispersion in dropout rates when comparing pre- and postreform data.

The bottom line of Duncombe and Johnston's analysis of dropout rates is that reform has resulted in small relative improvements. Flanagan and Murray reach conclusions similar to those reached in this chapter: Postreform dispersion in schooling outcomes has declined, but this decline in dispersion has been small. The results presented in this chapter indicate that, in Vermont, there have been, at most, small relative improvements in the test performance of fourth and eighth graders in those school districts with lower prereform per-pupil spending and per-pupil property wealth. Flanagan and Murray find that relative increases in postreform spending were translated into relative gains in postreform test performance, but these gains were quantitatively small.

Somewhat surprisingly, then, the results of these new case studies tend to echo the results of the earlier work on California. Thus far, the case studies have confirmed the conclusion of many of the researchers who have executed national-level analyses: The types of finance reforms that have been implemented in various states in response to court orders appear to have had little, if any, impact on the distribution of student test performance in those states.

Notes

Thanks to Tom Husted, Bill Mathis, Larry Kenny, Jim Wyckoff, John Yinger, Bob Strauss, and participants in the Economics Department seminar at the University of New Hampshire, in the Maxwell School's Conference on State Aid to Education, and in the 2001 meetings of the American Education Finance Association and the Association for Public Policy Analysis and Management for their helpful comments and suggestions. All errors of omission and commission are the responsibility of the author.

1. In the 2000–01 school year, the nominal property tax rate was 1.1 percent, and the foundation level was $5,200.

2. In the 1994–95 school year, 69 of the 248 towns in Vermont for which data were available had effective education property tax rates below $1.10 per $100 in assessed value. Although the percentage of towns with effective education rates below $1.10 had undoubtedly declined by the 1997–98 school year, the last year before the phasing in of Act 60 began, the reality was still that Act 60 forced a sizable fraction of the towns in Vermont to increase their property tax rates.

3. The correlation between each town's effective education property tax rate in 1994–95 and the fraction of that town's property that was owned by town residents in 1998–99 was 0.5461. In other words, towns with low effective property tax rates prior to Act 60

also tended to be towns in which a large fraction of the property tax burden was exported.

4. See Heaps and Woolf 2000 and Jimerson 2001 for efforts to evaluate both the implications of Act 60 for educational provision and the effects of Act 60 on property tax burdens.

5. Since towns that collected sufficient funds from individual contributions to pay for desired spending above the foundation level of spending could avoid participating in the sharing pool, in most gold towns education funds were established and property owners were encouraged to contribute to these funds. Participation rates varied across towns, ranging up to 87 percent in Manchester, where aggressive tactics, such as publication of the names of nonparticipants, were used to encourage giving. More traditional incentives were also used to encourage giving; in fiscal years 1999, 2000, and 2001, the Freeman Foundation matched individual donations to the funds.

6. For examples of references to California in the context of the Vermont reforms, see McClaughry 1997 and Mathis 1998.

7. The number of studies dealing with these varied topics are too numerous too cite. Evans, Murray, and Schwab (1999) and Downes and Figlio (1999, 2000) cite many of the relevant studies.

8. Generating comparable numbers for earlier years is difficult. Nevertheless, the best available data support the conclusion that these sharp differences in trends in the minority share of student populations in California versus those in other states predate the *Serrano*-inspired reforms. For example, calculations based on published information for California indicate the percentage minority in 1977–78 was 36.6 percent. Estimates based on the October 1977 Current Population Survey indicate that the percent minority nationally was 23.9 percent.

9. Husted and Kenny do find evidence consistent with the conclusion that, in states that undertake school finance reforms, these reforms have no impact on the standard deviation of SAT scores. Since, however, the standard deviation of test scores can remain unchanged even if cross-district inequality in performance has declined, this evidence fails to establish that finance reforms do not reduce cross-district performance inequality.

10. For instance, among the students in Card and Payne's low-parental-education group, in twenty-eight states in 1978 (twenty-five states in 1990) less than 10 percent took the SAT examination and in twenty states in 1978 (fifteen states in 1990) less than 3 percent took the SAT. Further, in no state in 1978 did more than 36.2 percent of the low-parental-education group take the SAT.

11. In the 2001–02 school year, 824 equalized pupils (see section 9.5.1) (out of 103,347 equalized pupils in the state) resided in towns or other areas in which all students were "tuitioned out" to other districts or private schools. Another 87 equalized pupils resided in towns that did not operate an elementary school but belonged to a union high school district.

12. In the 2001–02 school year, 15,274 equalized pupils (see section 9.5.1) resided in towns in which elementary students were served locally but high school students were tuitioned out. Of these 15,274 equalized pupils, less than half were tuitioned out.

13. If a town tuitions out either elementary or high school students, those students could be attending school in several surrounding districts. As a result, the town cannot be matched to a single elementary or high school district.

14. Means across schools of the percentage minority evidence the same stability. In 1995–96, the across-school mean was 2.1 percent; in 1999–2000, it was 2.8 percent.

15. Since categorical aid is fungible, increases in categorical aid do increase the opportunities even for those students toward whom the aid is not targeted.

16. The pattern of Gini coefficients for current expenditures per pupil in these districts is very similar: 0.0801 in 1995–96, 0.0776 in 1996–97, 0.0835 in 1997–98, 0.0796 in 1998–99, 0.0776 in 1999–2000, and 0.0690 in 2000–01.

17. In addition to K–12 districts and elementary districts located in towns that belong to union or joint high school districts, the other large group of districts is elementary districts located in towns that tuition-out their high school students.

18. Again, the pattern of Gini coefficients for current expenditures per pupil in these districts is very similar. The values of the Gini coefficients were 0.1177 in 1995–96, 0.0955 in 1996–97, 0.1015 in 1997–98, 0.1044 in 1998–99, 0.1013 in 1999–2000, and 0.1107 in 2000–01.

19. Because of data limitations, equalized assessed valuation can be calculated only as far back as 1998–99. The 1998–99 values are therefore used throughout this analysis. Although pre–Act 60 measures of property wealth would probably be preferable, Act 60–induced changes in property values were unlikely to be apparent in 1998–99, the first year of the phase in of Act 60.

It is not possible to separate capital expenditures out of this measure of per-pupil expenditures. No clear indication exists as to whether the correlation of this expenditure measure with assessed valuation overstates or understates the correlation of current expenditures with assessed valuation. Thus, some caution must be exercised in interpreting correlations between budgeted expenditures per pupil and the measures of taxable resources considered here.

20. Given the available data, it was not possible to quantify directly the correlation between expenditures and wealth measures prior to implementation of Act 60. The results of Baker (2001a), however, provide an indirect indication of the strength of the correlation. In regressions that are analogous to those in part 3 of table 9.2b, Baker generates values for R-squared ranging from 0.47 to 0.51 for the school years from 1994–95 to 1998–99. Further, the highest value for R-squared occurs in 1998–99, the first year of the Act 60 phase in. The implication, then, is that the correlation between expenditures and the wealth measures considered in this chapter was probably strong and stable in the years leading up to Act 60.

21. All of these regressions have also been estimated in log-log form and with contemporaneous measures of per-pupil equalized assessed value and adjusted gross income per exemption replacing the lagged measures used in tables 9.3a, 9.3b, 9.4a, and 9.4b. The implications of the results that are generated from these alternative specifications are the same as those reported here.

22. Jimerson (2001) observes a similar decline in the correlation between equalized assessed value per pupil and the percentage of fourth graders at or above the standard for the NSRE.

23. Results for the performance of second and eighth graders tend to mirror those in tables 9.3 and 9.4. In no instance is there evidence that student performance has become less equal post–Act 60.

Appendixes

A

A Guide to State Court Decisions on Education Finance

Yao Huang, Anna Lukemeyer,
and John Yinger

The vast majority of states have experienced some school finance litigation. The most important cases have involved challenges to property tax–based funding systems on the grounds of equal protection or education clauses in the state constitution. This appendix provides an overview of the major school finance decisions by state courts that involve challenges of this type.[1]

Appendix table A.1 classifies states in terms of the outcome and status of litigation as of June 2003. Appendix table A.2 describes the major school finance decisions in each state. Because this litigation is so extensive and active, appendix table A.2 is, for the most part, limited to decisions by a state's highest court.[2] State supreme court decisions addressing issues other than the merits of plantiffs' challenges to the state's education finance system, such as mootness or attorney's fees, are not included. Lower-court decisions are included only selectively, primarily if they represent the only decision in the state or if they are the most recent decision in the state and differ significantly from the state's latest high-court decision. Pending litigation is also included to the extent that we were aware of it at the time we composed the appendix.

As shown in appendix table A.2 and summarized in appendix table A.1, five states (Delaware, Hawaii, Mississippi, Nevada, and Utah) have not been parties to any education finance litigation.[3] In addition, a suit was filed in Indiana but was withdrawn, before any court decision, after the state developed a new funding system. A suit also was recently filed in Iowa, but a decision in that case is still pending.

Appendix tables A.1 and A.2 also reveal that eighteen states' education finance systems have been overturned by the state's highest court (Alabama,[4] Arkansas, Arizona, California, Connecticut, Kentucky, Massachusetts, Montana, New Hampshire, New Jersey, New York,

Table A.1
Outcomes of education finance litigation as of June 2003

Outcome and status	Number of states	States
No case	6	Delaware, Hawaii, Indiana, Mississippi, Nevada, Utah
Case pending, no decision	1	Iowa
System overturned by highest court		
No new reform litigation pending[a]	6	Arkansas, New York, Tennessee, Vermont, Washington, Wyoming
Subsequent reforms upheld	1	Texas[b]
Further reform litigation pending	9	Arizona,[c] California, Connecticut, Kentucky, Massachusetts, Montana, New Hampshire, New Jersey, West Virginia
System overturned, no enforcement	2	Alabama, Ohio
Highest court reversed lower-court dismissal of reformers' claims; litigation continues	4	Idaho,[d] Kansas,[d] North Carolina, South Carolina[d]
System overturned by trial or intermediate appellate court; no high-court reversal of decision		
Reformed system upheld by high court	1	Missouri
Capital funding system only overturned; rulings subject to possible appeal	2	Alaska, New Mexico
System upheld[e]		
System upheld	15	Georgia, Illinois, Louisiana, Maine, Michigan, Minnesota, Nebraska, North Dakota, Oklahoma, Oregon, Pennsylvania, Rhode Island, South Dakota, Virginia, Wisconsin
Further reform litigation pending	2	Colorado, Florida[f]
Subsequent lower-court ruling for plaintiffs	1	Maryland

Source: Table A.2.
Notes:
a. In some of these cases, the courts may have retained jurisdiction.
b. This classification of Texas does not consider the most recent decision by the state's supreme court, which calls for further litigation in a case claiming that the Texas reforms went too far.
c. The supreme court's decision in Arizona concerned capital funding only.

Table A.1
(continued)

d. The highest courts in Idaho, Kansas, and South Carolina have all issued opinions in prior cases addressing school finance reform suits. In Idaho and South Carolina, the court upheld the existing funding system against plaintiffs' claims. In Kansas, the court upheld legislative reforms resulting from lower-court action.

e. Despite their highest court's acceptance of the existing system, some of these states (notably Colorado, Oregon, Maryland, and Michigan) have enacted significant reforms without any push from the courts. Oregon's reforms include a state constitutional amendment strengthening the education clause.

f. After the Florida supreme court ruled against reform, voters enacted, in 1998, a state constitutional amendment strengthening education clause guarantees. In 2000, another suit was filed.

Ohio, Tennessee, Texas, Vermont, Washington, West Virginia, and Wyoming). The courts in Alabama and Ohio, however, have backed away from their initial decisions and made them unenforceable. In Arizona, the court's decision was limited to the state's capital funding system.

A number of the states in which the highest court overturned the finance system are participants in ongoing litigation, either in the form of new suits seeking further reforms (Arizona, California, Connecticut, Kentucky, Massachusetts, and Montana) or additional challenges to the state's implementation of earlier court orders for reform (Arizona, New Hampshire, New Jersey, and West Virginia). In four states (Idaho, Kansas, North Carolina, and South Carolina), the high court reversed a lower-court ruling dismissing reformers' claims and re-manded the suit for evidentiary hearing. In North Carolina a lower-court decision is once again before the high court. In addition, trial courts in Alaska and New Mexico recently declared their states' capital funding systems unconstitutional. These decisions have not yet been reviewed by the high courts in those states.

Finally, several courts have upheld reform legislation passed in re-sponse to an earlier decision overturning their state's education finance system. These include the highest courts in Texas, Missouri, and Kan-sas and an intermediate appellate court in California. The decisions in California and Kansas have been followed by other, still-pending chal-lenges to the state's reformed education finance system.

In contrast, the state supreme court has refused to strike down the education finance systems in fifteen[5] states (Colorado, Florida, Georgia, Illinois, Maryland, Michigan,[6] Minnesota, Nebraska, North Dakota, Oklahoma, Oregon, Pennsylvania, Rhode Island, Virginia, and

Table A.2
Significant school finance decisions by state, January 1971–June 2003

Case citation	Level of court	Outcome
Alabama		
Opinion of the Justices No. 338, 624 So.2d 107 (1993) (*Equity Funding Cases I*)	Highest court	Holding that trial court decision that current system violates constitution is binding unless appealed
Ex parte James, 713 So.2d 869 (1997) (*Equity Funding Cases II*)	Highest court	Vacating trial courts' remedial plan, directing legislature to enact a constitutional system, and remanding case to trial court
Ex parte James, 836 So.2d 813 (2002) (*Equity Funding Cases III*)	Highest court	Concluding that court imposition of a specific remedy would be a judicial intrusion into legislative matters and dismissing case
Alaska		
Kasayulie v. Alaska, 3-AN-97-3782 Ci. (Alaska Super.) (September 1, 1999)[a]	Trial court	Granting plaintiffs' motion for partial summary judgment that system for funding facilities violates education clause
Arizona		
Shofstall v. Hollins, 110 Ariz. 88, 515 P.2d 590 (1973)	Highest court	Reversing trial court summary judgment in favor of plaintiffs
Roosevelt Elementary School District No. 66 v. Bishop, 179 Ariz. 233, 877 P.2d 806 (1994) (*Roosevelt ESD I*)	Highest court	Requiring reform of capital funding system
Hull v. Albrecht, 190 Ariz. 520, 950 P.2d 1141 (1997) (*Roosevelt ESD II*)	Highest court	Requiring further reform of capital funding system (on review of reform legislation)
Hull v. Albrecht, 192 Ariz. 34, 960 P.2d 634 (1998) (*Roosevelt ESD III*)	Highest court	Requiring further reform of capital funding system (on review of reform legislation)
Hull v. Albrecht, No. CV-98-0238-SA (July 20, 1998)	Highest court	Upholding reform legislation
Roosevelt Elementary School District No. 66 v. Hull, No. CV-1999-019062/ CV-2002-011568 (October 17, 2002)	Trial court	Requiring state to restore funds to state's Building Renewal Fund (on appeal)
Crane Elementary School District v. Arizona	Trial court	Pending
Arkansas		
DuPree v. Alma School District No. 30, 279 Ark. 340, 651 S.W.2d 90 (1983)	Highest court	Requiring reform

Table A.2

(continued)

Case citation	Level of court	Outcome
Lake View School District No. 25 v. Huckabee, 351 Ark. 31, 91 S.W.3d 472 (2002), *cert. denied sub nom. Wilson v. Huckabee* (May 19, 2003)	Highest court	Requiring reform
California		
Serrano v. Priest, 5 Cal.3d 584, 487 P.2d 1241 (1971)	Highest court	Reversing trial court decision against plaintiffs and remanding for further proceedings
Serrano v. Priest, 18 Cal.3d 728, 557 P.2d 929 (1976)	Highest court	Requiring reform
Serrano v. Priest, 200 Cal.App.3d 897, 226 Cal. Rptr. 584 (1986)	Intermediate appellate court	Upholding reform legislation
Williams v. California	Trial court	Pending
Colorado		
Lujan v. Colorado State Board of Education, 649 P.2d 1005 (1982)	Highest court	Upholding existing system
Haley v. Colorado Department of Education (No. 02CV5149)	Trial court	Pending (challenging system for funding special education under education, equal-protection, and due-process provisions)
Connecticut		
Horton v. Meskill, 172 Conn. 615, 376 A.2d 369 (1977)	Highest court	Requiring reform
Horton v. Meskill, 195 Conn. 24, 486 A.2d 1099 (1985)	Highest court	Upholding reform legislation in part; reversing trial court finding of unconstitutionality; remanding case for further reveiew based on new standard
Sheff v. O'Neill, 238 Conn. 1, 678 A.2d 1267 (1995)	Highest court	Requiring reform
Johnson v. Rowland	Trial court	Pending
Delaware: No cases		
Florida		
Coalition for Adequacy and Fairness in School Funding v. Chiles, 680 So.2d 400 (1996)	Highest court	Upholding existing system
Honore v. Florida	Trial court	Pending

Table A.2
(continued)

Case citation	Level of court	Outcome
Georgia		
McDaniel v. Thomas, 248 Ga. 632, 285 S.E.2d 156 (1981)	Highest court	Upholding existing system
Hawaii: No cases		
Idaho		
Thompson v. Engelking, 96 Idaho 793, 537 P.2d 635 (1975)	Highest court	Upholding existing system
Idaho Schools for Equal Educational Opportunity v. Evans, 123 Idaho 573, 850 P.2d 724 (1993)	Highest court	Reversing trial court's dismissal of plaintiffs' education clause claim
Idaho Schools for Equal Educational Opportunity v. Idaho, 132 Idaho 559, 976 P.2d 913 (1998)	Highest court	Reversing trial court summary judgment against plaintiffs on issue of facilities and remanding for further proceedings
Illinois		
Committee for Educational Rights v. Edgar, 174 Ill.2d 1, 672 N.E.2d 1178 (1996)	Highest court	Upholding existing system (issue nonjusticiable)
Lewis v. Spagnolo, 186 Ill.2d 198, 710 N.E.2d 798 (1999)	Highest court	Upholding existing system (issue nonjusticiable)
Indiana		
Lake Central v. Indiana, No. 56 C01-8704-CP81 (Newton Cir. Ct. 1987)	Trial court	Withdrawn after state revised funding system
Iowa		
Coalition for a Common Cents Solution v. Iowa	Trial court	Pending
Kansas		
Mock v. State, No. 91CV1009 (Shawnee County District Court unpublished opinion of October 14, 1991)	Trial court	Settlement with reform
Unified School District No. 229 v. Kansas, 256 Kan. 232, 885 P.2d 1170 (1994)	Highest court	Upholding reform legislation
Montoy v. Kansas, 257 Kan. 145, 62 P.3d 228 (2003)	Highest court	Reversing trial court judgment against plaintiffs and remanding for further proceedings

Table A.2
(continued)

Case citation	Level of court	Outcome
Kentucky		
Rose v. Council for Better Education, 790 S.W.2d 186 (1989)	Highest court	Requiring reform
Young v. Williams	Trial court	Pending
Louisiana		
Charlet v. Legislature, 713 So.2d 1199, *writ denied* 730 So.2d 934 (1998)	Intermediate appellate court	Upholding existing system
Maine		
School Administrative District No. 1 v. Commissioner, 659 A.2d 854 (1995)	Highest court	Upholding method of implementing funding reduction
Maryland		
Hornbeck v. Somerset County Board of Education, 295 Md. 597, 458 A.2d 758 (1983)	Highest court	Upholding existing system and endorsing adequacy standard
Bradford v. Maryland State Board of Education, No. 94340058/CE 189672 (Circuit Court for Baltimore City, June 30, 2000)	Trial court	Requiring reform
Massachusetts		
McDuffy v. Secretary, 415 Mass. 545, 615 N.E.2d 516 (1993)	Highest court	Requiring reform
Hancock v. Driscoll	Trial court	Pending
Michigan		
Milliken v. Green, 390 Mich. 389, 212 N.W.2d 711 (1973), *vacating* 389 Mich. 1, 203 N.W.2d 457 (1972)	Highest court	Vacating initial opinion, favoring plaintiffs, and dismissing cause[b]
Minnesota		
Skeen v. Minnesota, 505 N.W.2d 299 (1993)	Highest court	Upholding existing system
Mississippi: No cases		
Missouri		
Committee for Educational Equality v. Missouri, No. CV190-1371CC (Circuit Court of Cole County, January 15, 1993)	Trial court	Requiring reform
Committee for Educational Equality v. Missouri, 967 S.W.2d 62 (1998)	Highest court	Upholding reform legislation

Table A.2
(continued)

Case citation	Level of court	Outcome
Montana		
Helena Elementary School District No. 1 v. Montana, 236 Mont. 44, 746 P.2d 684 (1989), *as modified*, 784 P.2d 412 (1990)	Highest court	Requiring reform
Columbia Falls Elementary School District No. 6 v. Montana (No. BDV-2002-528)	Trial court	Pending
Nebraska		
Gould v. Orr, 244 Neb. 163, 506 N.W.2d 349 (1993)	Highest court	Upholding existing system
Nevada: No cases		
New Hampshire		
Claremont School District v. Governor, 138 N.H. 183, 635 A.2d 1375 (1993)	Highest court	Reversing trial court dismissal of plaintiffs' claims and remanding for further proceedings
Claremont School District v. Governor, 142 N.H. 462, 703 A.2d 1353 (1997)	Highest court	Requiring reform: Current finance system violates constitutional provision requiring taxes to be proportionate and reasonable
Opinion of the Justices (School Financing), 142 N.H. 892, 712 A.2d 1080 (1998)	Highest court	Reviewing proposed reform legislation
Claremont School District v. Governor, 144 N.H. 210, 744 A.2d 1107 (1999)	Highest court	Holding that phase-in provision of reform legislation violates constitutional requirement that taxes be proportionate and reasonable
Opinion of the Justices (Reformed Public School Financing System), 145 N.H. 474, 765 A.2d 673 (2000)	Highest court	Reviewing proposed reform legislation
Claremont School District v. Governor, 147 N.H. 499, 794 A.2d 744 (2002)	Highest court	Requiring further reform (on review of reform legislation)
New Jersey		
Robinson v. Cahill, 62 N.J. 473, 303 A.2d 273 (1973), *cert. denied sub nom. Dickey v. Robinson*, 414 U.S. 976 (1973)	Highest court	Requiring reform
Robinson v. Cahill, 69 N.J. 449, 355 A.2d 129 (1976)	Highest court	Upholding reform legislation as facially constitutional

Table A.2
(continued)

Case citation	Level of court	Outcome
Abbott v. Burke, 119 N.J. 287, 575 A.2d 359 (1990)	Highest court	Requiring reform
Abbott v. Burke, 136 N.J. 444, 643 A.2d 575 (1994)	Highest court	Requiring further reform (on review of reform legislation)
Abbott v. Burke, 149 N.J. 145, 693 A.2d 417 (1997)	Highest court	Requiring further reform (on review of reform legislation)
Abbott v. Burke, 153 N.J. 480, 710 A.2d 450 (1998)	Highest court	Requiring implementation of specific reforms and remedial measures
Abbott v. Burke, 163 N.J. 95, 748 A.2d 82 (2000)	Highest court	Clarifying required reforms (regarding preschool education)
Abbott v. Burke, 164 N.J. 84, 751 A.2d 1032 (2000)	Highest court	Clarifying required reforms (regarding capital financing)
Abbott v. Burke, 172 N.J. 294, 798 A.2d 602 (2002)	Highest court	Granting in part and denying in part state's request for delay in implementing remedial measures
Abbott v. Burke (April 29, 2003)	Highest court	Ordering parties to mediation
New Mexico		
Zuni School District v. New Mexico, CV-98-14-11 (McKinley County District Court, 1999)	Trial court	Granting partial summary judgment on plaintiffs' claims (funding for facilities)
New York		
Board of Education, Levittown Union Free School District v. Nyquist, 57 N.Y.2d 27, 439 N.E.2d 359 (1982)	Highest court	Upholding existing system
Reform Educational Financing Inequities Today v. Cuomo, 86 N.Y.2d 279, 655 N.E.2d 647 (1995)	Highest court	Upholding dismissal of plaintiffs' claims
Campaign for Fiscal Equity, Inc. v. State, 86 N.Y.2d 307, 655 N.E.2d 661 (1995)	Highest court	Reversing dismissal of plaintiffs' claims and remanding for further proceedings
Campaign for Fiscal Equity, Inc. v. New York, No. 74 (New York, June 26, 2003) (slip opinion)	Highest court	Requiring reform
North Carolina		
Leandro v. North Carolina, 346 N.C. 336, 488 S.E.2d 249 (1997)	Highest court	Reversing dismissal of plaintiffs' claim and remanding for further proceedings

Table A.2
(continued)

Case citation	Level of court	Outcome
Hoke County Board of Education v. North Carolina, No. 95 CVS 1158 (2002)	Trial court	Requiring reform (in proceedings after remand of *Leandro*; decision currently under review by high court)
North Dakota		
Bismarck Public School District No. 1 v. North Dakota, 511 N.W.2d 247 (1994)	Highest court	Upholding existing system
Ohio		
Board of Education v. Walter, 58 Ohio St.2d 368, 390 N.E.2d 813 (1979), *cert. denied*, 444 U.S. 1015 (1980)	Highest court	Upholding existing system
DeRolph v. Ohio, 78 Ohio St.3d 193, 677 N.E.2d 733 (1997), *as clarified*, 78 Ohio St.3d 419, 678 N.E.2d 886 (1997)	Highest court	Requiring reform
DeRolph v. Ohio, 89 Ohio St.3d 1, 728 N.E.2d 993 (2000)	Highest court	Requiring further reform (on review of reform legislation)
DeRolph v. Ohio, 97 Ohio St.3d 434, 780 N.E.2d 529 (2002)	Highest court	Holding system unconstitutional, but vacating prior remand and ending court's jurisdiction over case
Ohio v. Lewis, 99 Ohio St.3d 97, 789 N.E.2d 195 (2003)	Highest court	Preventing trial court from holding compliance conference or supervising state's compliance with *DeRolph* orders (on petition for writ of prohibition)
Oklahoma		
Fair School Finance Council v. Oklahoma, 746 P.2d 1135 (1987)	Highest court	Upholding existing system
Oregon		
Olsen v. Oregon, 276 Or. 9, 554 P.2d 139 (1976)	Highest court	Upholding existing system
Coalition for Equitable Funding Inc. v. Oregon, 311 Or. 300, 811 P.2d 116 (1991)	Highest court	Upholding existing system
Pennsylvania		
Danson v. Casey, 484 Pa. 415, 399 A.2d 360 (1979)	Highest court	Upholding existing system (issue nonjusticiable)
Marrero v. Commonwealth, 559 Pa. 14, 739 A.2d 110 (1999)	Highest court	Upholding existing system (issue nonjusticiable)

Table A.2
(continued)

Case citation	Level of court	Outcome
Rhode Island		
City of Pawtucket v. Sundlin, 662 A.2d 40 (1995)	Highest court	Upholding existing system (issue nonjusticiable)
South Carolina		
Richland County v. Campbell, 294 S.C. 346, 364 S.E.2d 470 (1988)	Highest court	Upholding existing system
Abbeville County School District v. South Carolina, 335 S.C. 58, 515 S.E.2d 535 (1999)	Highest court	Reversing dismissal of plaintiffs' claim and remanding for further proceedings
South Dakota		
Bezdichek v. South Dakota, CIV 92-209 (1994)	Trial court	Upholding existing system
Tennessee		
Tennessee Small School Systems v. McWherter, 851 S.W.2d 139 (1993)	Highest court	Requiring reform
Tennessee Small School Systems v. McWherter, 894 S.W.2d 734 (1995)	Highest court	Requiring further reform in part (teachers' salaries)
Tennessee Small School Systems v. McWherter, 91 S.W.3d 232 (2002)	Highest court	Requiring further reform (teachers' salaries)
Texas		
Edgewood Independent School District v. Kirby, 777 S.W.2d 391 (1989)	Highest court	Requiring reform
Edgewood Independent School District v. Kirby, 804 S.W.2d 491 (1991)	Highest court	Requiring further reform (on review of reform legislation)
Carrolton–Farmers Branch Independent School District v. Edgewood Independent School District, 826 S.W.2d 489 (1992)	Highest court	Striking down reform legislation as violating constitutional provisions governing ad valorem property taxes (challenge brought by wealthy districts)
Edgewood Independent School District v. Meno, 893 S.W.2d 450 (1995)	Highest court	Upholding reform legislation
West Orange–Cove Consolidated Independent School District v. Alanis, No. 02-0427 (slip op., May 29, 2003)	Highest court	Reversing trial court dismissal of challenge to recapture provision of reform legislation
Utah: No cases		
Vermont		
Brigham v. Vermont, 166 Vt. 246, 692 A.2d 384 (1997)	Highest court	Requiring reform

Table A.2
(continued)

Case citation	Level of court	Outcome
Virginia		
Scott v. Commonwealth of Virginia, 247 Va. 379, 443 S.E.2d 138 (1994)	Highest court	Upholding existing system
Washington		
North Shore School District No. 417 v. Kinnear, 84 Wash.2d 685, 530 P.2d 178 (1974)	Highest court	Upholding existing system; substantially overruled by *Seattle School District No. 1*
Seattle School District No. 1 v. Washington, 90 Wash.2d 476, 585 P.2d 71 (1978)	Highest court	Requiring reform
West Virginia		
Pauley v. Kelly, 162 W.Va. 672, 255 S.E.2d 859 (1979)	Highest court	Reversing judgment against plaintiffs and remanding for further proceedings
Pauley v. Bailey, 174 W.Va. 167, 324 S.E.2d 128 (1984)	Highest court	Ordering implementation of "master plan," developed in response to trial court order, for establishing a constitutional educational system
Tomblin v. West Virginia Board of Education, Civil Action No. 75-1268 (January 3, 2003)	Trial court	Declaring reformed system constitutional and ending jurisdiction over the case (motion for reconsideration pending)
Wisconsin		
Kukor v. Grover, 148 Wis.2d 469, 436 N.W.2d 568 (1989)	Highest court	Upholding existing system
Vincent v. Voight, 236 Wis.2d 588, 614 N.W.2d 388 (2000)	Highest court	Upholding existing system
Wyoming		
Washakie County School District No. 1 v. Herschler, 606 P.2d 310, *cert. denied*, 449 U.S. 824 (1980)	Highest court	Requiring reform
Campbell County School District v. Wyoming, 907 P.2d 1238 (1995)	Highest court	Requiring reform
Campbell County School District v. Wyoming, 19 P.3d 518 (2001)	Highest court	Requiring further reform in part
Campbell County School District v. Wyoming, 32 P.3d 325 (2001)	Highest court	Clarifying issues raised in petition for rehearing, including "the issue of capital construction"

Table A.2
(continued)

Sources: ACCESS 2003; Minorini and Sugarman 1999b, tables 2.2–2.6; Murray, Evans, and Schwab 1998; and Enrich 1995.

Notes: This table compiles significant state supreme court decisions addressing the merits of equal protection or education clause challenges to property tax–based school funding systems. Because the state of this litigation is so fluid, only selected lower-court cases are reported here, as when no high-court decision exists. State supreme court cases addressing issues other than the merits of plaintiffs' challenges, such as mootness or attorney's fees, are also omitted.

a. Minorini and Sugarman (1999b) include *Matanuska-Susitna Borough School District v. Alaska*, 931 P.2d 391 (Alaska 1997). This case involved an atypical equal-protection challenge. Plaintiff's claim was based on the school funding system's differential treatment of regional educational attendance area (REAA) schools rather than its reliance on property tax revenues as such.

b. In a later case, an intermediate appellate court rejected the merits of plaintiffs' constitutional challenges and upheld the existing school finance system. *East Jackson Public Schools v. Michigan*, 133 Mich. App. 132, 348 N.W.2d 303 (1984).

Wisconsin). In addition, lower courts have upheld the existing education finance system in two states (Louisiana and South Dakota), with no reversal by the highest court in the state, and the Maine Supreme Court upheld the state's method for implementing a reduction in education funding.

The impact of these decisions is sometimes mitigated by subsequent events. Maryland and Michigan implemented major education finance reforms despite the decisions by their supreme courts, for example, and voters in Florida and Oregon responded to the supreme court decisions in their states by amending the education clauses in their states' constitutions. New suits challenging the state education finance systems have also been filed in Colorado and Florida.

In summary, state supreme courts have struck down school finance systems in eighteen states (including Alabama and Ohio) and have refused to do so in sixteen states. Of these thirty-four states, at least eleven currently have ongoing litigation in which plaintiffs are seeking further reform or, in the case of earlier losses, presenting new evidence and legal theories. In an additional four states, state supreme courts have issued interim decisions favorable to plaintiffs and litigation continues. Finally, suits are pending in three states with no supreme court decisions on the issue of education finance: Alaska, Iowa, and New Mexico. In these cases, plaintiffs have gained trial court victories in Alaska and New Mexico.

Notes

The authors thank Molly A. Hunter of the Advocacy Center for Children's Educational Success with Standards for her review of the appendix and helpful suggestions.

1. The sources for this appendix are ACCESS 2003; Enrich 1995; Minorini and Sugarman 1999b; and Murray, Evans, and Schwab 1998.

2. We use the terms "highest court," "high court," and "supreme court" as synonyms, even though the highest court is not literally called the "supreme court" in some states, such as New York, where it is called the "Court of Appeals."

3. It is not possible to challenge local education finance in Hawaii, which has a state school system.

4. The Alabama court did not address the merits of the school finance system but upheld a decision by a lower court on procedural grounds.

5. In addition to these fifteen states, high courts in Idaho and South Carolina have issued opinions upholding the school funding system against plaintiffs' claims. These opinions were issued before 1990. In later, ongoing litigation, these two courts have issued interim opinions favorable to plaintiffs.

6. In Michigan, the court vacated an earlier opinion favorable to plaintiffs and dismissed the case. This action was taken with no majority opinion on the merits, only a concurring opinion. In a later case, an intermediate appellate court reached an opinion on the merits and upheld the school finance system (see appendix table A.2).

A Guide to State Operating Aid Programs for Elementary and Secondary Education

Yao Huang

Introduction

This appendix summarizes state aid for elementary and secondary education in all fifty states. Appendix table B.1 broadly outlines each state's education finance system. It shows spending per pupil, the shares of revenue provided by different levels of government, and the spending gap facing high-poverty school districts. As shown in the table's first row, in the average state, spending per pupil is $7,284, the state pays 49.9 percent of the tab, and low-poverty districts receive almost $1,000 more per pupil than do high-poverty districts.

Appendix table B.2 provides more detailed information on the types of aid programs available in each state. In particular, it shows the shares of state revenue that come through formula assistance, compensatory programs, programs for students with handicaps, vocational programs, transportation programs, other programs, and state payments that aid school districts without going directly to them. An example of spending in the last category is state payment of teacher pensions. The first row of this table reveals that on average in U.S. states, 67.7 percent of state aid comes through formula assistance, whereas only 1.9 percent comes in the form of compensatory programs, and only 6.2 percent in the form of programs for students with handicaps.

Appendix tables B.3 through B.6 describe the features of state aid to school districts in more detail. These tables draw heavily on National Center for Education Statistics 2001c, which provides detailed information on state aid systems in 1998–99. A variety of sources have been found and used to update the information on state aid systems presented in these tables to reflect changes that may have occurred since

Table B.1
Education finance systems, by state, 2001

	Spending per pupil	Sources of funding (%)			Spending gap facing high-poverty district
		State	Local	Federal	
United States	$7,284	49.9	43.0	7.1	$966
Alabama	5,845	59.6	30.8	9.6	991
Alaska	9,165	55.3	27.4	17.3	n.a.
Arizona	5,100	46.4	43.7	9.9	845
Arkansas	5,852	72.0	18.7	9.3	76
California	6,965	60.5	31.2	8.3	59
Colorado	6,515	41.6	52.9	5.5	587
Connecticut	9,236	38.4	57.5	4.1	6
Delaware	8,603	67.2	25.9	6.9	n.a.
Florida	6,020	49.4	42.1	8.5	46
Georgia	6,909	48.5	45.3	6.2	−6
Hawaii	6,558	89.8	1.8	8.4	n.a.
Idaho	5,616	61.4	30.7	7.9	157
Illinois	7,585	36.7	55.5	7.8	2,060
Indiana	7,287	50.7	44.4	4.9	210
Iowa	6,912	49.4	44.5	6.1	471
Kansas	6,521	61.6	31.9	6.5	66
Kentucky	6,077	60.1	30.1	9.8	−133
Louisiana	5,934	48.7	39.7	11.6	793
Maine	8,178	44.2	49.7	6.1	148
Maryland	8,077	37.3	56.8	5.9	912
Massachusetts	9,038	41.1	54.2	4.7	−530
Michigan	8,029	64.7	28.6	6.7	1,103
Minnesota	7,447	61.8	33.6	4.6	−601
Mississippi	5,179	53.9	32.4	13.7	133
Missouri	6,593	46.6	46.8	6.6	284
Montana	6,671	47.5	41.1	11.4	1,535
Nebraska	6,946	35.0	57.8	7.2	516
Nevada	5,778	60.5	34.5	5.0	−280
New Hampshire	7,065	52.1	43.4	4.5	733
New Jersey	10,893	40.6	55.6	3.8	−324
New Mexico	6,115	71.3	14.9	13.8	86
New York	10,922	46.9	47.5	5.6	2,152
North Carolina	6,368	62.7	30.5	6.8	114
North Dakota	6,318	38.8	48.0	13.2	93
Ohio	7,499	42.9	51.3	5.8	394
Oklahoma	6,012	56.3	33.8	9.9	−57

Table B.1
(continued)

| | Spending per pupil | Sources of funding (%) | | | Spending gap facing high-poverty district |
		State	Local	Federal	
Oregon	7,511	56.7	36.1	7.2	−371
Pennsylvania	8,191	37.3	56.3	6.4	1,248
Rhode Island	8,755	41.9	52.5	5.6	273
South Carolina	6,570	53.9	38.2	7.9	332
South Dakota	6,063	35.9	52.2	11.9	171
Tennessee	5,622	45.0	46.1	8.9	−497
Texas	6,460	41.2	50.2	8.6	518
Utah	4,625	57.9	33.8	8.3	−422
Vermont	8,706	72.5	21.5	6.0	939
Virginia	7,278	42.5	51.8	5.7	885
Washington	6,613	63.6	29.3	7.1	145
West Virginia	7,450	59.8	29.6	10.6	199
Wisconsin	8,158	54.5	40.7	4.8	151
Wyoming	7,833	50.2	41.2	8.6	715

Sources: Columns 1 through 6 come from U.S. Census Bureau (2003, tables 5 and 8); column 7 comes from Education Trust (2002, table 1).
Notes: Formula assistance is defined as "revenue from general noncategorical state assistance programs" plus "revenue dedicated from major state taxes" (U.S. Census Bureau 2003, p. A-4). Other assistance includes compensatory, handicapped, vocational, and transportation, capital, and miscellaneous programs. The spending gap is the difference in spending per pupil in 2000 between school districts at the 25th percentile of the poverty-rate distribution and those at the 75th percentile. States marked with "n.a." (for not applicable) either have only one district or have little variation in the poverty rate. See Education Trust (2002).

1998–99, but no systematic update exists, and recent changes in some states may have been overlooked. These additional sources include Association of Alaska School Boards 1998; Carey 2002; Fowler and Monk 2001; Hunter 2003; Idaho School Superintendents' Association and the Idaho State Department of Education, Finance Division 2002; Illinois State Board of Education 2001; Mills 1996; New York State Education Department, State Aid Unit 2000; New York State Education Department, Elementary, Middle, Secondary, and Continuing Education 2003; New York State Office of the State Comptroller 1997; Maine School Management Association and the Department of Education General Purpose Aid Team 2003; Maryland Commission on Education Finance, Equity, and Excellence 2002; State of Alaska 2003; State of

Table B.2
Types of state aid for public elementary and secondary schools, by state, 2000–01 (in percentages)

	Formula assistance	Compensatory programs	Programs for students with handicaps	Vocational programs	Transportation programs	Other and nonspecified state aid	State payments on behalf of local education authority
United States	67.7	1.9	6.2	0.5	1.7	18.6	3.4
Alabama	85.0	1.1	0.7	0.0	6.3	6.9	0.0
Alaska	88.4	0.0	0.0	0.0	6.0	5.6	0.0
Arizona	81.0	0.0	0.0	0.4	0.0	18.6	0.0
Arkansas	69.9	3.8	1.1	0.6	0.0	23.7	0.9
California	52.1	2.7	7.9	0.0	1.8	32.7	2.7
Colorado	92.0	0.0	3.2	1.1	1.6	2.0	0.0
Connecticut	47.3	1.1	13.9	0.1	2.0	24.8	10.8
Delaware	69.4	0.0	0.3	0.0	6.1	23.9	0.4
Florida	38.5	0.0	15.7	2.9	4.4	38.5	0.0
Georgia	84.9	0.0	0.0	0.0	0.0	13.2	1.9
Hawaii	73.3	0.7	10.8	0.4	1.4	13.4	0.0
Idaho	69.8	0.0	0.1	0.8	5.3	23.9	0.1
Illinois	52.9	1.1	7.5	0.7	5.1	19.3	13.3
Indiana	81.2	0.3	0.6	0.1	0.8	3.8	13.2
Iowa	90.8	0.6	0.0	0.2	0.4	8.0	0.0
Kansas	84.7	0.0	8.8	0.8	0.0	1.8	3.9
Kentucky	67.4	0.0	0.0	0.3	0.0	13.9	18.3
Louisiana	93.8	0.0	1.0	0.0	0.0	5.2	0.0
Maine	70.4	0.0	0.0	0.0	0.0	9.6	20.0

Maryland	55.2	5.5	5.5	0.1	4.2	16.9	12.5
Massachusetts	69.1	0.0	0.0	0.0	2.4	14.3	14.2
Michigan	87.0	2.9	6.3	0.5	0.0	3.2	0.0
Minnesota	59.1	4.8	12.1	0.5	1.1	22.4	0.0
Mississippi	80.6	10.0	0.0	2.0	0.0	7.5	0.0
Missouri	57.1	0.0	7.5	1.0	4.7	29.7	0.0
Montana	85.5	0.0	0.7	0.1	2.0	11.8	0.0
Nebraska	72.9	0.0	17.4	0.0	0.0	9.7	0.0
Nevada	35.0	0.0	4.7	0.1	0.0	60.3	0.0
New Hampshire	93.2	0.0	0.0	0.4	0.0	5.6	0.8
New Jersey	49.0	16.1	11.9	0.5	4.4	7.9	10.1
New Mexico	88.3	0.2	0.0	0.0	5.3	6.1	0.0
New York	61.9	0.0	13.6	0.0	0.0	24.5	0.0
North Carolina	92.1	0.0	0.0	0.0	0.0	6.3	1.6
North Dakota	81.5	0.0	6.9	1.3	5.8	4.4	0.0
Ohio	80.8	3.1	0.1	0.2	0.2	15.6	0.0
Oklahoma	69.0	0.0	0.1	1.5	0.0	27.6	1.7
Oregon	90.7	0.0	0.0	0.0	1.1	8.2	0.0
Pennsylvania	60.3	0.7	13.6	1.1	8.3	16.0	0.0
Rhode Island	82.6	0.0	0.0	0.0	0.0	12.0	5.4
South Carolina	25.0	4.2	9.0	5.9	1.4	50.4	4.2
South Dakota	84.4	0.0	11.1	0.0	0.0	1.9	2.7
Tennessee	93.4	0.0	0.0	0.0	0.0	6.5	0.0
Texas	78.7	0.0	0.0	0.0	0.0	11.2	10.1
Utah	49.8	0.0	1.3	8.8	2.5	3.2	34.4
Vermont	81.5	12.2	0.9	0.1	2.6	2.6	0.0

Table B.2
(continued)

	Formula assistance	Compensatory programs	Programs for students with handicaps	Vocational programs	Transportation programs	Other and nonspecified state aid	State payments on behalf of local education authority
Virginia	76.2	3.9	6.9	1.3	0.0	11.1	0.6
Washington	75.7	2.8	8.5	0.0	3.8	9.2	0.0
West Virginia	66.0	0.0	0.0	0.0	0.0	26.9	7.1
Wisconsin	84.0	0.0	7.0	0.0	0.4	8.6	0.0
Wyoming	92.0	0.0	0.0	0.0	0.0	8.0	0.0

Source: U.S. Census Bureau 2003, table 3.

Note: According to U.S. Census Bureau 2003, "formula assistance" is "[r]evenue from general noncategorical state assistance programs"; "compensatory programs" include "[r]evenue for at risk or other economically disadvantaged students"; "other aid" includes programs for "bilingual education, gifted and talented programs, food services, debt services, instructional materials, textbooks, computer equipment, library resources, guidance and psychological services, driver education, energy conservation, enrollment increases and losses, health, alcohol and drug abuse, AIDS, child abuse, summer school, pre-kindergarten and early childhood, adult education (excluding vocational), desegregation, private schools, safety and law enforcement, and community services"; "unspecified aid" is revenue that covers more than one of the other categories; and "payments on behalf of LEA" (local education authority) include "[s]tate payments that benefit school systems but are not paid directly to school systems," such as payments into teacher retirement programs.

Table B.3
Types of state aid formula

Type of formula	Number of states	List of states
Foundation		
Foundation with no educational cost adjustments	2	Nevada, South Dakota
Foundation plus supplemental aid with educational cost adjustments	13	Alabama, Arizona, Arkansas, California, Idaho, Illinois, Maine, Michigan, New Jersey, North Dakota, South Carolina, Utah, West Virginia
Foundation with built-in educational cost adjustments	15	Alaska, Colorado, Connecticut,[a] Massachusetts,[a] Minnesota,[a] Mississippi, Nebraska, New Hampshire, New Mexico,[a] New York,[b] Ohio,[a] Oregon, Tennessee, Virginia,[a] Wyoming
Two-Tiered		
Foundation (first tier) plus GTB (second tier)	10	Florida,[c] Georgia,[a] Iowa,[c] Kansas,[c] Kentucky,[a,c] Maryland,[a,c] Montana,[a,c] Oklahoma,[a,c] Texas,[a,c] Vermont[c]
Foundation (first tier) plus matching (second tier)	1	Louisiana[c]
Flat grant (first tier) plus GTB (second tier)	1	Delaware[d,e]
Guaranteed tax base	3	Indiana,[a,f] Missouri,[f,g] Wisconsin[a]
Other	5	Hawaii,[h] North Carolina,[a,e] Pennsylvania,[e] Rhode Island,[a,e] Washington[a,h]

Sources: Carey 2002; NCES 2001c; ACCESS 2003, tables B.4 and B.5.

Notes: This table indicates the existence of educational-cost adjustments for cost of living, poverty, or limited English proficiency but does not indicate whether these adjustments are sufficient to account for actual cost differences across districts.

a. These states also have supplemental aid programs, which could be categorical or non-categorical, with an educational cost adjustment.

b. New York has several noncategorical operating aid programs; the largest program, Basic Operating Aid, has a foundation formula with minor cost adjustments; several other noncategorical programs also have cost adjustments. See New York State Education Department, State Aid Unit, 2000.

c. These states also have educational-cost adjustments built into their foundation aid formula.

d. Delaware provides matching grants adjusted for wealth, a formula very similar to GTB.

e. These states provide flat grants with little or no equalization; the grants are based on teacher units in Delaware, on pupils in North Carolina, and on past history in Pennsylvania and Rhode Island.

f. These states also impose a minimum required local tax rate.

g. This state includes a cost adjustment in its GTB program.

h. These states provide full state funding of their basic aid programs; technically, Hawaii does not provide aid since it has a state-run education system.

Colorado 2003a; State of Colorado 2003b; State of Delaware, Department of Finance 2003; State of Idaho 2003; State of Maryland 2003; and State of West Virginia 2003.

The descriptions of aid formulas in NCES 2001 and these other references are based on information provided by each state and are not organized on the basis of a standardized framework. Consequently, the information from different states varies dramatically in terms of the way the aid system is described and the level of detail provided. This appendix reorganizes this material using a framework designed to identify the program components most relevant for determining the impact of the program on the adequacy and equity of each aid formula. Whenever the information contained in NCES 2001c is not sufficient to answer all the questions raised by this framework for a particular state (which is the rule rather than the exception), I turn to the relevant codes and statutes for that state to ensure the completeness and accuracy of our program descriptions.

Appendix table B.3 provides an overview of the aid formulas states use to distribute aid to their school districts. This table focuses on noncategorical aid, although it also indicates whether any categorical aid programs include educational cost adjustments. The table shows that the vast majority of states distribute noncategorical aid using a foundation formula. To be specific, thirty states use a foundation formula alone, and eleven more states use a foundation formula as the first tier of their aid system. Only three states rely exclusively on a GTB formula, and a GTB formula is used in the second-tier program for eleven states with a two-tiered system. Louisiana combines a first-tier foundation program and a second-tier matching grant with no equalization, and Delaware combines a flat matching grant per teacher unit with a GTB-like formula that has a higher matching rate in lower-wealth districts. Three states, North Carolina, Pennsylvania, and Rhode Island, provide flat grants with little or no equalization, and two other states, Hawaii and Washington, provide full state funding for basic operating spending. Hawaii, of course, does not have any local school districts.

Appendix table B.3 also reveals that only three states (Nevada, Pennsylvania, and South Dakota) distribute aid without any type of cost adjustment. (It cannot be determined from available sources whether Hawaii considers educational costs when it decides how much revenue to give each of its school districts.) Moreover, adjustments for educational costs are built into the foundation formula in twenty-four states, including nine of the states with a two-tiered system. The remaining states make adjustments for educational costs through supplementary noncategorical aid programs or through categorical aid programs.

The Framework

The framework we use builds on the three main approaches to state aid formulas: foundation, GTB, and two-tiered (which combine the foundation and GTB approaches). These approaches, and their link to the framework, are briefly explained here. Further explanations of the formulas can be found throughout the book.

A foundation formula ensures that the combined contributions of the state and a school district will provide a predetermined minimum level of expenditure per pupil, called the foundation level. A foundation formula says nothing about spending above the foundation level. It neither restricts a district's spending beyond the foundation level nor provides any equalization for a district that wants to go beyond its required (or expected) minimum contribution. (Some states do restrict supplementation or provide additional equalization, but not as part of the foundation formula.)

A foundation formula takes the following form:

$$Aid_i = (Foundation \times Pupil\ count_i) - Local\ share_i,$$

where Aid_i equals state aid to school district i, $Foundation$ equals the statewide minimum expenditure per pupil, $Pupil\ count_i$ equals the number of pupils in district i (perhaps with different weights for different types of students), and $Local\ share_i$ equals the required local contribution for district i.

Within a foundation formula, the main issues of interest are (1) How is the foundation level determined? (2) How should the local share be determined? and (3) Are some districts compensated for the higher cost of educating disadvantaged students? (And if so, how is this compensation being implemented?) Appendix table B.4 addresses the first two questions, and appendix table B.5 addresses the third. Some additional features of aid programs are described in appendix table B.6.

Foundation Level

The foundation level is the state-defined minimum spending per pupil. Unfortunately, no source or combination of sources provides

Table B.4
Provisions of foundation aid programs

State	Foundation covers capital	Method to find foundation level	Required levy?	Minimum state share?	Restrictions on supplementation?
Alabama	No	Teacher unit	Yes	No	Yes, total restriction[a]
Alaska	No	Annual	Yes	Yes	Limit on supplement tax rate and amount
Arizona	Yes	Annual	No	No	Limit on supplement amount
Arkansas	No	Annual	Yes	No	Recapture half of supplement amount
California	No	Base plus inflation factor	Yes	Yes	Yes, total restriction[a]
Colorado	No	Base plus increase ≥ inflation rate	No	Yes, with recapture[b]	Limit on supplement amount
Connecticut	No	Annual	Required local share	No	None
Florida	No	Annual	Yes	Yes	Limit on supplement tax rate
Georgia	No	Annual	Yes	No	Tax rate cap and limit on revenue increase
Idaho	No	Teacher unit	Yes	No	None
Illinois	No	Annual	No	Yes	None
Iowa	No	Base plus increase ≤ revenue growth rate	Yes	Yes	Tax rate cap
Kansas	Yes	Annual	Yes	Yes	Limit on supplement amount

Kentucky	No	Annual, ≥1989–90 level	Yes	No	Limit on supplement amount
Louisiana	No	Annual	No	No	Tax rate cap
Maine	Yes	Base plus increase = average of two most recent CPI increases	Target local share, with penalty	Yes	None
Maryland	No	Teacher unit	Required local share	Yes	None
Massachusetts	No	Teacher unit plus inflation adjustment	Required local share	Yes	Tax rate cap and limit on tax rate growth
Michigan	No	Base plus increase that depends on revenue growth	Yes	No	Limit on supplement tax rate, with phased-out "hold-harmless" exceptions
Minnesota	Yes	Annual	Target rate, with penalty	No, with recapture	Limit on supplement amount
Mississippi	No	Teacher unit	Yes	Yes, variable	Tax rate cap and limit on tax revenue growth
Montana	No	Annual	Required local share	Yes	Limit on supplement amount
Nebraska	No	Annual	Target rate, with penalty	No, with recapture	Limit on spending growth, inversely related to previous year's spending
Nevada	No	Teacher unit	Yes	Yes	Yes, total restriction
New Hampshire	No	Teacher unit	No	No, with recapture	None
New Jersey	No	Teacher unit plus adjustment with CPI increase	Required local share	No	None

Table B.4
(continued)

State	Foundation covers capital	Method to find foundation level	Required levy?	Minimum state share?	Restrictions on supplementation?
New Mexico	No	Annual	Yes	No	None
New York	No	Annual	No	Yes	Tax rate cap for big cities
North Carolina	No	Teacher unit	No	Yes	Tax rate cap
North Dakota	No	Annual	No	No	None
Ohio	No	Annual	Yes	No	None
Oklahoma	No	Annual	Yes	No	Limit on supplement tax rate
Oregon	No	Annual	No	No	Tax rate cap
South Carolina	No	Annual	Required local share	No	Varies by district (from strict to none)
South Dakota	No	Base year plus increase = lesser of inflation rate and 3%	No	No	None
Tennessee	No	Teacher unit	Required local share	Yes	None
Texas	No	Annual	Yes	No	Limit on supplement tax rate
Utah	No	Annual	Yes	No, with recapture	Limit on supplement tax rate
Vermont	No	Base plus increase = average of two most recent increases in CPI	No	Yes	Recapture

			Required local share		
Virginia	No	Teacher unit	No	No	None
West Virginia	No	Teacher unit	No	No	Tax rate cap
Wyoming	No	Teacher unit	Yes	No, with recapture	None

Sources: NCES 2001c and the state sources listed in the text of appendix B.

Notes: The first column indicates whether the foundation grant in the state is intended to cover capital spending; the second indicates the method used to calculate the foundation level; the third indicates whether districts are required to levy a minimum tax rate or to contribute a minimum share of the revenue needed to reach the foundation level; the fourth indicates whether there is a legally specified minimum state share for the foundation program; and the fifth indicates whether (and in what manner) the state restricts supplementation of the foundation level of spending. In the fourth column, "recapture" means that a school district might have to pay money back to the state under some circumstances. In the last column, a requirement for voter approval is not considered a restriction on supplementation. As shown in appendix table B.3, 11 states also take steps to equalize supplementation efforts with a second-tier GTB formula.

a. These states have a tax rate cap that is the same as the required minimum local rate, which implies that no supplementation is allowed.

b. Colorado has a complicated formula for determining the state share; the recapture provision implies that some districts might have to pay back the state for some categorical grants, but they never have to exceed the previous year's tax rate to do so.

Table B.5
Educational-cost adjustments in state aid formulas

State	Poverty funding method	Cost of living	Limited English proficiency	Grade	District size
Alabama	Categorical	None	None	Yes	None
Alaska	None	Yes	Yes	None	Yes
Arizona	Categorical	None	Yes	Yes	Yes
Arkansas	Categorical	None	None	None	Yes
California	Categorical	None	None	None	Yes
Colorado	Pupil weights	Yes	Yes	None	Yes
Connecticut	Pupil weights and categorical	None	Yes	None	None
Delaware	None	None	None	Yes	None
Florida	None	Yes	Yes	Yes	None
Georgia	Categorical	None	None	Yes	None
Idaho	None	None	None	Yes	None
Illinois	Categorical	None	None	Yes	None
Indiana	Formula supplement and categorical	None	None	None	None
Iowa	Formula supplement	None	Yes	None	None
Kansas	Pupil weights	None	Yes	None	Yes
Kentucky	Pupil weights and categorical	None	None	None	None
Louisiana	Pupil weights	None	None	None	Yes
Maine	None	None	None	None	None
Maryland	Categorical	Yes	Yes	None	None
Massachusetts	Pupil weights and categorical	Yes	None	None	None
Michigan	Categorical	None	None	None	None
Minnesota	Pupil weights and categorical	None	None	Yes	Yes
Mississippi	Pupil weights	None	None	None	None
Missouri	Pupil weights	None	None	None	None
Montana	None	None	None	Yes	Yes
Nebraska	Pupil weights	None	None	None	Yes
Nevada	None	None	None	Yes	None
New Hampshire	Pupil weights	None	None	None	None
New Jersey	Categorical	None	Yes	Yes	None
New Mexico	Pupil weights	None	Yes	Yes	None

Table B.5
(continued)

State	Poverty funding method	Adjustment for			
		Cost of living	Limited English proficiency	Grade	District size
New York	Formula supplement and categorical	None	None	Yes	None
North Carolina	Categorical	None	None	Yes	Yes
North Dakota	None	None	Yes	Yes	Yes
Ohio	Categorical	Yes	None	Yes	None
Oklahoma	Pupil weights	None	Yes	Yes	None
Oregon	Pupil weights	None	Yes	Yes	None
Pennsylvania	None	None	None	None	None
Rhode Island	Categorical	None	None	None	None
South Carolina	Categorical	None	None	Yes	None
South Dakota	None	None	None	None	Yes
Tennessee	Formula supplement	Yes	None	None	Yes
Texas	Pupil weights and categorical	Yes	Yes	None	Yes
Utah	Categorical	None	None	None	None
Vermont	Pupil weights	None	Yes	Yes	Yes
Virginia	Categorical	Yes	None	None	None
Washington	Categorical	Yes	Yes	Yes	None
West Virginia	None	None	None	None	None
Wisconsin	Categorical	None	None	None	None
Wyoming	Formula supplement	Yes	None	Yes	Yes

Sources: NCES 2001c; Carey 2002; and the state sources listed in the text.

Note: The first column indicates the method the state uses, if any, to adjust its aid for the higher costs associated with poor students. The next four columns indicate whether a state has any program to account for the higher educational costs in a district associated with teacher costs (as measured by the cost of living or some other index), students with limited English proficiency, the distribution of students by grade, and district size, respectively. Hawaii is not included in the table because it has a state-run education program and thus does not provide aid, per se, to localities.

Table B.6
Noncost adjustments in education aid programs

	Adjustment for		
State	Gifted program	Test scores	Teacher experience
Alabama	None	None	Yes
Alaska	Yes	None	None
Arizona	Yes	None	None
Arkansas	None	None	None
California	Yes	None	None
Colorado	Yes	None	None
Connecticut	None	Yes	None
Delaware	None	None	None
Florida	Yes	None	None
Georgia	Yes	None	Yes
Idaho	Yes	None	Yes
Illinois	Yes	None	None
Indiana	Yes	Yes	None
Iowa	None	None	None
Kansas	Yes	None	None
Kentucky	Yes	Yes	None
Louisiana	Yes	None	None
Maine	Yes	None	None
Maryland	None	None	None
Massachusetts	Yes	Yes	None
Michigan	Yes	None	None
Minnesota	Yes	Yes	Yes
Mississippi	Yes	None	None
Missouri	None	None	None
Montana	Yes	None	None
Nebraska	Yes	None	None
Nevada	None	None	None
New Hampshire	None	None	None
New Jersey	None	None	None
New Mexico	Yes	None	Yes
New York	Yes	Yes	None
North Carolina	Yes	None	Yes
North Dakota	Yes	None	None
Ohio	Yes	None	None
Oklahoma	Yes	None	Yes
Oregon	Yes	None	Yes
Pennsylvania	None	Yes	None

Table B.6
(continued)

State	Adjustment for		
	Gifted program	Test scores	Teacher experience
Rhode Island	None	None	None
South Carolina	Yes	None	Yes
South Dakota	None	None	None
Tennessee	Yes	None	None
Texas	Yes	Yes	None
Utah	Yes	None	Yes
Vermont	None	None	None
Virginia	Yes	Yes	None
Washington	Yes	None	Yes
West Virginia	Yes	None	Yes
Wisconsin	None	None	None
Wyoming	Yes	None	Yes

Sources: NCES 2001 and the state sources listed in the text.
Note: The columns in this table indicate whether a state has any aid program that adjusts a district's award amount for the presence in the district of a program aimed at gifted students, for high or low test scores, or for teacher experience, respectively. Hawaii is not included in the table because it has a state-run education program and thus does not provide aid, per se, to localities.

this information for every foundation aid program in existence in the states. Among states for which we were able to obtain this information (largely from NCES 2001c), the foundation level for 1998–99 varies from $1,239 in Oklahoma to $6,899 in New Jersey. Foundation levels are inherently difficult to compare across states, however, because foundation aid programs are accompanied by various other aid programs. In New Jersey and Oklahoma, for example, the foundation level is not intended to cover transportation costs or capital spending. In a few other states, including Arizona and Georgia, both of these items are included in the foundation level. A full comparison across states requires a look at all aid programs, which is beyond the scope of this appendix. Nevertheless, as a link to the material in appendix C, the first column in appendix table B.4 indicates whether capital spending in each state is covered by the foundation grant in that state.

The second column of appendix table B.4 indicates the method used to determine the foundation level in each state. Broadly speaking, three different methods are used: (1) annual determination, (2) a base

amount plus an annual statutory increase, and (3) a calculation to estimate actual educational costs in a real or hypothetical sample school
district. For states in the first category, the state legislature determines
the foundation amount each budget year. This process takes into account historical data, the state's fiscal situation for that year, and the
state's priority for supporting elementary and secondary education
compared with other items in the state budget. The details of the legislative process to determine the foundation amount vary widely from
state to state, of course, and no attempt is made to describe these
details here.

An annual (or biannual) debate about the foundation level leaves
state aid subject to the danger of erosion under the influence of inflation, budget pressure, and competing political priorities. Nine states
attempt to minimize the potential for such erosion through a law that
ensures a minimum annual increase in the foundation level, based on
the inflation rate or a predetermined percentage. Duncombe and Johnston show in chapter 5, for example, that the foundation level in Kansas, which does not have this type of protection, grew only 7.5 percent
between 1992 and 2001, from $3,720 to $3,870 per pupil. During this
same period, the consumer price index increased by 19 percent, which
implies that the real value of the foundation amount declined considerably. The provisions in these nine states are designed to prevent this
from occurring.

The third method states use to determine their foundation amounts
is to estimate the actual cost of providing an adequate education in
the state. This type of calculation can be based on a state-determined
number of teachers per student or on the expenditures in a real or hypothetical sample school. At present, twelve states use some version of
this method, although interest in it appears to be increasing.

Other Features of a Foundation Formula

Appendix table B.4 also indicates whether states impose a minimum
tax rate (or a minimum local share) on school districts (third column),
whether their state aid legislation specifies a minimum state contribution (fourth column), and whether this legislation specifies limits on
state supplementation of the foundation level (fifth column).

Two methods are used to determine the minimum local share in
states that have one: a suggested or required minimum local property
tax rate or a local share inversely related to the district's wealth. As

shown in appendix table B.4, the first method is far more common. States also vary in the extent to which they limit local supplementation beyond the foundation level of spending. Most states allow some local supplements, with various limitations, some quite strict, but fifteen states have no significant restrictions on supplementation, and three states do not allow any local supplementation at all.

As shown in appendix table B.3, ten states with foundation aid programs make some attempt to equalize local supplementation, that is, to give low-wealth districts the same opportunities for supplementation as wealthy districts have. In practice, this means that these ten states have a second, equalizing tier of aid on top of a foundation level of spending. Normally, the second tier of a foundation level takes the GTB form:

$$Aid_i = t_i(V^* - V_i) \times Pupil\ count_i,$$

where Aid_i equals state aid to district i for equalization purposes, t_i equals the additional tax rate selected by district i, V^* equals the state's guaranteed tax base, V_i equals the actual tax base in district i, and $Pupil\ count_i$ equals the number of pupils (possibly weighted) in district i.

This kind of formula ensures that the increase in expenditure per pupil resulting from a district's extra tax effort depends only on the additional tax rate the district is willing impose—not on the district's tax base. The main issue in the design of this kind of formula is the level of the guaranteed tax base, V^*. Two states set V^* above the property value of the wealthiest district, and nine states set it below that level.

The GTB approach has been used mainly as an equalization strategy for states to use in dealing with the local supplement beyond the foundation level. As shown in appendix table B.3, only three states, Indiana, Missouri, and Wisconsin, use it as a base formula, and one state, Delaware, combines a GTB formula with flat grants.

Cost Adjustments

In the discussion so far, the foundation level in a state has been intended to indicate the minimum necessary expenditure for an average student in an average district in the state. As discussed throughout this book, adjustments are needed to compensate districts for the higher costs of attracting teachers to some districts and for the higher costs of educating disadvantaged students. Appendix table B.5 provides some information on educational cost adjustments in each state. In particular, the first column of this table indicates the method each state uses to account for the high costs of educating students who come from impoverished backgrounds. The remaining columns indicate whether the state makes an adjustment for the cost of living or some other measure of teacher costs (second column), for the share of students with limited English proficiency (third column), for the distribution of students across grades (fourth column), and for district size or density (fifth column).

As discussed elsewhere in this book, cost adjustments can be made by multiplying the foundation amount by a cost index, by using pupil weights that vary with pupil characteristics, or by implementing categorical grant programs to fund programs for high-cost pupils. The entries in the first column of appendix table B.5 indicate which of these methods is used to account for student poverty. The most common methods are adjusting the student weights and adding a categorical aid program for programs designed to help poor students. The extra weight given to a poor student varies widely. Among states where the weights can be determined, they range from 5 percent in Mississippi to 110 percent in Maryland and for the highest-poverty districts in New Hampshire.

As shown by Carey (2002), aid adjustments for poor students use several different measures of poverty, including the share of students eligible for a free or reduced-price lunch or the official poverty rate in the district. Each definition has somewhat different implications for the number of students who are counted as poor.

Carey also calculates funding per low-income student in each state. He divides the total poverty-based funding programs in the state for 2001–02, including both the portion of the main formula due to the addition of low-income weights and the various supplemental funds that account for poverty, by the number of students in households with income below the poverty line. According to Carey's calculations, funding per low-income student ranges from $111 in Arkansas to $5,199 in Massachusetts.

The last three columns of appendix table B.5 indicate which states have aid programs or provisions that reflect other educational cost factors. Among these provisions, adjustments for the cost of living are least popular (eleven states), and adjustments for the distribution of students by grade are most popular (twenty-two states).

As in the case of poverty adjustments, there is no guarantee that these (largely ad hoc) adjustments are sufficient to offset the higher costs associated with these factors. The additional weight given to an LEP student (in states where this weight can be determined) ranges from 6 percent in Arizona to 100 percent in Maryland, with a modal weight of 20 percent.

The table's fourth column indicates states with aid provisions that account for the distribution of students across grades. The most common practice is to use higher weights for pupils in grades K–3 and 9–12 and lower weights for pupils in grades 4–8. The additional weights assigned to pupils in various categories vary among the states.

Adjustments made for district size are quite diverse across states, as well. Six states provide additional funds only to districts below a certain size. In addition, twenty-four states use different pupil weights for districts of different sizes. Three of these twenty-four states give favorable weights to both large and small districts; the other twenty-one states give favorable weights only to the smallest districts. States' definitions of "small" and "large" districts vary dramatically, of course.

Other Adjustments

Appendix table B.6 examines several provisions that appear in many state aid programs but are not related either to wealth or to educational costs. Specifically, the table tracks whether states adjust aid amounts for gifted programs, high or low test scores, and teacher experience. As explained in chapter 1, these provisions are actually antiequalizing in the sense that they give more aid to high-wealth or low-cost districts instead of to low-wealth or high-cost districts.

The first column of the table indicates whether each state has an aid program for gifted students. Such programs are fairly common but also tend to be very small. For example, only two states have a gifted categorical aid program accounting for more than 1 percent of total state aid. The last two columns indicate that two other antiequalizing provisions of aid programs, based on test scores and teacher experience, exist in only a few states. In the case of adjustment for teacher experience, thirteen states reward districts whose average level of teacher experience is higher than the state average. In Arizona, for example, a teacher experience index is calculated annually for all teachers in the state, and additional funds are provided to districts with above-average levels of teacher experience. Specifically, the number of weighted pupils is increased by 2 percent for each year that the district's index is above the state average.

C

A Guide to State Building Aid Programs for Elementary and Secondary Education

Wen Wang

States exhibit a variety of approaches to supporting the construction of school buildings and other capital spending for schools. As shown in appendix table C.1, thirty-seven states support school capital spending through grants, Hawaii has full state funding, and twelve states provide no grants for new capital spending.

This appendix provides a state-by-state comparison of state aid to support capital spending by school districts. Appendix table C.1 provides a summary of the approaches of the various states. Appendix table C.2 describes the basic approach to state aid used in each state. In particular, this table focuses on whether a state uses lump-sum aid, matching aid, or both. Several states have more than one building aid program. In these states, the table lists the name of each program and gives it a number for ease of reference in later tables. Details of the programs are offered when they can be determined from published sources.

A lump-sum grant is an award for a predetermined amount that does not depend on a contribution from the recipient. The grant amount may be paid in several partial payments or in one payment at project completion. Some of these lump-sum grants are set at a certain amount per student in the district. The number of students in the district is usually measured on the basis of average daily membership or average daily attendance.

A matching grant supplements funds raised by the recipient at a predetermined rate. Matching grants can be divided into open-ended and closed-ended grants. A grant is said to be open-ended when there is no limit on the amount of funding or the number of projects that can be funded in each district, though the cost of each individual project may be capped. A closed-ended grant places a ceiling on the amount of funds that a district may receive.

Table C.1
States' approaches to building aid

Type of aid	Number of states	List of states
Building aid program	38	
Lump-sum aid	6	Arizona, Florida, South Carolina, Texas, Utah, West Virginia
Matching aid	23	Alaska, California, Connecticut, Delaware, Georgia, Illinois, Kansas, Maine, Maryland, Massachusetts, Minnesota, Montana, New Hampshire, New Jersey, New York, Pennsylvania, Rhode Island, Texas, Vermont, Virginia, Washington, Wisconsin, Wyoming
Both lump-sum and matching aid	9	Alabama, Arkansas, Colorado, Indiana, Kentucky, Mississippi, New Mexico, North Carolina, Ohio
Full state funding	1	Hawaii[a]
No grants for capital spending	11	Idaho, Iowa, Louisiana, Michigan,[b] Missouri, Nebraska, Nevada, North Dakota,[b] Oklahoma, Oregon, South Dakota

Source: Appendix table C.2.
Notes:
a. Hawaii has no local school districts.
b. Michigan and North Dakota do not provide grants but do provide loans.

Appendix table C.2 shows that building aid takes the form of lump-sum grants in six states, the form of matching grants in twenty-three states, and the form of a combination of lump-sum and matching grants in nine states. (This information reflects that presented in appendix table C.1.) Appendix table C.2 also indicates that nine states provide low-interest loans to school districts as a supplement to, or replacement for, building aid. In four states (Arizona, Kansas, Maine, and Minnesota), these programs are a supplement to the basic state aid formula, which is designed to cover capital spending as well as operating spending (appendix table B.4).

Appendix table C.3 describes the state-level constraints associated with school construction projects in the thirty-eight states with building aid programs. It indicates, for each of these states, whether voter approval of school construction projects is required, whether borrowing or associated taxes to pay for such construction projects are subject to tax limitations, whether such projects are reviewed, whether such

Table C.2
State building aid programs

State	Type of grant	Details of lump-sum grants	Details of matching grants	Loans
Alabama	Both	Flat grant per pupil (half of state funds)	Closed-ended; guaranteed tax base formula (half of state funds)	No
Alaska	Matching		Open-ended	No
Arizona	Lump-sum	(1) Soft capital, current funds (2) Deficiencies Collection Fund (3) Building Renewal Fund (4) New School Facilities Fund		No
Arkansas	Both	(1) General facilities	(2) Debt service supplement	Yes
California	Matching		Open-ended; 20–80% match	No
Colorado	Both	(1) $223–800 per pupil	(2) School Capital Construction and Renovation Fund; open-ended (3) School capital construction expenditures reserves; open-ended	No
Connecticut	Matching		Open-ended; 20–80% match	No
Delaware	Matching		Open-ended; 6–80% match	No
Florida	Lump-sum	(1) Public Education and Capital Outlay Fund (2) Capital Outlay and Debt Service Fund		No
Georgia	Matching		Closed-ended; 75–90% match	No
Hawaii	State funding			
Idaho	None			

Table C.2
(continued)

State	Type of grant	Details of lump-sum grants	Details of matching grants	Loans
Illinois	Matching		(1) School Construction Program; open-ended; 35–75% match	No
			(2) School Maintenance Grant Program; open-ended; 50% match	
Indiana	Both	$40 per pupil	Open-ended	No
Iowa	None			
Kansas	Matching		(1) New facilities weighting; open-ended	No
			(2) Debt service supplement; open-ended; 5% match for bond obligations before July 1, 1992; 25% match for bond obligations after July 1, 1992	
Kentucky	Both	(1) 1st level: $100 per pupil (3) 3rd level: lump-sum	(2) 2nd level: Facilities Support Program; open-ended	No
Louisiana	None			
Maine	Matching		(1) Revolving Fund, Renovation Program; open-ended; 30–70% match	Yes
			(2) School Construction Program; open-ended; circuit breaker sets maximum local share	
Maryland	Matching		Open-ended; 50–90% match	No
Massachusetts	Matching		Open-ended; 50–90% match	No
Michigan	None			Yes
Minnesota	Matching		(1) Health and Safety Revenue; open-ended	Yes
			(2) Debt Service Revenue; open-ended	
			(3) Alternative Facilities Bonding and Levy Program; open-ended	

Table C.2
(continued)

State	Type of grant	Details of lump-sum grants	Details of matching grants	Loans
Mississippi	Both	(1) Annual grants; $24 per pupil	(2) Mississippi Adequate Education Program; open-ended	Yes
Missouri	None			
Montana	Matching		closed-ended	No
Nebraska	None			
Nevada	None			
New Hampshire	Matching		open-ended; 30–55% match	No
New Mexico	Both	(2) Public School Capital Outlay Act; lump-sum (3) Direct legislative appropriations; lump-sum	(1) Public School Capital Improvements Act; open-ended	No
New Jersey	Matching		Open-ended; 40–100% match	Yes
New York	Matching		Open-ended; 10–95% match	No
North Carolina	Both	(1) Critical School Facilities Needs Fund; ends in 2003	(2) Public School Building Capital Fund; open-ended; 67% match	No
North Dakota	None			Yes
Ohio	Both	(2) Emergency Repair Program; lump sum	(1) Classroom Facilities Assistance Program; open-ended; 83.4% match, on average (3) Big Eight Capital Improvements Program; open-ended; 50% match (4) Exceptional Needs Program; open-ended	No
Oklahoma	None			
Oregon	None			
Pennsylvania	Matching		Open-ended	No
Rhode Island	Matching		Open-ended; 30–100% match	No
South Carolina	Lump-sum	Flat grant		No

Table C.2
(continued)

State	Type of grant	Details of lump-sum grants	Details of matching grants	Loans
South Dakota	None			
Tennessee	Lump-sum	Part of foundation grant		No
Texas	Matching		(1) Instructional Facilities Allotment Program; open-ended	No
			(2) Existing Debt Allotment Program; open-ended	
Utah	Lump-sum	Capital Outlay Foundation Grant		Yes
Vermont	Matching		Open-ended; 30% match	No
Virginia	Matching		(1) School Construction Program; open-ended; 20% match	Yes
			(2) State lottery revenues; open-ended; 18–80% match	
Washington	Matching		Open-ended; 20–90% match	No
West Virginia	Lump-sum	Comprehensive Educational Facilities Plan		No
Wisconsin	Matching		Closed-ended	No
Wyoming	Matching		Open-ended	No

Sources: New York State Education Department, Elementary, Middle, Secondary, and Continuing Education 2003; National Center for Education Statistics 2001c; New York State Office of the State Comptroller 2003; Opresko 2000; Gurley 2002; Wisconsin Department of Public Instruction 2003.

Note: Numbers in parentheses identify specific building aid formulas for reference in later appendix tables. "Guaranteed tax base" formula is defined in chapter 1.

Table C.3
State-level constraints associated with school construction projects

Overall		By program		
Voter approval	Debt limits	Review process	Project priority ranks	Restric- tions on spending
Alabama				
A bond issue requires a constitutional amendment, which requires voter approval		Project and capital needs plan	No	No
Alaska				
Voter approval required for bond issues		Project	No	No
Arizona				
Voter approval required for bond issues	15–30% of assessed value; 5–10% of assessed value after December 31, 1998	(1) None (2) Project (3) (4)	No	No No No Yes
Arkansas				
Voter approval required for millage increase	27–30% of assessed value		No	No
California				
Two-thirds majority required for bond issues	1% of assessed value; additional levies for debt service require two-thirds voter approval	Project (two stages)	Yes	No
Colorado				
Voter approval required for bond issues	Levy cannot exceed 10 mills or three years		No	No
Connecticut				
Majority vote required for bond issues	4.5 multiplied by the municipality's total tax revenue	Project	Yes	No
Delaware				
Voter approval required for bond sales (and for associated tax levy)	10% of assessed value; no more than two referenda in any twelve- month period	Project	No	Yes

Table C.3
(continued)

Overall		By program		
Voter approval	Debt limits	Review process	Project priority ranks	Restrictions on spending
Florida				
Voter approval required for bond sales and optional sales tax levy	10% of nonexempt assessed value (unless state board of education allows more); 6-mill, twenty-year limit on tax levy for school debt service; 2-mill limit on optional school construction tax levy	Project; five-year capital improvement plan	Yes	No
Georgia				
Voter approval required for bond issues, for tax levies, for local-option 1% sales tax, and for any tax rate above 20 mills	10% of assessed value (property assesses at 40% of market value)	Project; five-year capital improvement plan	Yes	No
Illinois				
Voter approval required for bond sales, new school construction, and optional tax cap	6% of equalized assessed value for elementary and secondary districts; 13% for unit districts	(1) Project (2) Project	Yes Yes	No Yes
Indiana				
None	2% of assessed value		No	Yes
Kansas				
Voter approval required for bond issues		(1) Project (2)	No	No
Kentucky				
None		(1) Project (2) Project (3) Project; facilities survey	No	No

Table C.3
(continued)

Overall		By program		
Voter approval	Debt limits	Review process	Project priority ranks	Restrictions on spending
Maine				
Voter approval required for bond issues		(1) Project	Yes	Yes
		(2) Project	Yes	No
Maryland				
Voter approval for bond sales required in Baltimore City and County only	None	Capital improvement plan	Yes	Yes
Massachusetts				
Voter authorization of project required		Project	Yes	No
Minnesota				
Voter approval required for bond issues and for a down-payment levy		(1) Project	No	No
		(2) Project		No
		(3) Project; ten-year facilities plan		Yes
Mississippi				
Voter approval required for bond issues	15% of assessed value		No	No
Montana				
Voter approval required for bond issues and/or establishing a building reserve fund	45% of assessed value	None	No	
New Hampshire				
Two-thirds majority required for bond sales except in single-city school districts	7% of assessed value; 10% of assessed value for cooperative school districts	Project (limited)	No	Yes
New Mexico				
Voter approval required for bond issues	6% of assessed value; levy cannot exceed 10 mills or five years	(1) (2) Project (3) Project	No	No

Table C.3
(continued)

Overall		By program		
Voter approval	Debt limits	Review process	Project priority ranks	Restrictions on spending
New Jersey Voter approval required for the local share of some construction projects		Project	No	Yes
New York Voter approval required for bond issues	5–10% of equalized assessed value, depending on type of school district	Project	No	Yes
North Carolina Voter approval required for bond sales and for local-option sales tax	8% of assessed value	(1) Project (2) Project; ten-year capital improvement plan	No	No
Ohio Voter approval required for bond levies	9% of assessed value	(1) Project (2) Project (3) Project; capital plan (4) Project	Yes No No Yes	No Yes No No
Pennsylvania Voter approval required to issue new debt if the debt limit is exceeded	225% of the local unit's borrowing base	Project	No	Yes
Rhode Island Most local governments require voter approval of school capital financing, unless a city public building authority is used	Many municipalities need enabling legislation from the state to sell bonds	Project	No	No
South Carolina A bond referendum is required	8% of assessed value		No	No

Table C.3
(continued)

Overall		By program		
Voter approval	Debt limits	Review process	Project priority ranks	Restrictions on spending
Tennessee				
None	None	None	No	Yes
Texas				
Voter approval required for bond sales and, if voters so petition, for lease purchase capital agreements		(1) None (2) None	Yes No	Yes Yes
Utah				
Voter approval required to incur indebtedness	4% of assessed value	None	No	No
Vermont				
Voter approval required for project funding		Project	Yes	No
Virginia				
Voter approval required for county-controlled, but not city-controlled, school district bonds	10% of assessed value	(1) None (2) Project	No No	No No
Washington				
Some bond issues must be approved by 60% of voters, with at least a 40% turnout; others (property acquisition or repair/remodeling) do not require voter approval	5% of equalized assessed value	Project	Yes	Yes
West Virginia				
Voter approval required for bond issues	5% of assessed value	Project; ten-year facilities plan	Yes	No
Wisconsin				
City-wide referendum required for bond issues or for construction tax levy of 0.6 mills or higher	5% of equalized assessed value	None	No	No

Table C.3
(continued)

Overall		By program		
			Project	Restric-
		Review	priority	tions on
Voter approval	Debt limits	process	ranks	spending
Wyoming				
None	10% of assessed value	No	No	No

Sources: New York State Education Department, Elementary, Middle, Secondary, and Continuing Education 2003; National Center for Education Statistics 2001c; New York State Office of the State Comptroller 2003; Opresko 2000; Gurley 2002; Wisconsin Department of Public Instruction 2003.

Notes: Numbers in parentheses, which apply to the last three columns of table C.3, identify the programs listed (and numbered) in appendix table C.2; items or entries left blank could not be determined from the sources consulted.

projects are selected on the basis of statewide priorities, and whether the state imposes restrictions on the amount a district may spend for various types of projects. Because some of these provisions vary by program, the last three columns of this table are linked by number to the specific programs identified in appendix table C.2 for several states.

Appendix table C.3 reveals that most states require voter approval for capital projects and that both borrowing or levy limits and project reviews are common. In contrast, only thirteen of these thirty-eight states use state-level priority rankings, and two of these thirteen states (Ohio and Texas) do so in only some of their building aid programs. Similarly, fifteen states place restrictions on project spending, but this restriction applies to only some building aid programs in five of these states (Arizona, Illinois, Maine, Minnesota, and Ohio).

Finally, appendix table C.4 describes key provisions in states' building aid formulas. In particular, it explains whether there is an adjustment in each state's formula for fiscal capacity and whether there is one for construction or educational costs. As in appendix table C.3, there is a link by number to specific programs in some states.

This table indicates that twelve of the thirty-eight states with building aid have no programs that adjust for property wealth or some other measure of fiscal capacity. Adjustments for building or educational costs are even less common: Twenty-nine of these states have no programs that make an adjustment of this type.

Table C.4
Provisions of state building aid formulas

State	Adjustment for fiscal capacity	Adjustment for costs
Alabama	Property wealth	None
Alaska	Property wealth	None
Arizona	(1) Property wealth	Low enrollment, special needs, sparsity
	(2) None	None
	(3) None	Building age, student capacity of buildings, and prior cost of rennovation
	(4) None	Size of building, rural area
Arkansas	(1) Property wealth	None
	(2) None	None
California	None	None
Colorado	Property wealth	None
Connecticut	Property wealth, income	None
Delaware	Property wealth	None
Florida	None	Building age, high enrollment growth
Georgia	Property wealth	High enrollment growth
Illinois	(1) Property wealth	None
	(2) Property wealth	None
Indiana	None	None
Kansas	(1) None	None
	(2) Property wealth	None
Kentucky	(1) None	None
	(2) Property wealth	None
	(3) None	None
Maine	(1) Property wealth	None
	(2) Property wealth	None
Maryland	Property wealth	None
Massachusetts	Property wealth, income	None
Minnesota	(1) None	None
	(2) Property wealth	Enrollment, sparsity
	(3) None	Building space, building age
Mississippi	(1) None	None
	(2) Property wealth	None
Montana	Property wealth	None
New Hampshire	None	None

Table C.4
(continued)

State	Adjustment for fiscal capacity	Adjustment for costs
New Mexico	(1) None	None
	(2) None	None
	(3) None	None
New Jersey	Property wealth	High-need districts
New York	Property wealth	Construction costs
North Carolina	None	None
Ohio	(1) Property wealth	None
	(2) None	None
	(3) None	None
	(4) Property wealth	Severity of needs
Pennsylvania	Property wealth	None
Rhode Island	Property wealth	None
South Carolina	None	None
Tennessee	None	None
Texas	(1) Property wealth	None
	(2) Property wealth	None
Utah	Property wealth	Housing conditions, student growth
Vermont	None	None
Virginia	(1) None	None
	(2) Property wealth, income, retail sales	None
Washington	Property wealth	None
West Virginia	None	None
Wisconsin	None	None
Wyoming	None	None

Sources: New York State Education Department, Elementary, Middle, Secondary, and Continuing Education 2003; National Center for Education Statistics 2001c; New York State Office of the State Comptroller 2003; Opresko 2000; Gurley 2002; Wisconsin Department of Public Instruction 2003.

Notes: The numbers in parentheses, which apply to both columns of table C.4, identify the programs listed (and numbered) in appendix table C.2. States with no building aid are not included in this table.

Note

The author is grateful to William Duncombe for extensive assistance with this appendix.

References

Advocacy Center for Children's Educational Success with Standards (ACCESS). 2003. "State by State" page. Available at ⟨http://www.accessednetwork.org/statesmain.html⟩ (accessed October 1, 2003).

Alexander, Celeste D., Timothy J. Gronberg, Dennis W. Jansen, Harrison Keller, Lori L. Taylor, and Philip Uri Treisman. 2000. *A Study of Uncontrollable Variations in the Costs of Texas Public Education*. A summary report prepared for the 77th Texas Legislature. Austin: Charles A. Dana Center, University of Texas-Austin. Available at ⟨http://www.utdanacenter.org/researchpolicy/reportsandbriefs.html⟩.

Alexander, Kern, and Richard Salmon. 1995. *Public School Finance*. Boston: Allyn and Bacon.

Andrews, Matthew, William D. Duncombe, and John M. Yinger. 2002. "Revisiting Economies of Size in Education: Are We Any Closer to a Consensus?" *Economics of Education Review* 21(3):245–262.

Association of Alaska School Boards. 1998. "Senate Bill 36: Accountability under a New Funding Formula." *Critical Issues* (October). Available at ⟨http://www.aasb.org/PDFs/SB36.pdf⟩.

Augenblick, John, John Myers, Justin Silverstein, and Anne Barkis. 2002. *Calculation of the Cost of a Suitable Education in Kansas in 2000–2001 Using Two Different Analytic Approaches*. Report submitted by Augenblick and Myers, Inc., to the State of Kansas Legislative Coordinating Council. Topeka, KS: Augenblick and Myers.

Baker, Bruce D. 2001a. "Balancing Equity for Students and Taxpayers: Evaluating School Finance Reform in Vermont." *Journal of Education Finance* 26(4):437–462.

Baker, Bruce D. 2001b. "Expert Witness Report on Behalf of Plaintiffs: Analysis and Opinions on the Suitability of the Kansas School District Finance Act." *Montoy v. State of Kansas*, No. 99-C01788 (Shawnee Country District Court).

Baker, Bruce D., and Michael Imber. 1999. "Rational Educational Explanation or Politics as Usual? Evaluating the Outcome of School Finance Litigation in Kansas." *Journal of Education Finance* 25(1):121–139.

Barro, S. M. 1992. "Cost of Education Differences Across States." Working paper, SMB Economic Research. Washington, DC.

Barrow, Lisa, and C. E. Rouse. 2000. "Using Market Valuation to Assess the Importance and Efficiency of Public School Spending." Working paper 2000-04, Federal Reserve Bank of Chicago, Chicago, IL.

Bènabou, Roland. 1996. "Equity and Efficiency in Human Capital Investment: The Local Connection." *Review of Economic Studies* 63 (April): 237–264.

Berends, Mark, Susan J. Bodilly, and Sheila Nataraj Kirby. 2002. *Facing the Challenges of Whole-School Reform: New American Schools after a Decade*. Santa Monica, CA: RAND.

Berger, Charles. 1998. "Equity without Adjudication: Kansas School Finance Reform and the 1992 School District Finance and Quality Performance Act." *Journal of Law and Education* 27(January):1–46.

Berne, Robert, and Leanna Stiefel. 1984. *The Measurement of Equity in School Finance: Conceptual, Methodological and Empirical Dimensions*. Baltimore: Johns Hopkins University Press.

Berne, Robert, and Leanna Stiefel. 1999. "Concepts of School Finance Equity: 1970 to the Present." In *Equity and Adequacy in Education Finance*, ed. H. F. Ladd, R. Chalk and J. S. Hansen, 7–33. Washington, DC: National Academy Press.

Bettinger, Eric. 1999. "The Effect of Charter Schools on Charter Students and Public Schools." Occasional paper no. 4, National Center for the Study of Privatization in Education, Teachers College, Columbia University, New York, NY.

Bifulco, Robert, Carolyn Bordeaux, William Duncombe, and John Yinger. 2002. *Do Whole-School Reform Programs Boost Student Performance? A Case of New York City*. Final report prepared for the Smith-Richardson Foundation, Center for Policy Research, Syracuse University, Syracuse, NY. Available at ⟨http://cpr.maxwell.syr.edu/cfap⟩.

Bifulco, Robert, and Stuart Bretschneider. 2001. "Estimating School Efficiency: A Comparison of Methods Using Simulated Data." *Economics of Education Review* 20(5):417–429.

Black, Sandra. 1999. "Do Better Schools Matter? Parental Valuation Of Elementary Education." *Quarterly Journal of Economics* 114(2) (May): 577–600.

Blume, Lawrence E. 1982. "The Sales and Use Taxes." In *Michigan's Fiscal and Economic Structure*, ed. Harvey E. Brazer and Deborah S. Lauren, 595–618. Ann Arbor: University of Michigan Press.

Bound, John, David A. Jaeger, and Regina Baker. 1995. "Problems with Instrumental Variables Estimation When the Correlation between the Instruments and the Endogenous Explanatory Variables Is Weak." *Journal of the American Statistical Association* 90 (June): 443–450.

Bradbury, Katharine L., Helen F. Ladd, Mark Perrault, Andrew Reschovsky, and John M. Yinger. 1984. "State Aid to Offset Fiscal Disparities across Communities." *National Tax Journal* 37 (June): 151–170.

Bradbury, Katharine L., Christopher J. Mayer, and Karl E. Case. 2001. "Property Tax Limits, Local Fiscal Behavior, and Property Values: Evidence from Massachusetts under Proposition $2\frac{1}{2}$." *Journal of Public Economics* 80(2):287–311.

Brunner, Eric, and Jon Sonstelie. Forthcoming. "School Finance Reform and Voluntary Fiscal Federalism." *Journal of Public Economics*.

Bundt, Julie. 1994. "State Education Finance Policy: The Question of Equity." In *Public Policy and the Two States of Kansas*, ed. H. George Frederickson, 51–63. Lawrence: University of Kansas Press.

Burkett, Elinor. 1998. "Don't Tread on My Tax Rate." *New York Times Magazine*, April 26, 42–45.

Burtless, Gary, ed. 1996. *Does Money Matter? The Effect of School Resources on Student Achievement and Adult Success*. Washington, DC: Brookings Institution Press.

Card, David, and A. Abigail Payne. 2002. "School Finance Reform, the Distribution of School Spending, and the Distribution of Student Test Scores." *Journal of Public Economics* 82 (January): 49–82.

Carey, Kevin. 2002. *State Poverty-Based Education Funding: A Survey of Current Programs and Options for Improvement*. Washington, DC: Center on Budget and Policy Priorities.

Casserly, Michael. 2002. *Beating the Odds: A City-by-City Analysis of Student Performance and Achievement Gaps on State Assessments*. Washington, DC: Council of the Great City Schools. Available at ⟨http://www.cgcs.org/pdfs/beatodds2.pdf⟩.

Center for Public Policy Priorities. 1998. "Measuring Up: The State of Texas Education— History of School Finance in Texas." Available at ⟨http://www.cppp.org/kidscount/ education/finance2.html⟩.

Chaikind, Stephen, and Hope Corman. 1991. "The Impact of Low Birth Weight on Special Education Costs." *Journal of Health Economics* 10(3):291–311.

Chambers, Jay G. 1995. *Public School Teacher Cost Differences across the United States*. Washington, DC: U.S. Department of Education, National Center for Education Statistics.

Chambers, Jay G. 1997. *A Technical Report on the Measurement of Geographic and Inflationary Differences in Public School Costs*. Prepared for the U.S. Department of Education, National Center for Education Statistics, Washington, DC.

Chambers, Jay G. 1998. "Geographic Variation in Public School Costs." Working paper 98-04. U.S. Department of Education, National Center for Education Statistics, Washington, DC. Available at ⟨http://nces.ed.gov/pubsearch/⟩.

Chambers, Jay G., Tom Parrish, Jamie Shkolnik, and Maria Perez. 2002. "A Report on the 1999–2000 Special Education Expenditures Project." Paper presented at special session at the annual research conference of the American Education Finance Association, Albuquerque, NM, March.

Citizens Research Council of Michigan. 1991. "Income, Spending, and Taxation— Michigan Compared to the U.S. Average." Council comments no. 997, Citizens Research Council of Michigan, Detroit, MI.

Clark, Catherine. 2001. "Texas." In *Public School Finance Programs of the United States and Canada, 1998–1999*, ed. John Dayton, C. Thomas Holms, Catherine C. Sielke, and Anne L. Jefferson. Washington, DC: National Center for Education Statistics, NCES-2001-309. Available at ⟨http://nces.ed.gov/edfin/state_finance/StateFinancing.asp⟩.

Clark, Melissa A. 2002. "Education Reform, Redistribution, and Student Achievement: Evidence from the Kentucky Education Reform Act." Working paper, Department of Economics, Princeton University, Princeton, NJ.

Clotfelter, Charles T., and Helen F. Ladd. 1996. "Recognizing and Rewarding Success in Public Schools." In *Holding Schools Accountable: Performance-Based Reform in Education*, ed. H. F. Ladd, 265–298. Washington, DC: Brookings Institution.

Clune, William H. 1992. "New Answers to Hard Questions Posed by *Rodriguez*: Ending the Separation of School Finance and Educational Policy by Bridging the Gap between Wrong and Remedy." *Connecticut Law Review* 24:721–755.

Cohen-Vogel, Lora Ann, and Daniel R. Cohen-Vogel. 2001. "School Finance Reform in Tennessee: Inching Toward Adequacy." *Journal of Education Finance* 26, 3 (Winter): 297–318.

Coleman, James, Ernest Q. Campbell, Carol J. Hobson, James McPartland, Alexander M. Mood, Frederic D. Weinfeld, and Robert L. York. 1966. *Equality of Educational Opportunity*. Washington, DC: U.S. Government Printing Office.

Coons, John, William H. Clune III, and Stephen D. Sugarman. 1970. *Private Wealth and Public Education*. Cambridge, MA: Harvard University Press.

Courant, Paul N., Edward Gramlich, and Susanna Loeb. 1995. "A Report on School Finance and Education Reform in Michigan." In *Midwest Approaches to School Reform*, ed. Thomas A. Downes and William Testa, 5–33. Chicago: Federal Reserve Bank of Chicago.

Courant, Paul N., and Susanna Loeb. 1997. "Centralization of School Finance in Michigan." *Journal of Policy Analysis and Management* 16 (Winter): 114–136.

Cullen, Julie Berry. 2003. "The Impact of Fiscal Incentives on Student Disability Rates." *Journal of Public Economics* 87(August):1557–1589.

Cullen, Julie Berry, and David N. Figlio. 1998. "How Effective Are Intergovernmental Incentives?" Working paper, University of Florida, Gainesville, FL, and University of Michigan, Ann Arbor, MI.

Cullen, Julie Berry, and Susanna Loeb. 2002. "Fiscal Substitution in the Context of School Finance Equalization." Working paper, University of Michigan, Ann Arbor, MI, and Stanford University, Palo Alto, CA.

Cullen, Julie Berry, and Randall Reback. 2002. "Tinkering toward Accolades: School Gaming under a Performance Accountability System." Working paper, University of Michigan, Ann Arbor, MI.

Cutler, David M., Douglas W. Elmendorf, and Richard Zeckhauser. 1999. "Restraining the Leviathan: Property Tax Limitation in Massachusetts." *Journal of Public Economic* 71(3):313–334.

Dayton, John. 1993. "Correlating Expenditures and Educational Opportunity in School Funding Litigation: The Judicial Perspective." *Journal of Education Finance* 19:167–182.

Dee, Thomas. 2000. "The Capitalization of Education Finance Reforms." *Journal of Law and Economics* 53 (April): 185–214.

Detroit News. 1995. "Kalkasa Schools Still Battling Cash Shortage." January 2, 1995.

Detroit News. 2000. "Merit Test Is Biased, ACLU Says." June 28, 2000.

Detroit News. 2001a. "Accreditation Threatened." May 7, 2001.

Detroit News. 2001b. "Choice Plan Shifts Funds for Schools." December 2, 2001.

Detroit News. 2001c. "Detroit Pulls out Stops to Enroll Pupils." August 23, 2001.

Detroit News. 2001d. "Kalkaska Saved by Funding Law, but Small District Still Has Problems." August 28, 2001.

Detroit News. 2001e. "State Flunks 600 Schools." April 11, 2001.

Dewey, James, Thomas A. Husted, and Lawrence W. Kenny. 1999. "The Ineffectiveness of School Inputs: A Product of Misspecification?" *Economics of Education Review* 19(1):27–45.

Dillon, Sam. 2003. "States Cut Test Standards to Avoid Sanctions," *New York Times*, May 22. Available at ⟨http://www.nytimes.com/2003/05/22/education/22EDUC.html⟩.

Downes, Thomas A. 1992. "Evaluating the Impact of School Finance Reform on the Provision of Public Education: The California Case." *National Tax Journal* 45(4):405–419.

Downes, Thomas A., and David N. Figlio. 1999. "What Are the Effects of School Finance Reforms? Estimates of the Impact of Equalization on Students and on Affected Communities." Working paper, Tufts University, Medford, MA.

Downes, Thomas A., and David N. Figlio. 2000. "School Finance Reforms, Tax Limits, and Student Performance: Do Reforms Level-Up or Dumb Down?" Working paper, Tufts University, Medford, MA.

Downes, Thomas A., and Thomas F. Pogue. 1994a. "Accounting for Fiscal Capacity and Need in the Design of School Aid Formulas." In *Fiscal Equalization for State and Local Government Finance*, ed. John Anderson, 55–83. New York: Praeger.

Downes, Thomas A., and Thomas F. Pogue. 1994b. "Adjusting School Aid Formulas for the Higher Cost of Educating Disadvantaged Students." *National Tax Journal* 47 (March): 89–110.

Downes, Thomas A., and Mona Shah. 1995. "The Effect of School Finance Reform on the Level and Growth of Per Pupil Expenditures." Working paper no. 95-4, Tufts University, Medford, MA.

Downes, Thomas A., and Jeffrey E. Zabel. 2002. "The Impact of School Characteristics on House Prices: Chicago 1987–1991." *Journal of Urban Economics* 52(1):1–25.

Drake, D. C. 2002. *A Review and Analysis of Michigan Tax Policies Impacting K–12 Finances.* Lansing, MI: Michigan Association of School Administration.

Duncombe, William D. 2002. "Estimating the Cost of an Adequate Education in New York." Working paper no. 44, Center for Policy Research, Maxwell School of Citizenship and Public Affairs, Syracuse University, Syracuse, NY.

Duncombe, William D., John Ruggiero, and John M. Yinger. 1996. "Alternative Approaches to Measuring the Cost of Education." In *Holding Schools Accountable: Performance-Based Reform in Education*, ed. H. F. Ladd, 327–356. Washington, DC: The Brookings Institution.

Duncombe, William D., and John M. Yinger. 1996. "School Finance Reform: Aid Formulas and Equity Objectives." Metropolitan Studies Program Occasional Paper no. 175, Center for Policy Research, The Maxwell School of Citizenship and Public Affairs, Syracuse University, Syracuse, NY.

Duncombe, William D., and John M. Yinger. 1997. "Why Is it So Hard to Help Central City Schools?" *Journal of Policy Analysis and Management* 16 (Winter): 85–113.

Duncombe, William D., and John M. Yinger. 1998. "School Finance Reform: Aid Formulas and Equity Objectives." *National Tax Journal* (June): 239–262.

Duncombe, William D., and John M. Yinger. 1999. "Performance Standards and Educational Cost Indexes: You Can't Have One without the Other." In *Equity and Adequacy in Education Finance: Issues and Perspectives*, ed. H. F. Ladd, R. Chalk and J. S. Hansen, 260–297. Washington, DC: National Academy Press.

Duncombe, William D., and John M. Yinger. 2000. "Financing Higher Student Performance Standards: The Case of New York State." *Economics of Education Review* 19 (October): 363–386.

Duncombe, William D., and John M. Yinger. 2001a. "Alternative Paths to Property Tax Relief." In *Property Taxation and Local Government Finance*, ed. W. E. Oates, 243–294. Cambridge, MA: Lincoln Institute of Land Policy.

Duncombe, William D., and John M. Yinger. 2001b. "Does School District Consolidation Cut Costs?" Working paper no. 33, Center for Policy Research, Maxwell School of Citizenship and Public Affairs, Syracuse University, Syracuse, NY.

The Education Trust 2002. *The Funding Gap: Low-Income and Minority Students Receive Fewer Dollars*. Washington, DC: The Education Trust. Available at ⟨http://www.edtrust.org/main/documents/investment.pdf⟩.

Enrich, P. 1995. "Leaving Equality Behind: New Directions in School Finance Reform." *Vanderbilt Law Review* 48:101–194.

Epple, Dennis, Radu Filimon, and Thomas Romer. 1993. "Existence of Voting and Housing Equilibrium in a System of Communities with Property Taxation." *Regional Science and Urban Economics* 23(5):585–610.

Epple, Dennis, and Glenn Platt. 1998. "Equilibrium and Local Redistribution in an Urban Economy When Households Differ in Both Preferences and Income." *Journal of Urban Economics* 43(1):23–51.

Evans, William N., Sheila E. Murray, and Robert M. Schwab. 1997. "Schoolhouses, Courthouses, and Statehouses after *Serrano*." *Journal of Policy Analysis and Management* 16 (Winter): 10–31.

Evans, William N., Sheila E. Murray, and Robert M. Schwab. 1999. "The Impact of Court-Mandated School Finance Reform." In *Equity and Adequacy in Education Finance: Issues and Perspectives*, ed. H. F. Ladd, R. Chalk and J. S. Hansen, 72–98. Washington, DC: National Academy Press.

Evans, William N., Sheila E. Murray, and Robert M. Schwab. 2001. "The Property Tax and Education Finance, Uneasy Compromises." In *Property Taxation and Local Government Finance*, ed. Wallace E. Oates, 209–235. Cambridge, MA: Lincoln Institute of Land Policy.

Feldstein, Martin. 1975. "Wealth Neutrality and Local Choice in Education." *American Economic Review* 61 (March): 75–89.

Ferguson, Ronald. 1991. "Paying for Public Education: New Evidence on How and Why Money Matters." *Harvard Journal on Legislation* 28(2):465–498.

Ferguson, Ronald, and Helen F. Ladd. 1996. "How and Why Money Matters: A Production Function Analysis of Alabama Schools." In *Holding Schools Accountable: Performance-Based Reform in Education*, ed. H. F. Ladd, 265–298. Washington, DC: The Brookings Institution.

Fernandez, Raquel, and Richard Rogerson. 1997. "Education Finance Reform: A Dynamic Perspective." *Journal of Policy Analysis and Management* 16 (Winter): 67–84.

Fernandez, Raquel, and Richard Rogerson. 1998. "Public Education and Income Distribution: A Dynamic Qualitative Evaluation of Education Finance Reform." *American Economic Review* 88 (September): 813–833.

Figlio, David N. 1997a. "Did the 'Tax Revolt' Reduce School Performance?" *Journal of Public Economics* 65(3):245–269.

Figlio, David N. 1997b. "Teacher Salaries and Teacher Quality." *Economic Letters* 55:267–271.

Figlio, David N. 2002. "Aggregation and Accountability." In *No Child Left Behind: What Will It Take?* ed. C. Finn. Washington, DC: Thomas B. Fordham Foundation.

Figlio, David N. 2003. "Fiscal Implications of School Accountability Initiatives." *Tax Policy and the Economy* 17:1–36.

Figlio, David N., and Marianne Page. 2003. "Can School Choice and School Accountability Successfully Coexist?" In *The Economic Analysis of School Choice*, ed. C. Hoxby, 49–66. Chicago: University of Chicago Press.

Figlio, David N., and Lawrence Getzler. 2002. "Accountability, Ability and Disability: Gaming the System?" Working paper no. 9307, National Bureau of Economic Research, Cambridge, MA.

Figlio, David N., and Maurice Lucas. 2000. "What's in a Grade? School Report Cards and House Prices." Working paper no. 8019, National Bureau of Economic Research, Cambridge, MA.

Figlio, David N., and Kim Rueben. 2001. "Tax Limits and the Qualifications of New Teachers." *Journal of Public Economics* 80(1):49–71.

Fischel, William A. 2001. *The Homevoter Hypothesis: How Home Values Influence Local Government Taxation, School Finance, and Land-Use Policies*. Cambridge, MA: Harvard University Press.

Fisher, Glenn W. 1995. "The History of the Property Tax in Kansas." In *Report of the Governor's Tax Equity Task Force*. Topeka, KS: Office of the Governor.

Fisher, Ronald C., and Leslie Papke. 2000. "Local Government Responses to Education Grants." *National Tax Journal* 53 (March): 153–168.

Flanagan, Ann, and Sheila Murray. 2002. "A Decade of Reform: The Impact of School Reform in Kentucky." Working paper, RAND Corporation, Washington, DC.

Fowler, J. William, and David H. Monk. 2001. *A Primer for Making Cost Adjustments in Education*. Washington, DC: National Center for Educational Statistics. Available at ⟨http://nces.ed.gov/pubsearch/pubsinfo.asp?pubid=2001323⟩.

Friedman, Lee, and Michael Wiseman. 1978. "Understanding the Equity Consequences of School Finance Reform." *Harvard Educational Review* 48:193–226.

Friedman, Milton. 1962. *Capitalism and Freedom*. Chicago: University of Chicago Press.

Fullerton, Don, and Diane Lim Rogers. 1993. *Who Bears the Lifetime Tax Burden?* Washington, DC: Brookings Institution.

Garing, Caprice. 2002. "Antipoverty Programs, Parental Incentives and the Identification of Disabled Children." Working paper, University of Florida, Gainesville, FL.

Gess, Larry R., Paul A. Montello, David L. Sjoquist, and John F. Sears. 1996. "Public School Finance: A Rational Response to Reform Pressures." In *Proceedings of the Eighty-Eighth Annual Conference on Taxation*, ed. Larry Ebel, 92–97. Washington, DC: National Tax Association.

Gill, Brian, P. Michael Timpane, Karen E. Ross, and Dominic J. Brewer. 2001. *Rhetoric versus Reality: What We Know and What We Need to Know about Vouchers and Charter Schools*. Santa Monica, CA: RAND Corporation.

Glasnapp, Douglas R., and John P. Poggio. 2001. *Adequacy of Education Programs and Opportunities in Kansas*. Report prepared for the State of Kansas, Center for Educational Testing and Evaluation, University of Kansas, Lawrence, KS.

Goertz, Margaret E., and Mark C. Duffy, with Kerstin Carlson Le Floch. 2001. *Assessment and Accountability Systems in the Fifty States: 1999–2000*. Consortium for Policy Research in Education Research Report Series RR-046. Philadelphia: University of Pennsylvania.

Goertz, Margaret E., and Malik Edwards. 1999. "In Search of Excellence for All: The Courts and New Jersey School Finance Reform." *Journal of Education Finance* 25(1):5–31.

Gold, Steven, David Smith, and Stephen Lawton. 1995. *Public School Finance Programs in the United States and Canada 1993–1994*. Vol. 1. Albany, NY: American Education Finance Association and the Nelson A. Rockefeller Institute of Government.

Goldhaber, Dan, and Dominic Brewer. 1997. "Evaluating the Effect of Teacher Degree Level on Educational Performance." In *Developments in School Finance, 1996*, ed. W. J. Fowler Jr., 197–210. Washington, DC: U.S. Department of Education, National Center for Education Statistics.

Gray, Jerry. 1999. "Whitman Signs Bills Cutting Property Taxes." *New York Times*, April 14, p. B4.

Guilfoyle, Jeffrey R. 1998. *The Effect of Property Taxes and School Spending on House Prices: Evidence from Michigan's Proposal A*. Lansing, MI: Michigan Department of Treasury.

Gurley, Richard. 2002. *School Capital Funding: Supplementary State Profiles*. Nashville: Tennessee Comptroller of the Treasury, Office of Education Accountability. Available at ⟨http://www.comptroller.state.tn.us/orea/reports/schcapsupp.pdf⟩.

Guryan, Jonathan. 2000. "Does Money Matter? Regression-Discontinuity Estimates from Education Finance Reform in Massachusetts." Working paper no. 8269, National Bureau of Economic Research, Cambridge, MA.

Guthrie, James W., and Richard Rothstein. 1999. "Enabling 'Adequacy' to Achieve Reality: Translating Adequacy into State School Finance Distribution Arrangements." In *Equity and Adequacy in Education Finance: Issues and Perspectives*, ed. H. F. Ladd, R. Chalk and J. Hansen, 209–259. Washington, DC: National Academy Press.

Hansen, Janet S. 2001. "21st Century School Finance: How Is the Context Changing?" Issue paper, Education Commission of the States, Denver, CO.

Hanushek, Eric A. 1996. "School Resources and Student Performance." In *Does Money Matter? The Effect of School Resources on Student Performance and Adult Success*, ed. G. Burtless, 43–73. Washington, DC: Brookings Institution Press.

Hanushek, Eric A. 1997. "Accessing the Effects of School Resources on Student Performance: An Update." *Educational Evaluation and Policy Analysis* 19(2):141–164.

Hanushek, Eric A., John Kain, and Steven Rivkin. 1998. "Teachers, Schools and Academic Achievement." Working paper no. 6691. National Bureau of Economic Research, Cambridge, MA.

Hanushek, Eric A., and Margaret E. Raymond. 2001. "The Confusing World of Educational Accountability." *National Tax Journal* 54(2):365–384.

Harvey, Lynn R. 1995. "1994 Michigan School Finance and Property Tax Reform." In *Increasing Understanding of Public Problems and Policies, 1994*, ed. Steve A. Halbrook and Teddee E. Grace, 171–178. Oak Brook, IL: Farm Foundation.

Hendrie, Caroline. 2001. "N.J.'s 'Whole School' Approach Found Hard for Districts." *Education Week*, February 21, p. 12.

Heaps, Richard, and Arthur Woolf. 2000. "Evaluation of Act 60: Vermont's Education Financing Law." Photocopy. Northern Economic Consulting, Burlington, VT.

Hickrod, G. Alan, Edward R. Hines, Gregory P. Anthony, John A. Dively, Gwen B. Pruyne. 1992. "The Effect of Constitutional Litigation on Education Finance: A Preliminary Analysis." *Journal of Education Finance* 18:180–210.

Hines, James R., Jr., and Richard H. Thaler. 1995. "The Flypaper Effect." *Journal of Economic Perspectives* 9 (Fall): 217–226.

Horn, Jerry, and Gary Miron. 2000. *An Evaluation of the Michigan Charter School Initiative: Performance, Accountability, and Impact*. Kalamazoo, MI: Western Michigan University, The Evaluation Center.

Hoxby, Carolyn M. 2001. "All School Finance Equalizations Are Not Created Equal." *Quarterly Journal of Economics* 66 (November): 1189–1232.

Hunter, Molly A. 2003. "Maryland Enacts Modern, Standards-Based Education Finance System: Reforms Based on 'Adequacy' Cost Study and Parallel Court Funding Principles." Advocacy Center for Children's Educational Success with Standards. Available at ⟨http://www.accessednetwork.org/resources/mdbrief4-02.htm⟩.

Husted, Thomas A., and Lawrence W. Kenny. 2000. "Evidence on the Impact of State Government on Primary and Secondary Education and the Equity-Efficiency Trade-Off." *Journal of Law and Economics* (April): 285–308.

Idaho School Superintendents' Association and the Idaho State Department of Education, Finance Division. 2002. *Financing Idaho's Public Schools*. Available at ⟨http://www.idschadm.org/PDFs/financing_Id_school_broc.pdf⟩.

Ihlanfeldt, Keith R. 1982. "Property Tax Incidence on Owner-Occupied Housing: Evidence from the Annual Housing Survey." *National Tax Journal* 35(1):89–97.

Illinois State Board of Education. 2001. *Illinois School Funding*. Available at ⟨http://www.isbe.state.il.us/board/meetings/oct01meeting/schfund2001.pdf⟩.

Inman, Robert P. 1978. "Optimal Fiscal Reform of Metropolitan Schools." *American Economic Review* 68(1):107–122.

Inman, Robert P. 1979. "The Fiscal Performance of Local Governments: An Interpretive Review." In *Current Issues in Urban Economics*, ed. Peter Mieszkowski and Mahlon Straszheim, 270–321. Baltimore, MD: Johns Hopkins University Press.

Inman, Robert P., and David Rubinfeld. 1979. "The Judicial Pursuit of Local Fiscal Equity." *Harvard Law Review* 92:1662–1750.

Jacob, Brian A. 2002. "The Impact of High-Stakes Testing on Student Achievement: Evidence from Chicago." Working paper, Harvard University, Cambridge, MA.

Jennings, M. 1990. "School Reform and Tax Bill Becomes Law." *Louisville Courier Journal*, April 12, p. A1.

Jensen, Robert M. 1997. "Advancing Education through Education Clauses of State Constitutions." *Brigham Young University Education and Law Journal* 6:1–47.

Jimerson, Lorna. 2001. *A Reasonable Equal Share: Educational Equity in Vermont*. Report. Washington, DC: Rural School and Community Trust.

Johns, Thomas L. 1976. "1975 School Aid Legislation: A Look at Three States." *Journal of Education Finance* 1 (Winter): 397–406.

Johnston, Jocelyn M., and William D. Duncombe. 1998. "Balancing Conflicting Policy Objectives: The Case of School Finance Reform." *Public Administration Review* 58(2):145–158.

Kane, Thomas, and Douglas Staiger. 2002. "Improving School Accountability Measures." Working paper, University of California at Los Angeles, Los Angeles, CA.

Kansas Association of School Boards. 1994. *Overview of Public Education in Kansas*. Topeka: Kansas Association of School Boards.

Kansas Association of School Boards, School Finance Coalition. 2001. *School Finance: Shifting the Burden from State to Local Taxes*. Available at ⟨http://www.accesskansas.org/kasb/issue_paper4.pdf⟩ (accessed June 5, 2002).

Kansas Legislative Research Department. 1991. *Kansas School District Equalization Act (as Amended through 1991)*. Topeka: Kansas Legislative Research Department.

Kansas Legislative Research Department. 2001a. *Amendments to the 1992 School District Finance and Quality Performance Act and the 1992 School District Capital Improvements State Aid Law (Finance Formula Components)*. Topeka: Kansas Legislative Research Department.

Kansas Legislative Research Department. 2001b. *School District Finance and Quality Performance Act and Bond and Interest State Aid Program*. Topeka: Kansas Legislative Research Department.

Kansas State Department of Education. 2000. *Quality Performance Accreditation Manual*. Topeka: Kansas State Department of Education.

Karoly, Lynn A., Peter W. Greenwood, Susan M. Sohler Everingham, Jill Hoube, M. Rebecca Kilburn, C. Peter Rydell, Matthew R. Sanders, and James R. Chiesa. 1998. *Investing in Our Children: What We Know and Don't Know about the Costs and Benefits of Early Childhood Interventions*. Santa Monica, CA: RAND Corporation.

Kentucky Department of Education. 1996. *Core Content for Assessment*. Frankfort, KY: Kentucky Department of Education.

Kentucky Department of Education. Various years. *Annual Financial Reports*. Frankfort, KY: Kentucky Department of Education.

Kentucky Department of Education, Office of District Support Services, Division of School Finance. Various years. *SEEK Bulletin*. Frankfort, KY: Kentucky Department of Education.

Kentucky Education Reform Act of 1990 (KERA). 1990. House Bill 940, 1990 Session, Frankfort, KY.

Knittel, Matthew J., and M. P. Haas. 1998. *Proposal A: A Retrospective*. Report. Michigan Department of Treasury. Lansing, MI.

Koretz, Daniel M., and Sheila I. Barron. 1998. *The Validity of Gains in Scores on the Kentucky Instructional Results Information System (KIRIS)*. Santa Monica, CA: RAND Corporation.

Kramer, Liz. 2002. "Achieving Equitable Education through the Courts: A Comparative Analysis of Three States." *Journal of Law & Education* 31(1):1–51.

Krueger, Alan B. 1999. "Experimental Estimates of Education Production Functions." *Quarterly Journal of Economics* 114(2):497–532.

Krueger, Alan B. 2002. "Economic Considerations and Class Size." Working paper no. 8875, National Bureau of Economic Research, Cambridge, MA.

Krueger, Alan B., and Diane M. Whitmore. 2001. "The Effect of Attending a Small Class in the Early Grades on College-Test Taking and Middle School Test Results: Evidence from Project STAR." *Economic Journal* 11 (January): 1–28.

Ladd, Helen F. 1976. "State-Wide Taxation of Commercial and Industrial Property for Education." *National Tax Journal* 29(2):143–153.

Ladd, Helen F. 1999. "The Dallas School Accountability and Incentive Program: An Evaluation of Its Impacts on Student Outcomes." *Economics of Education Review* 18(1):1–16.

Ladd, Helen F. 2001. "School-Based Educational Accountability Systems: The Promise and the Pitfalls." *National Tax Journal* 54(2):385–400.

Ladd, Helen F., and Janet S. Hansen. 1999. *Making Money Matter: Financing America's Schools*. Washington, DC: National Academy Press.

Ladd, Helen F., and Randall P. Walsh. 2002. "Implementing Value-Added Measures of School Effectiveness: Getting the Incentives Right." *Economics of Education Review* 21(1):1–17.

Ladd, Helen F., and John M. Yinger. 1991. *America's Ailing Cities: Fiscal Health and the Design of Urban Policy*. Updated ed. Baltimore: Johns Hopkins University Press.

Ladd, Helen F., and John M. Yinger. 1994. "The Case for Equalizing Aid." *National Tax Journal* 47(1):211–224.

Lankford, R. Hamilton, and James Wyckoff. 1996. "The Allocation of Resources to Special Education and Regular Instruction." In *Holding Schools Accountable: Performance-Based Reform in Education*, ed. H. F. Ladd, 221–257. Washington, DC: The Brookings Institution.

Lauver, Sherri C., Gary W. Ritter, and Margaret E. Goertz. 2001. "Caught in the Middle: The Fate of the Non-urban Districts in the Wake of New Jersey's School Finance Litigation." *Journal of Education Finance* 26(3):281–296.

Legislative Budget Board. 2000. *Fiscal Size-Up: Biennium Texas State Service*. Austin: Texas Legislature.

Legislative Budget Board. 2001. *Financing Public Education in Texas—Kindergarten through Grade 12: Legislative Primer*, 3rd ed. Austin: Texas Legislature.

Legislative Budget Board. 2003. *Fiscal Size-Up; 2004–05 Biennium*. Table 89: State and Local Revenue for Texas Public Schools. Austin: Texas Legislature. Available at ⟨http://www.lbb.state.tx.us/Fiscal_Size-up/Fiscal_Size-up_2004-2005_1203.pdf⟩.

Levin, Henry. 1989. "Financing the Education of At-Risk Students." *Education Evaluation and Policy Analysis* 11:47–60.

Levine, Gail F. 1991. "Meeting the Third Wave: Legislative Approaches to Recent Judicial School Finance Rulings." *Harvard Journal on Legislation* 28:506–542.

Loeb, Susanna. 2001. "Estimating the Effects of School Finance Reform: A Framework for a Federalist System." *Journal of Public Economics* 80(2):225–247.

Loeb, Susanna, and Marianne Page. 2000. "Examining the Link between Teacher Wages and Student Outcomes: The Importance of Alternative Labor Market Opportunities and Non-pecuniary Variation." *Review of Economics and Statistics* 82(3):393–408.

Lukemeyer, Anna. 2001. "Poor Children in Poor Schools: Can Reform Litigation Provide the Resources They Need?" Paper presented at the 43rd Annual Conference of the Western Social Science Association, Reno, NV.

Lukemeyer, Anna. 2003. *Courts as Policymakers: School Finance Reform Litigation*. New York: LFB Scholarly Publishing.

Maine School Management Association and the Department of Education General Purpose Aid Team. 2003. *Maine's Current School Funding Formula*. Available at ⟨http://www.state.me.us/education/data/subsidy/meffml03.htm⟩.

Manwaring, Robert L., and Steven M. Sheffrin. 1995. "The Effects of Education Equalization Litigation on the Levels of Funding: An Empirical Analysis." Working paper, Department of Economics, University of California–Davis, Davis, CA.

Manwaring, Robert L., and Steven M. Sheffrin. 1997. "Litigation, School Finance Reform, and Aggregate Educational Spending." *International Tax and Public Finance* 4 (May): 107–127.

Maryland Commission on Education Finance, Equity, and Excellence. 2002. *Final Report*. Baltimore: Maryland Commission on Education Finance, Equity, and Excellence. Available at ⟨http://mlis.state.md.us/other/education/final/2002_final_report.pdf⟩.

Mathis, William J. 1995. "Vermont." In *Public School Finance Programs of the United States and Canada, 1993–94*, ed. Steven D. Gold, David M. Smith, and Stephen B. Lawton, 617–619. Albany: Nelson Rockefeller Institute of Government, State University of New York.

Mathis, William J. 1998. *Act 60 and Proposition 13*. Montpelier, VT: Concerned Vermonters for Equal Educational Opportunities. Available at ⟨http://www.act60works.org/oped1.html⟩.

Mathis, William J. 2001. "Vermont." In *Public School Finance Programs of the U.S. and Canada: 1998–99*, ed. C. C. Sielke, J. Dayton, C. T. Holmes and A. L. Jefferson. Washington, DC: U.S. Department of Education, National Center for Education Statistics. Available at ⟨http://www.nces.ed.gov/edfin/state_finance/statefinancing.asp⟩.

McCarthy Snyder, Nancy. 1995. *The Use of the Property Tax for Public School Finance in Kansas*. Report of the Governor's Tax Equity Task Force. Topeka, KS: Governor's Tax Equity Task Force.

McCarty, Therese A., and Harvey E. Brazer. 1990. "On Equalizing School Expenditures." *Economics of Education Review* 9(3):251–264.

McCarty, Therese A., and Suthathip Yaisawarng. 1993. "Technical Efficiency in New Jersey School Districts." In *The Measurement of Productive Efficiency: Techniques and Applications*, ed. H. Fried, C. Lovell and S. Schmidt, 197–277. New York: Oxford University Press.

McClaughry, John. 1997. *Educational Financing Lessons from California*. Concord, VT: Ethan Allen Institute. Available at ⟨http://www.ethanallen.org/commentaries/1997/educatingfinancial.html⟩.

McClaughry, John. 2001. *School Children First: Replacing Act 60*. Report. Concord, VT: Ethan Allen Institute.

McMahon, W., and S. Chang. 1991. *Geographical Cost-of-Living Differences: Interstate and Intrastate*. Washington, DC: Center for the Study of Educational Finance.

McMillan, Kevin R. 1998. "The Turning Tide: The Emerging Fourth Wave of School Finance Reform Litigation and the Courts' Lingering Institutional Concerns." *Ohio State Law Journal* 58:1867–1903.

McMillan, Robert. 1999. "Competition, Parental Monitoring and Public School Quality." Working paper, Stanford University, Stanford, CA.

Meyer, Lori, Greg F. Orlofsky, Ronald A. Skinner, and Scott Spicer. 2002. "The State of the States." *Education Week* (Special Report), January 10.

Michigan Department of Education. Various years. Bulletin 1014, Michigan K–12 financial data files, available at ⟨www.michigan.gov/mde_for_the_years_1992-2002⟩.

Michigan House and Senate Fiscal Agencies. 1994. "Appendix A." In *The Michigan School Aid Act Compiled and Appendices*. Lansing, MI: House Fiscal Agency/Senate Fiscal Agency.

Mills, Morris H. 1996. "The Indiana Senate Republicans' Approach to Funding 294 School Corporations." *Policy Perspectives* 1 (1). Available from the Indiana Educational Policy Center at ⟨http://www.indiana.edu/~iepc/welcome.html⟩.

Minorini, Paul A., and Stephen D. Sugarman. 1999a. "Educational Adequacy and the Courts: The Promise and Problems of Moving to a New Paradigm." In *Equity and Adequacy in Education Finance: Issues and Perspectives*, ed. H. F. Ladd, R. Chalk and J. S. Hansen, 175–208. Washington, DC: National Academy Press.

Minorini, Paul A., and Stephen D. Sugarman. 1999b. "School Finance Litigation in the Name of Educational Equity: Its Evolution, Impact and Future." In *Equity and Adequacy in Education Finance: Issues and Perspectives*, ed. H. F. Ladd, R. Chalk and J. S. Hansen, 34–71. Washington, DC: National Academy Press.

Mishel, Lawrence, and Richard Rothstein. 1997. "Measurement Issues in Adjusting School Spending across Time and Place." Paper presented at annual data conference, National Center for Education Statistics, Washington, DC.

Moak, Lynn. 2002. "Economic Development versus Equity." Paper presented at annual conference of the American Education Finance Association, Albuquerque, NM.

Monk, David H. 1990. *Education Finance: An Economic Approach.* New York: McGraw-Hill.

Montgomery, Lori. 2002. "Md. Seeks 'Adequacy,' Recasting School Debate." *Washington Post*, April 22, p. A01.

Murnane, Richard J., and Frank Levy. 2001. "Will Standards-Based Reforms Improve the Education of Students of Color?" *National Tax Journal* 54 (June): 401–415.

Murray, Sheila E. 2001. "Kentucky." In *Public School Finance Programs of the United States and Canada, 1998–1999,* ed. John Dayton, C. Thomas Holms, Catherine C. Sielke, and Anne L. Jefferson. Washington, DC: U.S. Department of Education, National Center for Education Statistics. Available at ⟨http://www.nces.ed.gov/edfin/state_finance/statefinancing.asp⟩.

Murray, Sheila E., William N. Evans, and Robert M. Schwab. 1998. "Education-Finance Reform and the Distribution of Educational Resources." *American Economic Review* 88(4):789–812.

National Center for Education Statistics, U.S. Department of Education (NCES). Various years. *Digest of Education Statistics.* Washington, DC: U.S. Government Printing Office. (For years after 1995, available at ⟨http://www.nces.edu.gov/edstats/⟩.)

National Center for Education Statistics, U.S. Department of Education (NCES). 1995. *Digest of Education Statistics.* Washington, DC: U.S. Government Printing Office.

National Center for Education Statistics, U.S. Department of Education (NCES). 2000. *Digest of Education Statistics, 1995.* Washington, DC: U.S. Government Printing Office.

National Center for Education Statistics, U.S. Department of Education (NCES). 2001a. *Statistics in Brief. Revenues and Expenditures for Public Elementary and Secondary Education: School Year 1998–99.* Washington, DC: U.S. Department of Education, National Center for Education Statistics. Available at ⟨http://nces.ed.gov/pubs2001/2001321.pdf⟩ (accessed October 2, 2003).

National Center for Education Statistics, U.S. Department of Education (NCES). 2001b. "Table 4: Enrollments in Grades K–12 in Public Elementary and Secondary Schools, by Region and State, with Projections: Fall 1993 to Fall 2011." In *Projections of Education Statistics to 2011.* Washington, DC: U.S. Department of Education, National Center for Education Statistics. Available at ⟨http://nces.ed.gov/pubs2001/proj01/tables/table04_1.asp⟩.

National Center for Education Statistics, U.S. Department of Education (NCES). 2001c. *Public School Finance Programs of the United States and Canada: 1998–99.* Washington, DC: U.S. Department of Education, National Center for Education Statistics. Available at ⟨http://nces.ed.gov/edfin/state_finance/StateFinancing.asp⟩.

Nechyba, Thomas J. 1996a. "A Computable General Equilibrium Model of Intergovernmental Aid." *Journal of Public Economics* 62(3):363–398.

Nechyba, Thomas J. 1996b. "Public School Finance in a General Equilibrium Tiebout World: Equalization Programs, Peer Effects, and Private School Vouchers." Working paper no. W5642, National Bureau of Economic Research, Cambridge, MA.

Nechyba, Thomas J. 1997a. "Existence of Equilibrium and Stratification in Local and Hierarchical Public Goods Economies with Property Taxes and Voting." *Economic Theory* 10(2):277–304.

Nechyba, Thomas J. 1997b. "Local Property and State Income Taxes: The Role of Interjurisdictional Competition and Collusion." *Journal of Political Economy* 105(2):351–384.

Nechyba, Thomas J. 1999. "School Finance Induced Migration Patterns: The Case of Private School Vouchers." *Journal of Public Economic Theory* 1(1):1–46.

Nechyba, Thomas J. 2000. "Mobility, Targeting and Private School Vouchers." *American Economic Review* 90(1):130–146.

Nechyba, Thomas. 2003a. "Introducing School Choice into Multi-district Public School Systems." In *The Economics of School Choice*, ed. Caroline Hoxby, 145–194. Chicago: University of Chicago Press.

Nechyba, Thomas. 2003b. "School Finance, Spatial Income Segregation and the Nature of Communities." *Journal of Urban Economics* 54(1):61–88.

Nechyba, Thomas. 2003c. "Centralization, Fiscal Federalism and Private School Attendance." *International Economic Review* 44(1):179–204.

Nechyba, Thomas J., and Michael Heise. 2000. "School Finance Reform: Introducing the Choice Factor." In *City Schools: Lessons from New York City*, ed. J. Viteritti and D. Ravitch. Baltimore, MD: Johns Hopkins University Press.

New York State Education Department, Elementary, Middle, Secondary, and Continuing Education. 2003. *Debt Limit*. Albany: New York State Education Department. Available at ⟨http://www.emsc.nysed.gov/mgtserv/debtlimi.htm⟩.

New York State Education Department, State Aid Unit. 2000. *State Formula Aids and Entitlements for Schools in New York*. Albany: New York State Education Department. Available at ⟨http://stateaid.nysed.gov/hndbk00.pdf⟩.

New York State Office of the State Comptroller. 1997. *Meeting School Facilities Needs: A Conceptual Proposal for Consideration in the 1998–99 State Budget*. Albany: New York State Office of the State Comptroller. Available at ⟨http://www.osc.state.ny.us/reports/schools/1997/12-97.htm⟩.

New York Times. 2002. "Public Schooling for Profit." Editorial, May 26, p. 4–10.

Norman, Geoffrey. 1998. "Vermont's Class Act." *American Spectator* 31 (August): 22–27.

Nowak, John E., and R. D. Rotunda. 2000. *Constitutional Law*, 5th ed. St. Paul, MN: West Group.

Oates, Wallace E. 1972. *Fiscal Federalism*. New York: Harcourt Brace Jovanovich.

Odden, Allan R. 1992. "School Finance and Education Reform: An Overview." In *Rethinking School Finance*, ed. A. R. Odden. San Francisco: Jossey-Bass.

Odden, Allan R. 1999. "Improving State School Finance Systems: New Realities Create Need to Re-engineer School Finance Structures." Occasional Paper Series OP-04, Consortium for Policy Research in Education, University of Pennsylvania, Philadelphia, PA.

Odden, Allen R., and Lawrence O. Picus. 1992. *School Finance: A Policy Perspective.* New York: McGraw Hill.

Opresko, Alan. 2000. "School Construction: The Nation and Selected States." Inter-office memorandum, New York State Division of the Budget, Albany, October 25.

O'Sullivan, Arthur. 2001. "Limitation on Local Property Taxation: The United States Experience." In *Property Taxation and Local Government Finance*, ed. Wallace E. Oates, 177–200. Cambridge, MA: Lincoln Institute of Land Policy.

Papke, Leslie E. 2001. "The Effects of Spending on School Inputs and Outputs: Evidence from Michigan." Working paper, Michigan State University, Lansing, MI.

Picus, Lawrence O., and Linda Hertert. 1993. "Three Strikes and You're Out: Texas School Finance after *Englewood III*." *Journal of Education Finance* 18 (Spring): 366–389.

Picus, Lawrence O., Allan Odden, and Mark Fermanich. 2001. *Assessing the Equity of Kentucky's SEEK Formula: A Ten-Year Analysis.* Prepared for the Kentucky Department of Education, Frankfort, KY.

Prince, Hank. 1996. *Proposal A and Pupil Equity.* Fiscal Focus Report. Lansing: Michigan House Fiscal Agency.

Putterman, Louis, John Roemer, and Joaquim Silvestre. 1990. "Does Egalitatianism Have a Future?" *Journal of Economic Literature* 36(2):861–902.

Ratcliffe, Kerry, Bruce Riddle, and John M. Yinger. 1990. "The Fiscal Condition of School Districts in Nebraska: Is Small Beautiful?" *Economics of Education Review* 9 (January): 81–99.

Rebell, Michael A. 2002. "Education Adequacy, Democracy, and the Courts." In *Achieving High Educational Standards for All: Conference Summary*, ed. T. Ready, C. Edley Jr. and C. E. Snow, 218–268. Washington, DC: National Academy Press.

Reschovsky, Andrew. 1994. "Fiscal Equalization and School Finance." *National Tax Journal* 47 (March): 185–198.

Reschovsky, Andrew, and Jennifer Imazeki. 1998. "The Development of School Finance Formulas to Guarantee the Provision of Adequate Education to Low-Income Students." In *Developments in School Finance, 1997: Does Money Matter?* ed. W. J. Fowler Jr., 121–148. Washington, DC: U.S. Department of Education, National Center for Educational Statistics.

Reschovsky, Andrew, and Jennifer Imazeki. 2000. *Developing a Cost Index for School Districts in Illinois.* Report submitted to the Illinois State Board of Education. Madison, WI: La Follette School of Public Affairs, University of Wisconsin–Madison.

Reschovsky, Andrew, and Jennifer Imazeki. 2001. "Achieving Educational Adequacy through School Finance Reform." *Journal of Education Finance* 26(4) (Spring): 373–396.

Reschovsky, Andrew, and Jennifer Imazeki. 2003. "Let No Child Be Left Behind: Determining the Cost of Improving Student Performance," *Public Finance Review* 31 (May): 263–290.

Robelen, Erik W. 2002. "ESEA to Boost Federal Role in Education." *Education Week*, January 9.

Ross, Stephen L., and John M. Yinger. 1999. "Sorting and Voting: A Review of the Literature on Urban Public Finance." In *Handbook of Urban and Regional Economics*, ed. Edwin S. Mills and Paul Cheshire, vol. 3, *Applied Urban Economics, 2001–2060*. Amsterdam: North-Holland.

Roth, Jeffrey, David Figlio, Yuwen Chen, Doug Grove, Randy Carter, Changxing Ma, Mario Ariet, Sam Wu, and Michael Resnick. 2002. "Educational Costs of Low Birth Weight." Working paper, University of Florida, Gainesville, FL.

Rouse, Cecilia. 1998. "Private School Vouchers and Student Achievement: An Evaluation of the Milwaukee Parental Choice Program." *Quarterly Journal of Economics* 113(2):553–602.

Rouse, Cecilia. 2000. "School Reform in the 21st Century: A Look at the Effect of Class Size and School Vouchers on the Academic Achievement of Minority Students." Working paper no. 440, Industrial Relations Section, Princeton University, Princeton, NJ.

Russo, Charles J., Richard Donelan, and Eddy J. Van Meter. 1993. "The Kentucky Education Reform Act and School-Based Decision Making: A Not So Modest Governance Plan." *Record in Educational Administration and Supervision* 14(1):71–77.

Sielke, Catherine C. 2001. "Funding School Infrastructure Needs across the States." *Journal of Education Finance* 27(2) (Fall): 653–662.

Silva, Fabio, and Jon Sonstelie. 1995. "Did *Serrano* Cause a Decline in School Spending?" *National Tax Journal* 48(2):199–215.

Slemrod, Joel, and Jon Bakija. 1996. *Taxing Ourselves*. Cambridge, MA: MIT Press.

Solon, Gary. 1992. "Intergenerational Income Mobility in the United States." *American Economic Review* 82(3):393–409.

Sonstelie, Jon, Eric Brunner, and Kenneth Ardon. 2000. "For Better or for Worse? School Finance Reform in California." Report. Public Policy Institute of California, San Francisco, CA, February.

Staiger, Douglas, and James H. Stock. 1997. "Instrumental Variable Regression with Weak Instruments." *Econometrica* 65(3):557–587.

State of Alaska. 2003. "School Size Factor." Public Law 14.17.450. Available at ⟨http://touchngo.com/lglcntr/akstats/Statutes/Title14/Chapter17/Section450.htm⟩.

State of Colorado. 2003a. "Statewide Base per Pupil Funding—Increases." Public Law 22-55-106. Available at ⟨http://198.187.128.12/colorado/lpext.dll?f=templates&fn=fs-main.htm&2.0⟩.

State of Colorado. 2003b. "District Total Program." Public Law 22-54-104. Available at ⟨http://198.187.128.12/colorado/lpext.dll?f=templates&fn=fs-main.htm&2.0⟩.

State of Delaware, Department of Finance. 2003. *Delaware's System for Financing Education*. Available at ⟨http://www.state.de.us/finance/publications/efr/part4.pdf⟩.

State of Idaho. 2003. "Foundation Program—State Aid—Apportionment." Public Law Title 33, Chapter 10. Available at ⟨http://www3.state.id.us/cgi-bin/newidst?sctid=330100002.K⟩.

State of Kansas, Legislative Division of Post Audit. 1996. *Performance Audit Report: Reviewing the Use of State Assessment Tests in Kansas*. Report no. 96-49. Topeka: State of Kansas Legislative Division of Post Audit.

State of Maryland. 2003. "State Financial Assistance for Public Education." Public Law 5-202. Available at ⟨http://198.187.128.12/maryland/lpext.dll?f=templates&fn=fs-main.htm&2.0⟩.

State of West Virginia. 2003. "Abbreviated Summary of the Public School Support Program for the 2002–03 Year." Available at ⟨http://wvde.state.wv.us/finance/data/2003/pdfs/2003AbbreviatedSummary.PDF⟩.

Strauss, Robert P., Lori R. Bowes, Mindy S. Marks, and Mark R. Plesko. 2000. "Improving Teacher Preparation and Selection: Lessons from the Pennsylvania Experience." *Economics of Education Review* 19(4):387–415.

Stricker, Alex, and John M. Yinger. 2003. "Capitalization and Equalization: The Feedback Effects of Foundation Aid for Schools." Working paper, Center for Policy Research, Syracuse University, Syracuse, NY.

Tallman, Mark. 1993. "The 1992 Kansas School Finance Act: A Political and Legislative History." Master's degree field project, Department of Public Administration, University of Kansas. Lawrence, KS.

Tallman, Mark (Assistant Executive Director for Advocacy, Kansas Association of School Boards). 2002. Interview by Jocelyn Johnston, Kansas Association of School Boards, Topeka, Kansas, March 4.

Texas Association of School Boards. 1996. *The Basics of Texas Public School Finance*, 6th ed. Austin: Texas Association of School Boards.

Texas Education Agency. 2000. *Snapshot 2000: 1999–2000 School District Profiles*. Austin: Texas Education Agency, Division of Performance Reporting. Available at ⟨http://tea.state.tx.us/perfreport/snapshot/2000/pdf/snap001.pdf⟩.

Texas Education Agency. 2002a. "Table: Students." In *Pocket Edition 2000–01: Texas Public School Statistics*. Austin: Texas Education Agency, Division of Performance Reporting. Available at ⟨http://www.tea.state.tx.us/perfreport/pocked/2001/panel3.htm⟩ (accessed June 6, 2002).

Texas Education Agency. 2002b. "Grade 3 Report." In *TAAS 2003 Early Indicator Summary Report: Comparison of Results at Current and Higher Standards*. Austin: Texas Education Agency. Available at ⟨http://www.tsha.utexas.edu/handbook/online⟩ (accessed July 29, 2002).

Texas Education Agency. 2003. *CPTD Tax Preliminary: Tax Year 2002 and School Funding Year 2003–2004*. Austin: Texas Education Agency. Available at ⟨http://www.tea.state.tx.us/school.finance/⟩.

Texas State Historical Association. 2001. "*Edgewood ISD v. Kirby*." In *Handbook on Texas Online*. Available at ⟨http://www.tsha.utexas.edu/handbook/online⟩ (accessed July 29, 2002).

Theobald, Neil. 2002. *From Proposal A to Proposal A+: A Discussion of Issues and Options Regarding the Financial Requirements of Public Education in Michigan*. Report to the Michigan State Board of Education from Tom Watkins, Superintendent of Public Instruction and the School Finance Task Force. Lansing, MI: Michigan State Board of Education.

Thomas, Stephen B., and Billy Don Walker. 1982. "Texas Public School Education." *Journal of Education Finance* 8 (Fall): 223–281.

Thompson, David C., David S. Honeyman, and R. Craig Wood. 1993. "The Kansas School District Equalization Act: A Study of Fiscal Equity of Funding Categories." *Journal of Education Finance* 19(1):36–68.

Thro, W. 1990. "The Third Wave: The Impact of the Montana, Kentucky, and Texas Decisions on the Future of Public School Finance Litigation." *Journal of Law and Education* 19:219–250.

Thro, W. 1994. "Judicial Analysis during the Third Wave of School Finance Litigation." *Boston College Law Review* 35:597–617.

Trimble, C. Scott, and Andrew C. Forsaith. 1995. "Achieving Equity and Excellence in Kentucky Education." *University of Michigan Journal of Law Reform* 28(3):599–601.

U.S. Census Bureau. 2003. *Public Education Finances, 2001*. Washington, DC: U.S. Census Bureau. Available at ⟨http://www.census.gov/govs/school/01fullreport.pdf⟩.

U.S. Census Bureau. 1992. *State and Local Government Finances by Level of Government and State, 1991–1992*. Washington, DC: U.S. Census Bureau. Available at ⟨http://www.census.gov/govs/estimate/92censusviewtabss.xls⟩.

U.S. Census Bureau, Department of Commerce. Various years (1987, 1992, 1997). Census of Governments: School System Finance (F-33) file.

U.S. Department of Education. 2002. "The No Child Left Behind Act of 2001: Executive Summary." Washington, DC: U.S. Department of Education. Available at ⟨http://www.ed.gov/offices/WESE/esea/exec-summ.html⟩ (accessed July 29, 2002).

Westhoff, Frank. 1977. "Existence of Equilibria in Economies with a Local Public Good." *Journal of Economic Theory* 14(1):84–112.

Widerquist, Karl. 2001. *The Regressive Effects of STAR*. New York: Education Priorities Panel. Available at ⟨http://www.edpriorities.org/Pubs/Report/STAR.pdf⟩.

Wisconsin Department of Public Instruction. 2003. *School Financial Services*. Available at ⟨http://www.dpi.state.wi.us/dpi/dfm/sfms/tier.html⟩.

Wright, S., S. Horn, and W. Sanders. 1997. "Teacher and Classroom Context Effects on Student Achievement: Implications for Teacher Evaluation." *Journal of Personnel Evaluation in Education* 11(1):57–67.

Wyckoff, Paul G. 1995. "Capitalization, Equalization, and Intergovernmental Aid." *Public Finance Quarterly* 23(4):484–508.

Wyckoff, Paul G. 2001. "Capitalization and the Incidence of School Aid." *Journal of Education Finance* 27(1):585–607.

Yinger, John M. 2001. "Fixing New York's State Education Aid Dinosaur: A Proposal." Policy brief no. 21, Center for Policy Research, Syracuse University, Syracuse, NY.

Zimmerman, David. 1992. "Regression toward Mediocrity in Economic Stature." *American Economic Review* 82(3):409–429.

Court Cases

Abbott v. Burke, 119 N.J. 287, 575 A.2d 359 (New Jersey 1990) (*Abbott II*).

Abbott v. Burke, 136 N.J. 444, 643 A.2d 575 (New Jersey 1994) (*Abbott III*).

Abbott v. Burke, 149 N.J. 145, 693 A.2d 417 (New Jersey 1997) (*Abbott IV*).

Abbott v. Burke, 153 N.J. 480, 710 A.2d 450 (New Jersey 1998) (*Abbott V*).

Abbott v. Burke, 163 N.J. 95, 748 A.2d 82 (New Jersey 2000) (*Abbott VI*).

Abbott v. Burke, 164 N.J. 84, 751 A.2d 1032 (New Jersey 2000) (*Abbott VII*).

Abbott v. Burke, 172 N.J. 294, 798 A.2d 602 (New Jersey 2002) (*Abbott VIII*).

Board of Education v. Walter, 58 Ohio St.2d 368, 390 N.E.2d 813 (Ohio 1979), *cert. denied*, 444 U.S. 1015 (1980).

Board of Education, Levittown Union Free School District v. Nyquist, 57 N.Y.2d 27, 439 N.E.2d 359, 453 N.Y.S.2d 643 (New York 1982) (*Levittown*).

Brigham v. Vermont, 692 A.2d 384 (Vermont 1997) (*Brigham*).

Buse v. Smith, 74 Wis.2d 550, 247 N.W.2d 141 (Wisconsin 1976).

Campaign for Fiscal Equity (CFE) v. The State of New York (June 26, 2003) (not yet filed).

Campbell County School District v. Wyoming, 907 P.2d 1238 (Wyoming 1995) (*Campbell County I*).

Campbell County School District v. Wyoming, 19 P.3d 518 (Wyoming 2001) (*Campbell County II*).

Carrollton–Farmers Branch Independent School District v. Edgewood Independent School District, 826 S.W.2d 489 (Texas 1992).

Claremont School District v. Governor, 138 N.H. 183, 635 A.2d 1375 (New Hampshire 1993) (*Claremont SD I*).

Claremont School District v. Governor, 142 N.H. 462, 703 A.2d 1353 (New Hampshire 1997) (*Claremont SD II*).

Claremont School District v. Governor, 147 N.H. 499, 794 A.2d 744 (New Hampshire 2002).

Claremont School District v. Gregg, 635 A.2d 1375 (New Hampshire 1997).

Coalition for Adequacy and Fairness in School Funding, Inc. v. Chiles, 680 So.2d 400 (Florida 1996) (*Coalition for Adequacy*).

Committee for Educational Rights v. Edgar, 174 Ill.2d 1, 672 N.E.2d 1178 (Illinois 1996) (*Committee for Educational Rights*).

DeRolph v. Ohio, 78 Ohio St. 3d 419; 677 N.E.2d 733 (Ohio 1997).

DuPree v. Alma School District No. 30, 279 Ark. 340, 651 S.W.2d 90 (Arkansas 1983) (*DuPree*).

Durant v. State of Michigan, 456 Mich. 175, 566 N.W.2d 272 (Michigan 1997).

Edgewood Independent School District v. Kirby, 777 S.W.2d 391 (Texas 1989) (*Edgewood I*).

Edgewood Independent School District v. Kirby, 804 S.W.2d 491 (Texas 1991) (*Edgewood II*).

Edgewood Independent School District v. Meno, 893 S.W.2d 450 (Texas 1995) (*Edgewood IV*).

Fair School Finance Council v. Oklahoma, 746 P.2d 1135 (1987) (*Fair School Finance*).

Helena Elementary School District No. 1 v. Montana, 236 Mont. 44, 769 P.d. 684 (Montana 1989), *as modified*, 784 P.2d 412 (Montana 1990) (*Helena ESD*).

Horton v. Meskill, 172 Conn. 615, 376 A.2d 359 (Connecticut 1977) (*Horton I*).

Horton v. Meskill, 195 Conn. 24, 486 A.2d 1099 (Connecticut 1985) (*Horton III*).

Hull v. Albrecht, 190 Ariz. 520, 950 P.2d 1141 (Arizona 1997) (*Roosevelt ESD II*).

Kukor v. Grover, 148 Wis.2d 469, 436 N.W.2d 568 (Wisconsin 1989) (*Kukor*).

Lake View School District No. 25 v. Huckabee, 351 Ark. 31, 91 S.W.3d 472 (Arkansas 2002) (*Lake View*), *cert. denied sub nom. Wilson v. Huckabee*, 71 U.S.L.W. 3721 (2003).

Leandro v. North Carolina, 346 N.C. 336, 488 S.E.2d 249 (North Carolina 1997).

Lewis v. Spagnolo, 710 N.E.2d 798 (Illinois 1996).

Lujan v. Colorado State Board of Education, 649 P.2d 1005 (Colorado 1982) (*Lujan*).

McDaniel v. Thomas, 248 Ga. 632, 285 S.E.2d 156 (Georgia 1981) (*McDaniel*).

McDuffy v. Secretary of the Office of Executive Education, 415 Mass. 545, 615 N.E.2d 516 (Massachusetts 1993) (*McDuffy*).

Millikin v. Green, 390 Michigan 389, 212 N.W.2d 711 (Michigan 1973).

Montoy v. Kansas, No. 99-C-1738 (Shawnee county, Nov. 21, 2001).

Montoy v. Kansas, 275 Kan. 145, 62 P.3d 228 (Kansas 2003).

Olsen v. Oregon, 276 Ore. 9, 554 P.2d 139 (Oregon 1976). (*Olsen*).

Opinion of the Justices (Reformed Public School Financing System), 145 N.H. 474, 765 A.2d 673 (New Hampshire 2000).

Pauley v. Kelly, 162 W.Va. 672, 255 S.E.2d 859 (West Virginia 1979) (*Pauley*).

Robinson v. Cahill, 62 N.J. 473, 303 A.2d 273 (New Jersey 1973) (*Robinson I*), *cert. denied sub nom. Dickey v. Robinson*, 414 U.S. 976 (1973).

Robinson v. Cahill, 69 N.J. 133, 351 A.2d 713 (New Jersey 1975) (*Robinson IV*).

Robinson v. Cahill, 69 N.J. 449, 355 A.2d 129 (New Jersey 1976) (*Robinson V*).

Robinson v. State, 117 F.Supp.2d 1124 (D. Kan. 2001).

Roosevelt Elementary School District Number 66 v. Bishop, 179 Ariz. 233, 877 P.2d 806 (Arizona 1994) (*Roosevelt ESD I*).

Rose v. Council for Better Education, Inc. 790 S.W.2d 186 (Kentucky 1989) (*Rose*).

San Antonio Independent School District v. Rodriguez, 411 U.S. 1, 93 S.Ct. 1278, 36 L.Ed.2d 16 (1973) (*Rodriguez*).

School Administrative District No. 1 v. Commissioner, 659 A.2d 854 (Maine 1995) (*SAD1*).

Seattle School District No. 1 v. Washington, 90 Wash.2d 476, 585 P.2d. 71 (Washington 1978) (*Seattle SD*).

Serrano v. Priest, 5 Cal.3d 584, 487 P.2d 1241 (California 1971) (*Serrano I*).

Serrano v. Priest, 18 Cal.3d 728, 5557 P.2d 929 (California 1976) (*Serrano II*).

Skeen v. Minnesota, 505 N.W.2d 299 (Minnesota 1993) (*Skeen*).

Tennessee Small School Systems v. McWherter, 851 S.W.2d 139 (Tennessee 1993) (*Tennessee Small Schools*).

Unified School District No. 229 v. Kansas, 256 Kan. 232, 885 P.2d 1170 (Kansas 1994) (*USD No. 229*).

Washakie County School District No. 1 v. Herschler, 606 P.2d 310 (Wyoming 1980), *cert. denied*, 449 U.S. 824 (1980).

West Orange–Cove Consolidated ISD v. Nelson, 78 S.W.3d 529 (Tex. App.-Austin 2002).

Zelman v. Simmons-Harris, U.S. Supreme Court, Nos. 00-1751, 00-1777, and 00-1779 (Othio 2002).

Contributors

Julie Berry Cullen Julie Berry Cullen is an assistant professor of economics at the University of Michigan. She received her Ph.D. from the Massachusetts Institute of Technology in 1997. Her research and teaching are in the field of public economics, with an emphasis on social-insurance programs and the economics of education. Her recent papers in education explore how school district behavior responds to special education finance policies, school finance equalization policies, and accountability policies.

Thomas Downes Thomas Downes is an associate professor of economics at Tufts University. He received his B.A. from Bowdoin College in 1982 and his Ph.D. from Stanford University in 1988. His research focuses in part on the evaluation and construction of state and local policies to improve the delivery of publicly provided goods and to reduce inequities in the delivery of these goods, with particular attention paid to public education. He has also pursued research that considers the roles of the public and private sectors in the provision of education. He has advised policymakers in several states; an example of this advisory work is his contribution to *Educational Finance to Support High Learning Standards*, the final report of a symposium sponsored by the New York State Board of Regents.

William Duncombe William Duncombe is a professor of public administration and a senior research associate in the Center for Policy Research at the Maxwell School of Syracuse University. He received his B.A. in economics from the University of Washington and his M.A. and Ph.D. in public administration from Syracuse University. His research specialties include school aid design, educational costs and efficiency, program evaluation, demand and costs of state and local government services, budgeting, and fiscal health. His work has appeared in numerous journals in public administration and economics. He is coauthor with Roy Bahl of *Economic Growth and Fiscal Planning: New York in the 1990s* (Center for Urban Policy Research, Rutgers University, 1991). He has taught courses in education policy and finance, public financial administration, state and local public finance, program evaluation, policy analysis, economics, and statistics. Before coming to Syracuse University, he taught at the University of Georgia.

David N. Figlio   David N. Figlio is the Walter J. Matherly Professor of Economics at the University of Florida and a faculty research fellow at the National Bureau of Economic Research. He earned his Ph.D. in economics from the University of Wisconsin–Madison and previously taught at the University of Oregon. His research on education and welfare policy and political economy has been published in prominent journals such as the *American Economic Review, Quarterly Journal of Economics, Journal of Public Economics, Journal of Law and Economics* and *Journal of Urban Economics* and has been funded by numerous federal agencies and private foundations. His current work focuses on the implications of school accountability systems and the systemic effects of school choice programs.

Ann E. Flanagan   Ann E. Flanagan is a consultant at RAND. She holds a Ph.D. in economics from George Washington University. Her principal area of research is education with an emphasis on the estimation of econometric models of education efficiency and productivity. Her dissertation analyzed district-level education expenditures in Kentucky in an attempt to find statistical evidence of increased efficiency among Kentucky public school districts after the Kentucky Education Reform Act. She has analyzed state and national scores on the National Assessment of Educational Progress, Illinois district-level test scores, and Kentucky district-level test scores. Her research objective has been to identify and quantify the role of family characteristics and educational expenditures in student achievement. Her analyses of test score data have examined differential achievement by race, leveraged effects of targeting resources to students with given family characteristics, and threshold effects of resource allocation.

Yao Huang   Yao Huang is a master's degree student in the Departments of Public Administration and Statistics at the Maxwell School of Syracuse University.

Jennifer Imazeki   Jennifer Imazeki is an assistant professor of economics at San Diego State University, where she teaches courses in public finance and applied microeconomics. She received her Ph.D. in economics from the University of Wisconsin–Madison, where she also worked as a researcher for the Consortium for Policy Research in Education. In 1999–2000, she received a Spencer Foundation Dissertation Fellowship for Research Related to Education. Her current research focuses on school finance reform and teacher labor markets.

Jocelyn M. Johnston Jocelyn M. Johnston is an associate professor in the Edwin O. Stene Graduate Program in Public Administration at the University of Kansas, where she teaches state and local public finance, intergovernmental relations, and research methods. Since 1997, she has also served as a field research associate for the Rockefeller Institute's State Capacity Study of state-level welfare and Medicaid reforms. Her research, which currently focuses on intergovernmental policy and management and on government social-service contracting, has been published in several public administration journals. She was a co-recipient of the 2001 award for the best public administration paper presented at the American Political Science Association's annual conference and is chair-elect of the National Association for Budgeting and Financial Management.

Susanna Loeb Susanna Loeb is an assistant professor of education at Stanford University, specializing in the economics of education and the relationship between schools and federal, state, and local policies. She received her Ph.D. in economics in 1998 from the University of Michigan, from which she also received her master's degree in public policy. She studies resource allocation, looking specifically at how the structure of state finance systems affects the level and distribution of funds to districts and how teachers' preferences affect the distribution of teaching quality across schools. She is particularly interested in issues of equity. She also studies poverty policies, including welfare reform and early-childhood education programs. Her dissertation won the American Education Finance Association Jean Flanigan Outstanding Dissertation Award and the Association for Public Policy Analysis and Management Dissertation Award. Her recent papers include "Estimating the Effects of School Finance Reform: A Framework for a Federalist System," in the *Journal of Public Economics*; "Examining The Link between Teacher Wages and Student Outcomes: The Importance of Alternative Labor Market Opportunities and Non-pecuniary Variation," with Marianne Page, in the *Review of Economics and Statistics*; and "Centralization of School Finance in Michigan," with Paul Courant, in the *Journal of Policy Analysis and Management*.

Anna Lukemeyer   Anna Lukemeyer is an assistant professor of public administration at the University of Nevada, Las Vegas, where she teaches administrative law, fiscal administration, and research design. She received a J.D. from Southern Methodist University School of Law in 1986 and a Ph.D. in public administration from Syracuse University in 1999. Her research interests center on the interaction of law and public policy.

Sheila E. Murray   Sheila E. Murray is an economist at RAND and a visiting associate professor in policy sciences at University of Maryland's Baltimore County campus. She received her Ph.D. in economics from the University of Maryland, College Park. Prior to joining RAND, she was a National Academy of Education/Spencer Foundation postdoctoral fellow, a visiting scholar at the Northwestern University/University of Chicago Joint Center for Poverty Research, and an assistant professor of public policy and economics at the University of Kentucky. She is a member of the U.S. Department of Education National Center for Education Statistics Finance Technical Review Panel and training director for the RAND/Spencer Foundation Post-doctoral Fellowship in Education Policy. Her current research interests are in education finance reform, comprehensive school reform, inequality, and state and local economic tax policy and development.

Thomas J. Nechyba   Thomas J. Nechyba joined the Duke University faculty in 1999 after spending five years on the faculty at Stanford University. He received his Ph.D. from the University of Rochester in 1994. He has lectured as a visiting professor at the Fundacao Getulio Vargas in Rio de Janeiro and the Center for Economic Studies at the University of Munich, and he held a yearlong national fellowship at the Hoover Institution on War, Revolution and Peace at Stanford University in 1998–99. He is currently a research associate at the National Bureau of Economic Research, and he serves as associate editor for the *American Economic Review* and the *Journal of Public Economic Theory*. He also serves as the director of undergraduate studies in the Department of Economics at Duke. His research, which has been funded by agencies such as the National Science Foundation and the Spencer Foundation, lies in the field of public economics, with particular focus on primary and secondary education, federalism, and the functioning of local governments, as well as public policy issues relating to disadvantaged families.

Andrew Reschovsky   Andrew Reschovsky is a professor in the Robert M. La Follette School of Public Affairs and the Department of Agricultural and Applied Economics at the University of Wisconsin–Madison. He has a Ph.D. in economics from the University of Pennsylvania. He teaches public finance, microeconomic policy analysis, and urban economics. His research focuses on tax policy and on intergovernmental fiscal relations. He has conducted research for a number of state and local governments around the country and spent a year working on federal tax policy in the Office of Tax Analysis at the U.S. Treasury and a year at the Organization for Economic Cooperation and Development in Paris. He is serving as an advisor to the government of South Africa on the design of grants for the financing of education, health care, and social welfare and on the fiscal reform of local governments. Other recent projects include the design of formulas to distribute state aid for elementary and secondary education, tax policies to increase the rate of home ownership for low- and modest-income households, and state government fiscal responses to block grants for welfare. He has written numerous articles in professional journals and has contributed chapters to a number of books.

Wen Wang   Wen Wang is a Ph.D. student in the Department of Public Administration at Syracuse University.

John Yinger   John Yinger is Trustee Professor of Public Administration and Economics at the Maxwell School, Syracuse University, and director of the Education Finance and Accountability Program in the Maxwell School's Center for Policy Research. Before coming to Syracuse in 1986, he taught at Harvard University and at the University of Michigan and served as a senior staff economist on the President's Council of Economic Advisers. His recent publications include scholarly articles on education finance, the incidence of the property tax, the costs of housing discrimination, and the causes of housing discrimination. He has also authored or coauthored four books, two on topics in local public finance, one on discrimination in housing markets, and one (the most recent) on discrimination in mortgage lending.

Name Index

Subject Index